1992

University of St. Francis
GEN 860.992 B742

Women writers of contemporary

W9-ADV-281

WOMEN WRITERS
OF CONTEMPORARY SPAIN

Women Writers
of Contemporary Spain

Exiles in the Homeland

Edited by
Joan L. Brown

DELAWARE

Newark: University of Delaware Press
London and Toronto: Associated University Presses

LIBRARY
College of St. Francis
JOLIET, ILLINOIS

© 1991 by Associated University Presses, Inc.

All rights reserved. Authorization to photocopy items for internal or personal use, or the internal or personal use of specific clients, is granted by the copyright owner, provided that a base fee of $10.00, plus eight cents per page, per copy is paid directly to the Copyright Clearance Center, 27 Congress Street, Salem, Massachusetts 01970. [0-87413-386-6/91 $10.00 + 8¢ pp, pc.]

Associated University Presses
440 Forsgate Drive
Cranbury, NJ 08512

Associated University Presses
25 Sicilian Avenue
London WC1A 2QH, England

Associated University Presses
P.O. Box 39, Clarkson Pstl. Stn.
Mississauga, Ontario
Canada L5J 3X9

The paper used in this publication meets the requirements
of the American National Standard for Permanence of Paper
for Printed Library Materials Z39.48-1984.

Library of Congress Cataloging-in-Publication Data

Women writers of contemporary Spain/edited by Joan L. Brown.
    p.   cm.
Includes bibliographical references.
ISBN 0-87413-386-6 (alk. paper)
    1. Spanish literature–Women authors–History and criticism.   2. Spanish literature–20th century–History and criticism.
I. Brown, Joan Lipman, 1952–
PQ6055, W66 1991
860.9'9287'0904—dc20

89–40296
CIP

PRINTED IN THE UNITED STATES OF AMERICA

860.992
B742

Contents

Preface 7

Acknowledgments 9

Women Writers of Spain: An Historical Perspective
JOAN L. BROWN 13

1 Carmen Laforet: The Dilemma of Artistic Vocation
GUSTAVO PÉREZ FIRMAT 26

2 Writing against the Current: The Novels of Elena Quiroga
PHYLLIS ZATLIN 42

3 Dolores Medio: Chronicler of the Contemporary Spaniard's
Interaction with Society
MARGARET E. W. JONES 59

4 Carmen Martín Gaite: Reaffirming the Pact between Reader
and Writer
JOAN L. BROWN 72

5 The Fictional World of Ana María Matute: Solitude,
Injustice, and Dreams
JANET PÉREZ 93

6 Mercè Rodoreda's Subtle Greatness
RANDOLPH D. POPE 116

7 Ana María Moix's Silent Calling
ANDREW BUSH 136

8 Esther Tusquets's Fiction: The Spinning of a Narrative
Web
MIRELLA SERVODIDIO 159

9 Marina Mayoral's Narrative: Old Families and New Faces
from Galicia
CONCHA ALBORG 179

10 Lourdes Ortiz: Mapping the Course of Postfrancoist
Fiction
ROBERT C. SPIRES 198

6   CONTENTS

11 Montserrat Roig and the Creation of a Gynocentric
    Reality
    CATHERINE G. BELLVER   217
12 Rosa Montero: From Journalist to Novelist
    JOAN L. BROWN   240
13 Writing Ambiguity and Desire: The Works of Adelaida
    García Morales
    ELIZABETH J. ORDÓÑEZ   258

Works Available in English Translation   278
Contributors   279
Index   283

Preface

This volume introduces thirteen major women writers of the Franco and post-Franco eras in Spain, in essays by eminent scholars in the field of contemporary Spanish literature. Each essay features original literary analysis, as well as fundamental biographical data, a review of the author's works, and both primary and annotated secondary bibliographies. Singly these chapters present outstanding writers who are less well known than their talents warrant. Together they provide the first broad literary history of the best contemporary Spanish fiction by women.

Acknowledgments

I thank Mirella Servodidio and Aaron and Zelda Lipman for their reviews of my introductory chapter and Eunice Myers for her critical comments about my chapter on Rosa Montero.

I am especially grateful to Mark J. Brown for his encouragement and support.

WOMEN WRITERS
OF CONTEMPORARY SPAIN

Women Writers of Spain:
An Historical Perspective

Joan L. Brown

Until recently women authors have been rare in Spanish literature. Only in the contemporary era—the Franco period and the post-Franco years to date—has there been a sizable contingent of women writers in Spain. This should come as no surprise in a culture whose concept of masculine superiority is so strong as to be known in other languages by its Spanish name.

The representation of female authors in the canon in Spain since the Renaissance is appreciably less than that of women in England and, to a smaller degree, in the United States and France, as judged by their presence in literary histories and "masterworks" anthologies. This is especially true over the past two centuries. From the second half of the eighteenth century through the early twentieth century, the period in which a large proportion of literature in English is the work of women, female writers did not contribute substantially to the literature of Spain. There simply has not been a cadre of "literary women," defined by American critic Ellen Moers as "writers we . . . shall always read whether interested or not in the fact that they happened to be women."[1] Any attempt to trace a female literary tradition, comparable to those carried out with English-language novelists,[2] is for scholars of Spanish literature either an abbreviated enterprise or else a search outside the canon.

The purpose of this volume is twofold: to correct previous neglect of excellent writers and to illustrate the diversity of literature by women in contemporary Spain.

Spanish Women Writers in the Eras Before Franco

From the biased perspective of the modern age, Spanish literature by women can be divided arbitrarily into three periods: before Franco (1100–1936), during the Franco era (1936–75), and after

13

Franco (1975 to the present). The first period, lasting eight centuries, had the fewest women writers, while the most recent, a fifteen-year period, has yielded the most. In the intervening thirty-nine-year span, female writers first began to contribute to Spanish literature in substantial numbers.[3] This disparate representation highlights the recent productivity of Spanish women writers; it also reveals their near-total exclusion from Spanish literary history.

Only a half-dozen female authors had entered the canon in Spain before 1936, the first year of the Spanish civil war. They are Santa Teresa de Jesús in the sixteenth century, María de Zayas y Sotomayor in the seventeenth century, and Cecilia Böhl de Faber (who wrote under the pseudonym Fernán Caballero), Gertrudis Gómez de Avellaneda, Rosalía de Castro, and Emilia Pardo Bazán in the nineteenth century. These few women writers are as well known to the general public and to scholars of Spanish literature as their male counterparts.

A survey of the women writers who secured places in the official history of Spanish literature can serve as a prelude to a study of the women who came after them and to consideration of the question of a feminine tradition in Spanish letters. This study of female forebears has become an active area of research on women writers: Virginia Woolf's dictum that "we think back through our mothers if we are women" has been amplified by feminist critics to include the hypothesis that female predecessors are crucial to the self-definition of the woman artist.[4]

A review of canonical Spanish women writers must begin in the sixteenth century. The first female literary eminence in Spain remains the most revered woman author in Spanish history: Santa Teresa de Cepeda y Ahumada, known as Santa Teresa de Jesús or Santa Teresa de Avila. She is the writer credited with taking mystic literature to its loftiest heights. A Carmelite nun who was the daughter of converted Jews, Santa Teresa (1515–82) is the one Spanish woman writer who appears to have been known as a genius in her own lifetime, an achievement made more remarkable by the fact that she did not begin writing until she was forty-seven. Santa Teresa wrote with the goal of reforming her religious order, a duty with which she was charged by Church authorities. Of her more than a dozen books of prayers, autobiography, poems, and reflections, Santa Teresa's most significant masterpiece is *Moradas del castillo interior* (1588) (English translation by E. Allison Peers, *Interior Castle*, 1961), in which the life of the spirit is represented as a journey through the interior of a castle that leads to a union with God.

In the seventeenth century, María de Zayas y Sotomayor (1590?– 1661?) is recognized today as a major contributor to the genre of the *novela corta* (novelette). Her works were popular in Spain and abroad and were published in as many editions as those of her most illustrious male contemporaries, including Cervantes and Quevedo. Unjustly, in retrospect, her reputation never approached theirs.[5] Zayas was very conscious of her boldness in entering the male preserve of literature and defended the ability of women to do so. Both of the identically-titled narrative collections for which she is known (*Novelas ejemplares y amorosas*, 1637 and 1647; English translation by John Sturrock, *A Shameful Revenge and Other Stories*, 1963) depict the theme of the battle of the sexes, in the tradition of French writer Christine de Pisan's fifteenth-century defense of women. The brief pieces in Zayas's second collection are entitled *desengaños* (*desengañar* is to free from a deception), a familiar political theme in this era when embattled Spain was forced to realize that its Golden Age was transitory. The purpose of these witty tales, all narrated by women, is to expose the treachery of men.

The eighteenth century did not yield any women's entries into the "masterpiece" anthologies of Spanish literature, although this neoclassical era saw the introduction of a new subgenre of essay: the male intellectual's defense of women. The first and most lucid example was written by a brilliant Benedictine monk named Fray Benito Jerónimo Feijoo, who above all defended women's intellectual capacity.[6]

In the nineteenth century, four first-class figures have been recognized. The first is Cecilia Böhl de Faber, who adopted the pseudonym Fernán Caballero.[7] A prolific writer of best sellers in Spain in the 1850s and 1860s, she is most valued now for her *cuadros de costumbres* (depictions of customs and folklore) in Andalucía. Her most widely known work is *La gaviota* (1856) (English translation by Joan MacLean, *The Sea Gull*, 1965), whose convoluted and melodramatic plot traces the social defiance and ultimate defeat of an ambitious and talented woman. Although consistently represented in histories of literature, Fernán Caballero, as she is always known, is in my opinion the weakest of the canonical women writers.

The second nineteenth-century woman to earn widespread fame is Gertrudis Gómez de Avellaneda (1814–73), who was born in Cuba, a Spanish colony at that time, and raised in Spain. Although she cultivated many genres, she is best known for her poetry, as is her contemporary Rosalía de Castro (1837–85). This third author, Rosalía de Castro, is widely considered to be on a par with her more famous colleague, poet Gustavo Adolfo Béquer. The last and best-known nineteenth-century major woman author is Emilia Pardo Bazán (1851–1921), who is popularly known as the second most famous woman writer of Spain (after Santa Teresa). Pardo Bazán, a university professor, was especially concerned with the education of women. She began her career as a literary critic; after traveling to France and reading Zola, she introduced naturalism to Spain. Her elaboration of this aesthetic, most observable in her famous novel *Los pazos de Ulloa* (1886) (Ulloa's manor; English translation by Ethel Harriet Hearn, *The Son of the Bondwoman*, 1908) focuses on the inexorable encroachment of nature as it erodes the weakly rooted effects of socialization on human beings.

Evidently there are not many consecrated women writers through whom contemporary authors have the opportunity to "think back." Nevertheless, these few predecessors are held in high esteem by literary historians. In addition to these first-rank figures, some other Spanish women writers, notably María Zambrano, Rosa Chacel, Carmen Conde, and Concha Espina, achieved a measure of recognition in the first third of the twentieth century. One woman writer from Latin America also gained admission to the Spanish canon prior to the modern era. She was the brilliant Mexican poet Sor Juana Inés de la Cruz, a seventeenth-century nun who remains the most admired female in the Spanish-American literary pantheon.

Evidence of Underreporting of Women Writers

Despite the impressive achievements of a few, there is increasing evidence that accomplished women writers in Spain were excluded from the canon. This suspicion is substantiated by newly collected publication statistics on literature by women and by the recent reevaluation of their works.

A comprehensive reference book of Spanish literature by women has been compiled by a group of seventy-nine Hispanists, under the direction of Carolyn Galerstein. Entitled *Women Writers of Spain*, this 1986 bibliography builds on the findings of neglected older sources[8] and documents a surprisingly large number of women writers. This reference lists thirty women authors in Spain before the nineteenth century (one in the fourteenth century, four in the fifteenth century, eight in the sixteenth century, ten in the seventeenth century, and seven in the eighteenth century), sixty-one known women writers in the nineteenth century, and one hundred ninety-eight in the twentieth century. This listing includes poets as well as writers of narrative fiction but does not include writers whose work was composed in Catalan; this category, not subdivided by century, includes seventy additional names.[9] Another bibliographic resource is Janet Pérez's 1988 volume entitled *Contemporary Women Writers of Spain*, which includes major and minor Spanish women authors who wrote in Castilian and in the vernacular languages, and briefly introduces fifty-one authors from the twentieth century and seven from the nineteenth century.[10]

Why Women Writers Were Excluded

The disparity between the number of legacies being reclaimed by current scholarship and the number of consecrated female authors before the modern era forces the question of why women were excluded from the canon. Recent evidence dispels the myth that women did not write in substantial numbers and refutes the notion that women's writing was uniformly inferior to men's. The standard impediments to women's writing, including the inaccessibility of education and the sanctions against women's nondomestic achievement, did not preclude exceptional women from producing fine literature; in Spain, as elsewhere, these obstacles were surmounted. But when Spanish women did create literature, their contributions appear to have been ignored or denied.

An example of the process of denial is the recent controversy surrounding the authorship of the *kharjas*, the first Spanish lyric poetry. These verses were almost certainly created by women. However, from the time they were discovered this fact has been evaded by literary historians. The *kharjas*, written in the tenth century, are early Castilian verses attached as culminating stanzas to longer Arabic and Hebrew poems. Nearly all of the verses are composed in the voice of a woman. One prevailing theme is the longing of a young girl for her lover, another is a girl's lament over her lover's infidelity. Despite the female protagonists and themes of these verses, historians of Spanish literature have not only denied the possibility of female authorship, but they have invented explanations for how these important verses must have been created by men. The *kharjas* were seen as tropes, as representations of the male artist and his patron. Not until 1985, in an essay entitled "Spain's First Woman Writers," did a leading (British) medievalist grant that "it seems far more probable that the popular oral poets with whom the tradition began were women."[11]

The resolute avoidance of this conclusion highlights the bias that has excluded women from the canon from the tenth century forward. In my opinion this prejudice is rooted in the inability of the mainstream culture to accept artistic achievement by women. It is only with great difficulty that intellectual status can be granted to women in a social system characterized by the ethic of machismo. Even a traditional literary critic such as Gonzalo Sobejano finds that "atavisms," along with economic (under)development and religion, have historically functioned to enforce women's intellectual inequality in Spain, and that the scarcity of women's literature can be explained by their inferior status.[12] Until recently the recognition of great women artists in Spain has produced cognitive dissonance, the conflictive disequilibrium brought about by actions that are inconsistent with basic beliefs.[13] Efforts to avoid cognitive dissonance in the realm of literary history have been strenuous and, with the few exceptions already discussed, entirely successful.

The Contemporary Era: An Increasing Corpus of Literature by Women

The factors that militated against the acknowledgment of women writers in Spain are now diminished. In Spain and the United States, scholarly literature reflects a surge of interest in Spanish fiction by women. In histories of contemporary fiction and in academic books and articles, female writers are the subject of growing critical attention. While their numbers are still small, the increased appearance of women writers in twentieth-century literary histories reflects a substantial gain when compared to their scarce presence in accounts of Spanish literature over the preceding eight centuries.[14] Nevertheless, parity with male authors in encyclopedic literary histories is still far from sight.[15]

Scholarly publications on twentieth-century women writers have also increased significantly over the past decade, although as in literary histories the absolute number of contributions is much less than the number devoted to male counterparts. In 1984 Janet Pérez reported that "a survey in the late 1970's discovered that only 21 (1.8 per cent) of 1,145 doctoral dissertations in relevant fields produced in this country during the five-year period 1972–76 had major Spanish women writers as subjects. A similar review of five major periodicals for Hispanists (*Hispania, Hispanic Review, Hispanófila, Revista de Estudios Hispánicos, Revista Hispánica Moderna*) over a ten-year period turned up only 26 articles on Spanish women writers."[16]

The growth of scholarship on literature by women that has been evident to specialists over roughly the past decade, from the late seventies to the late eighties, is reflected in the entries contained in the Modern Language Association Bibliographies for the years in question. Between 1978 and 1988, the most recent year for which data are available in 1990, there were fifty-two American doctoral dissertations on Spanish women writers, five hundred thirty-six articles, and twenty-three books. This compilation includes peninsular writers of all eras. Santa Teresa remains the most popular subject for study, with one hundred fifty bibliographic entries over the analyzed years. Rosalía de Castro is second with eighty-nine entries, including two volumes of conference proceedings, and Emilia Pardo Bazán is third with seventy-seven entries. However, present-day writers are gaining ground. Carmen Martín Gaite is the most studied of the contemporary group, with fifty-nine entries. The rest of the ten most-studied Spanish women authors are as follows: Ana María Matute, with twenty-four entries; María de Zayas y Sotomayor with twenty; Carmen Laforet and María Zambrano with fifteen each; and Cecilia Böhl de Faber (Fernán Caballero) and Elena Quiroga with eleven each. A review covering 1978 to 1988 of the same five journals mentioned yields a total of forty-nine articles on women writers, close to twice as many as reported in the earlier survey, despite the fact that one of the journals (*Revista Hispánica Moderna*) was not published during most of the decade in question.

Seventy-one Spanish women writers have elicited critical articles over the last reported decade, as recorded by the MLA Bibliographies for 1978 through 1988. Even when the few pretwentieth-century names are subtracted, it is obvious that there has been exponential growth in the number of recognized women writers in Spain during and after the Franco regime.

Major Women Writers of Contemporary Spain

Of the many talented women writers of contemporary Spain, the thirteen who appear in this volume are among the most widely known and, arguably, the most outstanding. They include all members of the established "old guard" who came to prominence in the 1940s, 1950s, and early 1960s, as well as some of the most notable recent writers of the late 1960s, 1970s, and the 1980s. According to all available measures, including literary prizes, critical praise, and quantity of scholarly attention, these authors are important presences in modern Spanish literature. The major women writers of the Franco and post-Franco eras are presented here according to the order in which they gained recognition in Spain. The authors in this collection who came to prominence in the Franco era are Carmen Laforet, Elena Quiroga, Dolores Medio, Carmen Martín Gaite, Ana María Matute, and Mercè Rodoreda; the post-Franco group is comprised of Ana María Moix, Esther Tusquets, Marina Mayoral, Lourdes Ortiz, Montserrat Roig, Rosa Montero, and Adelaida García Morales. Of course, this selection is incomplete. Others who could have been included are Concha Alós, Mercedes Salisachs, and Elena Soriano from the first era, and Soledad Puértolas, Cristina Fernández Cubas, Carme Riera, and Beatriz Poteccher from the second. Their works argue strongly for a second volume of critical essays.

For those who are not familiar with the reputations of the authors presented here, a note about each will highlight the best-known aspects of their fiction. Carmen Laforet (b. 1921) is widely considered to be the premiere existential novelist of the 1940s and 1950s, a label that refers to the sensibility (rather than an express philosophy) evident in Spanish fiction of the immediate postwar period. The novels of Elena Quiroga (b. 1921) are distinguished by great technical innovation and experimentation and by the oblique presentation of themes that were forbidden under censorship. Dolores Medio (b. 1914) achieved fame through her unflinchingly realistic documentation of middle-class, postwar Spanish society. Carmen Martín Gaite (b. 1925) is known for her contributions to the development of the contemporary novel, from social realism to fantastic literature and metafiction. Ana María Matute (b. 1926) combines lyricism and committed social realism in a fashion that is personal and unique. Mercè Rodoreda (1909–83), whose works were first published in her native Catalan, is admired for the brilliance of her spare prose and for her parodies of popular genres.

Ana María Moix (b. 1947), a Catalan author who writes primarily in Castilian, creates novels that are linguistically and technically complex. Catalan writer and editor Esther Tusquets (b. 1936), who also composes in Castilian, is associated with the most innovative techniques of the modern novel. Marina Mayoral (b. 1942), a Galician who writes in Castilian, uses essentially traditional novelistic form to create memorable characters. The terms *traditional* and *experimental* both apply to Lourdes Ortiz (b. 1943), whose fiction is noted for its wide stylistic range. Montserrat Roig (b. 1946), who writes in Catalan and has been translated into Castilian, is the author of historical novels that uncover truths about Spanish society. Rosa Montero (b. 1951) offers issue-oriented testimony of contemporary Spanish life; a second strand of her work incorporates metafiction. Adelaida García Morales (b. 195?) creates haunting fictional worlds that are at once familiar and fantastic.

The Question of a "Women's Literature" in Spain

Because these thirteen novelists are representative of the larger body of literature by women in contemporary Spain, they provide a useful measure by which to gauge current assumptions about that literature. Specifically, they afford evidence that challenges the notion of a monolithic "women's literature" in Spain. There are those who argue that literature by women is homogeneous, that it is an outgrowth of styles and themes derived from a feminine sensibility. However, as the following essays demonstrate, the most striking characteristic of the work of these authors (like that of their female predecessors) is its diversity.

In the breadth of their range, and also in their affinities with male writers of each era, these eminent Spanish women authors suggest that gender is secondary to the writer's historical moment and individual experience as a basis for literary direction. This is accepted for men (since they are part of the dominant culture, it is not an issue), but it is also true for women. Although women writers may belong to a muted subgroup within the mainstream, they nevertheless are products of the received culture of their nationality and era, regardless of their sex.

This does not mean that literature by women is identical to literature by men, nor does it discount important dissimilarities. Recently gender studies and feminist criticism have focused on "reading for difference," meaning the difference between female writers and male writers. Unique gender-based literary qualities are unquestionably evident in the work of women writers of Spain (as elsewhere).[17] These differences are most striking in the areas of characters and themes. It is much more difficult to establish the influence of gender on novelistic structure, despite the efforts of French theorists to link anatomy and technique, or on language (with the exception of women's reported speech).

It is possible to argue that the major difference between literature by women and literature by men lies in the female characters created by women writers. The proportion of women heroes in literature by women vastly surpasses that found in literature by men. These characters illustrate feminist concerns, such as the search for matrilineal roots and the dilemma of the woman artist whose inherited models and myths undermine her self-esteem. This locus of difference explains the ubiquity of character studies in feminist criticism: most commonly psychoanalytic, following Freud or the contemporary French psychoanalyst Jacques Lacan, they also include developmental, linguistic, archetypal, sociohistorical, and even biological analyses of women characters created by female authors.

Evidence of specific gender-based differences in other aspects of fiction by contemporary Spanish women is lacking: the political issues, language, treatment of literary conventions, and even the degree of seriousness of women writers are both similar to and different from male authors and each other. The authors in this collection, which spans forty years, reveal differences from one another that are much more striking than shared differences from their male counterparts of any given decade. From Carmen Laforet's baroque evocations of psychological development to Lourdes Ortiz's escapist detective novels, this is a richly varied group of writers who also (though not coincidentally) are women.

Perspectives on Contemporary Spanish Literature by Women

This volume was written by twelve scholars who have special expertise in contemporary Spanish literature. What emerges from their chapters is a broad and many-faceted picture: in addition to providing readers with the necessary fundamental information, these essays offer new insights into writers whose fame still has not caught up with their talent. Gustavo Pérez Firmat studies the question of female authorship with regard to Carmen Laforet's "case" of early success followed by long silence. Phyllis Zatlin shows how the literature of Elena Quiroga could not have been fully appreciated when it appeared, and she documents its achievements for the contemporary reader. Margaret E. W. Jones demonstrates that the fiction of Dolores Medio is closely allied with the literature and philosophy of nineteenth-century Spain.

My essay on Carmen Martín Gaite discusses how she adopts the same role in her fiction as she does in her historical investigations—that of an anthropologist to her own culture who reports to an esteemed reader. Janet Pérez's essay on Ana María Matute shows how for this writer, more than any other, the experience of the civil war from a child's vantage point is obsessive: Matute's entire opus can be seen as a representation of this conflict.

Randolph D. Pope considers the fiction of Mercè Rodoreda in

terms of this author's triple exile from the mainstream culture as a member of the defeated enemy, as a Catalonian writing in a repressed language, and as a woman. Andrew Bush analyzes the work of Ana María Moix with regard to its underlying exploration of language and silence. Mirella Servodidio explores the fiction of Esther Tusquets as an extended narrative web and illuminates the complex psychological characteristics and interrelationships from which the author creates a detailed universe. Concha Alborg shows how the fiction of Marina Mayoral is defined and unified by themes and techniques that pervade all of her novels.

Robert C. Spires offers a succinct history of the post-Franco novel, distinguishing two literary poles and plotting the literature of Lourdes Ortiz from one to the other. Catherine G. Bellver shows how Montserrat Roig rewrites traditional, gender-bound history to focus instead on a "female-centered reality." In my essay on Rosa Montero, I argue that her novels demonstrate a progressively stronger rejection of the conventions of journalism in favor of ambiguity and invention. Elizabeth J. Ordóñez analyzes the fictional worlds created by Adelaida García Morales with regard to the genre of fantastic literature in structural, thematic, and also cultural terms.

Taken as a whole, the essays in this volume support my contention that literature by women in modern Spain, though united by important gender-based commonalities, is characterized even more by diversity. There does not appear to be a monolithic literature by contemporary Spanish women, any more than there exists a monolithic Spanish literature by men. It is ironic, though not unexpected, that only a book devoted to literature by women can challenge the validity of its own existence. Still, the question must be asked: Given its diversity, should fiction by women be separated out from the literature of the country?

For Spain, the answer is yes. At present, this affirmative action is necessary to bring outstanding, underappreciated literature to the attention of a wider readership. However, once introduced, it is unlikely that the work of these authors will need any special treatment in order to be featured in literary anthologies or bookstore displays. The fiction produced by these writers is fascinating, eloquent, comic, thoughtful, provocative, insightful, witty, innovative, stimulating, and impressive, as the essays that follow will show.

Notes

1. Ellen Moers, *Literary Women* (New York: Doubleday, 1976), xi.
2. The classic study is Elaine Showalter's *A Literature of Their Own: British*

Women Novelists from Brontë to Lessing (Princeton: Princeton University Press, 1977). For Spanish literature, the only comparable investigation is Carmen Martín Gaite's 1987 book, revealingly entitled *Desde la ventana: Enfoque femenino de la literatura española* (From the window: A feminine focus on Spanish literature) (Madrid: Espasa Calpe), in which she discusses four authors who wrote before the civil war and three contemporary writers.

3. Because of the effects of censorship on Spanish literature during the civil war and postwar years, the period of Franco's rule is distinguished as a unique era for writers. However, within this period, women authors did not establish a significant presence until the early 1950s. See Ymelda Navajo, *Doce relatos de mujeres* (Madrid: Alianza, 1982), Prólogo, 9, and José María Martínez Cachero, *La novela española entre 1936 y 1980: Historia de una aventura* (Madrid: Castalia, 1985), 229.

4. See Woolf, *A Room of One's Own* (New York and London: Harcourt Brace Jovanovich, 1929), 79, and also Sandra M. Gilbert and Susan Gubar, *The Madwoman in the Attic: The Woman Writer and the Nineteenth-Century Literary Imagination* (New Haven and London: Yale University Press, 1979). Mary Jacobus summarizes this postulate when she states that for women writers, "thinking back through the mother becomes a gesture at once of recuperation and revision." In *Reading Woman: Essays in Feminist Criticism*, ed. Mary Jacobus (New York: Columbia University Press, 1986), 39.

5. Sandra M. Foa, "María de Zayas y Sotomayor: Sibyl of Madrid (Spanish 1590?–1661?), " in *Female Scholars: A Tradition of Learned Women Before 1800*, ed. J. R. Brink (Montreal: Eden Press Women's Publications, 1980), 54–67.

6. In her 1975 collection *Antología del feminismo* ([Madrid: Alianza], 227–333), Amalia Martín-Gamero devotes a chapter to the essays of "Men Who Defended Women," including Luis Vélez de Guevara in the sixteenth century, King Carlos III in the eighteenth century, and turn-of-the-century playwright Gregorio Martínez Sierra (whose wife has been shown by scholar Patricia O'Connor to have authored a number of plays attributed to him).

7. A thoughtful discussion of this author's male pseudonym, and of the conflicts relating to anxiety of authorship for a woman in nineteenth-century Spain, is offered by Susan Kirkpatrick in "On the Threshold of the Realist Novel: Gender and Genre in *La gaviota*," *PMLA* 98 (May 1983): 323–40.

8. The primary older reference is the exhaustive turn-of-the-century bibliography of women writers from 1404–1833 compiled by historian Manuel Serrano y Sanz, which lists over a thousand names. The most substantial contemporary resource before those of the current decade is Isabel Calvo de Aguilar's 1954 *Antología biográfica de escritoras españolas* (Madrid: Biblioteca Nueva), which profiles eighty-five modern writers.

9. Carolyn L. Galerstein, ed., *Women Writers of Spain: An Annotated Bio-Bibliographical Guide* (New York and Westport, Conn.: Greenwood Press, 1986).

10. Janet Pérez, *Contemporary Women Writers of Spain* (Boston: Twayne Publishers, 1988).

11. Alan Deyermond, "Spain's First Women Writers," in *Women in Hispanic Literature: Icons and Fallen Idols*, ed. Beth Miller (Berkeley and Los Angeles: University of California Press, 1983), 27–52; quote is on 28.

12. Gonzalo Sobejano, *Novela española de nuestro tiempo*, 2d ed. (Madrid: Prensa Española, 1975), 145.

13. This concept was originated by Leon Festinger and explained in his *A Theory of Cognitive Dissonance* (Stanford, Calif.: Stanford University Press, 1957). The term was originally applied to individual conflictive reactions, although in popular

usage it has been extended to include the collective reactions of homogeneous groups, such as that of the men with common cultural conditioning who comprise the critical elite in Spain.

14. Examples are the literary history published in 1956 by Gonzalo Torrente Ballester, which discusses seventeen women writers; Juan Luis Alborg's 1958 volume, which includes six women writers; and the reference by Eugenio de Nora, published in 1962, which presents nineteen. Gonzalo Sobejano's 1975 literary history discusses five women authors, the 1973 book by José Domingo presents twelve, and the 1983 edition of the history of twentieth-century literature by Angel Valbuena Prat includes sixteen. Ignacio Soldevila Durante's 1980 literary history features thirty-three women authors, and José María Martínez Cachero's 1985 history of postwar literature includes thirty-four. See Gonzalo Torrente Ballester, *Panorama de la literatura española contemporánea* (Madrid: Guadarrama, 1956); Juan Luis Alborg, *Hora actual de la novela española* (Madrid: Taurus, 1958); Eugenio de Nora, *La novela española contemporánea* (Madrid: Gredos, 1962); Gonzalo Sobejano, *Novela española de nuestro tiempo*, 2d ed. (Madrid: Prensa española, 1975); José Domingo, *La novela española del siglo XX, tomo dos* (Barcelona: Editorial Labor, 1973); Angel Valbuena Prat, *Historia de la literatura española*, vol. 4 (Barcelona: Gustavo Gili, 1983; 1st ed. 1963); Ignacio Soldevila Durante, *La novela desde 1936* (Madrid: Alhambra, 1980), and José María Martínez Cachero, *La novela española entre 1936 y 1980: Historia de una aventura* (Madrid: Castalia, 1985).

More recently, the premiere Spanish cultural journal *Insula* devoted an issue to a review of major developments in the Spanish novel from 1976–85. The mention of over a dozen women authors in this overview comprised of essays by eminent male critics supports the observation of writer Esther Tusquets, who when asked to characterize the past decade noted first of all that greater attention has been paid to novels by women. See "Diez años de la novela en España (1976–1985)," *Insula* 464–465 (1985). Tusquets's statement is on p. 11.

15. Proportional page totals allotted to male and female writers attest to a continuing imbalance: Torrente Ballester devotes 29 of 815 pages to literature by women, Alborg allots 29 of 333, de Nora devotes 18 of 515, Sobejano allocates 42 of 461, Valbuena Prat allots 32 of 975, José Domingo devotes 17 of 173, Soldevila Durante designates close to 100 pages of 470, and Martínez Cachero allocates approximately 120 pages of 480.

16. Janet Pérez, "Some Desiderata in Studies of Twentieth-Century Spanish Fiction," *Siglo XX/Twentieth Century* 1 (Spring 1984): 6. Reprinted in her *Contemporary Women Writers of Spain*, p. 1.

17. A recent issue of the primary scholarly journal devoted to contemporary Spanish literature carried this title: "Reading For Difference: Feminist Perspectives on Women Novelists of Contemporary Spain," ed. Mirella Servodidio (*Anales de la Literatura Española Contemporánea* 12: 1987). Although they deal exclusively with fiction by Spanish writers, the essays in this volume demonstrate the formative influence that American and French feminist theory and criticism have had on this field. Among the most frequent sources of theoretical foundations for research on Spanish fiction by women are the writings of American critics Elaine Showalter, Susan Gilbert and Sandra Gubar, Judith Fetterley, Annette Kolodny, and Annis Pratt, and of French critics Hélène Cixous, Luce Irigaray, and Julia Kristeva.

144165⁴

LIBRARY
College of St. Francis
JOLIET, ILLINOIS

1

Carmen Laforet: The Dilemma of Artistic Vocation

Gustavo Pérez Firmat

Carmen Laforet was born in Barcelona in 1921. As a young child she moved to the island of Gran Canaria, where her father, an architect, taught at an industrial arts school. There she spent her childhood and adolescence. At the end of the Spanish civil war in 1939, she left the Canary Islands to pursue university studies in Barcelona and later in Madrid. Although she took courses in both literature and law, she did not complete her studies. Her literary career was launched in 1944, when she was awarded the Nadal Prize for her first novel, *Nada* (English translations by Inez Muñoz, *Nothing*, 1958, and by Charles F. Payne, *Andrea*, 1964), which was published and received great critical acclaim the following year. Along with Camilo José Cela's *La familia de Pascual Duarte* (Pascual Duarte's family) (1942), *Nada* marked the resurgence of Spanish literature after the civil war and placed Laforet at the forefront of the novelists of her generation. In 1946 Laforet married Manuel Cerezales, a journalist and publisher, with whom she had five children (the marriage broke up twenty-four years later, in 1970). Laforet's second novel, *La isla y los demonios* (The island and the demons), appeared in 1952 and was also well received by critics and readers. That same year she published a volume of short stories, *La muerta* (The dead woman), followed two years later with a collection of four novellas, *La llamada* (The calling). Laforet's third novel, *La mujer nueva* (The new woman), a byproduct of the author's conversion to Catholicism in the early 1950s, appeared in 1954; her fourth novel, *La insolación* (Sunstroke), was published in 1963. Although *La insolación* was advertised as the first volume in a trilogy to be called *Tres pasos fuera del tiempo* (Three steps outside time), Laforet has yet to publish the other two. The second volume of the trilogy, *Jaque mate* (Checkmate), was completed, but on reading the

26

galleys for the book, Laforet became disillusioned with the project and decided not to see it into print. She has not published—and apparently not written—any other novels since then. Laforet's most recent book is a readable account of a trip to the United States, *Paralelo 35* (Thirty-fifth parallel) (1967).

Not long ago Carmen Laforet was universally regarded as one of the leading novelists of contemporary Spain. Few modern Spanish novels have had as much critical and popular success as *Nada*; even today, more than forty years after its original publication, *Nada* continues to be read and discussed. Yet Laforet's place in the canon of modern Spanish fiction is no longer secure. Her prolonged silence, combined with the changes in literary fashion that have taken place in the last twenty years, has turned her into something of a marginal figure. The consensual opinion seems to be that Laforet never lived up to the expectations created by her early work, and one senses that Laforet's output as a whole and *Nada* in particular are quickly becoming curiosities—texts of considerable historical interest but dwindling literary significance. Indeed, for the contemporary student of Spanish literature, Laforet's "case"—great early success followed by a long, enigmatic silence—is perhaps more intriguing than her novelistic production.

For this reason, the questions that one feels compelled to address to Laforet's *oeuvre* seem external to it. They have to do, above all, with the issue of artistic vocation, perhaps especially as it relates to the role of women in modern Spanish society. One wonders to what extent this author's career—like that of other women artists—has been constrained by familial and social pressures and expectations. Given Laforet's reticence and the pious attitude of some students of her work, it is possible that one may never be able to provide a biographical answer to these questions. Still, in this case biographical answers may not be appropriate or necessary, since the question of artistic vocation is in fact not external to Laforet's writings. Just the opposite is true: the dilemma of vocation, and particularly of female vocation, is a recurrent theme in all of Laforet's work, from *Nada* to *La insolación*. In this connection the title of her second collection of short fiction, *La llamada*, is key, especially since in context it refers specifically to the protagonist's artistic calling, "la llamada de su arte" [the calling of her art] (677). Indeed, I will argue that Laforet's work remains interesting, above all, for its sensitive discussion of the issue of vocation in general and of female authorship in particular. I refer specifically to her first two novels, *Nada* and *La isla y los demonios*, to the novella *La llamada*, and to a short story entitled "Rosamunda." Not only are these texts concerned, in diverse ways, with the problem of authorship (for Laforet it *is* a problem), but they also actually *anticipate* Laforet's much-discussed silence. The question that these novels and stories insistently take up is whether artistic vocation is compatible with a woman's calling, and they dispose of the question by providing a negative answer. Laforet's subsequent agraphia is inscribed, as it were, in several of her best-known narrations.

Nada is a first-person narration, set, like all of Laforet's novels, in the years immediately succeeding the Spanish civil war. The protagonist is Andrea, a young woman who has come to Barcelona to study at the university. She takes up residence at her ancestral family home in an elegant but run-down section of the city. Like the neighborhood, the family's fortunes have suffered with the war, and the house is decrepit. The family members themselves are a gallery of eccentrics and neurotics. Román, Andrea's uncle and at one time a promising composer, lives in the attic and seems bent on inflicting psychological torture on his brother, Juan, and on Juan's wife (and Román's former lover), Gloria. Juan dedicates himself to painting, but with little success, and Gloria is the one who actually supports the family by gambling on the sly. Andrea's maternal grandmother is a weak and feeble-minded old woman who, by design or accident, blinds herself to the sordid reality of the family's life. The cast is rounded out by a tyrannical and sinister maid who protects the kitchen as if it were her own private domain and by a spinster aunt, aptly named Angustias (anguish).

In the course of Andrea's stay several unexpected events alter the course of the family's life. Román commits suicide, and Angustias leaves the house to join a convent. After a year with her relatives, Andrea herself abandons Barcelona to continue her studies in Madrid. As several critics have pointed out, *Nada* has less to do with any incidents in the plot than with the effect that these incidents have on the developing sensibility of the eighteen-year-old protagonist. The focus of the narration never shifts away from Andrea, who records and reacts to the strange events that take place around her. In this respect the novel is both "egographic" and "egocentric": Andrea is both the medium and the subject of the story.[1]

The paradox of *Nada*—already insinuated in the title—is that Andrea is a narrator whose language insistently calls attention to itself but who is equally insistent in covering up or dissembling the act of narration. From the first pages of the novel it becomes clear that *Nada* is very much a literary account rather than the informal or inchoate or unselfconscious recollections of a character who does not adopt a writerly stance. There is here none of that artifice that consists of placing the narration in the hands of an incompetent narrator—a child, an illiterate, an aphasic. From the first sentences the reader is struck by the richness and intensity of Andrea's language, features that have led some critics to associate Laforet's novel with *tremendismo*, the name given to the tendency of some post-civil war writers to depict in stark fashion the sordid and the disagreeable aspects of life. As one example, from the description of the house on Aribau Street: "Parecía una casa de brujas aquel cuarto de baño. Las paredes tiznadas conservaban la huella de manos ganchudas, de gritos de desesperanza. Por todas partes los desconchados abrían sus bocas desdentadas rezumantes de humedad. Sobre el espejo, porque no cabía en otro sitio, habían colocado un bodegón macabro de besugos pálidos y cebollas sobre fondo negro. La locura sonreía en los grifos torcidos" [That bathroom looked like a witch house. The dirty walls bore the fingerprints of hooked hands, of shouts of despair. Oozing humidity, the peeling walls gaped like toothless mouths. On top of the mirror, because there was no room anywhere else, someone had placed a painting of pale giltheads and onions against a black background. Madness grinned from the twisted spigots] (28–29). The language of this passage is nothing if not *graphic*, in both senses of the word: Andrea's aim is to reproduce what she saw as vividly as possible, and this aim can be accomplished only with a highly contrived description—hence the proliferation of striking similes and adjectives. Like the walls in the bathroom, Andrea's language seems to call out to the observer: it is not only the walls that ooze; Andrea's prose itself spills over with rhetorical flourishes. Although this passage has been read (and rightly so) as reflective of the oppressive political and literary climate of post-civil war Spain,[2] it is also possible to see it as a kind of virtuoso scriptive performance. In descriptions like these Andrea is strutting her stuff, making her reader aware of the expressive resources at her command. The deep "purple prose" of these sentences can only call attention to the authorial hand that contrived them. If the walls of the house on Aribau Street conserve the *huellas* or fingerprints of its ghostly inhabitants, Andrea's language is similarly marked by the hand of its creator.

The problem, however, is that throughout the whole novel Andrea herself remains something of a "ghost," a writer who does not acknowledge her labors. Discussing the impressionistic narrative technique of the novel, Laforet has asserted that Andrea "es casi una sombra que cuenta" [is almost a shadow who speaks].[3] As a writer, Andrea is indeed a shadowy presence, a ghost, since she never owns up to the act of composition. *Nada* is a novel where language occupies center stage but where the scriptive act and the will that produced that language are nowhere in evidence. The autobiographical act supposes the continuity of narrator and protagonist; it supposes that, with the passage of time and the unfolding of the narrative, the latter will merge into the former. For this reason, one of the essential plotlines of an autobiographical narrative is to retrace the steps that have led the protagonist from character to narrator, from actor to author. Because of this, the plot of an autobiography is always double, since the reader's attention can focus on the act of narrative or on the events in the plot. An autobiography always contains a secondary or recessed story: the story of how the story gets told. In *Nada*, however, this second story is elided, since the reader never finds out how Andrea comes to write her account. As Ruth El Saffar has pointed out, "the fictional author is not shown in her novel developing out of the character whom she presents on page one" (El Saffar 1974, 119). Andrea's stance as writer, the "graphic" component of her autobiography, remains hidden from view, although every single word in the novel bears witness to it.

This situation contrasts sharply with what obtains in other first-person narrations, where much information is furnished about the circumstances under which the story is composed. In Cela's *Pascual Duarte*, just to give one example from a novel to which *Nada* is often compared, the reader has a clear picture of Pascual the writer: we know that he writes from his jail cell as he awaits execution for the murders he has committed; Pascual even provides information about his writing implements, his work habits, and the room from which he writes. In *Nada* this kind of information is lacking, for there are no references whatsoever to the circumstances of the story's composition. Andrea focuses on her past and avoids any explicit reference to her present. In fact, the one passage in the novel that gives a glimpse of Andrea's writerly self is a sentence spoken not by Andrea but by Román, who says to her reproachfully, "Ya sé que estás siempre soñando cuentos con nuestros caracteres" [I know that you are always dreaming up stories with our characters] (46). Román's reproach actually forms the nucleus of *Nada*, which is indeed the *cuento* [story] Andrea dreams up around the characters (in both senses) that inhabit the house on Aribau. Román here accuses Andrea of what Andrea will never admit—that she is a writer.

Andrea's reticence about her writing becomes more puzzling when one recalls how often she draws attention to the differences between her younger and older selves, between Andrea as actor and Andrea as author. Throughout the novel she repeatedly states that she is not now—at the time of writing—the person she was when she arrived in Barcelona. At the end of the novel, as she is about to leave for Madrid, she reflects:

> Bajé las escaleras despacio. Sentía una violenta emoción. Recordaba la terrible esperanza, el anhelo de vida con que las había subido por primera vez. Me marchaba ahora sin haber conocido nada de lo que confusamente esperaba: la vida en su plenitud, la alegría, el interés profundo, el amor. De la casa de la calle de Aribau no me llevaba nada. Al menos, así creía yo entonces.

> I went slowly down the stairs. I felt a violent emotion. I remembered the hopefulness, the longing for life with which I had gone up those stairs for the first time. I was leaving now without having known anything of what I confusedly was expecting: life in its fullness, happiness, deep interests, love. From the house on Aribau Street I was taking nothing. At least, that's what I thought then. (260)

Passages like this one, where there is a clear separation between Andrea's twin identities as protagonist and narrator, are scattered throughout the text.[4] The ''entonces'' [then] of the last sentence clearly points to an ''ahora'' [now] from which Andrea, older and wiser, records and interprets her experiences during the year at Aribau. The paradox is that this time frame—the here-and-now of writing—is everywhere evoked but nowhere rendered.

The somewhat puzzling title, *Nada*, reflects this aspect of the novel. In a passage that strongly echoes Andrea's statement above, Laforet explained the title in this way: ''Andrea pasa por el relato con los ojos abiertos, con curiosidad, sin rencor. Se va de él sin nada en las manos. Sin encontrar nada . . .'' [Andrea passes through the story with her eyes open, curious, without rancor. She leaves empty-handed. Having found nothing . . .][5] Yet it is clear that Andrea does come away from her experiences with something; not only does she believe that she is more lucid or perceptive than she was before, but she has also produced an account entitled ''Nada'' of her stay in Barcelona (internal allusions make it clear that ''Nada'' is as much Andrea's title as it is Laforet's). The point is that the choice of title is part of the protagonist's propensity to elide or downplay the act and fact of writing. Calling the novel *Nada* is still another self-deprecating gesture that suggests the reluctance with which Andrea assumes the role of author.

In Laforet's second novel the implicit reluctance of *Nada* becomes an explicit refusal. *La isla y los demonios* is set in the city of Las Palmas, on the island of Gran Canaria, where Laforet grew up. Although this time the narration is given in the third person, the protagonist is again a young woman, Marta, who is sixteen years old. Like Andrea, Marta is for all practical purposes an orphan since her mother has lapsed into catatonia and her father is dead; also like Andrea, Marta is surrounded by a coterie of odd relatives and acquaintances. As several critics have remarked, almost all of the characters in *La isla* have their corresponding types in *Nada*: the role of Román, the neurotic and failed artist, is now played by Pablo, a painter with whom Marta becomes infatuated; the role of Angustias is now played by Pino, Marta's step-sister-in-law; the role of Juan is taken by José, Marta's half-brother and head of the household; the role of the grandmother is taken by Vicenta, the *majorera* (the name given by the islanders to those born on the island of Fuerteventura); and the character of Honesta, Pablo's wife, reminds one of Gloria. Like *Nada*, *La isla* ends with the protagonist's departure from the family home to make a life for herself, and, as in the first novel, the civil war is a hovering presence but is not directly portrayed. Although the action of *La isla* takes place during the war, in the Canaries the conflict remains in the background: the temporal distance of the first novel finds an analogue in the spatial distance of the second.

Because of these and other similarities, *La isla y los demonios* may be seen as a rewriting or "reiteration" of Laforet's first novel.[6] For my purposes, however, the two works display a crucial difference: unlike Andrea, Marta acknowledges her literary ambitions, and an important thread in the novel's plot is her development as a writer. These ambitions materialize in her collection entitled "Legends of Alcorah," stories based on the mythology of the Canaries (where Alcorah is an island god), as well as in her journal and a spate of poems. Throughout the novel one finds repeated references to these texts, which Marta hides zealously in her room. If *Nada* is a *bildungsroman*, a novel of formation, *La isla* belongs to the subgenre of the *künstlerroman*, a novel of formation that deals specifically with the growth of an artist's vocation. In this respect *La isla* fills in the gap between action and narration that was present in *Nada*. When Marta locks herself up in her room to record her impressions in a journal, the reader seems to be witnessing the process that will eventually lead to the composition of an auto-biographical account like *Nada*.

Curiously, the climactic moment in the novel occurs when Marta decides to *forsake* her literary ambitions. Seeking approval, Marta shows some of her legends to several of her relatives, who have arrived from the mainland. Instead of encouraging her, they tell her that she has no talent and should give up writing altogether. Marta believes them and decides to burn all of her manuscripts. The book burning is the final event in the novel. Roberta Johnson has interpreted this scene as the culmination of Marta's entrance into adulthood and of her "emergence from her dream-world and girlish illusions" (Johnson 1981, 75). Marta herself, remarking that "La niña que había escrito aquellas cosas no era ella ya" [She was no longer the child who had written those things] (634), thinks that by burning her writings she is destroying her adolescent self: "Aquello era, verdaderamente, convertir en cenizas su adolescencia" [In truth, that was tantamount to converting her adolescence into ashes] (634).

While it is certainly the case that Marta's destruction of her manuscripts is portrayed in the novel in a favorable light (that is, Marta's interpretation of this incident is endorsed by the omniscient narrator), the novel's conclusion remains puzzling. Any novel that ends with a book burning is rather curious, especially when the manuscripts being incinerated to some extent mirror the novel itself (since one can consider the novel a transposition into the third person of the contents of Marta's journal). The fact that *La isla* is a novel of formation makes this self-consuming quality even more puzzling, for one is being told that Marta's maturation entails a passage from writing to agraphia. Writing is a symptom of immaturity; growing up means recognizing the folly of her literary vocation: "Despacio, acabó de vaciar su cartera. Arrugó los papeles que quedaban allí; de nuevo frotó una cerilla para prenderlos. Las leyendas que no quiso leer nadie, se quemaron, crepitando, humeando, como la víctima de un sacrificio a un dios pagano. Al fin, quedaron sólo unas cenizas retorcidas. Marta las aventó" [Slowly, she finished emptying her portfolio. She crumpled the papers that were left inside; again, she struck a match to set them on fire. The legends that no one wanted to read burned, crackling, smoking, like the victim of a sacrifice to a pagan god. Finally, only a few twisted ashes remained. Marta tossed them into the wind] (635). Throwing the ashes into the wind is Marta's final action, an action with which she intends to signify her conversion, her break with the past. Her sacrifice drives away the psychological demons that have accosted her throughout her formative years. The price of the exorcism, however, is high: in order to dissipate the mental *recuerdo* (memory), Marta must destroy its scriptive record; the memoir must be destroyed along with the memories.

Rather than making overt the motivation implicit in *Nada*, *La isla y los demonios* actually subverts the autobiographical impulse. If Andrea had been Marta, the first-person account of *Nada* would not have come to be. Significantly, the principal structural difference between these two novels is that the later novel is narrated by an impersonal omniscient narrator—a choice of narrative perspective consistent with the protagonist's abdication of both recollection and writing. Marta's will-to-forget would have made an autobiographical account impossible. *La isla* thus represents a rather rare genre: not a portrait of an artist's growth and maturation but a portrait of the sacrifice of vocation, of the abdication of authorship, which is what Marta must relinquish if she is to leave adolescence behind. One of the underlying claims of this novel is that emotional maturity and artistic vocation are incompatible.

Considered jointly, Laforet's first two novels paint a rather gloomy picture of the possibilities and significance of artistic achievement. In the first novel, giving artistic shape to one's past—turning memory into memoir—is reduced to "nothing"; in the second novel, the same gesture is reduced to ashes. Some of Laforet's shorter fiction offers further corroboration of the notion that artistic vocation is incompatible with adult female behavior. *La llamada*, a novella that engages the subject of artistic vocation already in its title, complements the treatment of vocation present in the two novels. In *Nada* and *La isla*, the protagonist is an artist-to-be; in *La llamada* the protagonist is an artist who never was. The novels portray the drama of an aborted vocation; the novella provides an epilogue by showing the long-term consequences of the decision to abandon art. The protagonist of this tale is a middle-aged woman who, having given up her desire to pursue a career as an actress many years before, has settled into an unhappy domestic existence as wife and mother. Hearing by chance about a relative who lives in Barcelona, she abandons family and home and goes to the city to pursue her long-deferred career. Once there she manages to perform at a nightclub for aspiring actors, but her debut is a fiasco and she is driven from the stage by hoots and whistles. Chastened by the experience, Mercedes returns to her town and resigns herself to her lot. This is how she rationalizes the decision to return home: "Mercedes sentía una gran paz y, sí, alegría .... Era como si hubiera estado muy enferma y un medicamento fuerte la hubiera curado. Todo se volvía de pronto tan natural, tan sencillo, tan limpio" [Mercedes felt a great peace and, yes, happiness .... It was as if she had been very ill and a strong medicine had cured her. All of a sudden everything became so natural, so simple, so clean] (685).

In the context of Laforet's first two novels, the metaphor of vocation as disease acquires more than casual significance. Mercedes's "illness" is equivalent to Marta's "demons." In both cases a drastic remedy is required—the "sacrifice" of Marta's writings in one instance and the "strong medicine" of public embarrassment in the other. It is important to underscore that Mercedes's choice of language is not treated ironically; for the reader, Mercedes's decision to become an artist is nothing short of folly, an access of lunacy from which she is indeed "cured" by her lack of success on the stage. Like Marta, Mercedes at the end sees the light; that is, she realizes that her true calling is that of wife and mother. Still, one suspects that Laforet has deliberately stacked the cards against her protagonist by making her a pathetic figure bereft of any real talent (recall that a similar opinion was expressed about Marta's writing). A pattern begins to emerge: the three narrations examined above elaborate the traditional novelistic theme of the passage from illusion to reality. In *Nada* and *La isla y los demonios*, this passage is cast in the form of an adolescent's maturation; in *La llamada*, it takes the form of a midlife crisis that is resolved when the protagonist belatedly discovers her true calling. In all three cases the female protagonists have some connection to art, and this connection is severed as part of the protagonists' development.

Curiously, Laforet's one portrayal of successful artistic vocation focuses on a male artist, Martín, the painter-protagonist of *La insolación*. In contrast to Laforet's first two novels, *La insolación* focuses on a male adolescent who undergoes a sexual and artistic awakening. The action of the novel takes place during three summers that Martín spends in a resort town with his father and stepmother (the motif of orphanhood that had been prevalent in the first two novels reappears here). Most of the events have to do with Martín's relationship with two neighbors—Carlos, who is Martín's age (fifteen when the novel begins), and his sister, Anita, who is a year old. Like *Nada* or *La isla*, *La insolación* is less a coordinated sequence of actions than a series of episodes connected by the presence of the protagonist. The climactic scene in the novel occurs when Martín's father discovers Martín and Carlos sleeping in the same bed and, enraged at the suspicion of homosexual behavior between the two adolescents, beats his son, who shortly thereafter leaves his father's house and returns to live with his grandparents in Alicante. This decision entails a commitment to the life of art. As Martín says to Carlos in his culminating speech, "Ayer me di cuenta de lo que es una vocación de artista, Carlos . . . . Ayer, en aquellas horas que pasé pensando, sentí lo que es la verdadera liberación. No sé cómo explicártelo. No sé si alguna vez tú te has planteado problemas de ataduras religiosas, políticas o familiares, no lo sé. Nunca hemos hablado .... Yo me sentí liberado de todo eso como si hubiera roto esas ataduras" [Yesterday I realized what an artist's vocation is, Carlos .... Yesterday, during those hours I spent thinking, I felt what true liberation is. I don't know how to explain it to you. I don't know whether you have ever faced problems of religious, political, or family ties. I don't know, we've never talked about that .... I felt freed from all that as if I had broken all of those ties] (320).

One can contrast Martín's assertion with the corresponding one by Marta from *La isla y los demonios*: "Le parecía que la vida que iba a empezar era tan nueva que no quería meterse en ella cargada de recuerdos viejos. Rompió sin compasión la pequeña agenda en que, día a día, había resumido durante varios meses, en unas frases cortas, sus impresiones" [It seemed to her that the life she was about to begin was so new that she didn't want to embark on it weighted down with old memories. Feeling no regret, she tore up the small notebook where, day by day, she had summarized, in short phrases, her impressions over the last several months] (633–34). For Marta, abdicating her artistic vocation is a mark of maturity; for Martín, precisely the opposite is true, for only when he decides to dedicate himself completely to his art does he achieve adulthood. Whereas *La insolación* follows the traditional pattern of the *künstlerroman*, *La isla* places itself in opposition to it. Both novels end with the protagonists' liberation, with the severing of familial and social ties, but in *La isla* this liberation entails a disengagement from art. In order to find herself Marta not only has to break with her family, but she also needs to "tear up" her journal (the verb in Spanish is the same—*romper*).

One can also usefully contrast Martín and Mercedes. In order to recover from her illness, Mercedes has to give up her acting ambitions; in *La insolación*, however, it is the forgetting of art that is a kind of disease, the "sunstroke" referred to in the title (327). For Laforet's one male protagonist, art is health; for her female protagonists, it is a symptom of mental illness or immaturity. One cannot find in Laforet's corpus one single artist-heroine; all of the women with artistic vocation fail or are frustrated; it is only the male artist who has the talent and determination to impose his vocation on adverse circumstances. Leaving aside for the moment the question of how this gloomy portrait of women artists reflects Laforet's problematic assumption of her own literary vocation, the conclusion to be drawn from these texts is fairly unequivocal: art is a legitimate calling only when its subject is male; when a woman hears "the call of art," she is regarded as acting out of folly or self-delusion.

In fact, the only vocation (other than the traditional one of wife and mother) that is successfully pursued by Laforet's female protagonists is a religious one. This is the subject of Laforet's third novel, *La mujer nueva*. The Pauline resonances of the title already suggest the religious dimension of the novel. The protagonist (whose name, expectedly, is Paulina) is no longer an orphaned adolescent but a married woman in her middle thirties who undergoes a sudden religious conversion. In the first part of the novel, Paulina, who has led a turbulent and free-thinking youth, settles down to a loveless marriage with Eulogio, a member of a wealthy land-owning family, and an intermittent affair with Antonio, a man she met during the war. In the brief second part Paulina, while riding on a train, undergoes a mystical experience that leads her to Catholicism. The last part of the novel describes the "new woman" she becomes as she attempts to reconcile her newly acquired faith with her obligations as wife and mother. The novel concludes with Paulina's decision to return to her husband and son. Unlike *Nada* and *La isla*, both of which end with a sense of expectancy, *La mujer nueva* takes expectancy into accomplishment, hopefulness into faith.[7]

A look at an additional text, a short story entitled "Rosamunda," will summarize the argument thus far and probe further into Laforet's problematic view of female artistic vocation. This early story, published originally in *La muerta*, is in several respects an encapsulated version of *La llamada*. As in *La llamada*, the protagonist is a middle-aged, impoverished woman whose artistic inclinations are regarded as foolish and unrealistic. While riding third class in a train, Felisa (a name not without irony since it suggests "felicidad" or happiness) relates to a young soldier her achievements on the stage, where she was known as both an actress and poet. In telling her story, much of which is doubtless fabrication (indeed, perhaps this is the one true work of art that Felisa has produced), Felisa talks about herself in the third person, all the while referring to herself by her stage name, Rosamunda. The young man is both intrigued and repulsed by the spectacle of this haggard, ill-dressed woman, and the story concludes when he invites her to have breakfast. The woman accepts and asks the young man to call her Rosamunda, in this way installing herself definitively in the dream world that she has created in the course of the train ride. The parallels and contrasts with *La mujer nueva* are worth noting. Like the novel, this story details the protagonist's forging of a new identity; the subject of "Rosamunda," like that of the novel, is the birth of a "new woman"; and, as in the novel, the change takes place on a train.[8] Unlike Paulina's, however, Felisa's new identity is seen as ridiculous and inauthentic. If Paulina's conversion inspires respect, Felisa/Rosamunda's provokes only laughter. The moral seems clear: as far as women are concerned, religion is health and art is disease.

This short story can be juxtaposed with the autobiographical prologue Laforet wrote for *La niña* (The girl) (1970), a collection of previously published narrations that includes this story. Although several decades separate the composition of the story from the writing of the prologue, there are two significant points of contact between Laforet's image of herself as writer and her portrayal of Felisa/Rosamunda. First, Laforet's description of how real-life anecdotes become fiction employs a language that harks back to the theatrical atmosphere of the story: "Estas anécdotas se airearon como los trajes viejos que se guardan en el desván de las casas antiguas y se sacan cuando hace falta disfrazarse para representar una comedia" [These anecdotes were taken out to be aired like old suits that one keeps in the attic of old houses only to take them out when one needs to put on a costume in order to act in a comedy] (Laforet 1970, 9). The transformation of reality into fiction is analogous to Felisa's transformation into Rosamunda. Writing is a form of theatrical imposture, a way of dressing up or disguising true stories to make them presentable or representable in public. Laforet seems to look upon her literary creations much as she looks upon Felisa's fabrications: although they are harmless enough, they possess little real worth; they are almost "nothing."

The other similarity between the prologue and the story is that Laforet, like Felisa, speaks about herself in the third person. "Carmen Laforet está casada. En la época en que escribió los relatos que tenéis entre manos era madre de algunos niños convertidos ya en mujeres y hombres. Su hijo más joven no había nacido entonces y tiene en la época que escribo este prólogo 12 años" [Carmen Laforet is married. At the time when she wrote the stories you have in your hands she was the mother of children who are now grown men and women. Her youngest son had not been born yet and he is now, as I write, twelve years old] (13). The striking oscillation between past and present and third person and first, encapsulated in the opposition between "escribió" (she wrote) and "escribo" (I write), endows Laforet with twin identities: Laforet the writer—the one who "wrote" all these stories—and Laforet the nonwriter, or the writer only of marginalia—the one who "writes" the prologue. This split is significant for the distance that it establishes between Laforet's scriptive and nonscriptive selves. Although the prologue to *La niña* was written approximately in 1970, this distancing mechanism goes back to Laforet's first novel, *Nada*, where a similar distancing occurred between the Andrea as narrator and Andrea as character. In this prologue Laforet views herself much as Andrea views her younger self; indeed, Laforet's autobiographical remarks echo one of the key passages in *Nada*. Speaking of one of the photographs included in her complete works, she states: "En la primera aparece una muchacha aún no marcada, libre—o al menos eso creía ella—de elegir su destino en la tierra" [In the first one there appears a girl not yet marked by fate, free—at least that's what she thought—to choose her destiny on earth] (11). The teasing parenthetical interpolation in this sentence is almost a direct quotation from *Nada*: "De la casa de la calle Aribau no me llevaba nada. Al menos, así creía yo entonces" [From the house on Aribau Street I was taking nothing. At least that's what I thought at the time] (260).

   These parallels between Laforet's autobiographical statements and her fiction provide a glimpse of the real-life vexations that may lie behind Laforet's literary silence; more important, they add another facet to Laforet's delineation of the problematic of female authorship. For reasons that she never makes explicit but that doubtless have something to do with societal and family obligations—in this context the reference above to her inability to elect freely her lot in life is obviously significant—Laforet's career (and I use this term to encompass both fictional texts and autobiographical subtexts) insistently dramatizes the failure or abandonment of artistic vocation. What makes Laforet arresting to this day is her intricate depiction of the problems that afflict an artist—especially a female artist—in whom "the call of art" conflicts with other, perhaps louder or more insistent, callings. Laforet's legacy may well be a trail of smoke, exactly like the one produced when Marta, at the end of *La isla y los demonios*, sets fire to her manuscripts and watches her literary career turn into nothing.

Notes

1. I take the notion of an "egographic narrator" from Steven Kellman, *The Self-Begetting Novel* (New York: Columbia University Press, 1980).

2. See Kronik 1981.

3. Carmen Laforet, *Mis páginas mejores* (My best pages), (Madrid: Gredos, 1956), 13.

4. This aspect of the novel has been studied by Perelmuter Pérez (1980).

5. Laforet, *Mis páginas mejores*, 13.

6. The term *reiteration* appears in Eugenio G. de Nora, *La novela española contemporánea* (Madrid: Gredos, 1970), 3: 109.

7. It is worth noting that *La isla y los demonios* also features a conversion scene of sorts: Marta's "conversion" of her manuscripts into ashes, which is likened to a "sacrifice to a pagan God" (635).

8. It is a curious coincidence that in *La llamada*, the poem that the protagonist recites during her debut on the stage is Campoamor's "El tren expreso" (The express train).

Bibliography

1. PRIMARY WORKS

1945. *Nada*. Barcelona: Destino.

1952a. *La isla y los demonios*. Barcelona: Destino.

1952b. *La muerta*. Barcelona: Destino.

1954. *La llamada*. Barcelona: Destino.

1955. *La mujer neuva*. Barcelona: Destino.

1963a. *La insolación*. Barcelona: Planeta.

1963b. *Novelas*. Barcelona: Planeta.

1970. *La niña y otros relatos*. Madrid: Editorial Magisterio Español.

2. SECONDARY WORKS

Carrasco, Hugo. 1982. "Las narraciones concurrentes en *La isla y los demonios*." *Estudios Filológicos* 17: 23–38. One of the few sustained discussions of a novel other than *Nada*.

Collins, Marsha. 1984–85. "Carmen Laforet's *Nada*: Fictional Form and the Search for Identity." *Symposium* 38: 298–310. Studies the novel as both romance and *bildungsroman*.

El Saffar, Ruth. 1974. "Structural and Thematic Tactics of Suppression in Carmen Laforet's *Nada*." *Symposium* 28: 119–29. An insightful discussion of the novel's dual narrative perspective.

Foster, David William. 1966. "*Nada* de Carmen Laforet (ejemplo de neo-romance en la novela contemporánea)." *Revista Hispánica Moderna* 32: 43–55. Places the novel in the tradition of the Gothic romance.

Johnson, Roberta. 1981. *Carmen Laforet*. Boston: Twayne. The best, most complete book-length study on Laforet.

Jones, Margaret E. W. 1979. "Dialectical Movement as Feminist Technique in the Works of Carmen Laforet." In *Studies in Honor of Gerald E. Wade*, ed. Sylvia Bowman *et al*, 109–20. Madrid: Porrúa. On the structuring function of character pairs in the novels and novellas.

Kronik, John W. 1981. "*Nada* y el texto asfixiado: Proyección de una estética." *Revista Iberoamericana* 116–17: 195–202. Analyzes the images of enclosure in the novel.

Perelmuter Pérez, Rosa. 1980. "Acontecimiento y escritura en *Nada* de Carmen Laforet." *Taller Literario* 1: 11–15. Cogent discussion of the distance between action and narration.

Spires, Robert C. 1978. "La experiencia afirmadora de *Nada*." In *La novela española de posguerra: Creación artística y experiencia personal*, 51–73. Madrid: Cupsa. Thoughtful analysis of the evolution of the protagonist in the context of her two roles as character and narrator.

2

Writing against the Current:
The Novels of Elena Quiroga

Phyllis Zatlin

When Elena Quiroga's *Viento del Norte* (Northwind) won the Nadal Prize for 1950, this virtually unknown writer quickly gained national recognition. Carmen Laforet won the first Nadal in 1944, and Quiroga was the second woman to be so honored. In the 1950s, four other women novelists were awarded the coveted prize. Three of these—Dolores Medio, Carmen Martín Gaite, and Ana María Matute—joined Laforet and Quiroga in a group of postwar Spanish women novelists that has been the subject of continuing scholarly interest.

This interest, however, has not always been evenly distributed across the group. Quiroga, in particular, despite winning the Critics' Prize in 1960 for *Tristura* (Sadness), for many years was not given the critical attention her works deserved. Thus in January 1983, when she became the second woman elected to the Real Academia Española, even some specialists in the contemporary Spanish novel were caught by surprise; the related feature story in the Madrid newspaper *Cambio 16* was entitled "Elena Quiroga, la olvidada" (Elena Quiroga, the forgotten woman). The poet Carmen Conde, the first woman member of the Academy, was quoted in the article as justifying her support of Quiroga's candidacy on the grounds that in difficult times Quiroga had written of things that involved taking a real risk (Llopis 1983, 89). Quiroga's novelistic production to date consists of ten full-length and three short novels. Her recent distinction has brought new editions of several books and has introduced an important author not only to a younger generation of readers but also to those who failed to discover her daring, innovative novels at the time of their first publication.

Elena Quiroga, the sixteenth of seventeen children, was born 26 October 1921 in Santander.[1] Her mother, Isabel Abarca Fornés, who died when Elena was not yet two years old, returned to her family's home in Santander to give birth. Quiroga, however, tends to identify herself as Galician. Her father, José Quiroga Velarde, was a landowner from Villoria in the province of Orense, and it was there that Quiroga spent her early childhood. At the age of nine, she was sent to a boarding school near Bilbao and began spending her vacations with her maternal grandmother in Santander rather than returning to Galicia.

In 1936, when Spain was on the verge of civil war, Quiroga decided that she could no longer tolerate the restrictive atmosphere of Catholic school. Her father agreed to send her to Rome, where she studied at a school specializing in arts and humanities. She considers her time in Italy to have been an important influence on her future career as a writer. Rome itself was, for her, a revelation. At Christmas 1937, in the middle of Spain's civil conflict (1936–39), she returned home via southern France and she spent the duration of the war in the relative tranquility of a Galician village.

Largely self-educated, Quiroga took full advantage of her paternal grandfather's collection of books—a collection she labels "Voltairian"—and of the library in La Coruña, the coastal city to which she and her father moved in 1942. For several years she occupied her time by reading, walking, and exploring the Galician countryside on rickety old buses. Aside from one long-forgotten newspaper article, her earliest effort at writing was *La soledad sonora* (Sonorous solitude), a novel completed in 1948 and published the following year. Quiroga dates the real beginning of her novelistic career from *Viento del Norte*, the work that brought her national fame and initiated a decade of great literary productivity.

In 1950 Quiroga married the Galician historian and genealogist Dalmiro de la Válgoma, and the couple moved to Madrid, where they still reside. Since 1968, when he was named permanent librarian and secretary of the Real Academia de Historia, they have lived in the History Academy building on the Calle de León. Until her own appointment to the Real Academia Española, with the resultant flurry of interviews, speaking invitations, and commitments to judge literary contests, Quiroga lived a quiet, even isolated life in the sanctity of her study in Madrid and at the couple's *pazo* (country estate) in Galicia.

Quiroga's own experiences are reflected thematically in her novels, although not always in direct, autobiographical ways. She clearly empathizes with motherless children, often examining the psychology of the orphaned or lonely, alienated individual. Her knowledge of and love for Galicia is shown in her choice of that region as the background for several of her major works, but often the action is divided between two locales (Galicia and Santander, Galicia and Madrid), building upon the same division at different moments in her life. In *Tristura* and *Escribo tu nombre* (I write your name) (1965), the first two novels in a planned trilogy, she draws most extensively on her past. Her protagonist Tadea, a motherless child who is sent from Galicia to be raised by her maternal relatives in Santander and who ultimately rebels against the narrowness and hypocrisy of her Catholic boarding school, has much in common with the young Elena Quiroga.

Viento del Norte, still Quiroga's most widely read novel and one that also gained popularity as a movie, has a traditional novelistic structure. There is a third-person omniscient narrator, and time is linear. Because of these narrative aspects and the setting in rural Galicia, a number of critics quickly labeled it "nineteenth century" and sought to link it with the novel of Emilia Pardo Bazán (1851–1921). Perhaps the superficiality of their critical approach can be attributed to two biases: a male-centered focus that tended to put all women writers, and certainly all Galician women writers, in the same category, and a Madrid-centered focus that failed to appreciate the realities of twentieth-century Galicia.

Quiroga remembers a conversation she had years later with a scholar who had called *Viento del Norte* "nineteenth century." When he finally visited Galicia, he discovered that the ambience of her novel was reflective of rural life with its sharp divisions between social classes. She asked him when he would write a retraction of his previous views, but to her knowledge he has never done so. Although other Galicians, such as Gonzalo Torrente Ballester (b. 1910) and Marina Mayoral (b. 1942), have since written novels in Castilian that are set in their native region and show a related reality, old labels are hard to erase. The tendency to brush off Quiroga's works as out-of-date was even more unfair because her subsequent novels, whatever the setting, differed greatly from her Nadal Prize-winner in novelistic technique.

Although *Viento del Norte* is atypical of Quiroga's dominant, Faulknerian narrative structure, it introduces elements that are prevalent throughout her work: penetrating psychological analysis, creation of authentic characters within a given sociohistorical circumstance, poetic style, and themes of orphanhood, alienation, and class prejudice.

Quiroga's next novel, *La sangre* (Blood) (1952), is also atypical. The most lyrical of her novels, it is a first-person account of four generations of a family told from the perspective of a chestnut tree.

Because the chestnut's vantage point is limited, and it can recount only what it sees and hears, the result is an effective ironic distancing. Critics at the time failed to note the relationship with Faulkner, but in various respects *La sangre* is a transitional work that already reveals affinities with the North American writer. Like Faulkner's Mississippi, Quiroga's Galicia is a decadent society. Her lyricism coexists with a naturalistic perception of characters doomed to degeneracy. Gone is the strict linear time of *Viento del Norte*, as the consciousness of the narrator freely flows from past to present.

Paradoxically, while Quiroga's *oeuvre* long bore the initial label "nineteenth century," some critics did recognize such innovative works as *Algo pasa en la calle* (Something's happening in the street) (1954), *La enferma* (The sick woman) (1955), and *La careta* (The mask) (1955) as being "Faulknerian." Unfortunately, they also rejected these novels as being too difficult. Accustomed to the dominant current of social realism, they were left confused by novels that introduced multiple perspectives, simultaneous time, and stream of consciousness narration, and that anticipated that the reader would become immersed in the novelistic world in order to give meaning to the text. In some cases, translations of Quiroga's innovative novels were more readily accepted in other European countries than the original texts were within Spain. Overlooking Quiroga, histories of Spanish literature generally recognize Luis Martín-Santos's *Tiempo de silencio* (1962) (*Time of Silence*, 1964) as being the landmark novel that broke away from the monochord realism previously in vogue.

The initial failure to recognize Quiroga's originality may be attributed not only to the relative lack of sophistication of her readers, but also to her tendency to work, as Carmen Conde noted in the *Cambio 16* article, with topics that implied a certain risk. *Algo pasa en la calle* touches in depth on the taboo subject of divorce. There are no published reviews of *Algo pasa en la calle* that correctly identify divorce as the novel's theme. Quiroga recalls that her controversial work was approved for publication because the censor never read it; he assumed that it would be in the vein of *Viento del Norte* and approved it on the spot. *La careta*, while probing the psychological aftermath of the civil war, daringly suggests that atrocities were committed on both sides. This novel passed censorship with comparable ease but later could not be openly displayed in bookstores.

Algo pasa en la calle and *La enferma* are both multiple perspective novels with shifting narrative points of view. They both also emphasize the female experience and form part of a cluster of

Quiroga's novels that have attracted feminist scholars in recent years. Quiroga has successfully created male protagonists, notably the alienated Moisés of *La careta* through whose consciousness most of the action is screened, and the three bullfighters in *La última corrida* (The last bullfight) (1958). In *Algo pasa en la calle* and her most recent novel, *Presente profundo* (Deep present) (1973), she develops sympathetic male characters who serve a pivotal function in contrasting the various narrative strands. In general, however, it is Quiroga's probing analysis of female experience that strikes the reader as being daring for that time and singularly perceptive even today.

In *La enferma* Quiroga juxtaposes two women—the unnamed narrator and Liberata. The latter, in response to being abandoned by the man she loves, retreats into silence and immobility; her madness is the epitome of inner exile and may indeed be interpreted as a political metaphor for the Galician situation.[2] While on the surface the narrator, a married woman who comes from the city to visit Liberata's village, has nothing in common with the sick woman, the reader ultimately realizes that both women lead empty, meaningless lives. Liberata is a mirror in which the narrator sees her own reflection.

A similar juxtaposition underscores the novella *Plácida, la joven* (The young Plácida) (1956). The narrator is visiting the Galician village where a young peasant woman, lacking proper medical care, dies in childbirth. Like Mercedes Salisachs (b. 1916), whose *Una mujer llega al pueblo* (1956) (*The Eyes of the Proud*, 1960) also revolves around a postpartum death, Quiroga is angered by class distinctions that produce such tragedies. In attempting to reconstruct Plácida's life and imagine how she thought and felt, the narrator also explores her own existence and her sense of responsibility to other women. Significantly both the narrator and Plácida are orphans, and Plácida's baby girl is left motherless.[3]

The sources of inspiration for Quiroga's novels are varied. She has commented that coming from such a large family, she never lacked material for potential stories and characters. In the cases of Liberata and Plácida, the author builds her fiction on real people and events in Galician villages. With *Tristura* and *Escribo tu nombre*, however, she turns, to some extent, to her own life. While the novels are not autobiographical per se, they ring with authenticity. In *Tristura*, the narrative point of view is that of a lonely little girl. In the seven-hundred-page *Escribo tu nombre*, the author reveals in vivid detail the world of the convent school and shows in the microcosm of Tadea's experience the moral hypocrisy and social prejudice that led to the Spanish civil war. The name Tadea writes is "Liberty," but liberty within and beyond the boarding school is short-lived. With good reason *Escribo tu nombre* was selected in 1967 to represent Spain in the first international contest for the Rómulo Gallegos Novel Prize.

In the decade following the 1951 publication of *Viento del Norte*, Quiroga wrote intensively, completing six novels and three novelettes. She then spent four years writing the massive *Escribo tu nombre*. Her productivity since then has been slight. Her only novel of the 1970s was *Presente profundo*. In the 1980s she has published no new works of fiction although she has long proposed a final volume in the Tadea trilogy to deal with the civil war years.

For the purpose of examining Quiroga's contribution to the contemporary Spanish novel, I have chosen four of her major works for more detailed discussion: *Algo pasa en la calle*, *La careta*, *Tristura*, and *Presente profundo*.[4] Written over a period of twenty years, they vary in structure and theme. Taken collectively, they present an excellent picture of the author's social and intellectual concerns as well as of the range of her narrative art.

In the early 1950s, when Quiroga began writing her experimental novels, the dominant narrative current in Spain was "objective" realism. Representative titles include Camilo José Cela's *La colmena* (1951) (*The Hive*, 1953), Luis Romero's *La noria* (The treadmill), winner of the Nadal Prize for 1951, and Rafael Sánchez Ferlosio's *El Jarama* (1956) (The Jarama River; translated into English as *The One Day of the Week*, 1962), winner of the Nadal Prize for 1955. Critics at the time viewed these works as being devoid of subjective elements. Description was cinematic, including only that which could be observed by the movie camera. Dialogue was purely naturalistic and might have been merely overheard and recorded. The authors' very creativity was placed in doubt, but the narrative technique was generally applauded.

Quiroga was quite capable of producing works in this same style; her novelette *Trayecto uno* (Bus one) (1953) falls well within this mode. The salient characteristic of *Algo pasa en la calle*, however, is the break from nominally objective, external narration. Like the objective novels, *Algo pasa en la calle* has a fragmentary structure and multiple protagonists; the action, however, is not viewed through the uniform perspective of the camera's eye but rather from the shifting, subjective points of view of the various characters. Quiroga juxtaposes several interior monologues, sometimes written in the first person, sometimes in an indirect third person, and briefly in a second person, which might be considered an antecedent to

Michel Butor's *La Modification* (1957) (*A Change of Heart*, 1959).
There are minor intrusions by an omniscient third-person narrator,
but generally there is no guide. As is true with much of the work of
Faulkner and the French New Novel, the various narrative strands
may be seen as a puzzle to be reconstructed by the reader. The
characters often contradict each other, may have only incomplete
information on the reality of the other characters, and sometimes are
reluctant to discover the truth about themselves. The reader must
weigh the evidence and reach an independent conclusion.

In *Algo pasa en la calle* the action in the fictive present—a spring
day in 1954—is precipitated by the accidental death of Ventura, a
liberal, idealistic philosophy professor. The characters, whose
interior monologues constitute the novel, are his wealthy first wife,
Esperanza; their daughter, Agata; Agata's husband, Froilán;
Ventura's second wife, Presencia; and their teenage son, Asís.
Through the individuals' memories and flashbacks the reader is
informed of a relative past extending back to the 1920s.

Absent from the novel is an overt explanation of the sociohistorical circumstance that underpins the action. Indeed, the word
divorce appears only once and then only in the final pages. In the
1930s, during the Republic, Spain developed a model divorce law,
complete with a no-fault provision. Following the civil war, the
Franco regime repealed the divorce law to bring the civil code into
conformity with Catholic doctrine. The retroactive effect was to
nullify civil second marriages and declare illegitimate any children
born to such marriages. Within the novelistic world—and in the
society that received Quiroga's novel in the 1950s—Presencia is
living in sin, and Esperanza is still Ventura's wife at the time of his
death. Asís, who has just learned the truth about his parents from
classmates, considers himself a bastard and his mother a whore—
although the labels themselves are only suggested.

The very fact that Spain ever had a divorce law was silenced. Not
until after Franco's death in 1975 could books that chronicled the
rise and fall of divorce and civil marriage be published. Playwright
Fernando Fernán-Gómez's box office hit *Las bicicletas son para el
verano* (Bicycles are for summer) (1982) is perhaps the first popular
literary work to deal with the subject. Quiroga's novel is therefore
surprising for the time period when it appeared, for the accuracy of
its oblique references to the law and its repeal, and for its sensitive
analysis of the sociological and psychological impact of divorce.

Quiroga's strength as a psychological novelist is particularly
apparent in her treatment of the broken marriage in *Algo pasa en la
calle*. Esperanza is aware that it would be socially and emotionally

easier for her and her daughter to accept Ventura's death than his leaving them. She secretly hopes that he will be killed in the war, and she lies to the child, telling her that her father is dead. When she learns the truth, the adolescent Agata's responses, which are all consistent with recent American studies on divorce and fatherless daughters, include her initial desire to reunite her parents and her feeling that somehow she was to blame for their separation; her disgust when she learns that her father is living with another woman; her subsequent search for a husband who will be a "father substitute"; and her lack of maternal feeling toward her own children.

Quiroga's daring as a social critic extends well beyond her willingness to deal with the divorce issue. Both Presencia and Esperanza recall how unjust it was that Ventura had been removed from his faculty position in a period of postwar political retaliation. Quiroga is probably the first writer within Spain to comment negatively on the abuses of the summer of 1939. Patricia W. O'Connor observes in her unpublished paper that a neighbor in the street blames Ventura's death—he falls when a balcony collapses—on the government's failure to inspect older buildings, and adds that the name of the street is "Los Desamparados" [the forsaken ones]. Quiroga thus points out the power structure's "benign neglect" of those not economically advantaged.

Through a technique of inversion, Quiroga leads her readers to question many of the assumptions perpetuated by the Franco era's National Catholicism. Froilán is startled when he meets Presencia after the accident; she is not at all the femme fatale he expects "the other woman" to be. Presencia, a nonconformist and nonbeliever, reveals herself to be a loving, understanding wife and mother and a basically good person who respects Ventura's deep religious convictions even when she does not share them. So that the dying Ventura may receive the priest's blessing, she voluntarily leaves the side of the man she loves. It is Esperanza, the traditional, churchgoing, legitimate wife, who would have denied her husband the comfort of his religion in the hour of his death.

Not only are practicing Catholics not necessarily good Christians, but also marriages blessed by the church may be less authentic than relationships like that of Ventura and Presencia. The essential incompatibility of Esperanza and Ventura becomes readily apparent as she remembers their past. She could not understand his intellectual pursuits; he was uncomfortable in her world of material possessions and frivolous social activities. He was attracted by her physical beauty; she was frigid. By mentioning the couple's sexual problems, Quiroga was, of course, touching upon another taboo topic. Even more daring is her veiled suggestion that Esperanza's best friend Reyes had attempted to seduce Ventura because her own husband was gay. In the 1950s in Spain, homosexuals could be punished by law, and the dominant ideology did not recognize the possibility that such deviation could occur in the best families. While Ventura is anguished by the loss of his daughter and his exclusion from the Catholic religion, the reader is given ample evidence that a good divorce is better than a bad marriage.

On a number of levels, *Algo pasa en la calle* places patriarchal authority in doubt. There is no monolithic approach to truth; no single religious path leads to goodness. As O'Connor notes, even Ventura's method of teaching, described by Presencia, is a refutation of Francoist ideology. Rather than lecturing to his students, Ventura invites them to participate in the discussion, to think for themselves, and to reach their own conclusions. By eschewing an omniscient narrator and a single narrative point of view, Quiroga extends the same invitation to her readers.

Although the narrative structure is quite different from that of *Algo pasa en la calle*, Quiroga also forces her readers to immerse themselves in the novelistic world of *La careta*, a work that Juan Villegas in his MLA paper has unreservedly called a masterpiece: "... me pareció envidiable, asombrosa en su precisa construcción, en los detalles significativos que hacen vivir o caracterizan a un personaje, el pequeño detalle insignificante que posteriormente adquiere importancia o que el análisis cuidadoso revela como clave, la gradación con que se entrega el mundo" [... it seemed to me enviable, astonishing in its precise construction, in the significant details that define or make a character live, the small, insignificant detail that later acquires importance or that a careful analysis reveals as a clue, the gradation with which the world is delivered].

Written in the indirect third person from the perspective of Moisés, *La careta* is a meticulous, gripping example of stream of consciousness. The fictive present is an evening in the midfifties; after some years of separation, Moisés is having a reunion dinner with his cousins. The narrative includes the degenerate protagonist's cynical view of his relatives—his mental efforts at tearing away their hypocritical masks; his often corrosive imagination, which is evident in the novel's opening image of his literally "exploding from laughter"; and the free flow of his thoughts from present to past, with a series of flashbacks that eventually allows the reader to relive with Moisés the traumatic moments at the beginning of the civil war that have shaped his alienated existence.

As with *Algo pasa en la calle*, the salient aspect of *La careta* is its brilliant narrative structure. The shifts from the real to the imaginary, from present to past, are achieved with great fluidity. They are typographically marked by parentheses and italics, respectively, but even so the reader must enter into Moisés's mind and participate in the reconstruction of his inner world. This task is complicated by the tendency to imbed flashbacks within other flashbacks, blurring two moments in time. In existentialist terms, Moisés's inner world simultaneously encompasses both past and present. As Quiroga clearly indicates in the title *Presente profundo*, she has studied the philosophical and psychoanalytical concept of existentialist time and incorporates it in *La careta* as well as in the later novel. Although the shifts from the fictive present to varying moments in the past are often achieved through a Proustian device—a sight or smell triggers the transition—Moisés is not in search of lost time; past and present are one.

Quiroga is among the first writers within Spain to deal with the psychological aftermath of the civil war, specifically with the question of guilt. She anticipates by some ten years a wave of literature that explores this very subject, including such closely related works as Antonio Buero Vallejo's tragedy *El tragaluz* (1967) (*The Basement Window*, 1981) and Ana María Matute's novel *La trampa* (The trap) (1969).

Moisés was twelve when the war broke out. His soldier father, caught in Republican Madrid, went into hiding but was eventually found and killed. The frightened child not only witnessed his father's death but also smothered his wounded mother in an effort to keep her from calling for help—and perhaps bringing the enemy back to kill him, too. His feelings of guilt about his parents' deaths are compounded by his relatives in Galicia treating him like a hero and by a variety of other emotions he does not fully understand. The reader, however, can readily analyze the young boy in terms of Freudian psychology. Before the outbreak of the war, Moisés had often had his mother's undivided attention but had admired his father's bravery; when his father remains hidden rather than going out to fight, the child begins to scorn him for being a coward and to become jealous of him and the love he inspires in Moisés's mother.

It is only near the end of the novel that the reader becomes fully aware of the cause of the adult Moisés's psychological problems and alienation. As Villegas indicates, however, all of the details have been skillfully introduced. For example, the children's game of hide-and-seek functions as a leitmotiv. In the flashbacks Moisés repeatedly relives his anguish of playing the game with his cousins in Galicia following his escape from Madrid. In retrospect, the reader can appreciate the child's unexpressed emotions. The deadly game of hide-and-seek that led to his father's death merges with the scenes from the more recent past in Galicia. The voices Moisés hears are sometimes the cousins at play, sometimes his parents in Madrid. The reader's ear must become attuned in order to distinguish between those voices and thus begin to solve the puzzle.

While the psychological portrait of Moisés is masterful, other aspects of the novel are equally worthy of attention. As in *Algo pasa en la calle*, there is provocative sociopolitical commentary. Again Quiroga inverts Franco-era stereotypes and anticipates by a decade the demythification of the civil war that became a widespread theme in the Spanish novel. The Communists killed Moisés's parents, but in Galicia he meets a boy whose father was assassinated by the winning Nationalist side. Moisés's aunt in Galicia is astonished that a leftist family helped the orphaned boy escape, first to France and then to the safety of Galicia. She is similarly amazed to find that she genuinely likes and respects her Protestant sister-in-law from Argentina. She wonders if it is possible that people can be good without being Francoist and Catholic.

In *Algo pasa en la calle*, Quiroga creates a sympathetic priest who offers comfort to the dying Ventura and understanding to Presencia. In *La careta* there is no counterpart figure. As an adolescent and as an adult, Moisés seeks confession in the vain hope of unburdening his overwhelming, self-destructive guilt. Both times he is turned away, first by a priest who does not take the "innocent" boy seriously and then by one who has no feelings of Christian charity for a drunken man. It is a daring but subtle criticism of the church.

Throughout most of the action in the present, Moisés, immersed in his own thoughts, fails to listen to his cousins' conversation. Because almost all of the novel is screened through the protagonist's consciousness, the reader can only "hear" the dialogue when Moisés does. Late in the evening when Felisa, the daughter of one of his cousins, returns home, Moisés becomes attentive, perhaps because this comparative stranger has no power to evoke his past.

Through Felisa, a rebellious young woman, Quiroga voices the most overt criticism of contemporary Spanish society. Felisa's harsh judgment of her elders in some ways reinforces Moisés's negative opinions of their hypocrisy and materialism, but she also takes to task all of the "bridge generation" that has used the civil war as an excuse for not building a better world. She is no more patient with Moisés, a "victim" of the war, than she is with any of the others. Quiroga is certainly one of the first Spanish writers to give full expression to this viewpoint, which represents a younger generation born during or after the war.

Villegas correctly notes that *La careta* offers multiple possibilities for sociopolitical analysis: "Desde el punto de vista ideológico, es un texto de una extraordinaria riqueza, tanto en lo que dice como en lo que no dice o no se podía decir en la España de 1955." [From the ideological point of view, the text has an extraordinary richness, in what it says as well as in what it does not say or what could not be said in Spain in 1955.] The same observation could be made about *Algo pasa en la calle.* In both of these works Quiroga focuses on Spanish society of the mid-1950s while simultaneously tracing back to the 1930s the causes of the social and psychological ills she describes. In *Tristura* she shifts to the prewar period itself, and through the use of an elliptical style forces the readers, much more extensively than in the earlier novels, to give meaning to the text by filling in the gaps, by discovering the unsaid.

The fictive present of *Tristura* is the two-year period 1929–30 when Tadea, the protagonist, is eight and nine years old. The first-person narration flows from present to past with flashbacks from Tadea's earlier experiences in Galicia and in Santander, where she lives with her mother's relatives. Although on occasion the reader is aware of an implied adult narrator, in general the perspective is that of the alienated, motherless child, and the action is screened through her consciousness.[5] There is no narrator-guide, no exposition, no direct explanation of the relationship among the various characters. In passages of dialogue the speakers are seldom identified. In passages of description there may be no verbs. The reader's viewpoint merges with that of the child; understanding comes only by entering Tadea's world. Because of the child's relative innocence, however, there is also an ironic distancing somewhat like that created by the chestnut tree's limited knowledge in *La sangre.*

Moisés in *La careta* is an anguished individual because of his secret guilt. Perhaps, as he believes, he is not alone in failing to communicate and in creating a mask for himself. Certainly young Felisa, who does not hesitate to speak her mind, criticizes her parents' generation for hiding behind the unsaid or the half-truth. In *Tristura* Tadea's world is dominated even more by silence. Badly treated by her aunt Concha and her cousins, the rejected child becomes increasingly taciturn, but her inability to communicate is also a response to an authoritarianism that prohibits language and suppresses thoughts. Aunt Concha's rigid ideas on bringing up children, on the division between social classes, on morality, and on politics mirror those of a reactionary society that would eventually rise up against the reforms of the Spanish Republic. Thus the elliptical style of the novel underscores both the psychological development of the protagonist and the sociological background.

The title of the novel means "sadness" but also implies emptiness—an emptiness that in Tadea's case is the existential anguish of a solitary individual who is alienated from the repressive, hypocritical society that surrounds her. She suffers from the absence of her dead mother; of a father who never comes to see her; of her brothers, her surrogate mother, and her dog in Galicia; of Galicia itself and the freedom it comes to signify for her; of the French governess who is unjustly fired by Aunt Concha; of her grandmother's "poor" cousin Julia, whose death is marked for the child by the arrival of the empty chest of drawers she has inherited. The grandmother, whose unspoken love for Tadea ultimately makes the child's existence bearable, says so little and intervenes so seldom in the affairs of the household that she is perceived as an object: "laabuelalabutaca" (thegrandmotherthearmchair).

Tadea's world is one of silences: words are not said because a child should not hear them, because those who might have said them are absent, because the potential speakers feel no affection for her, because Tadea herself or others are unable to communicate their feelings. By entering into the subjective, impressionistic perspective of the child, the reader experiences with her the anguish of absence, silence, and emptiness.

In quite different contexts, these same themes recur in the lives of the principal female characters of *Presente profundo*, Quiroga's novel about existential anguish in the 1970s. Returning to the use of multiple perspectives and shifting narrative point of view associated with *Algo pasa en la calle*, Quiroga juxtaposes the stories of Daría, an older, working-class woman in Galicia, and Blanca, a relatively young and sophisticated upper-class woman in Madrid. Despite the contrasts between their social classes and life styles, both commit suicide. The opening passage of the novel is written in third-person stream of consciousness from the perspective of Daría; it provides the clues to her suicide, but as in *La careta* these clues are initially incomprehensible to the reader. The following passage is the first-person narration of Rubén, a young doctor who serves as the link between the two stories as he seeks to understand the reasons for both deaths.

In Rubén's search for Blanca's truth, he sometimes addresses the absent woman in the second person, sometimes thinks to himself in the first person, and sometimes, in flashbacks, listens to the testimony of others. In the fictive present, he similarly hears Daría's family and friends give their individual opinions on the dead woman as he tries to comprehend why she drowned herself. Daría's story also includes sections related by an omniscient third-person narrator. Although Rubén offers his subjective interpretation of the other characters, as do Froilán in *Algo pasa en la calle* and the unnamed narrator in *La enferma*, the reader is once again called upon to participate in the novelistic world and draw his or her own conclusions. To a greater extent than in the earlier works, Rubén as narrator-character is introspective; by probing the two women's lives and deaths, he hopes to reach a greater understanding of himself.

In Martha A. Marks's paper the principal theme of *Presente profundo* is not necessarily Spanish society but rather Western society with all of the conflicts and confusion that have tormented it in the past quarter century. There is much within the novel to sustain her opinion. Blanca is Brazilian; she and her friends travel freely throughout the world. The song that serves as a leitmotiv to her meaningless life is the American "Strangers in the Night." The malaise that leads to Blanca's death stems from her loss of traditional values. The child of a broken marriage, divorced herself and separated from a second husband and the child she loves, the ostensibly "liberated" woman finds no real pleasure in her material possessions or her series of casual love affairs. Her earlier suicide attempt and her death from a drug overdose are her responses to the anguish of nothingness.

Daría faces a similar emptiness. At fifty-nine she finds that her children no longer need her, her husband has taken a young mistress, and even her work in the family bakery is threatened by a daughter-in-law who wants to put her in a corner. As she walks out into the sea, her last thoughts are of the sexual abuse she suffered as a young girl. Neither Daría nor Blanca has a meaningful existence of her own; feeling totally alienated from the family life they yearn for, they choose death.

Through Rubén and a series of secondary characters, Quiroga explores other aspects of the changing social patterns to which Marks refers. The young doctor has not fulfilled his parents' expectations; he plans to go off to America, and they have found a surrogate son to take on his father's business. Happiness, if it exists at all in this novelistic world, is certainly not based on family ties. Indeed the characters who appear to be most content with their lot in life are two women, one a friend of Daría and the other of Rubén, who have learned to be self-sufficient. The older Galician, Soledad, proudly proclaims that no man can "retire" her, as Daría's husband did to Daría, because she has no one. Marta, a doctor in Madrid, completed her education on her own after her parents' deaths, feels no need to marry her lover, and has no desire to have children. Like Presencia in *Algo pasa en la calle*, Marta is a nonconformist at peace with herself.

Throughout her narrative works, Quiroga skillfully probes the inner worlds of her characters, uncovering their psychological reality. Her search often reveals an alienated individual, a Moisés, a Tadea, or a Daría, who cannot communicate with the dominant society and who therefore retreats to silence, perhaps even to a path of self-destruction. Themes of orphanhood, alienation, and class prejudice persist throughout Quiroga's fiction.

Quiroga's novels do not belong to the category of objective realism; rather, they are characterized by a poetic style and innovative, Faulknerian narrative structures. Nevertheless, they are allied with objective realism in their presentation of a strong but subtle criticism of the sociopolitical background that gives rise to the individual situations that are examined in depth. There is no related criticism of the characters because the narrative structure forces the reader to reach conclusions without a narrator-guide and because Quiroga creates no villains. Perhaps her greatest strength as a psychological novelist is her ability to help the reader understand all of the characters in her novelistic world and see them all, in Ortega's terms, as themselves and their circumstances.

Notes

1. I first interviewed Elena Quiroga on 9 and 27 June 1975 when I was preparing my Twayne World Authors Series book. Since that time I have talked at length with her at least once a year during my annual trips to Spain. Biographical information and opinions attributed to Quiroga are drawn from these personal conversations.

2. Quiroga is only one of several writers to create passive, immobile female characters whose lives may be interpreted as political metaphors. See my article "Passivity and Immobility: Patterns of Inner Exile in Postwar Spanish Novels Written by Women," *Letras Femeninas* 14 (1988): 3–9.

3. I discussed this subject in greater depth in a paper delivered at the annual MLA convention in New York City in December 1986. Both Salisachs and Quiroga treat the death of the mother in childbirth as part of an ongoing tragedy—motherless daughters beget motherless daughters. Their novelistic situations thus stand in contrast with the works of male authors; the death of Fortunata in Pérez Galdós's 1886–87 masterpiece *Fortunata y Jacinta* (*Fortunata and Jacinta*, trans. by Agnes Moncy Gullón, 1986) with the subsequent adoption by Jacinta of the baby boy is one example. Fortunata's postpartum death restores harmony while the deaths of the female protagonists in the two novels written by women do not.

4. These are the four novels I selected for discussion at a special session on Quiroga at the MLA convention in Washington D.C. in December 1984. My fellow panelists and their topics were Patricia W. O'Connor, "Shattered Taboos in Elena Quiroga's *Algo pasa en la calle*"; Juan Villegas, "*La careta*: La familia y los valores degradados" (*La careta*: The family and degraded values); and Martha Alford Marks, "*Presente profundo*: Images of an Alienated Society." References to the opinions of these scholars in the section that follows are drawn from these unpublished MLA papers.

5. A number of critics have commented on the possible influence of Quiroga's *Algo pasa en la calle* on Miguel Delibes's *Cinco horas con Mario* (Five hours with Mario) (1966). The latter novel also deals with the unhappy marriage of an idealistic intellectual and his materialistic wife. To my knowledge no one has noted a similar parallel between *Tristura* and Delibes's *El príncipe destronado* (The dethroned prince) (1973), where the action is screened through the consciousness of a young child.

Bibliography

1. PRIMARY WORKS

1949. *La soledad sonora*. Madrid: Espasa-Calpe.

[1951] 1983. *Viento del Norte*. Reprint. Destinolibro, no. 198. Barcelona: Ediciones Destino.

[1952] 1981. *La sangre*. Reprint. Destinolibro, no. 136. Barcelona: Ediciones Destino.

1954. *Algo pasa en la calle*. Ancora y Delfín, no. 102. Barcelona: Ediciones Destino.

[1955a] 1987. *La careta*. Reprint. Barcelona: Plaza y Janés.

1955b. *La enferma*. Barcelona-Madrid-México: Editorial Noguer.

[1956] 1985. *Plácida, la joven y otras narraciones*. Reprint. Barcelona: Plaza y Janés.

1958. *La última corrida*. Barcelona: Editorial Noguer.

[1960] 1984. *Tristura*. Reprint. Barcelona: Plaza y Janés.

1961. *Carta a Cadaques*. Santander: Imprenta Bedia. Privately printed poetic work.

1963. *Envío al Faramello*. Madrid: Raycar. Privately printed poetic work.

[1965] 1985. *Escribo tu nombre*. Reprint. Barcelona: Plaza y Janés.

1973. *Presente profundo*. Ancora y Delfín, no. 416. Barcelona: Ediciones Destino.

1984. *Presencia y ausencia de Alvaro Cunqueiro: Discurso leído el 8 de abril en su recepción pública*. Madrid: Real Academia Española.

2. SECONDARY WORKS

Brent, Albert. 1959. "The Novels of Elena Quiroga." *Hispania* 42: 210–13. Helpful introduction to Quiroga's first six novels.

Landeira, Ricardo. 1983. "Múltiple variación interpretativa en *Algo pasa en la calle*, de Elena Quiroga." In *Novelistas femeninas de la postguerra española*, edited by Janet W. Pérez, 57–70. Studia Humanitatis. Madrid: Porrúa Turanzas.

Llopis, Silvia. 1983. "Elena Quiroga, la olvidada." *Cambio 16* 24 January: 89.

Marks, Martha Alford. 1980a. "Elena Quiroga's *Yo* Voice and the Schism between Reality and Illusion." *Anales de la Novela de Posguerra* 5: 39–55. Analysis of the narrator/protagonist's ironic quest for truth in the five first-person novels.

———. 1980b. "La perspectiva plural en dos novelas de Elena Quiroga." *Cuadernos Hispanoamericanos* 359: 428–33. Examination of shifting narrative point of view as a structuring device in *Algo pasa en la calle* and *Presente profundo*.

———. 1981. "Time in the Novels of Elena Quiroga." *Hispania* 64: 376–81. Application of A. A. Mendilow's concept of absolute present, fictive present, and relative past to several novels.

Villegas, Juan. 1968. "Los motivos estructurantes de *La careta*, de Elena Quiroga." *Cuadernos Hispanoamericanos* 75: 638–48. First major critical study of any of Quiroga's novels; discussion of her works from stylistic, structural, and thematic perspectives.

Zatlin-Boring, Phyllis. 1977a. *Elena Quiroga*. Twayne World Authors Series, no. 459. Boston: G. K. Hall. Overview of life and works. Only book to date on the author in any language.

———. 1977b. "Faulkner in Spain: The Case of Elena Quiroga." *Comparative Literature Studies* 14: 166–76. Stylistic analysis of selected novels.

———. 1984. "Divorce in Franco Spain: Elena Quiroga's *Algo pasa en la calle*." *Mosaic* 17: 129–38. An analysis from a sociological perspective of a subject considered taboo at the time the novel was written.

———. 1988. "Elena Quiroga's *Tristura*: The Anguish of Silence and Absence." *Modern Language Studies* 18: 89–96. Analysis of stylistic and thematic implications of the unsaid.

3

Dolores Medio: Chronicler of the Contemporary Spaniard's Interaction with Society

Margaret E. W. Jones

Dolores Medio was born in 1914 in Oviedo, the capital of Spain's northern province of Asturias. She spent her early childhood in a comfortable middle-class setting, where she seemed destined to take her place among the young ladies of Oviedo middle-class society. However, her situation dramatically changed when her adored father died, leaving the family in near penury. Young Dolores was forced to drop her art and music to pursue a teaching career, and in addition to her studies she held several part-time jobs to help support her family. She spent her summer months as a governess in the palatial home of the Marqués de Villaverde in Galicia. The luxurious lifestyle of the nobility contrasted sharply with the hard lot of the laborers and created a lasting impression on the young woman.

The historical milieu in Spain during Medio's formative years was marked by social and political unrest and accompanied by violence and war. Although she was too young to have experienced the First World War, the changing political scene in Spain produced wide swings in power, generating reforms and then counterreforms, with equally violent reactions as the power changed hands. One of the most traumatic results was the 1934 uprising in Asturias, fomented by Socialist and labor groups, which occasioned particularly extreme repressive measures. Medio, who was witness to many of the cruelties, began to formulate ideas concerning the effects of historical change on the individual and to note patterns of behavior.

Her teaching career began in 1936 in the small town of Nava, near Oviedo. Efforts to introduce new pedagogical methods were received with suspicion by the townspeople, who regarded her progressive theories as Marxist or Socialist. Relieved of her position the same year she began teaching, she was reinstated in 1940 because of insufficient cause for the dismissal.

However, the Spanish civil war (1936–39) caused even greater employment problems for Medio. Since the dismissal left her with no references, she could not resume teaching and simply survived by working at whatever was available—as a worker in a bottling factory, as a maid—and like others, she endured hunger and privation. She was detained several times for questioning, even though she was not affiliated with any political movement. She also suffered personal tragedies: her mother died during this period, and her fiancé was killed during the war.

As a child, she had shown a precocious interest in writing, and when she received the Concha Espina prize in 1945 for her short story "Niña," she decided to move to Madrid to pursue a career in writing. She worked primarily for the newspaper *Domingo* until its demise in 1945, publishing articles on a wide range of subjects, including a regular column of advice to the lovelorn. During this period she was fired and then reinstated after a trial in which she successfully disproved allegations by her employers.

In 1962 she was wrongly accused of participating in a women's march in favor of a pay raise for Asturian mine workers. Found in the vicinity, taken into custody, and unable to pay the fine, she was jailed for a month.

In addition to her work on the newspaper, Medio pursued her creative writing and finally broke into the literary world when in 1952 she received the prestigious Nadal Prize for her first novel, *Nosotros los Rivero* (We Riveros) (1953). She continued to work steadily on her fiction from that point on, alternating full-length novels with excellent short pieces. Her second novel, *Funcionario público* (Public servant) (1956), depicts the situation of a minor public servant in Madrid; *El pez sigue flotando* (The fish stays afloat) (1959) narrates life in Madrid through a cross-section of tenants in an apartment house; *Bibiana* (1963) and its sequel, *La otra circunstancia* (The other circumstance) (1972), describe the everyday world of a housewife and her family; *Farsa de verano* (Summer farce) (1973) moves again to the collective experience; and *El fabuloso imperio de Juan sin tierra* (The fabulous empire of John the Landless) (1981) uses a regional setting to narrate the interaction between Juan and the townspeople.

Medio has also produced superb short fiction, winning the Sésamo Short-Story Prize for her collection entitled *Andrés* (1967). In the realm of nonfiction, she has written a guidebook to her native region entitled *Asturias* (1973) and biographies of Queen Isabel II of Spain and Selma Lagerlof, the Swedish Nobel Prize-winning writer.

Any biographical information on Dolores Medio is doubly important to the critic of her works, since most of her literature incorporates her personal experience, thinly disguised by fiction. She has articulated very plainly a literary philosophy that posits everyday reality as the cornerstone of her works. The intermediary between objective reality and the written page is the filter of personal and artistic elaboration that converts the raw novelistic material into a "human" text. Medio's use of information from real life thus creates sources that produce a "documento humano, dándole un sentido de autenticidad, de precisión indiscutible, que puede faltar en una obra puramente imaginativa" [human document, giving (the novel) a sense of authenticity, of unquestionable precision, which could be lacking in a purely imaginative work].[1] Her works employ autobiography in the most basic sense of using episodes predominantly from her own life (most apparent in *Nosotros los Rivero*), as well as introducing a number of alter egos (Irene in *Diario de una maestra*; Lena in *La pez sigue flotando*; Marcela in *Farsa de verano*) or simply transferring isolated episodes from life to text (teaching experiences in *Diario de una maestra*, and the arrest and jail adventure in *Bibiana*).

Medio has been associated primarily with the "social novel" in Spain, a postwar literary movement that sought to provide a critical view of contemporary Spanish social, economic, and political reality in order to provoke reaction and reform. There are undeniable points of contact with the goals of the social novel, but exclusive association with this movement would not be completely accurate, since both style and intent may ally her more closely with the nineteenth-century Spanish realists and naturalists. Her descriptions of her own technique certainly suggest the procedures of the nineteenth-century novelists she so admired—observation, documentation, literature as a chronicle of contemporary life—and she has stated that one can study the contemporary history of Spain better through the daily lives of her characters than in a textbook.[2] Her interest in the theories of heredity and environment, clearly evident in *Nosotros los Rivero*, recall similar procedures of the nineteenth-century naturalists, particularly Leopoldo Alas (Clarín), a fellow writer from Oviedo whose influence is apparent in her work.

Medio's fiction is set in contemporary Spain; her favorite subjects, the common people (with whom she identifies), are individually and collectively the protagonists of her literature. The preference for the common person translates into a preponderance of lower- or middle-class characters, caught in the web of problems generally associated with modern times. One of the most prevalent dilemmas is the loss of individuality, the result of the dehumanization apparent in all levels of contemporary life. This process becomes fictionalized through the conflict of the protagonist with rigid structures within society and with institutions that do not sufficiently allow for individual differences and needs, and in the loneliness, isolation, and alienation of the characters who are unable to communicate with each other.

Medio's professional experiences as teacher and writer obviously colored her outlook and style. Conforming to her theory that the novel should be used for instructional purposes, she creates direct, uncomplicated prose. Such a deliberately clear style also addresses the requisite of nonexclusionary literature, accessible to more than a minority of educated readers.

Medio's first novel, *Nosotros los Rivero*, reflects her interest in combining realistic techniques with personal experience as it recounts in fictional form much of her early life in Oviedo. It is a *bildungs-roman* in its chronicling of the maturation of a young person who becomes aware of her surroundings and the various demands (social, familial, professional) to which she will be subjected. This central issue is placed within a national setting, which is crucial to both personal and historical levels since the growth and development of the main character seems tied to that of Spain.

The circular structure begins as the mature, successful writer Lena Rivero returns to the Oviedo of her youth. Her exploration of the city evokes memories of her childhood, and thus the reader accompanies her on a journey into the past. Her tightly knit family circle is shattered with the death of her father, leaving them nearly destitute and forcing the family to move to inferior lodgings and to get work wherever they can.

Family dynamics also play an important role in the developing saga. Mrs. Rivero is a traditionalist who refuses to change with the times: she is appalled at Lena's escapades into freedom and constantly talks about the proper behavior for a young lady. She obviously prefers her son, Ger, the only man in the family, and pins her hopes on him. Two other sisters form a complementary pair: the religious, self-effacing María and the rebellious Heidi.

Medio thoroughly explores Lena's growing awareness of her place in the world and portrays her primarily in an adversarial role as she questions the status quo of society: her rejection of the hypocritical attitudes of adults, her reluctance to give up childhood to accept adult responsibility, and her dislike of her mother's rigid social expectations. As she matures, Lena provides a fresh viewpoint in her reconsideration of institutions and traditions, always opting for a refreshingly innocent, tolerant attitude that is based on common sense.

The inner turmoil that Lena experiences as she matures parallels national and regional political upheavals. The proclamation of the Second Republic is followed by the occupation of Oviedo by revolutionary forces and accompanied by a great deal of violence. Ger disappears and is presumed dead; Mrs. Rivero dies. The victory of the government troops marks the end of an era for Spain and the end of Lena's childhood.

Nosotros los Rivero presents the main character within the context of the middle class that was so fascinating to Medio because of its values, problems, and human interest. Thus Lena's development as an individual takes place as a factor within a given environment, and Medio is particularly adept at weaving a dense background fabric of people, incidents, and historical circumstances that give depth to the novel. True also to naturalist interests, Medio openly posits the effects of heredity and environment on the individual through discussions between characters and through events themselves.

As in any novel of development, the adolescent faces a series of obstacles that he or she must overcome. In Lena's case the issue of woman's place within society and as an individual comes to the fore. The former is represented by aspirations to social prestige and tenacious adherence to middle-class tradition (as epitomized in the pretentious, maladjusted Mrs. Rivero). The individual perspective (the quest for liberty and self-fulfillment) is stifled by the restrictive social norms associated with the era preceding the Second Republic.

Lena and the reader discover that the opportunities open to a young woman are evident in various role models symbolized by secondary female characters: the older generation that refuses to face change (the mother); the spinster, with no life of her own, dependent on and subservient to a family (Aunt Mag); the rebel who is an outcast (Heidi, Aunt Carina); or the other acceptable profession for the unmarried woman—the church (María).

The emergence of a new, liberated woman who is not dependent on family or a husband to fulfill her life is a possibility open to the individual. Although the specific means of attaining this goal are not investigated as thoroughly as descriptions of traditional society, Lena's outlook on life certainly takes nothing for granted—she is an individual first and a member of the group second. However, her return as a successful novelist suggests that such a life is certainly an alternative, an option explored more fully in later works.

Funcionario público appeared in 1956, marking a decided shift in outlook as well as considerable growth in narrative technique. Medio combines three different perspectives—personal, social, and economic—to display a bleak but apparently typical picture of urban postwar life in Spain. She again turns to the middle class for inspiration, noting the preeminent role of the social system in contemporary existence, which affects the individual in every aspect, from work to private life (*Discurso*, p. 20).

Pablo Marín is employed as a telegraph operator in Madrid, but his salary is barely enough to make ends meet. This causes tension in his relationship with his wife, Teresa, who is dissatisfied with their meager standard of living that includes lodgings in a sublet room in an apartment, a typical situation caused by the housing shortage in Madrid at that time. Pablo relieves the monotony of his life by fantasizing about winning the lottery or a bet and by tracking down the owner of a notebook he finds on the street, the mysterious Natalia, who represents the unattainable. The novel traces the downward spiral of his life: severe marital problems, exacerbated by a complete breakdown in communication; the difficult economic situation; unpleasant living conditions; his negative attitude toward his work; frustration at his lack of personal and professional success. When he finally comes home with the news that he has received a raise, he is greeted with a note saying that his wife has left him.

The two major aspects of the novel—the individual and the representative—converge in a portrait of urban postwar Spanish life. The housing shortage, constant financial problems, low wages, and the corruption that such an economy entails are dramatized by brief, ancillary episodes that illustrate the human perspective. Most important, however, is the continual leitmotiv of the dehumanized individual, who is alienated and alone. One of the most frequent metaphors suggests the individual as a cog in a huge machine, appreciated only for his or her role in helping to make that machine run smoothly.

Pablo's personal failures are bound inextricably to the enveloping social environment. Accepting his dehumanized role, or lacking the willpower to change his life, he drifts along, indecisive and discontented. In fact, this lack of control causes his personal failure, for he allows circumstances to rule him.

A considerable advance in literary technique moves the narrative focus from an exterior description to an inner reality. A restricted perspective reinforces the personal limitations of the protagonist: the reader is privy only to Pablo's musings, Teresa's thoughts, and random comments by the author. Thus the realism of the situation (the postwar ambiance) is transmitted from a uniquely personal narrow point of view.

Wider-reaching implications are present in characters whose function may be representative and symbolic, such as fellow employees embodying issues pertaining to the work situation (living on a low salary, chances of advancement, group dynamics); individuals representing varying attitudes toward life; and characters symbolizing dream and reality (Natalia/Teresa). Connections with the social novel are evident in the representative function of many characters, the critical implications, the exposé of the problems inherent in postwar Spain, and finally, the plight of the middle-class public servant. The success of *Funcionario público*, however, lies in the skillful blending of both social and personal perspectives, providing an individual and collective experience of contemporary life.

Further exploration of narrative possibilities appears in *El pez sigue flotando*, a novel that combines elements from the first two works and develops them in new ways. The story takes place in Madrid and centers around an apartment house with its typical inner courtyard, a space that allows a natural flow of multiple characters. Short chapters introduce one tenant after another in brief sketches of moments in their lives, which Medio begins, drops, and picks up later in random patterns. The common denominator, however, seems to be deprivation (emotional or economic), disillusionment, and isolation.

The two main plot lines comprise the story of the shopkeeper Morales, who wants to change his lonely, middle-aged existence and creates a fantasy that ends in disillusionment, and that of the poor, young typist Marta, who longs for independence from the obligation to support herself and her old servant Tata. Both stories resolve in the unhappiness and disappointment of the characters, setting a pessimistic perspective from which to judge the other cases, less fully developed but no less poignant. Most deal with unhappiness, shattered dreams or hopes, lack of communication, alienation, and solitude.

The novelist Lena Rivero reappears here. She lives on the top floor of the building and undergoes her own interior struggle, albeit in a more analytical way than the others. For the most part, Lena's comments on her neighbors and on life reflect the author's own opinions.

The narrative presentation is fragmented, and there may be pieces of any number of stories going on at the same time. The aggregate of all the individual experiences produces a sense of totality emanating from the microcosm of the apartment. This novelistic technique has a philosophical parallel in José Ortega y Gasset's theories on perspectivism, which suggest that absolute truth can only be obtained by the sum of individual, partial truths.

The use of the multiple character and simultaneous action also provides an interesting wide-screen perspective that underlines complementary behavior and interdependence of motive and thought, and allows obvious conclusions or even commentary to arise from situation rather than explanation. This experimental technique was popular during the postwar period, perhaps due to the influence of cinematographic experiments that used visual juxtaposition for commentary. A sense of totality lends itself to generalizations about human nature, suffering, alienation, and other modern themes that are efficiently expressed by the multiplication of characters, creating a fellowship of the anonymous. The episodic novel confers on the reader a certain measure of cocreative autonomy because of his or her unique ability to draw conclusions from the wider picture—in this case, a very pessimistic one concerning human loneliness, economic and emotional deprivation, and disillusionment in the frustration of hopes and dreams.

Despite the guise of objectivity implied in this technique, Medio still attempts to provide a rounded picture of human nature. Surface action becomes the means of entry into an inner world revealed by interior monologue, so that the novel presents simultaneity of actions in the apartment house as well as simultaneity of exterior and interior reality.

A later experiment with multiple characters and interwoven stories appears in *Farsa de verano*, where the unifying factor is a vacation tour taken by a diverse group. Excellent thumbnail sketches reveal each person's character and quirks, causing a concomitant move away from the more critical stance associated with the earlier works. However, the middle- and lower-class interest is still strongly evident, as is the presence of an alter ego for the author—this time Marcela Abril, a poet. A surprising, tragic finale provides an unpleasant jolt to the ending and adds an unusually ironic and incongruous note.

Diario de una maestra, published in 1961, adds the character Irene Gal to the list of alter egos in Medio's novels. Through Irene, Medio describes her work as a rural teacher, and by extension airs her own views on education. That much of the novel is based on Medio's own life can be corroborated by the publication of *Atrapados en la ratonera: Memorias de una novelista* (Caught in the mousetrap: Memoirs of a novelist), which recounts her personal experiences in the civil war.[3] A comparison between the two works reveals the extent to which the author has relied on autobiographical elements as inspiration for her fiction. The personal side of the character emerges in her affair with her teacher, Máximo Saenz. Although most of the work is narrated in the third person (belying the form associated with the "diary" in the title), the thoughts and impressions are so personal that they would only be revealed through such an intimate medium.

Although Irene's innovative teaching methods are looked on with suspicion by the people in the small town to which she is assigned, her good will and affection for all win over children and adults alike. Using love as the basis for her philosophy of life, she tries to understand everyone—even the soldiers on the other side during the civil war—as human beings with problems and needs. Thus Ortega's philosophy of perspectivism translates here into human qualities of tolerance, understanding, and forgiveness.

After the war, Irene waits for Max to be released from prison, but he unexpectedly terminates their relationship. A brief temptation to commit suicide is truncated when she realizes how much the children need her, and Irene returns to the village where she will help others, thereby acknowledging the primacy of life and duty.

Bibiana is the first novel of a projected trilogy entitled *Los que vamos a pie* (We who go by foot). The title character is a middle-aged housewife and mother of five children whose entire life centers around home and family. The novel shifts between scenes depicting family dynamics, most of which include Bibiana, and some unusual, rather comical misadventures that stem from the character's own sheltered, naive perspective on the world but that are also subtly tied to themes of women's issues. As such, the presentation of Bibiana's personality is more of an unfolding of static qualities rather than the development and growing awareness one would associate with the *bildungsroman*. Her misadventures are the direct result of her dependence on her home life to the exclusion of anything else, yet these excursions into the outside world seem to carry with them a lesson for the housewife—one must not venture beyond the prescribed limits of one's "job." For example, Bibiana wins a prize for having selected a certain food product at the store. She shows a typical inability to cope with the unexpected, but when told that she is to appear on a radio program, she suddenly feels her own importance and decides that this is her first incursion into life as a liberated woman. Not unexpectedly, her family downplays the event, complaining because dinner is not ready. A more serious episode involves Bibiana in a women's demonstration: she has no idea what she is protesting or the real implications of this action, and she is amazed when she is arrested.

Her experiences occur in her home life, where she is secure, and in the outside world, where she is totally unprepared. Her upbringing has obviously sheltered her from life; marriage was simply the continuation of that arrangement. Her failure to see beyond her limited sphere of interest prevents Bibiana from grasping the seriousness of her position: her idea of a "modern" woman comes from simplistic generalities about social life. The comic element, based on Bibiana's extreme naiveté, is a subtle way of disguising the inherent tragedy: a woman, educated in the traditional mold, is unprepared to understand and participate in contemporary society.

The sequel, *La otra circunstancia*, continues the saga of the family, but moves the focal point from Bibiana to Marcelo. The historical setting affords a glimpse at how economic ease can affect the "little man," who is still the major interest of Medio. Her theories of how environmental determinism influences character are quite apparent here—the addition of a single factor to Marcelo's life causes apparently latent, unpleasant characteristics to appear.

El fabuloso imperio de Juan sin tierra employs Juan, who has returned home from America after many years' absence, as a catalyst to reveal the personalities and foibles in a small town. A chatty tone, quick sketches and tales concerning these people, and a style peppered with colloquialisms and regionalisms make the town come alive.

Medio has written several collections of fine short fiction, showing her skill at capturing human nature and behavior with a quick, deft touch. Although the stories are understandably varied, there is the common element of middle- or lower-class characters who are generally placed in situations that point out a pathetic or ironic perspective on their lives. These people are victims of adverse economic or personal circumstance, who are for the most part lonely and misunderstood, and who perceive a gap between their dreams and the grim reality that will never change. "El señor García" learns that he will soon be promoted, but after a day of fantasizing about his rosy future, he discovers that someone with connections has gotten the job. Children are often protagonists in similar situations; their bewilderment or shattered innocence is a masterful device for revealing humanity's disillusionment. Young Andrés insists on giving up his schooling to earn money so that his mother will no longer have to support the family by prostitution; in the same collection, the honest resolution of a poor boy's temptation to keep a lost wallet ends ironically in a lack of appreciation for his honesty (in a story entitled "Injusticia"). Dashed hopes and early and unpleasant initiation into adulthood are indications of the human condition.

Several nonfiction works also reinforce themes present in Medio's fiction—her love of her region, in the guidebook to Asturias; her fondness for children, in a Christmas book for children; and her interest in women's issues, in the biographical studies of Isabel II of Spain and of the Swedish writer Selma Lagerlof (both of which stress the human as well as historical issues). Her 1980 *Atrapados en la ratonera: Memorias de una novelista* removes the fictional separation between experience and the written page and offers an excellent document of the civil war through the eyes of a civilian—and a woman.

Dolores Medio is one of the generation of postwar novelists whose major works appeared in the 1950s and 1960s. Like the other writers of this period, she shows a great interest in displaying contemporary Spanish life through the experiences of the average person, who is generally a victim of forces beyond his or her control. The plots invariably show the effects of the postwar conditions on humanity, and use the themes of solitude, disillusionment, shattered hopes, lack of communication, and financial difficulties to reinforce the characters' more personal stories. The interweaving of historical moment with individual concerns, the influence of environment on character development, and the juxtaposition of social pressures and personal goals suggest that Medio considers the clash between exterior demands and individual aspirations to be important in her fictional works. Her critical intentions appear most clearly in her use of characters who transcend their individuality to represent their class or group. The individual can thus provide commentary on society as a whole, while retaining enough singularity to allow human interest and psychological depth to the story.

Medio is also recognized as a member of this generation because of her connections with social realism: her critical stance, certain formal techniques (realism, objectivism), and contemporary lower- and middle-class themes. However, she has not yet been fully appreciated in her role as feminist writer. Her works clearly document and comment on the position of the Spanish woman in the early postwar years, a portrayal made even more poignant by the realization that much of what her female characters undergo is a faithful reflection of her own experiences. Thus a major contribution to Spanish fiction and to women's studies centers around the female characters in Medio's works, which may be divided into two rough groupings. The young, successful professionals (Lena, Irene,

Marcela) evoke aspects of the writer's own life; they often go through an initiation process, generally precipitated by some personally or nationally traumatic experience. Others, either a principal character (Bibiana) or one of the myriad secondary females who populate these works, appear in a static role that seems to reflect on the inequitable situation of women in contemporary Spain. Their lack of power to influence others, much less to direct their own lives, is made apparent in every aspect of their existence. Even the more liberated women—those who seem to have more control over their lives or who have more contemporary, if cynical, outlooks (such as Bibiana's daughter)—have lives that are filled with personal and professional problems and questions, suggesting that mere liberation is not a total solution to human problems.

Medio's fiction can be appreciated as a reflection of the literary preoccupations of her time—social realism, objectivism, critical intentions, as a faithful representation of contemporary social and historical reality that she herself experienced, and as a commentary on more universal, human concerns.

Notes

1. Untitled lecture in *El autor enjuicia su obra* (The author judges his own work). (Madrid: Editora Nacional, 1966), 156.
2. Dolores Medio, *Discurso* (Discourse). (Santander: Aldus Velarde, S.A., 1967), 16.
3. Dolores Medio, *Atrapados en la ratonera: Memorias de una novelista* (Madrid: Alce, 1980).

Bibliography

1. PRIMARY WORKS

1948. *El milagro de la noche de reyes*. Burgos: Hijos de Santiago Rodríguez.
1953. *Nosotros los Rivero*. Barcelona: Ediciones Destino.
1954a. *Compás de espera*. Barcelona: Ediciones G. P.
1954b. *Mañana. Cinco novelas*. La Novela del Sábado, V. Madrid: Ediciones Cid.
1956. *Funcionario público*. Barcelona: Ediciones Destino.
1959. *El pez sigue flotando*. Barcelona: Ediciones Destino.
1961. *Diario de una maestra*. Barcelona: Ediciones Destino.
1966. *El señor García*. La novela popular, no. 33. Madrid: Alfaguara.
1967a. *Andrés*. Oviedo: Richard Grandio.
1967b. *Bibiana*. Barcelona: Ediciones Destino.
1972. *La otra circunstancia*. Barcelona: Ediciones Destino.

1973. *Farsa de verano*. Madrid: Espasa Calpe.

1974. *El bachancho*. Madrid: Editorial Magisterio.

1981. *El fabuloso imperio de Juan sin tierra*. Barcelona: Plaza y Janés.

1982. *El urogallo*. Gijon: Noega.

2. SECONDARY WORKS

Alborg, Juan Luis. 1958. *Hora actual de la novela española*. Madrid: Taurus, vol. 2, 333–48. One of the earliest long analyses of Medio's novels, through *Diario de una maestra*.

de Nora, Eugenio G. 1962. *La novela española contemporánea (1927–1960)*. Madrid: Editorial Gredos, vol. 2, 207–10. Important work on the contemporary novel in general. Covers novels through *El pez sigue flotando*.

Galerstein, Carolyn L. 1982. "*Bibiana*: A Plea for the Liberation of Spanish Women." *Letras Femeninas* 8: 3–8. Describes Bibiana's traditional role and the changing place of women in contemporary Spain.

———. 1986. "Dolores Medio's Women in Wartime." *Letras Femeninas* 12 (Spring–Autumn): 45–51. Examines women's view of war and shows personal experiences converted into fiction.

Jones, Margaret E. W. 1974. *Dolores Medio*. New York: Twayne Publishers. Includes biographical information, material from interviews, and analysis of works. Covers Medio's writings through 1973. Bibliography includes articles and stories in periodicals.

Ordóñez, Elizabeth J. 1986. "*Diario de una maestra*: Female Heroism and the Context of War." *Letras Femeninas* 12 (Spring–Autumn): 52–59. An excellent interpretation of the female hero and the ironic perspective of the work.

Peñuel, Arnold M. 1973. "The Influence of Galdós' *El amigo manso* on Dolores Medio's *El diario de una maestra*." *Revista de Estudios Hispánicos* 7 (January): 91–96. Analyzes influences and similarities and speculates on reasons for divergences and role reversal in the dénouement.

Sandarg, Jana I. 1985. "Dolores Medio's *Milagro* for Children." *Monographic Review/Revista Monográfica* 1: 66–75. Provides Medio's ideas on children's literature and an analysis of the plot and style of the book.

Smoot, Jean J. 1983. "Realismo social en la obra de Dolores Medio." In *Novelistas femeninas de la postguerra española*, edited by Janet W. Pérez, 95–102. Madrid: José Porrúa Turanzas. Concentrates on *Bibiana*, *La otra circunstancia*, and *Farsa de verano* and deals generally with character, social import, and point of view.

Winecoff, Janet. 1966. "Fictionalized Autobiography in the Novels of Dolores Medio." *Kentucky Foreign Language Quarterly* 13: 170–78. Based on a series of interviews and letters from the novelist, the writer makes a striking case for the autobiographical elements in the novels.

4

Carmen Martín Gaite: Reaffirming the Pact between Reader and Writer

Joan L. Brown

Carmen Martín Gaite has been honored with her country's major literary awards over the past four decades. Even so, she has only recently been granted her place as one of the foremost writers of the postwar era. Many factors contributed to the lapse between achievement and recognition for this author, including the marginalization of women writers in most Spanish literary histories and a lack of self-promotion on her part. But however belatedly, Martín Gaite's stature now has been confirmed: in 1987 she became the first Spanish woman to be elected an honorary fellow of the Modern Language Association, joining an elite group of approximately seventy contemporary world authors (including three fellow Spaniards) who are considered by scholars to be the most significant.[1]

Underlying her election to the exclusive club of "the world's best authors" is the bond that Martín Gaite forges with her readers. The terms of the "narrative pact" between the reader and this writer are extremely generous: she goes to great lengths to promote reader involvement in as well as enjoyment of her texts. For Martín Gaite, the reader is a colleague. She has written in depth about the search for a conversational partner and has created important conversations within her novels. The most compelling conversation or communication in her work, however, is between text and recipient. As Servodidio and Welles observe, "Martín Gaite's writings are themselves not so much texts as 'utterances,' for throughout her pages the human voice is heard in rising and falling cadences, telling tales and weaving magic spells" (Servodidio and Welles 1983, 11–12).

Carmen Martín Gaite's singular voice reflects her particular way of apprehending the world, the unique "back room" from which her writing emanates. Martín Gaite's literary vision has been shaped by her gender, background, and historical moment. She was born in the provincial capital of Salamanca on 8 December 1925, the second of two daughters of a prosperous and cultured attorney and his highly intelligent and gracious wife. Martín Gaite ascribes many of the advantages that influenced her as a writer to her upbringing.[2] Her education, especially, was unusual for young women of her social station, who commonly received finishing-school training from nuns. Instead, she was taught by private tutors for the primary grades, and she attended a secondary school that stressed academics and included girls of varied backgrounds. Until she was eleven, Martín Gaite was primarily influenced by family activities. She was afforded tomboyish summers in the family's Galician country house, extended trips to Madrid, and the impressive cultural resources (especially the library) of her parents. From 1936 forward, however, her personal experience was molded as much by external events as internal ones: the civil war of 1936–39, in which her family's sympathies were with the defeated side, and the extended postwar era of Franco's dictatorship were critical determinants of her sensibility.

Martín Gaite was graduated from the University of Salamanca in 1948 and moved to Madrid to pursue a doctorate in history and philology. At the University of Madrid, she fell in with a group of seemingly negligent students who would later become some of the most important writers of the postwar era. These contemporaries include Ignacio Aldecoa (whom she knew in Salamanca), Medardo Fraile, Alfonso Sastre, Jesús Fernández Santos, and Rafael Sánchez Ferlosio. Martín Gaite is most commonly introduced in histories of Spanish literature as part of this almost exclusively male cohort, known to subsequent literary scholars as the Generation of Mid-Century. Distinguished by a commitment to social criticism, these writers shared the experience of the civil war from a child's vantage point and an interest in foreign (especially Italian) literature and film. They are associated with the "social novel" that eluded government censors and that offered the only objective testimony of life in Franco's Spain in the absence of a free press. Influenced by her friends and by her success in publishing short stories, Martín Gaite put aside her doctoral dissertation, deferring its completion for over twenty years, in favor of writing fiction.

Since she began writing fiction Martín Gaite has published five novels, two novellas, fifteen short stories, a collection of informal verses, and two novels for children. She has had concomitant success as a biographer, a historian, a writer of screenplays for television and film, a literary critic, and most recently a playwright. A brief review of these pursuits is appropriate background to a study of this author's fiction, since they coincide with what is categorized as her "creative writing." In both fields she effectively functions as an anthropologist to her own culture, reporting her findings to an esteemed reader.

Martín Gaite has two areas of specialization that span the critical gap between fiction and nonfiction: the social and literary history of Spain in the eighteenth century and the social and literary history of Spain in the modern era. In her forties she returned to scholarship, and to the completion of her doctorate in history and philology, with a study of an eighteenth-century figure who intrigued her: don Melchor de Macanaz. Seven years of investigating his life story yielded a historical biography published in 1969, entitled *El proceso de Macanaz: Historia de un empapelamiento* (The case of Macanaz: History of a lawsuit), reissued in 1975 as *Macanaz como otro paciente de la Inquisición* (Macanaz: Another victim of the Inquisition). This was followed by a volume of social and literary history entitled *Usos amorosos del siglo XVIII en España* (1972) (Love and courtship customs in eighteenth-century Spain). In this study, which focuses on the distinctive social patterns of the era (including the phenomenon of the platonic male companion for wealthy married women) in relation to the politics of the time, Martín Gaite uses literary as well as purely historical evidence for her analysis. Recent social and literary history has also been the subject of her scholarly inquiry. In her 1973 collection of essays, *La búsqueda de interlocutor y otras búsquedas* (The search for a conversational partner and other searches), she analyzes various aspects of the problematic nature of communication in modern society. The properties of narrative are explored in her 1983 best-seller, *El cuento de nunca acabar* (The never-ending tale). In this compendium of brief essays, subtitled *apuntes sobre la narración, el amor y la mentira* (notes on narration, love, and lies), the author probes the most absorbing questions of literary theory, especially the problem of why some stories are well told and others are not. The subject of politically conditioned relations between the sexes for her own generation of Spaniards who grew up under Franco is explored in her 1987 *Usos amorosos de la postguerra española* (Love and courtship customs in postwar Spain), another best-seller. Her most recent nonfiction work is a study of literary women in Spain entitled *Desde la ventana* (1987) (From the window).

In her personal life Martín Gaite has known both happiness and tragedy. She married fellow writer Rafael Sánchez Ferlosio in 1953; they separated in 1970 and divorced in 1987. The couple had two children; the first died in infancy, and the second as an adult. Solitude has contributed to her personal vision. "Yo no le temo a la soledad," she has affirmed, "me he acostumbrado a ella y la aguanto bastante mejor que la mayoría de la gente que conozco" [I am not afraid of being alone, I have become accustomed to it, and I tolerate it better than most of the people I know] (Brown 1987, Spanish 204; English 33). But good conversation is always welcomed: "Hablar con la gente de la más diversa condición y edad es algo que me encanta, y escuchar tanto o más que hablar" [To speak with people of the most diverse conditions and ages is something that delights me, and listening as much as or more than speaking] (Brown 1987, Spanish 204; English 33). Martín Gaite has reached conversational partners in Spain and abroad, including the United States, where she has been a visiting professor and invited lecturer at a number of colleges and universities.

Her impulse to communicate, to engage the mind of an interlocutor, permeates all of Martín Gaite's writings, especially her fiction. Two other concerns also unite the author's work: a preoccupation with the relationship between the nonconformist individual and society and an intense interest in the characteristics of narrative art. From the beginning of her career through her current novel-in-progress, she has demonstrated what John Kronik has termed a "developing but consistent production" (Kronik 1983, 49). The summaries of Martín Gaite's novels that follow demonstrate the breadth of her work over time: she develops enduring social concerns, using a range of techniques, and presents them to a reader who is tantamount to a conversational partner. What these summaries cannot reveal is another overriding characteristic of Martín Gaite's literature—her beautiful, fluid prose style, which is often reminiscent of the spoken word.

Martín Gaite's literary career began in 1954. Her first short novel *El balneario* (The spa) captured the Gijón Prize, an extremely prestigious award bestowed by an elite group of writers who recognized that *El balneario* was far ahead of its time. Its sophisticated technique, incorporating fantastic as well as realistic elements and utilizing all aspects of its structure to communicate the work's themes, would not become widespread in Spanish literature until the 1970s.

El balneario consists of two parts. The first section of the sixty-page novella begins with an apparently straightforward description of the arrival of the protagonist, an unremarkable middle-aged woman named Matilde who is accompanied by her husband, at a spa in the north of Spain. Without any marked transition, the narrative in the first part of the novella gradually moves from the mundane to the bizarre and terrifying adventures of the main character. Part 2 of the novella opens with a bellboy knocking on the door of "Miss Matilde," and it suddenly is clear that the entire first part of the work—the realistic portion as well as the surrealistic dreamed adventure—was part of Matilde's dream. Neither the protagonist's status as a married lady nor her exciting adventure was real. Resigned, Miss Matilde accepts the bellboy's invitation to join a game of cards that epitomizes the risk-free monotony of her summer vacation and her life.

Martín Gaite has explicitly stated the underlying themes of her first major work: the ambivalence felt by those who lead mundane lives toward the possibility of adventure and risk; the conversion of repressed impulses into dreams; the question of the provenance or true narrator of dreamed experiences.[3] The major achievement of *El balneario* lies in the author's involvement of the reader in formulating these fascinating and complex questions. Because the text has no signposts pointing to transitions between narrative planes, both the reader and the protagonist are not sure if what is transpiring is real. This shared hesitation is a distinguishing feature of fantastic literature, as defined by Tzvetan Todorov, the leading theoretician of the genre.[4] Because the second part of the work resolves this hesitation by advancing an explanation of the previous fantastic elements, the work falls into Todorov's classification of "l'étrange pur," or "the uncanny."

Martín Gaite's sophisticated first novel, with its unmarked transitions between narrative planes and its unexplained exploration of a character's subconscious, was ahead of the characteristically objective, realistic Spanish novel of the 1950s. The short stories included in the first anthology that carries the novella's title are much more representative of the literary modes of that time. With titles such as "La chica de abajo" (The girl from downstairs) and "Los informes" (References), most of these shorter works offer brief sketches of common people's lives.[5] Although the themes they deal with are close to those of her first novella, the avant garde complexity of *El balneario* would not be repeated in Martín Gaite's fiction for over two decades, when her next fantastic novel captured both Spain's National Book Award and the acclaim of critics in Spain and abroad.

While *El balneario* established Martín Gaite among the rarefied critical elite of her country, she did not achieve widespread fame until her second novel *Entre visillos* (1958) (Through the curtains; English translation by Frances López-Morillas, *Behind the Curtains*, 1990), received the most important literary prize in Spain, the Nadal Prize of 1957. The strength of this accolade firmly established Martín

Gaite's importance, as it had for earlier recipients, and guaranteed her a broad reading public.

Entre visillos is a panoramic documentary of traditional society in postwar Spain. It is set in the 1950s in an unnamed provincial city that the author has acknowledged is the Salamanca of her youth, and is structured around the four-month stay of a young high school teacher named Pablo Klein. Klein is one of the novel's two main characters; the other is his brightest pupil, Natalia Ruiz Guilarte, a sixteen-year-old experiencing a decisive year in her struggle with the conflict between personal aspirations and the circumscribed role options available to women. These characters are also the two first-person narrative voices in the novel: chapters told by the third-person narrator alternate with first-person chapters narrated by Pablo Klein, with the exception of two chapters drawn from Natalia's diary. Despite Klein's sex, both narrator-protagonists partially represent Carmen Martín Gaite.[6] In her first full-length novel the author returns to the city in which she grew up to capture its essence as if she were recording it on film. The town is elevated to the status of a huge protagonist. Its institutions, social patterns, and physical characteristics are described objectively by the omniscient narrator, by the idealistic male teacher, and by the iconoclastic schoolgirl. A cinematic metaphor conveys the subtleties of novelistic structuring that Martín Gaite employs: through multiple points of view, overlapping accounts of the same events are included in the novel as if the "director" were presenting all footage. It is up to the reader to edit the material.

As the reader assembles multiple narrative strands, what emerges is a complex view of the stultifying environment of a provincial capital in the postwar era. Censorship laws precluded explicit political criticism, but social analysis implicit in the novel reveals the constriction and tedium of the city in which it is set. As outsiders, both Pablo Klein and Natalia illustrate the suffocating environment from which he, at the novel's close, is the first to escape. Motifs such as nosy people peering through curtains and the giant eye of the cathedral clock watching over the town reinforce the limited horizons and enforced conformity that oppress individuals.

Beyond the broad social history visible in the novel, *Entre visillos* focuses particular attention on the lives of women. In fact, the novel was criticized when it was published for its presentation of the banal speech of high school girls, although subsequent analyses have discovered the logic and even the brilliance of this innovation. The plight of the woman who does not conform is foregrounded by contrasting it with the socially sanctioned traditional norm. What

Martín Gaite later would study as the feminine goal of the woman who was "muy mujer" (all woman), held up by the Franco government in the service of its postwar agenda,[7] is here illustrated by the unhappy female characters who internalize societal proscriptions regarding appropriate behavior and goals.

Despite themes that lend themselves to sociological summaries, such as the problem of conformity versus nonconformity in traditional society, *Entre visillos* is not a treatise. Rather it is a realistic, multilayered, and personal story of provincial society in Franco's Spain. Influenced by the prevailing realistic orientation in Spanish literature and taking Italian neorealist cinema as a source of inspiration, the novel also is a descendant of the sweeping Spanish social novel best represented by Leopoldo Alas (who lived from 1852–1901 and wrote under the pen name Clarín). Unlike her nineteenth-century predecessor, however, Martín Gaite invites her audience to be more than pleased spectators: in *Entre visillos* she characteristically assumes that readers will participate in assigning meaning.

Martín Gaite's next work of fiction is less structurally complex than *Entre visillos*, but it is thematically interrelated with her first major novel. *Las ataduras* (Binding ties) (1960) is a novella that explores the issue of emotional commitments, especially in the lives of women. Simultaneous vignettes explore the situations of Alina, a young wife and mother living in Paris, and her two parents in Spain. Flashbacks recall Alina's history, especially her father's disappointment in his daughter's failure to fulfill her own promise by abandoning her education to become a mother and wife. The protagonist, spurred by her parents' recent visit, resolves to accept them and to attempt to show them that she is content in the life she has chosen.

Unlike her groundbreaking first novella, *Las ataduras* fulfills the classic function of its genre, illustrating what Henry James originally described as a combination of thematic expansion with structural intensity. Martín Gaite presents and then reexamines a situation in order to elucidate an overarching theme.[8] She explores the issue of imposed versus chosen obligations, with the latter seen as the only truly authentic ties, in the context of the larger issue of personal freedom. The novella *Las ataduras* is followed in the title collection by six short stories. Distinct yet interrelated, they have been described as "un estudio literario de la familia" (a literary study of the family).[9]

In her second full-length novel, Martín Gaite shifted her focus from the internal dynamics of families to the issues facing a singular individual. *Ritmo lento* (A slower rhythm) (1962) explores the problematic relationship of a superior nonconformist to the society in which he finds himself obliged to function. The novel traces the development of a unique young man, David Fuente (whose last name means "source"), as he attempts to decipher the process of his own personality.

David Fuente is a lucid idealist who rejects the widespread hypocrisy and the shallow values of those around him. Raised by his father, a physician engaged in medical research, David assimilates the scientific method as well as his father's lofty principles and applies both codes in his life. His refusal to accept anything that he himself has not validated, along with his acute awareness of all sides of any question, lead to an overwhelming passivity: decisions and choices are nearly impossible for him to make. Although he is a gifted painter, he lacks the ambition necessary to pursue this or any other career. Instead he drifts into circumstances and plots his own activities with scant regard for the outside world. When a relative arranges outside employment for David in a bank, his disdain for money leads him to commit an impulsive prank that costs him his job and results in his being sent to a rest home to be "cured."

It is from this sanatorium that David's narrative emanates. Couched between two objectively narrated "bookends," most of the novel is comprised of David's first-person reminiscences about his life. Although he explicitly rejects his own duplicitous psychiatrist as well as psychiatry in general, David's recapitulation of his life is structured as if he were engaged in psychotherapy. However, as Marcia Welles has noted, the aim of his verbalization is "not . . . to cure, but to comprehend."[10] David's narrative is seemingly spoken, in the accurately captured natural patterns that characterize all of Martín Gaite's writings. His first-person voice desists when the increasingly tenuous thread joining him to the world finally snaps. A newspaper clipping recounts the novel's final violent episode, which leads to David's involuntary placement in an insane asylum.

The issue of the social definition of madness is one of the central themes in *Ritmo lento*. Mechanisms of social control and the escalating sanctions leveled against nonconformists are vividly illustrated by the responses of the majority to David Fuente. His derisive exposure of society's shortcomings is rooted in his absolute rationality, which leads him to reject the intense pursuit of material gain, the treatment of women as possessions (and also women's own perpetuation of their secondary status), and the encouragement of violence among children. As an instrument for social analysis, David Fuente differs from the collective protagonists so common in novels of social criticism in Spain in the 1950s. In *Ritmo lento* social criticism is communicated through one character whose conflicts with the prevailing social order point to society's deficiencies, since he is patently in the right. Through her iconoclastic and ultimately "crazy" protagonist, Martín Gaite effectively exposes the hypocrisy and inequity, as well as the difficulty of true communication, that characterized postwar Spanish society.

In addition to focusing social analysis through a singular lens, Martín Gaite's second full-length novel represents an innovative technical advance over the realistic narrative that dominated the Spanish novel at the time it was published. The complex psychological portrait of *Ritmo lento* is presented in the form of a retrospective collage. David's reminiscences, organized into chapters revolving around important people in his life, are not presented in chronological order. Nor do they always reflect an external logic. Influenced by the Italian master Italo Svevo, Martín Gaite crafts her protagonist's story by using free associations, stream-of-consciousness meanderings, internal discourse, and dreams. It is up to the reader to reassemble the chronology of this unusual character's life.

Curiously, at the time *Ritmo lento* was published the book did not attract a large number of readers. Its critical reception was influenced by unfortunate timing: the novel was the first runner-up for the respected Biblioteca Breve Prize of 1962, the first year that the prize was awarded to a South American writer, Mario Vargas Llosa. Perhaps discouraged by the dearth of reviews that greeted the novel, and certainly eager to resume her scholarly investigations, Martín Gaite did not publish another novel for over a decade.

Her next novel, entitled *Retahílas* (Yarns) (1974), shares with its predecessor the author's predilection for the confessional monologue. In this novel, Martín Gaite's fascination with spoken communication is fully actualized: *Retahílas* takes the form of a night-long conversation. Twenty-four-year-old Germán and his forty-five-year-old Aunt Eulalia arrive at the family's ancestral country home, summoned by the caretaker Juana upon the impending death of Eulalia's grandmother (Germán's great-grandmother). Over the course of six hours they engage in a conversation resembling a "bonfire," which is extinguished by the death of the grandmother at dawn. In a structure similar to that of *Ritmo lento*, the novel is framed by two objective chapters, here designated "Prelude" and "Epilogue," between which the characters' alternating first-person narratives constitute the central portion of the work.

Eulalia, whose name is Greek for "beautiful speech," has nearly twice as many pages for her monologues as does her nephew. This division is appropriate, since not only is she almost twice his age and more than doubly knowledgeable, she also is the object of her nephew's intense curiosity. Germán lost his mother when he was a young child, and Eulalia, his father's sister, was his mother's closest friend. Eulalia is able to share her knowledge of Germán's mother while at the same time disclosing her own personality. Both Eulalia and Germán present themselves through words: the communication of self is their overriding concern. Eulalia is a brittle, sophisticated, successful intellectual with strong ideals who now is mourning the end of a long marriage and questioning her decision not to have children. Germán, whom the author has acknowledged to be a supporting character,[11] is an earnest young man who is conscious of the superficiality of his own peer group.

The alternating discourses of Eulalia and Germán are verbal missives. In a form reminiscent of the epistolary novel, each character's spoken "letters" are transcribed without interruption, to be followed by the other's response. Salient topics predominate in each pair of chapters and are centered around important personal relationships in the lives of the speakers. The notion of an unraveling series of ideas, inherent in the work's title, functions as a central organizing principle. Skillfully blending "discourse" or abstraction and "story" or action, the spoken letters of Eulalia and Germán avoid the tedium that threatens lengthy reminiscences. The convention that the novel is spoken, not written, adds immediacy to each character's accounts of long-ago events and current longings.

Foremost among the characters' desires is the wish for communication through language, an urge that in *Retahílas* is expressed explicitly by the speakers as well as implicitly in the work's form. Other themes include the tyranny of gender-specific role definitions for both sexes, the deterioration of contemporary culture, and the problems of reconciling intellectual positions (such as the emancipated choice not to have children) with basic emotional needs. Dismayed with the decay evident in society and over signs of her own mortality, both of which are symbolized by the dilapidated yet once-grand house to which they have come, Eulalia repeatedly voices her creator's conviction that language is humanity's only salvation.

Within the novel Eulalia and Germán fulfill for one another the author's criteria for successful conversational partners, as outlined in several of her nonfiction essays. They are not "distorted mirrors" in that they know little of each other and do not harbor fixed preconceptions; they are sincerely interested in one another; and they feel no pressure to be elsewhere. The characters participate in the elusive, near-magical event described by Martín Gaite in her essay "La búsqueda de interlocutor," in which speakers surprise themselves by "contándole a un desconocido, de quien las circunstancias han hecho amigo ocasional, historias atrasadas, apenas latentes . . ." [telling a stranger, who by chance has become an acquaintance, our backlogged, barely latent stories . . .].[12] Not only are the nephew and his aunt compelling tellers of stories, but they are also supremely effective listeners, as of course the work's implicit conversational partner—the reader—also must be.

Martín Gaite's fourth novel, *Fragmentos de interior* (Inner fragments) (1976) is her least well known. The "interior" it describes is not the inner region of the mind but rather the inside view of a modern Madrid household. It is a novel of action that augurs the story-oriented literary trend of the late 1970s and 1980s, epitomized by the "novela negra," or detective novel. The superficial milieu criticized in *Retahílas* is here transformed into the backdrop for character sketches and rapidly unfolding events. Over the course of three days in 1975, the crucial year in which Franco died and Spain entered an anxious phase known as "pre-democracy," the microcosm of one household is revealed within the context of the macrocosm of Madrid.

The Alvar family and their household staff are at the center of *Fragmentos de interior*. The handsome forty-five-year-old Diego is a publishing executive who has unfulfilled dreams of writing a novel; he is separated from his still-beautiful fifty-year-old wife, Agustina, a poet, and is living with Gloria, an attractive though common thirty-year-old young woman. Diego and Agustina have two children. Isabel, bright and cynical, is active in dangerous leftist political movements; Jaime, it is suggested, is coming to terms with his homosexuality. The family's household retinue includes two traditional older women servants and a lovely young newcomer named Luisa, who is in service temporarily. Critic Carlos Feal has observed that the role of this character parallels that of the reader: she, like the reader, enters a new world and must organize the experience that awaits her.[13]

The frenzied actions of these characters include episodes that just years earlier would have been unthinkable in Spanish fiction: Isabel hides a political fugitive sought by the police; Gloria removes her clothing for a scene in a movie; Luisa smokes marijuana while waiting for a young man whom she barely knows but with whom she has been intimate. The culmination of the rapid plot of *Fragmentos de interior* also points to the central theme of the novel. Agustina's suicide is an extreme response to the isolation that plagues all of these characters (and has always preoccupied their author).

In addition to the difficulty of communication in the fast-paced life of the modern European capital, Martín Gaite's novel also focuses on the still-limited role options available to women and the relationship between members of the privileged class and their servants in an evolving social order. Once again Martín Gaite reveals hypocrisy, this time in the supposed "new freedom" that replaces commitment with casualness in relationships between men and women but does nothing to erase the ageist double standard by which the former judge the latter.

Similar to the British television serial "Upstairs, Downstairs," Martín Gaite's *Fragmentos de interior* has been characterized by the eminent Spanish critic Antonio Tovar as a "small epic." Though lacking the sweeping focus characteristic of the classical epic, the novel illustrates most other stylistic and thematic aspects of the genre. The world of the novel is a self-contained universe populated by characters who each have one distinguishing feature. Characters reveal themselves primarily through action and dialogue, rather than through the contributions of a privileged narrator, and consequently the author's hand is not perceived. The theatrical plot should not distract critical readers from the novel's considerable achievements. The dialogues are perfectly pitched and the "snapshots" of Madrid in the seventies are vivid. Recognizing the richness contained in this modern-day novel of manners, one Spanish critic who reviewed the novel when it first appeared offered an unusual instruction that might well be featured on the dust-jacket of the book: *Fragmentos de interior* is a novel that should be read twice (Brown 1987, 137).

Martín Gaite's most recent work of fiction for adults is her most acclaimed book. *El cuarto de atrás* (1978, English translation by Helen R. Lane, *The Back Room*, 1983) was a dazzling success when it appeared in Spain, winning the 1979 Premio Nacional de Literatura. On both sides of the Atlantic, this unique novel has continued to attract readers and fascinate scholars for more than a decade.

The novel's complexities are best appreciated in the context of its historical moment and of its author's stage of development. The novel was begun on the day of Franco's burial in 1975. With his death, the protracted postwar era officially expired. As Spain edged into "pre-democracy," the restraints of the fascist government gradually were loosened. In the realm of literature, the end of censorship gave rise to a plethora of memoirs: detail-laden confessions of now-ancient-seeming political activities glutted the shelves of booksellers, just as magazine racks were jammed with newly acceptable political and pornographic publications.

For Martín Gaite, political confessions held no appeal, although she also felt the need to come to terms with the end of the political era in which she had lived nearly all of her life. For her, one of the most important aspects of the new freedom was the new availability of foreign literature, which abetted her ongoing investigation of the properties of narrative art that would culminate in *El cuento de nunca acabar* (1982). The novel that interrupted her book of literary theory, while richly benefitting from it, was *El cuarto de atrás*. This novel is the result of Martín Gaite's reactions to her moment in history and to her preoccupation with questions of literary theory.

Martín Gaite's fifth novel is a technically complex work whose form makes it a unique hybrid. It is at once a fantastic novel and a "realistic" memoir or evocation of the life and literature of its creator. Over the course of an unexpected, late-night interview by a mysterious man dressed in black, whose appearance is preceded and followed by the introduction of a huge cockroach, a woman character who exactly resembles the author discusses long-repressed memories of growing up in Franco's Spain. The man in black is a consummate interlocutor. Using his considerable resources, including pharmacological as well as intellectual inducements to speech, he elicits and shapes the woman writer's recollections while a storm rages outside her penthouse windows. As the speakers continue their torrential conversation, a pile of pages grows mysteriously next to the author's typewriter. Finally, exhausted, she falls asleep. When she is awakened, she discovers that Alejandro, the man in black, has gone, but that two vestiges of his visit remain. One is a little gold box, and the other is the stack of pages that constitute the novel itself.

Because of the man in black, *El cuarto de atrás* is a fantastic novel. The unresolved hesitation that the woman protagonist shares with the reader over whether or not the minutely described interview can be considered "real" defines one of the modes of this unusual work of literature. This self-referential text, which highlights the process of its own creation, fulfills the author's desire (expressed in her own monologue and also in her conversation with her interviewer) to write a fantastic work of fiction. In so doing Martín Gaite skillfully creates what fellow novelist J. M. Caballero Bonald terms the "magical" sphere of the novel.[14]

Evoked from and filtered through the magical sphere, Martín Gaite's reminiscences about her youth and her literary career constitute the novel's second mode, the ostensibly "realistic" (mimetic) or, in Caballero Bonald's terminology, the "testimonial" realm. Free from the overt strictures of censorship, yet habituated to self-censorship and constrained by the unreality that characterizes all childhood memories but especially those of her generation of Spanish children, the author retrieves fragments of her past. Martín Gaite has acknowledged that for the first time she describes her own life: "cuento cosas de mi propia vida, sin enmascararlas bajo otros artificios" [I tell things from my own life, without using other devices to mask them].[15] But she avoids the tiresome banality of the memoir genre as she lets these memories surface freely: "Pero no son propiamente unas memorias," she has recognized, "sino una reflexión sobre las trampas de la memoria, una meditación sobre el paso del tiempo y sobre el caos de los recuerdos" [Yet strictly speaking they are not memoirs, but rather a reflection on the tricks that memory plays, a meditation on the passage of time and on the chaos of recollections].[16] The process by which these memories are recaptured has been aptly compared to the Freudian notion of "dreamwork," the mysterious process by which the unconscious retrieves symbols and narrates stories.[17]

Personal memories retrieved from the author's chaotic "back room" also reflect much of the common history of Martín Gaite's generation of Spaniards. Accounts of the civil war, as well as political references that were suppressed under censorship, are included here for the first time, as in the purely realistic memoirs of Martín Gaite's contemporaries. Social themes are vividly illustrated, such as the inhibition of freedom and the social pressures facing women, the deprivation that affected even a privileged family such as that of the author, and the difficulty of communication between individuals.

In this novel of personal development, Martín Gaite also documents what it was like to grow up as a gifted and highly intelligent woman during the civil war and postwar years. Social history is recorded in descriptions of female rites such as having dresses made, along with assessments of the impact of Franco's propaganda as it was received by young women fulfilling their mandatory social service commitment. Intellectual history also is presented in both societal and personal terms. The reading experiences of Martín Gaite's generation, including the textbooks that impeded learning, are chronicled with insight. Especially interesting is the impact of popular culture, transmitted through American movies and through women's formulaic romance novels, on young Spanish women in the 1940s and 1950s.

Literary themes also are abundant. The narrator and the man in black discuss literary topics at length; he even criticizes the author for "backing down" in the second part of her first novella *El balneario*, in which the fantastic first part is revealed to have been a dream. *El cuarto de atrás* has been shown to be a complete actualization of the author's principal tenets of literary theory. Martín Gaite's convictions that literature involves escapism, that it is inextricably tied to memory, that it exists in order to achieve much-needed communication, and that it affords its creator a spiritual catharsis are both specified in and embodied by this novel.[18]

Beyond conveying the author's own theories, *El cuarto de atrás* encourages readers to apply their own. The novel's multiple ambiguities, which Martín Gaite considers essential to good literature, are in effect the most gracious invitation imaginable. Critic Debra Castillo voices the delight of professional critics when she observes that in the novel "apparent polarities [of] memory and forgetfulness, history and literature, true and false, reality and fantasy...are suddenly, ambiguously, flung together in a celebration of riches."[19] One example of the vast possibilities for interplay with critics inherent in the novel is the plurality of interpretations of the man in black, which range from the devil incarnate to the author's idealized vision of the reader. Responding to a tantalizing gambit, of which there are many in this sophisticated and canny novel, literary scholars have entered into a dialogue with the work itself, one which has continued to intensify over the years. *El cuarto de atrás* is by far the most studied novel by Carmen Martín Gaite. It is also, according to the Modern Language Association Bibliographies for 1978 to 1988 (the most recent year for which data are available in 1990), the most frequently examined novel by a contemporary Spanish woman author over the past decade.

This overview suggests a number of conclusions about the most studied contemporary woman writer of Spain. It is clear that her stature rests on a body of work that is complex and varied but which reveals certain overriding consistencies. These include her effective, "conversational" prose, mastery of multiple techniques, skill as a social observer, and astute depictions of the lives of women.

The most pervasive quality in Martín Gaite's fiction is that it seems to be addressed, even spoken, to a respected colleague. For this author, the reader is a conversational partner who enables her to fulfill an urgent desire to communicate. In unpretentious yet expert prose, she captivates with storytelling skill at the same time that she engages the reader in assembling meaning from cues that range from the documentary—as in *Entre visillos*, to the playfully ambiguous—as in *El cuarto de atrás*. A related question of the characteristics, boundaries, and power of oral and written narrative is both explored and actualized in two of her novels, *Retahílas* and *El cuarto de atrás*, which consist of cathartic conversational interchanges. The precursor of these novels, *Ritmo lento*, focuses on the failure of a "talking cure" with a deficient conversational partner, a psychiatrist whom the patient holds in low regard.

Throughout her work Martín Gaite has experimented with new techniques and repeatedly has been ahead of her time in her choice of literary directions. Her first novella, *El balneario*, introduced techniques in 1954 that would not become widespread for at least twenty years, including a fantastic episode and an oneiric exploration of the main character's subconscious mind. Along with other members of the Generation of Mid-Century, she participated in the documentary realism of the 1950s; her cinematic descriptions and seemingly tape-recorded dialogues are among the most accomplished of her group. Her 1958 *Entre visillos* is the best example of this method, which is also represented by her 1960 *Las ataduras*. She went on to help introduce a new type of social novel in 1962 with *Ritmo lento*, in which objective realism was replaced by a synchronic narrative collage that probed the psychology of a maladapted yet superior individual. Martín Gaite created a new genre with her 1974 *Retahílas*, a series of spontaneous, interlocking verbal missives created by chance over the course of one night, and couched between the text's two objective "bookends." Her action-adventure story *Fragmentos de interior*, published in 1976, was a very early entry into the escapist action genre, a literary category that only recently has been taken seriously by the critical elite. In her 1979 *El cuarto de atrás*, the conversational format of *Retahílas* recurs, but with several twists: one of the conversational partners represents Carmen Martín Gaite herself, and the other may be an apparition. Neither the narrator nor the reader can resolve the ambiguity of this meta-fictional text, which mysteriously "writes itself."

Her techniques have always abetted Martín Gaite's observation of Spanish society. Over four decades she has been an anthropologist to her own culture, a social critic who analyzes Spanish society of the twentieth century with the trained eye that she uses in her nonfiction explorations of eighteenth-century Spain. Her social analysis began in the mainstream of Spanish neorrealism of the 1950s, which focused on everyday, "non-literary" people. In the 1960s she depicted the psychology of an individual who was sanctioned for being superior to the mediocre values of society. In the 1970s, Martín Gaite overtly criticized the decay of contemporary society, and especially the deterioration of language; the superficiality of the European youth culture also came under her scrutiny. When censorship ended, Martín Gaite retrieved recollections of the bizarre nature of life for her generation, who came of age in the civil war and lived in its repressive aftermath for close to forty years. Beyond her fascination with society as a whole, Martín Gaite is more specifically concerned with the lives of women. It can be argued that her acuity as a social observer is directly related to her gender and to the alienation felt by intellectual women of her generation in Spain, who could not help but resent the traditional social directives that would have had them limit their sights to being the mirror of a man. There are woman heroes in Martín Gaite's fiction, and they pursue what have been termed "quest plots" in their lives, seeking to fulfill personal ambitions and to accomplish individual goals.[20]

Not only have Martín Gaite's depictions of women been sensitive and compelling, they have been audacious. In the 1950s she ventured that proper spinsters can have repressed but furious longings for adventure (*El balneario*), and she devoted a serious novel to a year in the life of a provincial adolescent girl. The protagonist of her 1962 novel *Ritmo lento* criticized the prevailing notion of women as possessions, and with even greater insight, he attacked women who perpetuated this injustice. When social mores relaxed in the 1970s, Martín Gaite did not romanticize women's new freedom: she reported honestly on the ageist double standard that discriminated against women in *Retahílas* and in *Fragmentos de interior*, and ridiculed the "liberated woman" who traded sexual favors for job advancement in the latter novel. Martín Gaite's most recent representation of a woman was based on a presentation of her own autobiography and depicts a famous woman writer granting an interview to a male admirer.

As with other writers, the real-life persona of Carmen Martín Gaite can only be guessed at from her works. The figure of the woman writer in *El cuarto de atrás* and her published auto-biographical sketch are the fundamental sources of biographical information on Carmen Martín Gaite, and neither offers sufficient clues to the character of this woman writer. Readers will have to look to other sources for the answer to questions such as to what degree she herself is a conformist and to what degree she is an iconoclast. Recently, in accepting an award for lifelong literary achievement from the king of Spain, she laughingly noted that for a woman of her generation to give the acceptance speech for an award she shared with a man (the poet José Angel Valente) would have been unheard of: she should have kept in the background, she wryly noted, drinking a gin-fizz as he talked.[21] Although the inner forces that propelled her from provincial dances to the summit of Spanish literature may never be known, her acceptance speech for this most recent honor does reveal humor, honesty, and charm. These are qualities that are perceived by her friends and by her literary partners, her readers. Perhaps no less than her accomplished prose style, they underly the success of the person who helped to invent a new category in contemporary Spanish literature: the master writer who is a woman.

Notes

1. *MLA Newsletter* 19 (Summer 1987): 1.

2. This and subsequent autobiographical statements are quoted from Carmen Martín Gaite, "Un bosquejo autobiográfico" (An Autobiographical Sketch), in Brown 1987. The Spanish document appears in the appendix, 193–206; the English translation comprises chapter 2, 20–34.

3. Based on a personal note from Carmen Martín Gaite, published in Brown 1978. An English translation of the note appears in Brown 1987, 37–38.

4. Further evidence of the modernity of *El balneario* is the fact that the now-classic definition of the genre was published in 1971. See Tzvetan Todorov, *Introduction a la littérature fantastique* (Paris: Editions du Seuil, 1971). English translation by Richard Howard, *The Fantastic: A Structural Approach to a Literary Genre* (Ithaca, N.Y.: Cornell University Press, 1975).

5. Detailed critiques of Martín Gaite's two collections of short stories are found in Brown 1987, chaps. 3 and 5. An analysis of Martín Gaite's short stories in the order they were written is the subject of Joan Lipman Brown, "Martín Gaite's Short Stories, 1953–1974: The Writer's Workshop," in Servodidio and Welles 1983, 37–48.

6. While Natalia is naturally associated with the author as an adolescent, Pablo Klein represents Martín Gaite at the age at which she ventured back to reexamine the world of her youth as the author of the novel (Brown 1987, 71–72). John Kronik considers Pablo Klein the singular "implied author's mask-presumptive," which would readily be apparent were it not for readers' awareness of the real author's gender (1983, 53).

7. Carmen Martín Gaite, *Usos amorosos de la postguerra española* (Madrid: Anagrama, 1987).

8. Judith Liebowitz, in *Narrative Purpose in the Novella* (The Hague: Mouton, 1974), takes this reexamination as the critical distinction between the novella and the short story (79).

9. F. Sánchez Fontenla, "C. Martín Gaite: Las ataduras," *Insula* 178 (September 1961): 9.

10. Marcia L. Welles, "Carmen Martín Gaite: Fiction as Desire," in Servodidio and Welles 1983, 200.

11. Carmen Martín Gaite, from a delivered speech quoted in Brown 1987, 153.

12. Carmen Martín Gaite, "La búsqueda de interlocutor," in *La búsqueda de interlocutor y otras búsquedas*, 2d ed. (Barcelona: Destino, 1982), 25.

13. Carlos Feal, "Hacia la estructura de *Fragmentos de interior*," in Servodidio and Welles 1983, 98.

14. J. M. Caballero Bonald, "*El cuarto de atrás* de Carmen Martín Gaite: Complicidades de la memoria," *Diario 16* (19 June 1978): 19.

15. Carmen Martín Gaite, in an interview with Soledad Izquierdo, "Carmen Martín Gaite: La literatura como placer," *Crítica* 664 (March 1979): 19.

16. Carmen Martín Gaite, in an interview with Jorge Marfil, "Carmen Martín Gaite: La narración incesante," *El viejo topo* 19 (April 1978): 64.

17. Jean Alsina, "Temps, fiction et autobiographie: Reprise et reclassement dans *El cuarto de atrás* de Carmen Martín Gaite," in *L'autobiographie en Espagne*, ed. J. Diffusion and J. Lafitte (Aix-en-Provence: University of Provence, 1982), 324–33. Debra Castillo (1987) cites Alsina's metaphor and elaborates upon it in "Never-Ending Story: Carmen Martín Gaite's *The Back Room*."

18. Joan Lipman Brown and Elaine M. Smith, 1987.

19. Castillo, 822.

20. See Joan L. Brown, "The Challenge of Martín Gaite's Woman Hero," in *Feminine Concerns in Contemporary Spanish Fiction by Women*, ed. Roberto Manteiga, Carolyn Galerstein, and Kathleen McNerney (Potomac, Md.: Scripta Humanistica, 1988), 86–98.

21. Carmen Martín Gaite, "VIII Premios Príncipe de Asturias: Discurso de Carmen Martín Gaite dedicado a don Felipe de Borbón," *El País* (Madrid), 16 October 1988, 30.

Bibliography

1. PRIMARY WORKS

1954. *El balneario* [novella]. Madrid: Alianza, 1968 (2d ed.).

1958. *Entre visillos* [novel]. Barcelona: Ediciones Destino, 1967 (5th ed.). Translated by Frances López-Morillas and published as *Behind the Curtains* by Columbia University Press, 1990.

1960. *Las ataduras* [novella and six short stories]. Barcelona: Destino. Published by Barral in 1978 with only the title novella and an introduction by Ana María Moix.

1962. *Ritmo lento* [novel]. Barcelona: Seix Barral, 1974 (3d ed.); 1969 (2d ed., without epilogue).

1974. *Retahílas* [novel]. Barcelona: Destino, 1979 (2d ed.).

1976a. *Fragmentos de interior* [novel]. Barcelona: Destino.

1976b. *A rachas* [poetry]. Edited by Jesús Muñárriz. Madrid: Peralta.

1978a. *El cuarto de atrás* [novel]. Barcelona: Destino, 1978. Translated by Helen R. Lane and published as *The Back Room* by Columbia University Press, 1983.

1978b. *Cuentos completos* [all of the author's novellas and short stories]. Madrid: Alianza.

1981. *El castillo de las tres murallas* [children's novel]. Barcelona: Lumen.

1985. *El pastel del diablo* [children's novel]. Barcelona: Lumen.

1986. *Dos relatos fantásticos* [children's novels]. Barcelona: Lumen. Contains both of the author's children's novels.

2. SECONDARY WORKS

Bellver, Catherine G. 1980. "Carmen Martín Gaite as a Social Critic." *Letras Femeninas* 6 (Autumn): 3–16. Examines the "underlying ideal" of freedom for woman protagonists throughout Martín Gaite's fiction.

Boring, Phyllis Zatlin. 1977. "Carmen Martín Gaite, Feminist Author." *Revista de Estudios Hispánicos* 11 (October): 323–38. Analyzes the feminist concerns of all of the author's writings up to 1976.

Brown, Joan Lipman. 1978. " 'El balneario' by Carmen Martín Gaite: Conceptual Aesthetics and 'l'étrange pur.' " *Journal of Spanish Studies: Twentieth Century* 6 (Winter): 163–74.

———. 1981a. "A Fantastic Memoir: Technique and History in *El cuarto de atrás*." *Anales de la Literatura Española Contemporánea* 6: 165–76. Examines the novel's two modes, the fantastic and the realistic, to delineate their structural and thematic relationships.

———. 1981b. "The Nonconformist Character as Social Critic in the Novels of Carmen Martín Gaite." *Kentucky Romance Quarterly* 28: 165–76. Identifies and investigates the mechanisms by which nonconformist protagonists serve as instruments of social analysis in the author's first three novels.

———. 1982. "*Tiempo de silencio* and *Ritmo lento*: Pioneers of the New Social Novel in Spain." *Hispanic Review* 50 (Winter): 61–73. Investigates the previously unexplored parallels between the two novels that may have inaugurated a new social novel in Spain.

———. 1987. *Secrets from the Back Room: The Fiction of Carmen Martín Gaite*. University, Miss.: Romance Monographs. A comprehensive analysis of all of the author's fiction through 1984, including an autobiographical sketch by Martín Gaite and an extensive annotated bibliography of secondary sources in the United States and Spain.

Brown, Joan Lipman, and Elaine M. Smith. 1987. "*El cuarto de atrás*: Metafiction and the Actualization of Literary Theory." *Hispanófila*, no. 90: 63–70. Demonstrates how the novel both transmits and illustrates personal tenets of literary theory that the author detailed in interviews in the Spanish press.

Castillo, Debra. 1987. "Never-Ending Story: Carmen Martín Gaite's *The Back Room*." *PMLA* 102(5): 814–28. Using the metaphor of the sewing basket full of tangled threads that appears in the novel, this analysis emphasizes the ambiguities of the text.

Kronik, John W. 1983. "A Splice of Life: Carmen Martín Gaite's *Entre visillos*." In *From Fiction to Metafiction: Essays in Honor of Carmen Martín Gaite*, edited by Mirella Servodidio and Marcia L. Welles. Lincoln, Neb.: Society of Spanish and Spanish-American Studies, 49–60.

Matamoro, Blas. 1978. "Carmen Martín Gaite: El viaje al cuarto de atrás." *Cuadernos Hispanoamericanos* 351 (October): 581–605. Reviews the literature of Martín Gaite and her colleagues in the 1950s and examines *El cuarto de atrás* as a "questioning return" to this era.

Ordóñez, Elizabeth J. 1979. "The Decoding and Encoding of Sex Roles in Carmen Martín Gaite's *Retahílas*." *Kentucky Romance Quarterly* 27: 237–44. Analyzes the novel's use of language as a vehicle for the protagonists' self-definition and self-assessment in terms of male and female roles, and for their attempt to surpass traditional norms.

Palley, Julian. 1980. "El interlocutor soñado de 'El cuarto de atrás' de Carmen Martín Gaite." *Insula* 404–405: 22. A discerning analysis of the novel's structure and an examination of the man in black as the Jungian "positive animus" of his creator.

Roger, Isabel. 1988. "Carmen Martín Gaite: Una trayectoria novelística y su bibliografía." *Anales de la Literatura Española Contemporánea* 13: 293–317. Summarizes Martín Gaite's literary production and the major critical responses it has elicited. The accompanying bibliography is extensive; although the secondary bibliography is not annotated, many of the references are discussed in the essay.

Servodidio, Mirella, and Marcia L. Welles, eds. 1983. *From Fiction to Metafiction: Essays in Honor of Carmen Martín Gaite*. Lincoln, Neb.: Society of Spanish and Spanish-American Studies. Classic volume containing a lucid introduction, a previously published interview with the author, and fourteen essays by distinguished contributors that span all of Martín Gaite's fiction.

Sobejano, Gonzalo. 1975. *Novela española de nuestro tiempo (en busca del pueblo perdido)*. 2d ed. Madrid: Prensa Española, 493–502.

5

The Fictional World of Ana María Matute: Solitude, Injustice, and Dreams

Janet Pérez

For a quarter century during the Franco era, Ana María Matute constituted a significant intellectual and literary force. As Spain's most visible and influential woman novelist during the 1960s, Matute gained steadily in stature from the release of her first novel in 1948 to the appearance of her last long fiction to date in 1971. During these years she produced eighteen volumes for adult readers, along with nearly a dozen books of juvenile fiction, all imbued with her peculiar, immediately recognizable blend of lyricism and stark realism, somber intuition and determined sociopolitical *engagement*. Matute's writings for adults comprise nine novels, five collections of short stories and one of novelettes, plus three collections of literary or artistic essays and memoirs. Her work has been recognized by prizes and honorary mentions, most significantly the respected Critics' Prize (1958) and National Literary Prize (1959), then Spain's highest awards for the novel. Invited by foreign universities to be a guest lecturer and artist-in-residence, Matute saw her titles translated into Italian, Portuguese, French, English, and German. Her works for children were also recognized by national and international literary prizes, and she obtained de facto recognition in the United States when her works were included (along with those of Unamuno, Lorca, Neruda, and Borges) on the reading list for Spanish advanced placement credit on university entrance examinations. She even began to be mentioned as a candidate for the Nobel Prize. Unfortunately, failing health and myriad other problems during the 1970s and 1980s all but terminated her publishing career, and Matute is no longer a visible and forceful presence in the post-Franco era.

Ana María Matute, the second of five children of a Catalan industrialist, was born 16 July 1926 in Barcelona. Her mother's family, rural Castilian gentry, maintained a country home in the

village of Mansilla de la Sierra, in the mountainous uplands of la
Rioja near the boundaries of the provinces of Burgos, Soria, and
Logroño, where the family usually spent their summers. The
mountain village with its dignified, traditional, but miserably poor
people and backward sharecroppers—enormous contrasts to the
cosmopolitan progressiveness of Barcelona—strongly impressed the
sensitive girl, imprinting a lasting mark upon her fiction (in which the
names "la Artámila" and "Hegroz" are substituted for that of
Mansilla).

The future writer and her two sisters were educated in convent
schools, as was usual for girls of their class, studying at the
elementary level with an order of French nuns. Ana María, however,
acquired a most unusual educational experience when, following an
extended illness at age eight, she was sent to convalesce in the
mountains with her grandparents and to attend the village school.
Spain's public schools were then attended only by the most
impoverished students, who learned by rote in a room of the
schoolmaster's home, usually without books and often without heat.
Matute has recalled many times that the poverty of schoolteachers
was proverbial, and the gaunt, haggard, slightly feverish figure of the
village schoolmaster is familiar in her stories. The village schoolroom, dusty and bare and attended sporadically by children of
families who barely eked out a livelihood, also appears in many of
her tales. Matute as a mature writer has repeatedly identified that
experience as the origin of her social conscience, as portrayed in her
short story "Los chicos" (The boys), in *Historias de la Artámila*
(Tales of Artamila) (1961). The pathetic figures of children prematurely aged by poverty and stress, that are so characteristic of
Matute's fiction, undoubtedly evolved from this time.

Since the family life of the future writer and her sibling relationships appear to have been tranquil, happy, and close, the origin of
the pervasive sense of loneliness and alienation that fills her fiction,
populated with estranged children and adolescents, must therefore
be sought elsewhere. Because of her father's business, the family
maintained and resided alternately in homes in both Madrid and
Barcelona, traditional rivals with distinct ethnicities, languages, and
cultures. Catalonia has for centuries resented the central government
in Castilla, which is perceived as indifferent when not hostile to
Catalan interests, while Castilla (especially under Franco) recipro-
cated with a perception of Catalonia as rebellious, disloyal, and
alien. As a child, Matute sensed and suffered from the latent
hostility, feeling herself an outsider both in Madrid, where she was
"la catalana," and in Barcelona, where she was "la castellana." The

sensation of not belonging, of being somehow different and inexplicably at odds with society, characterizes Matute's protagonists almost without variation and creates an atmosphere of general existential solitude, incommunicativeness, and estrangement. One result of this childhood experience may be seen in her subtle rejection of Madrid, which at no time appears in Matute's fiction. Barcelona and Mansilla are Matute's most frequent settings, although she also uses Majorca (in her trilogy, *Los mercaderes* [The merchants]), and the Basque fishing village of Zarauz (in *Pequeño teatro* [Little theater] [1954]).

Another subtle literary effect of the family's residence pattern appears in the fact that Matute has never written in Catalan and, indeed, appears to have learned little or none of it, in spite of living in Barcelona during the culmination of Catalan nationalism. While the Franco regime's erstwhile ban on the vernacular languages could well explain the writing of Matute's postwar novels in Castilian, not even her earliest efforts (dating from age four) were composed in Catalan, nor has the post-Franco outpouring of literature in the vernaculars resulted in Matute's writing so much as a single story in Catalan, which has only faint traces in the Majorcan place names and patronymics of the trilogy. Her otherwise baffling ignorance of Catalan may be due to Matute's staunchly Castilian mother who—the writer once remarked—"era como el Cid."[1]

A third childhood experience, one whose impact would be even more decisive for the life and works of the future writer, was the Spanish civil war (1936–39), which erupted shortly before Matute's tenth birthday, at a moment when the family was on the point of leaving for the mountains to spend the summer with the maternal grandparents in Mansilla de la Sierra. The hostilities divided the country and confined the family to Barcelona, where the experience of conflict was particularly traumatic and intense since the Catalan capital experienced not only the war but also a violent social revolution. Like her childhood contacts with the mountain village and the alienation brought on by almost continuous changes of residence and culture, the war indelibly marked Matute's fiction. It appeared both directly (in *Las luciérnagas/En esta tierra* [Fireflies/In this land] [1955], in *Los hijos muertos* [The dead children, 1958; translated into English as *The Lost Children*, 1965], and in the trilogy), and symbolically (as the Cain/Abel conflict in *Los Abel* [The Abel family] [1948], in *Fiesta al noroeste* [Celebration in the northwest] [1959], and in *La torre vigía* [The watchtower] [1971]).[2]

Other writers who experienced the war as children—aware of hostility and danger, yet helpless to intervene—have likewise exorcised some of its lingering emotional effects via the depiction of conflict in their fiction, but for none of them does the war appear so obsessive as for Matute, whose entire work may be seen as a fictional representation of that strife, an exploration of its social roots, or— more rarely—its consequences. The novelist's family suffered less from the national tragedy than many, since none of them became wartime casualties, but they were directly affected in other ways: the father's factory was "nationalized" (appropriated by the socialist faction of Catalan nationalists during the autonomous Generalitat, the government of Catalonia), and the father was temporarily imprisoned. Their apartment was similarly appropriated as temporary housing for party members, an experience that Matute recaptured in the novel *Las luciérnagas/En esta tierra*. Unable to leave Barcelona, the family lived through months of terrorism and politically motivated assassinations, including the burning of convents and churches and killings of priests and members of religious orders. Matute has frequently alluded to the bewilderment of the family's children when officially "good" people suddenly, inexplicably became "bad," when priests and nuns—their teachers—went into hiding and no longer dared to wear religious habits. She has often evoked the atmosphere of fear as bodies appeared daily in the streets and vacant lots, the tension experienced as she, her siblings, and cousins crouched behind drawn shutters during bombardments or listened to the gunfire outside. Reflections of such moments appear in *Las luciérnagas*, *Los hijos muertos*, and *Los soldados lloran de noche* (The soldiers cry by night) (1964).

Schools throughout Spain were closed for the duration of the war, and the Matute children studied at home with a tutor. They also had long periods of enforced idleness, which the future writer spent in a series of literary pursuits, including the production of a sort of review of which she was editor, major contributor, publisher, and technician (samples are preserved in the Fundación Ana María Matute at the Mogar Library of Boston University). She wrote stories, poems, and news items, illustrating them with her own sketches. For the entertainment of the other children, she also gave theatrical performances, using a little theater (probably a marionette theater) and enacting various roles herself, most often in pieces of her own composition. This aspect of the writer's childhood is reflected in the main character Matia's possession of a similar little theater in *Primera memoria* (literally, First memoir; English translations use various titles) (1960), in the overall conception of *Pequeño teatro*, and in one piece of *Tres y un sueño* (Three [fantasies] and one dream) (1960).

Although Matute's formal schooling was resumed at war's end, it was to be brief. After studying only the first two years of the *bachillerato* (high school equivalency), Matute abandoned formal education in order to devote herself intensively to the study of violin and painting with well-known masters. This decision, reached when she was fourteen, was apparently based on her distaste for the prevailing texts and pedagogical methods as much as on her love of art. Interviews and biographical notes record Matute's dislike for the dull, exempla-laden didactic readings and oppressive regimentation that were the order of the day. The much-commented motif of Cain and Abel in her narratives, symbolizing the fratricidal conflict of the civil war, can be traced to the prints on the schoolroom walls, perhaps the only part of the *colegio* (private school) that Matute found fascinating. From this point on, Matute's literary formation became autodidactic, acquired through readings and, in her later teens, through association with other aspiring writers.[3] Traces of some five years' study of painting have been detected in Matute's characteristic use of somber color in her fiction, and in the pictorial conception of many narrative scenes.[4]

With free time, she read books more to her liking, especially fairy tales and works of fantasy such as the stories of Hans Christian Andersen and the Brothers Grimm, *Peter Pan*, and *Alice in Wonderland*—her "bible," with which she credits her understanding and acceptance of the absurd.[5] Andersen's dichotomous world-view—the division of material and spiritual riches, materialist and idealist souls—is reflected both in Matute's juvenilia and many of her adult works.

Matute did not completely abandon writing during her study of art, although not until the age of eighteen or nineteen did she seriously consider undertaking a literary career. Several extant pieces of juvenilia date from these years (the early and mid-1940s), including an unpublished play, *Cumbres* (Summits). Her only known theatrical piece, *Cumbres* represents the transition from her earlier stylized, idealized works to the concrete realism of *Los Abel*. In 1942, when Matute was sixteen, "El chico de al lado" (The boy next door), a short story and her first published work, appeared in the Barcelona magazine *Destino*. Encouraged by this and the completion of the manuscript of *Pequeño teatro* the following year, she interrupted her music and painting studies in 1943 to devote herself exclusively to literature. She was immediately plunged into the suffocating environment created by the rigid censorship of all publications, mass media, and entertainment, an atmosphere in which most foreign books were prohibited and even Spanish classics were expurgated. The average citizen—skeptical of the controlled press and unable to afford the high prices of contraband books—essentially gave up reading. Matute and the other young writers of her generation were motivated above all by the desire to denounce, to clamor for liberty, human rights, and social justice.[6]

Primarily an intuitive writer, lyrical and intensely subjective, Matute displays occasional touches of expressionism in her characterization as well in her typical rhetorical combinations that blend the poetic and the grotesque. Her protagonists are frequently orphans, which symbolizes and intensifies their solitude, alienation, and vulnerability. In fact, most of her major characters are children or adolescents. The few adult characters of any significance are typically engaged in extended retrospective recall of childhood and adolescent episodes. Seldom are women portrayed as wives or mothers, and those who are tend to be minor characters, rarely if ever happily married. Motherhood is depicted not as fulfillment but as the cause of endless sacrifice.[7] The unbroken family is a rarity in Matute's narratives, and only fleeting happiness exists beyond the charmed circle of childhood's fantasy world. So important is childhood in this writer's works that several studies have been devoted to this theme.[8] Matute's typical protagonist is an androgynous, half-tamed, rebellious adolescent, frequently having a Peter Pan complex. Often she portrays the passage to adulthood, the loss of innocence, illusions, or idealism that is essential for the preadult stage. Once a character becomes an adult (a state that by definition is conventional, practical, and materialistic), he or she seems to interest Matute much less. The alienation of Matute's adult characters is confirmed by Elizabeth Ordóñez's exploration of female experience between adolescence and aging.[9]

Written in 1945 and a finalist for the 1947 Nadal Prize won by Miguel Delibes, Matute's first published novel, *Los Abel*, employs the diary format in its updating of the biblical story of the struggle between brothers. The fratricidal conflict between the two eldest of the seven Abel children is motivated by the brothers' rivalry for possession of the family lands and the same woman. Matute's characteristic use of the technique of paired opposites (fair/dark, good/evil, innocent/perverse, victim/executioner, materialist/idealist, and so on) appears in the characters of the rival brothers, Aldo and Tito: the former is brusque, ascetic, rigid, hardworking, and potentially violent, while the latter is irresponsible, charming, seemingly happy and full of life, but superficial and somewhat empty inside. The two best-developed female characters, Valba (the elder daughter and author of the diary) and Jacqueline (her sometime friend and future sister-in-law), are similarly opposed: Valba is dark, slim, tomboyish, alienated, and rebellious, while Jacqueline is blonde, voluptuous, conventional, and hypocritical. The main plot details the decadence, disintegration, and sudden mysterious disappearance of the Abels, a large, prosperous family of provincial gentry who had lived fairly well, thanks to Aldo's administration of their holdings. Additional narrative lines concern the psychological development of Valba and the constant conflicts between family members (by no means limited to the rivalry of Aldo and Tito). The Cain and Abel motif that permeates almost all of the sibling relationships will be a constant theme in Matute's fiction and will be later integrated in a broader rhetorical complex of biblical imagery.

Although *Los Abel* resembles the nineteenth-century rural novel and occasionally evokes associations with Emilia Pardo Bazán's *Los pazos de Ulloa* (Ulloa's manor, English translation *The Son of the Bondwoman*, 1908), Matute's emphasis and intention diverge greatly from such precedents. She is concerned with the daily life and customs of the region not as local color (seen in the past century's regionalism) nor as symptoms evincing the effects of heredity and environment (as with naturalism) but as social inequity and injustice, as a problematic aspect of the overall Spanish panorama, as cause and/or effect of the individual's radical solitude, alienation, and despair. The mountain village in Old Castile that provides the setting for *Los Abel* subsequently becomes the novelist's most frequent locale, and her vision of this area harmonizes with similar descriptions in later works. Themes such as the tension between landowners and peasants, the love of some for the land and the desperate desire of others to escape it that are enunciated in this novel also assume increased significance in later works such as *Fiesta al noroeste*, *Los hijos muertos*, and *Historias de la Artámila*. Here they become part of the fabric of Matute's first tentative explorations of the underlying causes of the civil war, probed in greater depth in *Las luciérnagas*, *Fiesta al noroeste*, *Los hijos muertos*, and the trilogy. Matute develops the economic factor, never entirely absent, in association with social and historical factors; already this theme has influenced human events, foreshadowing its increased role in Matute's fiction.

Before the publication of this first novel, Matute had associated only with budding intellectuals and had met no professional writers. The success of her first novel brought her officially into literary circles in Barcelona, and her career began to gather momentum. In 1951, *Los Abel* was translated into Italian and Matute won her first literary prize for a short story, "No hacer nada" (Doing nothing;

presently included in the collection *El tiempo*). The prize—a purely symbolic twenty-five pesetas—was awarded by an informal literary gathering, the Tertulia Café del Turia, and the following year, the novelist received a similar but considerably more prestigious award, the Cafe Gijón Prize for her novelette *Fiesta al noroeste*, perhaps her most artistically perfect narrative. Also in 1952, despite the fact that marriage had never been part of her plans, Matute married Ramón Eugenio de Goicoechea, a would-be writer who later became her business manager, with disastrous results. The novelist, whose interviews are generously laden with details of her childhood and adolescence, has studiously avoided all mention of her life during the years of marriage and has maintained almost complete silence regarding her husband, but it appears clear that the marriage was in difficulty from an early date. Shortly after their marriage the couple moved to Madrid, which Matute had earlier disliked and hated later. The only positive result of the move was that it brought her into contact with most of Spain's important writers of the day, enormously increasing her literary sophistication. The one positive outcome of the marriage, from Matute's viewpoint, was the birth of her only child, Juan Pablo, in 1954. An increasingly significant part of her life and a compensation for matrimonial trials, her son also provided the impulse for the writing of juvenile fiction, in which Matute has achieved distinction and important awards.

Fiesta al noroeste symbolizes the conflicting forces in the civil war through another Cain/Abel dichotomy. Juan Medinao, the elder, deformed, and fanatically religious legitimate son of a landowner, represents the aristocracy, capitalism, and the Church (the groups that supported Franco), as well as *caciquismo* (local political bossism), and thus stands for a spectrum of conservative or reactionary positions. His handsome, illegitimate half-brother, Pablo, the "disinherited" son of a servant, is associated with labor movements and nascent socialism. Most of the novelette is an extended confession by Juan, who suffers a latent homosexual attraction toward Pablo and an obsessive need to control and thereby "possess" him. In their first confrontation (a strike in which Pablo supports the demands of the workers), Juan hopes to break and subdue Pablo, but learns to his chagrin that Pablo can lose without being beaten. Wealth permits Juan to buy Pablo's sweetheart from her destitute parents in an attempt to use her as bait to bring Pablo to his house. The strategem fails and Juan, finding himself with a wife who cares nothing for him and who interests him not at all, is abandoned by Pablo, who simply leaves. Later Juan rapes Pablo's mother as a symbolic way of possessing him. The background of these events—the depiction of Juan's mother's desperate unhappiness during his childhood, her helpless rage at his father's philandering, and her loneliness, vulnerability, and ultimate suicide—constitutes one of Matute's most memorable treatments of a minor character. Women appear merely as pawns in a game where all the stakes are held by men. They are not the only victims, however: the poor, insofar as they do not rise above material considerations (as Pablo is able to do), are generally exploited by those who control the wealth. This theme appears in *Fiesta al noroeste* in the truncated story of Dingo that begins the novel: this boyhood associate of Juan remains trapped in their love-hate friendship by the greed and venality that motivated him to begin the relationship years before. Matute ably exploits the framework of the confession to treat "sinful" and potentially censurable materials. Some of her most striking rhetorical figures appear in this powerful novelette that is both an allegory of the civil war and its surrounding events and a very realistic vision of rural poverty, backwardness, and degradation.[10]

Under increasing financial pressure, Matute submitted the manuscript of her unpublished novel, *Pequeño teatro*, to the competition for the Planeta Prize, winning it in 1954. Although Matute rewrote her previously censored version of *Las luciérnagas* and cut the last of three parts from the manuscript, publishing it in 1955 as *En esta tierra* (In this land), she continued to resent the financial exigency that forced her to capitulate to the censors' demands in order to have something to publish during the seven years that she devoted to working on *Los hijos muertos*. In *Pequeño teatro*, Matute utilizes motifs drawn from marionnette shows and the *commedia dell'arte* to suggest Nobel prize winning playwright Jacinto Benavente's theme in *Los intereses creados* (The bonds of interest) (1909) of vested interests that permit people to be manipulated like puppets.[11] The protagonist, Zazu, daughter of the town's only wealthy man, is typically dark, androgynous, and rebellious and is the scandal of the Basque fishing village in which the work is set. Engaged to marry an elderly sea captain, Zazu indulges her erotic urges (and suggested nymphomania) with visits to the fishermen's quarter. Much of the novel deals with sincerity versus hypocrisy by reconstructing the socially acceptable façades behind which the town's "respectable" people criticize and condemn Zazu for her forthrightness but duplicitously adulate her because of her father's position. The plot involves the arrival of Marco, a bizarre but mysteriously attractive stranger. Clearly a confidence man, he plays skillfully upon the greed and insincerity of the hypocritical village "establishment," but only the alienated Zazu is able to see his underlying falseness, although even she is hypnotized by his magnetism. Enslaved by her own sexuality, Zazu has nevertheless kept her heart untouched. When she senses the danger of being conquered by Marco, she walks off the end of the breakwater into a wild sea whipped up by a storm. Suicide, like adultery, was not permitted by censors of this period, so *Pequeño teatro*, together with several of Matute's other works, ends somewhat abruptly and inconclusively, without sufficient explanation of events and motives. Here, Zazu's demise, as well as her deliberate intent to end her life, must be deduced by the reader, who is told only that she walks into the sea. Matute's characteristic emphasis on the eyes and hair of her young protagonists appears in descriptions of Zazu, together with her predilection for boyish or childlike girls whose beauty is flawed; many of the other women are *esperpentos* (grotesque caricatures).[12]

Matute's fondness for contrast and antithesis appears in such techniques as the use of paired opposites, producing a constant reliance upon rhetorical figures such as the oxymoron and paradox. As part of an overall bipartite structure, she frequently employs parallel constructions, repetition of words and phrases, and repetition with variation of only one element. However, she also has a predilection for tripartite structures (a series of three adjectives or descriptive elements in a sentence) and is gifted in the invention of unusual, strikingly visual expressions of horror. *Fiesta al noroeste* is similarly introduced, with approximately the first third of the work narrated by Dingo, a puppeteer who had been the only childhood friend of Juan Medinao before absconding with their joint savings (filched by Juan from his father) that the two had planned to use to escape from La Artámila and to join a circus. When Dingo's wanderings once again bring him near the hated village years later, he accidentally runs down and kills a shepherd's child. In jail, he turns for help to Juan, which serves to introduce the character of the local *cacique* (political boss) and to explore his psyche via an extended introspective and retrospective confession. Dingo is essentially forgotten, abandoned in jail by the novelist, since the reader learns no more of his fate.

In the much longer novel *Los hijos muertos*, the narrative is structured as a family chronicle and spans three generations of the Corvo family (rural gentry much like the Abels). The third generation introduces the novel's protagonist, Miguel, a young convict in a nearby penal colony, with whom Mónica—the youngest Corvo—falls in love. This structuring may appear to be an artistic defect, especially if the principle of narrative economy is highly valued. However, it should be understood in the light of the prevailing censorship at the time Matute was writing. Such construction could effectively function as a "red herring": the censors (usually bureaucrats) would assume that the original narrator—the cousin of *Los Abel*, the puppeteer in *Fiesta al noroeste*, for example—was also the novel's protagonist, and so would concentrate on this character and his or her adventures. When the character disappeared, they would continue to anticipate his or her return, and thus distracted, pay inadequate attention to the major narrative, which contained more subversive elements. The narrative developed by Miguel in *Los hijos muertos* is an enormously powerful and subversive plea for liberty, whose approval by the censors was unquestionably facilitated by this "false overture" technique.

En esta tierra is the revised, expurgated, published version of *Las luciérnagas*, which was prohibited by the censors. In the novel Soledad, daughter of a bourgeois Barcelona family, sees their world destroyed by the civil war. Although she is not fully an alter ego or mask of Matute, she shares certain of the author's experiences, making this one of Matute's most autobiographical works.[13] Soledad sees her family's holdings appropriated by the socialistic faction of the Catalan nationalist Generalitat and part of their apartment taken to house leftist militia. One difference is that Soledad was not a ten-year-old child, as Matute was, but a young woman. Her family circumstances are also rather different, and she has only one brother instead of four siblings. During a bombardment Soledad is thrown together with Cristián when they are at first trapped in a ruined building. Unable to locate family members after the air raid, the two take refuge in an abandoned house and end up becoming lovers. When the Franco forces reach Barcelona, Cristián runs toward the advancing army, shouting, and is gunned down. It is unclear whether the shout was one of welcome, defiance, or despair.

The original, censored version of the novel contained a much more explicit third part that clarified the ending. With the arrival of the Franco forces, the two are jailed (Cristián as a draft evader). Soledad learns that she is pregnant while in jail. Cristián, mobilized into the Franco army, later escapes and marries Soledad. The young couple begins the postwar era with cautious optimism and an infant son. However, the economic realities of the Franco regime are harsh and Cristián is unable to support his family. Apprehended in a robbery when his son urgently needs medicine, Cristián is sentenced to a prison camp where most of the inmates are political prisoners.

Soledad lives nearby with her son but suffers hunger and many hardships, reflecting a less-than-ideal world under the new regime, even for those who had been nonaligned, and in spite of Soledad's family belonging to a class that had supported Franco. In this case, where marriage is freely chosen by both parties and their relationship is apparently satisfactory (rather unusual for Matute's fiction), external circumstances destroy happiness. The clearly political causes of their discontent adequately explain why this work was prohibited by Franco's censors.[14]

Many parallels exist between *En esta tierra* and *Los hijos muertos*. Matute's longest and most ambitious novel, *Los hijos muertos* was awarded the Critics' Prize as the best novel of 1958 and achieved "official" recognition the following year by winning the government-sponsored National Prize for Literature "Miguel de Cervantes." These two novels are unique among Matute's work in that they combine the settings of contemporary Barcelona and the Castilian village of Mansilla (called Hegroz in *Los hijos muertos*).

Los hijos muertos, however, is very specific in its presentation of the social background and underlying economic problems, especially such aspects as absentee landlordism, the misery of the peasants and sharecroppers, social tensions between rural gentry and day laborers, and the decadence of landowning families. As she did in *Los Abel* and *Fiesta al noroeste*, the novelist again explores underlying causes of the civil war, attempting to explain the conflict in terms of individual passions and frustrations by reducing the fratricidal conflagration to the dimensions of an intrafamilial struggle. Matute's hallmark, the Cain and Abel motif, reappears often in *Los hijos muertos* through the tangled hates and loves of the Corvos; its symbolism becomes explicit when two Corvos (cousins raised in the same household) fight on opposing sides in the civil war.[15] Portraying several generations of a family that acquired wealth in the nineteenth century, only to lose it early in the twentieth, *Los hijos muertos* presents opposing sets of values in the characters. Matute represents contrasting ideologies as the conflicts between youth and age, conventionalism or hypocrisy versus authenticity, and materialism versus idealism. Members of the older generation are characteristically defeated, hurt, disillusioned, and sterile, while the younger generation, which embodies humanity's brightest and best promise, is ultimately frustrated by the crushing weight of tradition, inertia, and circumstance.

Matute establishes a counterpoint between past and present, rural Castilla and urban Barcelona, youth and age, haves and have-nots, and the ossified Establishment and those who represent a potential for renewal. *Los hijos muertos* presents a vast canvas of characters, unsurpassed in Matute's work even by her trilogy, *Los mercaderes*. Here Matute again uses paired characters, but this time establishes a parallel between generations or epochs. The motif of the orphan, so common in her work, is especially frequent, with all of the major characters losing their parents by adolescence at the latest. There are several story lines, of which the most significant are two tales of young love and the chronicle of family decadence and disintegration. While much of the Corvo history is retrospective, the novel's "present" action begins around 1929, when the Great Depression provoked bank failures in Argentina, precipitating the family's ruin. This caused the suicide of Daniel's father, Elías, and the attempted suicide of Daniel's uncle Gerardo and his two daughters: vigorous, domineering Isabel and dreamy, rebellious Verónica.[16]

Daniel, the ostensible protagonist, embodies the class struggle. His mother was allegedly a mulatto servant in Cuba, resulting in Daniel's treatment as a second-class relative and his hatred of the leisure class, which makes of him an instinctive champion of the poor. Isabel's attempt to repair the family finances by an arranged marriage between fourteen-year-old Verónica and a wealthy older man, frustrated by Verónica's refusal, leads to another match of convenience planned by Isabel between her father, Gerardo, and Beatriz, a moderately prosperous never-married woman of forty, who dies within a year after giving birth to Mónica near the end of 1932.[17] After a jealous Isabel has provoked Daniel's expulsion, he and Verónica elope shortly before the war. Verónica and her unborn child are killed in an air raid, the first of the "dead children" of the title. Daniel's service in the Republican army results in his sentence of many years of forced labor in the mines, from which he returns after some fifteen years, prematurely aged, broken in body and spirit, to become the forester on the family estate.

Mónica represents the youth of the postwar generation, together with Miguel Fernández, an urban delinquent who is one of the few nonpolitical prisoners in a penal colony near the family manor. Their impossible love is perhaps symbolic of some sort of aspiration toward postwar rapprochement between discrete social strata, but Miguel—who is both a victim of the system and a personification of the all-consuming longing for liberty—is killed in an escape attempt after being hunted down like an animal at the same time that the annual wolf hunt takes place. Wolves play a significant symbolic role in Matute's work: they represent the disinherited, the poor, those who are forced to violence by necessity (although the novelist indicates that they do not kill wantonly but only when they are hungry).[18] Conversations between the aged Daniel and Diego Herrera, chief of the penal colony, constitute another effort to transcend the war's hurts and rancors: the two men, on opposing sides, had both lost children and consciously acknowledge the need for reconciliation.

This novel unfolds not in linear, chronological fashion, but through several juxtaposed time sequences. The end of the novel takes place in 1948, after Daniel's return to Hegroz, but this alternates with flashbacks and memories usually triggered by situations resembling or otherwise associated with those recalled. The juxtaposition of different times serves to underscore the confrontation of generations and establish parallels between the lives and situations of two different age groups, thereby insinuating that Franco's "Glorious Crusade" really changed nothing. Time is annihilated by the similarities between past and present, and the novel becomes a protest against the useless suffering and sacrifice of a futile conflict.[19] The "background" and secondary characters of this complex novel serve as vehicles to highlight the ever-present problems of the need for social justice and equity, for land reform, and for a remedy of the poverty and subhuman conditions suffered by dispossessed peasants in the forgotten mountain valleys of Castilla. The Barcelona proletariat, with their own hunger, suffering, and bitterness, constitute an impressionistic mosaic of causes underlying Catalonia's social revolution in the era of the Generalitat, although Matute by no means idealizes the lower classes: her message transcends partisanship. A civil war is a war without winners, but the special losers are the children, as is suggested by the work's title.[20]

Perhaps on the strength of the recognition achieved by *Los hijos muertos*, her most honored novel, Matute was awarded a grant by the Fundación March to work on her trilogy, *Los mercaderes*, of which she had just completed the first volume, *Primera memoria*, published in 1960. Winner of the Nadal Prize, it was translated in English as *School of the Sun*.[21] From this time on, excepting the rest of the trilogy, most works published by Matute have been books for children or collections of short fiction, both of which echo constants in her novels. Despite the help afforded by the grant, work on the remaining two volumes went slowly, complicated by problems in the writer's personal life. Definitively separated from her husband in January 1963, she was forced to live with a sister for three years during the legal process because laws promulgated by the Franco regime viewed the married woman as a perpetual minor, a ward of the husband unable to have a bank account or apartment without his permission. However, during this period, Matute began to reap the satisfactions of international recognition, as several novels were translated, appearing variously in French, German, Italian, English, and Portuguese. Having completed in 1964 the second volume of the trilogy, *Los soldados lloran de noche*, she traveled extensively in Europe and in the fall of 1964 made her first visit to the United States, lecturing at several universities. Matute returned to Indiana University as a visiting professor in 1965, after having won custody of her son. After completing the last volume of the trilogy, *La trampa* (The trap) (1969), she served as a visiting professor at the University of Oklahoma in the fall of 1969 and as writer-in-residence at the University of Virginia in 1978, and subsequently lectured at a number of other universities. During the 1970s, however, her health deteriorated considerably, and only two new titles have been published by the novelist in the nearly twenty years since the third part of *Los mercaderes*: *La torre vigía* (1971), her last novel to date for adults, and a children's book, *Solo un pie descalzo* (Only one bare foot) (1983).

Primera memoria returns to the Cain and Abel framework to portray symbolically and in miniature Spain's fratricidal civil conflict from the supposedly peaceful haven of the Balearic Islands. Matia, whose father is in the Loyalist army, is sent to live with her grandmother, a reactionary representative of the traditional order, uniting wealth and *caciquismo*, who is, quite logically, a Franco sympathizer, as is Matia's cousin Borja, whose father is with the Franco rebels. The novel takes the form of a memoir written years later by the mature Matia, the narrator and protagonist (who will reappear in the third novel as she approaches middle age). Matia relives a number of adolescent discoveries, all illuminated by the blindingly brilliant island sun: sordid adult sexuality, death, treachery, betrayal, and her own cowardice. An alienated figure in nearly all of her relationships (as is typical of a majority of Matute's characters), Matia feels disgust for the older generation, ambivalence toward Borja, and admiration only for Manuel.[22] Manuel's idealized figure, representing victims of exploitation and discrimination, frequently recalls biblical accounts of Christ and his passion.[23] Many minor conflicts (between juvenile gangs, between Matia and Borja, between unidentified proto-Fascists and the putative father of Manuel) mirror the civil war in miniature. The treachery whereby a jealous Borja frames Manuel for a crime he did not commit, resulting in Manuel's imprisonment when Matia dares not speak the truth in his defense, is a symbolic reproduction of the cowardice of the "silent majority" who did not protest the postwar purges, political imprisonment, and executions of untold thousands who were "guilty" of loyalty to the country's legally constituted government. So important is the theme of betrayal or treachery in Matute's work that it, too, has been the subject of a doctoral dissertation.[24] And betrayal, as both *Primera memoria* and many of Matute's stories make clear, can be a sin of omission as well as commission.

Los soldados lloran de noche, set shortly before the end of the civil war, begins with Manuel's release from the reformatory to which Borja's treachery had confined him until an unexpected inheritance made him wealthy. His release points to inequities of the Spanish judicial and criminal justice system, adding to the list of social injustices denounced by Matute. While in prison, Manuel met a charismatic communist organizer called Jeza who was later executed for his refusal to name his comrades. Jeza came to symbolize for Manuel uncompromising idealism (he is the first of the "soldiers," or heroes of the title). Manuel seeks out Jeza's widow, Marta, satisfying a deep psychological need to learn more of this lay martyr (another Christ figure of the trilogy).

From the moment Manuel and Marta begin to converse, the novel's structure becomes that of two extended, intercalated monologues that change speakers without indication or transition, as each person recreates the past. Marta's earlier life, sordid in the extreme, included an abusive mother who ran a tavern and apparently dealt in drugs and contraband. Escaping from her mother's lesbian partner and admirer, Marta ran away with the mother's young lover, Raúl, Jeza's brother. Abandoned by Raúl, she was rescued from her depraved existence by Jeza, who in effect becomes her "savior," marries her and fathers her child, but always maintains his mission as his first priority. Marta and Manuel resolve to complete Jeza's last mission of carrying documents to the mainland to his comrades, although both realize it may be suicidal. Under cover of fog, in a small boat, they reach Barcelona only hours before the arrival of the Franco forces. Convinced that it is better to die for an ideal, even a borrowed one, than to live without one, they occupy an abandoned machine-gun post on the road taken by the advancing army, where they are slain.

Matute divides humanity into two groups in the trilogy, the *mercaderes* or merchants (the vast majority)[25] and the soldiers or heroes (a minority of idealists). This structure applies in theory to the trilogy as a whole and may be extended implicitly to most of Matute's fiction, but is made explicit in the second novel of the trilogy. Obviously another biblical allusion (to the merchants or money-changers cast out of the temple by Christ), the "merchants" are by extension all those whose services, loyalty, or support can be bought or manipulated by self-interest in any form. Marta, Manuel, and Jeza, with their total renunciation of self-interest, illustrate the small group of idealists.

La trampa returns to the island of Majorca and most of the original cast of *Primera memoria*, who appear a quarter-century later, all aged and much the worse—morally and psychologically as well as physically—for the passage of time. Matia, fortyish and discontented after spending most of her life in a futile search for love and understanding, responds to a summons by the hated grandmother to attend her centennial celebration (the matriarch's longevity and decrepitude allude to Spain's social and political structures, as her function as a personification of *caciquismo* or bossism is now clearer). New characters introduced in *La trampa* include Bear, Matia's university-age son, and Mario, an allegedly idealistic revolutionary who has recruited Bear for a mission on the island. To provide a hiding place for the would-be terrorist until the time comes to strike, Bear plants Mario in his mother's quarters, counting correctly on their becoming lovers. Infatuated with Matia, Mario repents of his plan to use her son in what proves to be personal vengeance (the intended victim is not a key politician, as Bear has been told, but the man who killed Mario's father years before). Bear overhears Mario tell his mother that there will be no assassination, but before learning why, dashes off to commit the deed alone. Desirous of ruining the hated family (the grandmother, Borja, and what they represent), he makes no effort to conceal his identity and flees to an unspecified fate.

Contrasting youth and age, materialism and idealism, once again, Matute nonetheless seems less dualistic than in the previous two novels, for here the idealists are misguided and the cause is decidedly tarnished. Considered by many to be Matute's most mature and significant accomplishment, the trilogy has been studied more extensively than many of her works.[26]

La torre vigía initially seems to be a marked departure from Matute's established patterns. A neochivalric novel set in the tenth century, it takes place not in Spain but in an unnamed part of central Europe, thus abandoning her usually realistic time and place referents.[27] The watchtower, both real and symbolic, functions as an elevated lookout from which to distinguish the true from the false, and—as always in Matute's fiction—the material from the ideal. The narrator is a disembodied voice belonging to the spirit of a young squire killed by his jealous older brothers on the eve of attaining knighthood, a social variant of the Cain and Abel myth in which Cain is once again the representative of the disinherited (a victim of unfair paternal favoritism), while Abel has become three brothers instead of one. The young squire is sent to be raised in the castle of a baron who embodies the most sordid and degenerate materialism and amorality. Thus, the apprenticeship becomes a symbolic voyage of discovery, the discovery of evil. Slowly the protagonist realizes that the lord and lady are ogres, not chivalric models (both prey upon adolescents of both sexes). The abyss between human reality and presumed knightly ideals so disillusions the youth that during the vigil of his arms in the chapel prior to being knighted, he renounces knighthood, deciding never to become a warlord. Upon leaving the chapel to discuss his insights with the enigmatic and visionary watchman in the tower, he is stabbed by his brothers.

La torre vigía abounds in apocalyptic elements, beginning with its millennial chronology, but includes allegorical battles between the forces of good and evil such as the one played out in the spirit of the young protagonist and others in the visions of the watchman who describes in detail the clashes between black and white armies, including many signs and omens of the end of the world. Matute perceives many similarities between the tenth century, as she envisions it, and the twentieth, which helps to explain her interest in this period.[28] Another link with the novelist's earlier work comes in the form of biblical imagery and allusions, diabolic monsters, and mighty metaphysical combats that seem to come straight from the Book of Revelations. The alienated protagonist, the symbolic significance of time—usually linked with decadence and destruction, but here implicitly heralding the Day of Doom—the rites of passage motif, and the coincidence between loss of innocence and death, as well as the presence of war, are likewise constants of this writer's work. The motif of the tower has appeared several times before in her fiction, sometimes as an island within an island (in the trilogy), but also in *Pequeño teatro, Las luciérnagas*, and the prize-winning children's novel, *El polizón del Ulises* (Cabin boy of the "Ulysses") (1965), where it is also linked with discovery and rites of passage. Solitude, disillusionment, and the self-immolation motif also appear in many of Matute's fictions for both adults and children, making clear the essential unity of her narratives.

Among Matute's collections of brief fiction are *Los niños tontos* (The stupid children) (1956), which contains twenty-one lyric sketches, all dealing with children who are "different," many of whom die or disappear, often as the result of some traumatic disillusionment.[29] These artistically wrought tales were described by the contemporary novelist Camilo José Cela as "the most important work by a woman in Spanish since Emilia Pardo Bazán." *El tiempo*

(Time) (1957) brings together a heterogeneous group of previously published tales, many with social themes and critical intent. Time, as suggested by the title story, is a major concern of Matute that she often associates with decadence, destruction, and disappearance (as in *Los Abel*, the trilogy, and *Los hijos muertos*, all depicting several generations). The motifs of train and river are usually symbolic of time or its passage in Matute's works as well.[30] *Historias de la Artámila* (1961) is unified by the common geographical setting of the Castilian mountain village (also the setting of *Los Abel, Fiesta al noroeste, Los hijos muertos*, and a later collection of autobio-graphically inspired sketches, *El río* [The river] [1963]). Social themes predominate in the twenty-two tales, which emphasize poverty, illiteracy, the exploitation of sharecroppers, the cruelty of the strong toward the weak, and the daily suffering produced by indifference, selfishness, and insensitivity. By contrast, *El arrepentido* (The repentant one) (1961) has no discernible common theme or setting. *Libro de juegos para los niños de los otros* (Book of games for others' children) (1961), the title notwithstanding, is not a book for children. It depicts the "games people play" to perpetuate discrimination, class prejudice, and social injustice. *Tres y un sueño*, a trio of novelettes written in 1961, often hermetic and filled with highly personal symbolism, is undoubtedly Matute's least accessible work. Elsewhere her writing may occasionally raise questions because of enigmatic passages that are intended to circumvent the censors or because of the use of fantasy that invades reality, leaving the boundaries unclear. *Tres y un sueño*, Matute's most autobiographical work, is so full of surrealistic and oneiric imagery that few personal secrets are betrayed. *Algunos muchachos* (Some kids, 1968; translated into English as *The Heliotrope Wall and Other Stories*, 1989), unquestionably Matute's finest collection of brief fiction, is also one of her most mature and is highly recommended as "vintage Matute." Containing much variety in plots and techniques, the collection offers more of her most characteristic themes: the alienated individual—usually set against the ossified social structure—political and socioeconomic injustice, the loss of innocence, and passage from the magical world of childhood.[31]

Although Matute has written for all ages and covered a time period reaching back to the tenth century, her works have many unifying characteristics. Chief among these are certain repetitive, obsessive themes that function almost as leitmotifs throughout her work: these are childhood as a special magical world, alien to the adult mentality; the traumatic estrangement of adolescence; child-hood illness and death, or the orphan state (all of which intensify alienation and loneliness); a search for the roots of the civil war, as part of an effort to understand the conflict; the war itself, whether depicted realistically, or symbolically (as the Cain/Abel struggle); the pall of poverty and other economic hardships; ruralism; a lyric vision of nature, even at its most hostile; ethical and emotional commitment to "social" literature; altruistic denunciation of injustice; and the dichotomy between idealism and materialism. Combined with her intensely personal and poetic style, these elements demonstrate the accuracy of Matute's self-assessment when she stated that she always writes the same book, in different guises.

Notes

1. "She was just like el Cid." El Cid is Spain's national hero, famed for extending the territory of Castile at the expense of other ethnic groups. I interviewed Ana María Matute in Lubbock, Texas, in December 1978.

2. Detailed discussion of this aspect of Matute's work can be found in Mary Andrea Chacón, "The Spanish Civil War in the Works of Ana María Matute," Ph.D. diss., University of California at Los Angeles, 1974.

3. These writers included Juan and Luis Goytisolo, Carlos Barral, and Lorenzo Gomis. More detailed information on Matute's life, especially her formative years, appears in Díaz 1971.

4. Studied by Celia Barretini 1961, 405–12.

5. Pérez interview with Matute in New York, September 1965 (cited in more detail in Díaz 1971, 26).

6. See "A Wounded Generation," translated by A. Gordon Ferguson in *The Nation*, 29 November 1965.

7. Different conclusions from mine are drawn in the doctoral dissertation of Raquel Galbis Flores-Jenkins, "La mujer como individuo y como tipo en la novelística de Ana María Matute," University of Connecticut, 1980.

8. The most lengthy include a portion of Jones 1970 and a doctoral dissertation by Emilie Teresa Cannon, "Childhood as Theme and Symbol in the Major Fiction of Ana María Matute," Ohio State University, 1972.

9. Ordóñez studies this aspect especially in *La trampa* in her doctoral dissertation, "Woman as Protagonist and Creator in the Contemporary Spanish Novel," University of California, Irvine, 1976.

10. *Fiesta al noroeste* was edited as a text for American students and is an excellent introduction to Matute's work since it provides examples of her most characteristic style and themes. (In relation to this work see Winecoff 1966, 61–69.)

11. For extensive discussion of this motif, see Janet Díaz, "La *commedia dell'arte* en una novela de Ana María Matute," *Hispanófila* 40 (1970): 15–28.

12. See Janet Pérez, "Variantes del arquetipo femenino en la narrativa de Ana María Matute," *Letras femeninas* 10 (Fall 1984): 28–39.

13. A more detailed analysis of the relationship between life and literature in Matute's work appears in Díaz 1968, 139–48.

14. More extensive discussion of similarities and differences between the two versions appears in Díaz 1971, 62–70.

15. The significance of the Cain/Abel motif is studied at length in the doctoral dissertation by Michael Abel Fernández, "Temas bíblicos en la obra de Ana María Matute: Su expresión y significado," University of Colorado, 1979.

16. The women in *Los hijos muertos* are studied more extensively in Theresa Mary Hadjopoulos' dissertation, "Four Women Novelists of Postwar Spain: Matute, Laforet, Quiroga and Medio," Columbia University, 1974.

17. Since children who have lost one parent are *huérfanos* in Spanish, Mónica is "orphaned" almost from birth. Interestingly, far more of Matute's children and adolescents have lost mothers than have lost fathers, making it clear that the novelist is not representing children left fatherless by the war.

18. The French translation, *Plaignez les loups*, gives appropriate recognition to the importance of the wolf motif (which in Matute's work is not so much an embodiment of the notion that "man is a wolf to his own kind" as a variant of the disinherited or Cain figure).

Interestingly, Matute describes a number of characters as having eyes or teeth of wolves, and in a Christmas 1978 visit, presented me with a book on wolves as a gift.

19. Jones 1971, 282–88, explores Matute's treatment of time and its destructive passage, as well as how she manipulates time to comment on human behavior, time's use in characterization, and the contrasting of objective and subjective time, especially in *Los hijos muertos*, where historical progression is replaced by cyclic and spiral chronologies.

20. See Alexandre Kalda's interview with Matute in *Arts*, 17–23 April 1963.

21. American and British translations of *Primera memoria* appeared in the same year: *School of the Sun*, trans. Elaine Kerrigan (New York: Pantheon Books, 1963), and *Awakening*, trans. James Mason (London: Hutchinson and Co., 1963). The significant title changes in both cases stress the motif of discovery that runs throughout the novel.

22. Alienation in Matute's work is the subject of a doctoral dissertation by James Townsend entitled "Alienation in the Novels of Ana María Matute," Washington University, 1976.

23. See Jones 1968, 416–23. Matute's use of language in this and the second novel of the trilogy has been studied in "Rhetorical Elements in Two Novels by Ana María Matute, *Primera memoria* and *Los soldados lloran de noche*," a master's thesis by Constance Nock Brown, University of North Carolina, Chapel Hill, 1970.

24. For a lengthy study of the theme of treachery, see James Earl Alvis, "La traición en la obra de Ana María Matute," Ph.D. diss., University of Oklahoma, 1976.

25. Matute once observed that *mercader* in Catalan means "burgués," or upperclass, lending a more specifically social dimension to the title's significance.

26. The most extensive dissertations on the trilogy are Lilit María Zekhulin, "The Narrative Art of Ana María Matute in *Los mercaderes*," University of Toronto, 1979; and Michael Scott Doyle, "*Los mercaderes*: A Literary World by Ana María Matute," University of Virginia, 1981. Joan Brown's 1983 study of the linkages between the three novels considers thematic, stylistic, and other relationships, as well as characters, settings, and reiterated motifs as part of an attempt to elucidate the integration between the novels (19–32).

27. A similar period and setting were announced for "Olvidado Rey Gudú" ("Forgotten King Gudú"), a one-thousand-page novel that was advertised for imminent publication in the 1970s but that may never appear.

28. Interview with Matute, Lubbock, Texas, December 1978.

29. *The Stupid Children*, trans. Willis Barnstone, *Artes Hispánicas/Hispanic Arts* 1 (1967): 76–93.

30. See especially Janine Peters Ling, "Time in the Prose of Ana María Matute," Ph.D. diss., University of Wisconsin, 1972.

31. Story-by-story discussion of the individual titles in these collections appears in chapter 6 of Díaz 1971. The unpublished juvenilia are treated in chapter 7. Díaz

also studies Matute's books for children, but the novelist's juvenile fiction is examined more extensively in the dissertation of Mario Acevedo, "La creación literaria infantil de Ana María Matute," Texas Tech University, 1979.

Bibliography

1. PRIMARY SOURCES

1948. *Los Abel*. Barcelona: Destino.

1954. *Pequeño teatro*. Barcelona: Planeta.

1955. *En esta tierra*. Barcelona: Editorial Exito.

1956. *Los niños tontos*. Madrid: Ediciones Arión.

1957. *El tiempo*. Barcelona: Editorial Mateu.

1958. *Los hijos muertos*. Barcelona: Planeta. English translation by Joan MacLean, *The Lost Children*. New York: Macmillan, 1965.

1959. *Fiesta al noroeste*. Barcelona: Pareja y Borrás.

1960. *Primera memoria*. Barcelona: Destino. American translation by Elaine Kerrigan, *School of the Sun*. New York: Pantheon Books, 1963. Reissued in 1989; New York: Columbia University Press. British translation by James Holman Mason, *Awakening*. London: Hutchinson and Co., 1963.

1961a. *A la mitad del camino*. Barcelona: Editorial Rocas.

1961b. *El arrepentido*. Barcelona: Editorial Rocas.

1961c. *Historias de la Artámila*. Barcelona: Destino.

1961d. *Libro de juegos para los niños de los otros*. Barcelona: Editorial Lumen.

1961e. *Tres y un sueño*. Barcelona: Destino.

1963. *El río*. Barcelona: Editorial Argos.

1964. *Los soldados lloran de noche*. Barcelona: Destino.

1968. *Algunos muchachos*. Barcelona: Destino. English translation by Michael Scott Doyle, *The Heliotrope Wall and Other Stories*. New York: Columbia University Press, 1989.

1969. *La trampa*. Barcelona: Destino.

1971. *La torre vigía*. Barcelona: Editorial Lumen.

1976. *Obra completa*. 5 vols. Barcelona: Destino.

2. SECONDARY SOURCES

Barretini, Celia. 1961. "Ana María Matute, la novelista pintora." *Cuadernos hispanoamericanos* 48 (December): 405–12. Stresses Matute's use of painterly composition and coloration.

Brown, Joan L. 1983. "Unidad y diversidad en *Los mercaderes* de Ana María Matute." In *Novelistas femeninas de la postguerra española*, edited by Janet Pérez, 19–32. Madrid: Porrúa. A study of the fictional linkages between the second novel of the trilogy (*Los soldados lloran de noche*) and the other two. Questions whether the three parts are effectively integrated and reaches somewhat negative conclusions.

Díaz, Janet. 1968. "Autobiographical Elements in the Works of Ana María Matute." *Kentucky Romance Quarterly* 15: 139–49. An analysis of the influence of Matute's biographical experience upon her fiction up to the midpoint of the trilogy.

———. 1971. *Ana María Matute*. New York: Twayne Publishers. A comprehensive bio-bibliographical study of the life and works up to 1970 (does not include *La torre vigía*).

Doyle, Michael Scott. 1984. Review of Matute's *Solo un pie descalzo* (1983) in *Latin America in Books* 7 (July): 24–25. One of few references to Matute's last published novel (here classed as juvenile fiction, although before publication the author said it was not for children).

El Saffar, Ruth. 1981. "En busca de Edén: Consideraciones sobre la obra de Ana María Matute." *Revista Iberoamericana* 47: (July–December): 223–31. Studies especially *La torre vigía* in relation to Matute's persistent use of the garden and archetype of the "divine child."

Guillermo, Edenia, and Juana Amelia Hernández. 1970. "Ana María Matute." In *Novelística española de los sesenta*, edited by Edenia Guillermo and Juana Amelia Hernández, 153–91. New York: Eliseo Torres. Primarily studies *La trampa* for experimental techniques, novelistic structure, surrealist elements, and "técnica desrealizadora."

Hernández, Juana Amelia, and Edenia Guillermo. 1981. *Selecciones de Ana María Matute*. Princeton: FFH Publications. An anthology with a useful introduction stressing characteristic themes, language, style, structure, and archetypal characters.

Hickey, Leo. *Realidad y experiencia de la novela*. 1978. Madrid: Cupsa Editorial. Using principles extrapolated from contemporary linguistics and sociology, Hickey focuses upon the novel in relation to ethnographic context and empirical reality, with special reference to *La trampa*, 241–50.

Jones, Margaret W. 1967. "Antipathetic Fallacy: The Hostile World of Ana María Matute's Novels." *Kentucky Foreign Language Quarterly* 13 (1967): 5–16. An excellent study of Matute's distortion of nature through imagery of sun and flowers, particularly in *Fiesta al noroeste*, *Los hijos muertos*, and *Primera memoria*.

———. 1968. "Religious Motifs and Biblical Allusions in the Works of Ana María Matute." *Hispania* 51 (September): 416–23. A key analysis of Matute's use of biblical imagery.

———. 1970. *The World of Ana María Matute*. Lexington: University of Kentucky Press. A perceptive, detailed and careful examination of Matute's depiction of children and adolescents, and to a lesser degree, of adults.

———. 1971. "Temporal Patterns in the Works of Ana María Matute." *Romance Notes* 12: 282–88. Investigates the theme of the destructive passage of time and how Matute uses it to characterize and insert unobtrusive editorialization.

Kubayanda, José. 1982. "*La torre vigía* de Ana María Matute: Aproximación a una narrativa alegórica." *Revista de Estudios Hispánicos* 16 (October): 333–45. Emphasizes Matute's use and forms of allegory.

Thomas, Michael D. 1978. "The Rite of Initiation in Matute's *Primera memoria*." *Kentucky Romance Quarterly* 25: 153–64. Stresses Matia's encounter with death and symbolic motifs.

Valis, Noel. 1982. "La literatura infantil de Ana María Matute." *Cuadernos hispanoamericanos* 389 (November): 407–15. Good overview of Matute's juvenile fiction, with special attention to *El polizón del Ulises*.

Winecoff, Janet. 1966. "Style and Solitude in the Works of Ana María Matute." *Hispania* 49 (March): 61–69. An early essay in English focusing on rhetorical devices, use of color, and presence of existential themes; most stylistic examples are drawn from *Fiesta al noroeste*.

6

Mercè Rodoreda's Subtle Greatness

Randolph D. Pope

In September 1964 *Serra d'Or*, an important Catholic journal of Barcelona that records and studies Catalonian culture, surveyed literary critics and novelists to determine the works that they perceived as the most important written during 1939–63. The runner-up was *Bearn*, a refined narration of a family's decadence by Lorenç Villalonga, a revered writer whose intelligent and rich prose can be compared to works by the Cuban Alejo Carpentier or the Spaniard master of style Juan Benet. The clear winner was *La Plaça del Diamant* (Diamond Square), a Mercè Rodoreda novel published only two years before the survey was undertaken, when the author was over fifty years old. This novel, translated into English as *The Time of the Doves* in 1980, soon became a classic of peninsular literature and a popular film.

Behind this success story lies the reality of a life that had to affirm itself under the pressure of a triple banishment from the central and established culture of Spain. As a Catalonian writer writing in Catalan, Rodoreda did not receive the same attention nor did she have the same publishing opportunities as those who wrote in Spanish, such as Ignacio Agustí, a perceptive chronicler of the industrial and social transformation of Barcelona. As an exile in 1939 from the Spanish civil war, she spent most of her life abroad, not residing again in Barcelona until four years before her death. Rodoreda held menial jobs and had an unfortunate life as wife and lover. This marginal life, as contrasted to her assured central place in Hispanic literature, illustrates the obstruction of talent when it is found in a repressed language, in a defeated enemy, and in what has been considered the second sex.

Mercè Rodoreda was born in Barcelona on 10 October 1909, in a period when social unrest was frequent and the affirmation of Catalan language and culture was strong. She grew up in the neighborhood of Saint Gervasi, and her memories of childhood in a large house and a bountiful garden where she found her freedom are present in her writing. When she was only nine years old her grandfather became seriously ill and her mother decided to keep Mercè, her only child, at home from school to help with household chores. Years later she lamented that she never learned how to do division, to her a loss symbolic of her exclusion from many sectors of human enterprise and knowledge.[1] Rodoreda's texts would subsequently concentrate on love and life at home, while they would grow fuzzy and sound hollow when trying to describe the worlds of finance, commerce, or industry, a deficiency that contributed to the weakness of many of her male characters. In her novels the worlds of learning and the university are absent, reflecting her mother's crucial decision to pull her out of school.

While still a teenager, Rodoreda married a wealthy uncle, her mother's brother, but soon after having a child they decided to separate. She became active as a writer, publishing short stories in periodical publications such as *Mirador*, *La Rambla*, and in the children's page in *La Publicitat*, and editing a journal for young women, *Clarisme*. Although she wrote five novels between 1932 and 1937, several decades later Rodoreda completely rejected four of them by their exclusion from the edition of her complete works. Only the revised version of her fifth novel, *Aloma*, was considered legitimate enough to be included in the definitive family of her works. Since the topics and structures of these novels are not so different from her later work as to justify oblivion, her exclusion of them may be related to a wish to blank out a period of youthful experimentation that ended in personal failure at the time of a national tragedy. Her conversations with other writers at the Club dels Novellistes fed her interest in culture and brought her into contact with the rich inheritance of Catalan literature, the psychological novel, and interior monologue. During the civil war of 1936–39 Rodoreda backed the socialist UGT (Unión General de Trabajadores) and worked as a secretary at the Institució de les Lletres Catalanes. In January 1939, the war almost ended and lost by the Republican government, Rodoreda escaped the approaching Franco troops and joined thousands of Spaniards heading to France and a long exile. She left her son behind, and she did not publish a novel until twenty-three years later.

Rodoreda spent a few months in Toulouse and then went to Paris, where she helped to find a place for herself and a large group of intellectuals from Barcelona at a chateau at Roissy, forty miles from the French capital. She became the lover of the Catalan writer Joan Armand Obiols, who was married, and they were forced to move to a chateau in Saint Cyr because of the antagonism of the friends of Obiols's wife, Montserrat Trabal. From there they moved again, this time to a house belonging to friends of Anna Murià, a writer who had become a close friend and protector of Rodoreda but who left in January 1940 for the Dominican Republic. In June 1942 the Germans took over Paris and Rodoreda had to flee through an apocalyptic landscape that she recalls later in her novel *Quanta, quanta guerra* (So much war) (1980). She took refuge first in Limoges, then in Bordeaux. Her relationship with Obiols was unstable because he was unable or unwilling to sever his relationship with his wife, which fueled Rodoreda's skepticism towards love, for her a painful emotion that she saw as a frustrating effort to establish true and permanent communication. For Rodoreda, love was always fragile, frequently trapped in a triangular relationship and ending in betrayal and bitter memories. She wrote to her friend Anna Murià in a stormy moment of her relationship with Joan Armand Obiols: "El meu amor per en Joan ha estat el centre de la meva vida, en fallar-me aquest amor, m'ha fallat tot" [My love for Joan has been the center of my life, and when it failed me, everything failed].[2]

After the war, in 1948, Rodoreda visited Barcelona briefly, but found it so changed that she returned to her exile. Rodoreda established herself first in Paris and then moved in 1954 to Geneva, gaining her subsistence by sewing and later by translating. In the prologue to *Mirall trencat* (Broken mirror), she affirms that she is only moderately interested in her historical period and that she did not wish to become a chronicler of her time: "Però no he nascut per limitar-me a parlar de fets concrets" [But I was not born to limit myself to speak of things that have happened].[3] This disclaimer does not mean that she has ignored the experience of exile. On the contrary, it has been transmuted into a harrowing series of stories where men are feminized and swallowed while women barely survive at the animal level or are blotted out by hunger, old age, sickness, and neglect.[4] During a period in Geneva she devoted herself to painting (following the model of Klee), a discipline that glows through the carefully wrought texture of colors in her writing. She had begun slowly to write a few short stories in the late 1940s that were published in small journals in Mexico, but her health, her need to work with the needle instead of the pen in order to survive, and a writer's block probably occasioned by a long series of traumas sapped her energy.

In the 1950s she clandestinely entered Spain in a friendly embassy's car to visit her mother, who had planned a reconciliation of Rodoreda and her husband, but her life was firmly rooted in

Switzerland and France and she refused to return to a past she abhorred. In 1957 she received the Victor Català prize for her *Vint-i-dos contes* (Twenty-two short stories). However, full recognition came only with the enthusiastic reception by the general public of *La plaça del Diamant* in 1962, after it did not receive the Sant Jordi prize to which Rodoreda had submitted it, but had been recommended for publication by one member of the jury. For the rest of her life she remained apart from literary circles, occasionally visiting Spain and granting few interviews, until her death on 13 April 1983.

Rodoreda's first published novel, *Sóc una dona honrada?* (Am I an honest woman?) (1932), contains many elements that remained constant in her texts: a woman trapped in an unhappy marriage, the temptation of adultery, a man who is desired but who is also recognized as insensitive and brutal, and a search for a style that reproduces the spoken language of intimate confidences. In *Sóc una dona honrada?*, one of the main characters, Teresa, describes in her diary her enervating boredom and her evasions of sleep and dreams. The title is ironic, since Teresa may be an honest woman through conviction, fear, or sloth, but she certainly is not happy as prisoner of an unsatisfying role (wife) and a place (home). She will come to the realization that she cannot expect Prince Charming to come to her rescue: "La felicitat no existeix; la felicitat se l'ha de fer cadascú; si hom es refia dels altres per a assolir-la, està ben perdut" [Happiness does not just lie there; each one of us must make her own happiness; if you expect others to give happiness to you, you are completely lost] (188). This lesson of hard-won self-sufficiency is to be learned once and again with considerable pain by Rodoreda's characters, yet this insight is not a cause for celebration, since women in her novels are still left to fend for themselves with few resources other than their bodies in a world dominated by men.

If *Sóc una dona honrada?* showed a woman restricted by marriage and the constraints of city life, *Del que hom no pot fugir* (The inevitable) (1934) follows the destructive path of a young woman who falls in love with an older man, already married, and then, rejected and disenchanted, flees to the countryside only to find a harsher violence against women exerted by men and nature. While the warmth of early summer and the flowering of the earth invite the body to pleasure and sex, fall is the inevitable corollary, with the pain of childbirth, the decay of the body, and the scattering of the family. Rodoreda's character caves in, sliding from frustrated dreams into madness and, possibly, into suicide.

In *Un dia en la vida d'un home* (A day in the life of a man) (1934)

Rodoreda explores the same frustrations outlined in *Sóc una dona honrada?* but this time examines the point of view of a man suffocated by a plodding, "honest" wife and wrenched by the allure of an extramarital relationship with a younger woman. A shoddy and frustrated affair in a room rented by the hour, however, will not measure up with what books, movies, and his imagination have made Ramon Rampell anticipate. As his name indicates— "Rampell" means "whim"—his timorous action will have no lasting effect and he is condemned to the droning repetition evoked by the "ram-ram" of the name Ramon Rampell. A comparison of Ramon leaving the rented room with Adam being forced to leave paradise touches a chord frequently sounded by Rodoreda: the fallen condition of all life and the incessant longing for remembered happiness in a garden, before sex became an obligation with the painful consequence of childbirth and for a Golden Age with no financial obligations and a father to take care of the world.[5]

Crim (Crime) (1936), the last of the four novels later rejected by Rodoreda, is a parody of an English detective novel that, like the previous three novels, contains important elements that constantly preoccupied Rodoreda. This ironic warping of a popular genre, the detective novel, will reappear later in the suspense of an impending crime in *La plaça del Diamant* and in the mysteries of *El carrer de les Camèlies* (The street of the camellias) (1966). Rodoreda's fascination with romance and popular crime novels provided her with proven formulaic techniques for presenting her anecdotes and keeping readers interested, while at the same time demolishing the comfortable atmosphere of the bourgeois drawing room and bedroom, traditional places where mysteries are explained and differences reconciled.

Aloma (1938) received the Premi Crexells of 1937, an important honor that would have surely made Rodoreda's work better known if the civil war had not ended with a strong repression of Catalan culture. *Aloma* is a forceful novel, well paced, with clearly delineated characters and vivid glimpses of Barcelona. Rodoreda tells again the story of an adolescent awakening to the harsh reality of the female condition. "Aloma" is a name taken from Ramon Llul's *Blanquerna*, where it refers to a perfect wife, while in Rodoreda's novel it is only a nickname given by an old uncle to a child called Angela Rosa María. Aloma lives with her brother Joan, his wife, Anna, and their child, Dani, in the old family home with a lovely garden. At the start of the novel the reader immediately encounters bad omens: Aloma remembers that her brother, an ardent reader, commited suicide while still a teenager, leaving behind a note to

Aloma about the sadness of life. In front of Aloma's window a cat roams year after year, becoming more and more decrepit, always burdened by new kittens and assaulted by other cats, until she turns up dead, beaten on the head with a night guard's stick while delivering her last litter. Aloma helps at home but feels unappreciated and taken for granted. Her brother does not let her work outside the home, but here she feel trapped, "sense res per distreure's, sense que passés mai res" [with nothing to entertain her, nothing ever happening] (1: 62). She buys a romance novel and fantasizes about the freedom she could have as a married woman. Daydreaming is challenged by a warning nightmare: "Havia somiat el gat. Ressuscitava i li deia: —No et deixis enganyar, no et casis" [She had dreamed of the cat. She came back to life and told her: —Do not be fooled, do not get married] (1: 61). This negative attitude toward marriage is reinforced by the story of a couple that separates when their long-expected child is born, and by the visits of an older woman called Mercè, who frequently tells the story of her disappointing husband, always ending with a plea to Aloma not to get married (1: 86). What else has she been trained to do?

De petita li havien dit que quan seria gran es casaria, que havia de saber portar una casa perquè en tindria una de seva. Que s'hauria de casar per poder tenir fills. Que per fer-los créixer havien de ser dos, perquè ella sola no en sabria. La mare a fer el menjar; el pare a guanyar diners perquè no els faltés res. (1: 153)

[Since she was a little girl she had been told that when she grew up she would get married, that she had to know how to take care of a house because one day she would have one of her own. That she would have to get married to have children. That in order to take care of them they had to be two, because she would not be able to manage all by herself. The mother takes care of the kitchen; the father makes money so that they don't lack anything.]

Anna's brother Robert arrives from America in the spring and by late summer he has become Aloma's secret lover. He is insensitive to her feelings, especially when her nephew dies, and she comes to dislike the obligatory and clandestine sex. She has never been able to express her feelings to him, and only by writing letters to an imagined sailor with Robert's name can she bring into her life the tenderness she found in books. Joan has mortgaged the house to finance his affair with a young and attractive neighbor, a relationship endured with silent yet bitter resignation by his wife. When he is unable to make the payments, the family has to move to a small apartment. Robert decides to return to America and to his lover, Violeta. Aloma is left expecting a child, bereft of her ancestral home, friendless and surrounded by darkness. *Aloma* was revised by Rodoreda in 1968, with special attention given to the coherence of the narrator's point of view, who mostly reflects Aloma's emotions.[6] The prose that encompasses boredom, elation, love, and despair with equal economy and precision is a good example of Rodoreda's poetics: "Per escriure bé entenc dir amb la màxima simplicitat les coses essencials" [My belief is that writing well means to say the essential with the greatest simplicity] (Rodoreda 1974, 14).

With *Vint-i-dos contes*, which obtained the Victor Català prize of 1957, Rodoreda continued to explore the topics of love and marriage, mostly with dark colors dominated by pessimism, failure, and sadness. Some of the stories had been published in 1946 and 1947 in Mexico, among them "Felicitat" (Happiness), where a woman is happy next to her lover during the night but discovers in the morning that she has fallen out of love and decides to leave him. Yet moved by her lover's tender concern she stays on, occasioning a caustic remark from the narrator: "Arraulida hi havia una noia sense espines, sense exabruptes, una noia que es quedava, ignorant que tirànicament l'empresonaven quatre parets i un sostre de tendresa" [Kneeling there was a young woman without thorns, without nastiness, a young woman that stayed, ignoring that she was imprisoned by four walls and a ceiling of tenderness] (212). In most of the stories, however, conditions are described without commentary, with the characters frequently telling their own stories in their own voices, leaving readers to reach their own conclusions. In "La sang" (The blood), a woman discovers she is beginning to get old while her husband is infatuated with a younger woman, but she finally realizes that he too is old when he cries in her arms the day the girl is to be married. The blood in the title refers to menstruation, celebrated as womanhood and youth, but the story also reverberates with the "bad blood" created by the estranged marriage and the irrational, cruel, and beastly instinct driving the husband, who is ultimately rejected and despised.

"La sang," an obsessive monologue, is the first story in *Vingt-i-dos contes*; the last one, "Abans de morir" (Before dying), is a suicide letter interspersed with diary entries that reiterates the destructive effects of infidelity. In a brisk succession of memories that the twenty-year-old narrator stacks like a pile of postcards before commiting suicide, the reader learns that she married a charming lawyer, only to find out that he carried always and everywhere a case with the letters of his previous lover. The text of the story is an attempt to "fight fire with fire," or letters with letters, yet a brief moment of self-irony leads the narrator to acknowledge that her suicide may be an old-fashioned gesture. The pain of being displaced, of being used as a replacement of an idealized phantom, is persuasively conveyed and is reminiscent of the suffering that Rodoreda herself expressed to Anna Murià in a chilling letter, dated 17 March 1947:

L'Obiols m'ha dit categòricamente que vol tornar a casa seva. Jo no tinc una rival, Anna, el que que veritablement tinc és un *enemic*. I l'enemic és l'home que estimo. L'Obiols es va buscar una dona per passar l'exili, era massa complicat de fer venir la seva família i era més fàcil el que ha fet .... Viure amb ell, ara, és un suplici, sempre l'he sentit preocupat, però ara el sento absent .... He passat tres anys a Bordeus, Anna—això no està bè que ho digui—, treballant per l'Obiols, tot el pes fort de la casa queia damunt meu i ell anant escrivint cartes dient "ara ja falta poc." ¿T'imagines la meva capacitat de dissimulació, l'esforc immens per a salvar una mica de cosa d'aquest naufragi? ... Què espero? Per què aguanto? T'asseguro que cada dia em vaig morir una mica i que no puc més. Però encara el veig, si l'amor em manca, encara el tinc al costat, encara el sento vora meu a la nit .... Envejo la teca felicitat, el teu fill de l'home que estimes .... Bé, deixem els assumptes del cor.

[Obiols has told me that he definitely wishes to return to his house. I don't have a rival, Anna, what I really have is an *enemy*. And the enemy is the man I love. Obiols looked for a woman to accompany him during his exile, it was too complicated to have his whole family come and what he did was easier .... To live with him now is a torture, I have always felt he was worried, but now I feel that he is absent .... I have spent three years in Bordeaux, Anna—it is not proper for me to say that—working for Obiols, all the heavy work of the house fell on me and he meantime writing letters to her saying "now the end is near." Can you imagine my capacity to hide my feelings, the immense effort to save a tiny anything from this wreckage? ... What am I waiting for? Why do I stand it? I assure you that every day I die a little and that I can't take it any longer. Yet still I see him, even if love fails me, I still have him next to me, I still feel him next to me at night .... I envy your happiness, your son from a man you love .... Well, let's drop these matters of the heart.][7]

It is not simply that Rodoreda sublimated her own unhappy marriage and love affair into a series of reiterated meditations on the shortcomings of love, but that she examined her experience with great lucidity, dared speak about it, and then incorporated it into the hackneyed medium of popular literature. Her stories are reversals of the typical romance. They not only question the validity of the romance as a model, but they also reveal the deficiencies of more refined forms of literature, which tend to drop these "matters of the heart" or to present them from a man's point of view. Rodoreda is particularly acerbic about romantic love and marriage, and her bitter reports of wasted lives ring true. In *Vingt-i-dos contes* there are many subdued moments that are memorable and corrosive: the man who returns home to his sick wife and child but whose mind is still caught up in the vision of a young girl ("Estiu," [Summer]); the young lovers who have a fight and a disquieting thought that their marriage may not prove to be what they expect ("Tarda al cinema," [Afternoon at the movies]); the bride who lovingly remembers her previous lover ("El gelat rosa," [The pink ice cream]); the young lovers who examine each other's pockets and promise to have no secrets ("Promesos," [An engaged couple]); the man who sees in his daughter his lost lover ("En veu baixa," [In a low voice]); and the man who plans to seduce his secretary while his wife slaves at home ("Començament," [Beginnings]). Two stories in particular, "El gelat rosa" and "En veu baixa," are examples of unusual craftsmanship that compresses into very few lines a complex intensity of feelings and a tangled web of experience and memories.[8]

In 1962 Rodoreda published *La plaça del Diamant*, a novel generally acknowledged to be her masterpiece and one of the best in contemporary peninsular literature.[9] The reader is pulled in as an eavesdropper while a woman recounts her life to a silent listener. The speaker is Natalia, an innocent victim who will descend into hell before reaching the serene and conciliatory tone of her compelling voice. As her name implies—"Nadal" in Catalan means "Christmas"—she brings life to herself through her actions and narration. When her story begins Natalia is remembering the main event of her youth, the meeting of a young carpenter, Quimet, who will become her first husband. At the time she worked in a candy store and her life seemed pleasant, even if without direction. Her mother had been dead for years and her father had remarried. Left to herself, "joveneta i sola a la plaça del Diamant" [young and alone in Diamond Square] (354), she is tempted by a friend, Julieta, to attend the street dances of the festivities of Saint John, which is the same type of popular surge of life that had precipitated Aloma's fall. This is a transgression of social mores since Natalia has a boyfriend, Pere, who washes dishes. Quimet is first a voice that tempts her to dance and later promises that she will be his wife and queen. Although he looks like a monkey, he attracts Natalia with his fast talk and dominating character. Just as Gabriel brings news to Mary about her destiny, Quimet informs Natalia about his plans. He changes her name to Colometa ("Little Pigeon"), a symbol at this stage of the domesticity, faithfulness, and subservience that he expects from her. Her attempt to escape is frustrated by what is for her a shameful episode: her slip falls and she must leave it behind on the ground. The episode, told in a breathless manner, suggests a rape. It is a good example of Rodoreda's many-layered writing because under the seemingly trivial anecdote—girl meets boy at a dance—a whirlwind of contradictory implications opens the text to deeper interpretation with allusions to the encounter of Romeo, the betrayal of the previous lover (with anticipated punishment), baptism, Cinderella, rape, and loss of innocence.

The second chapter introduces an important element, sex, that is immediately displaced and repressed. Natalia is waiting outside of Guell Park for Quimet to arrive when an unknown young man, calling from a window where he stands in his pajamas, asks her to approach him. When she innocently complies, Natalia discovers that she has been taken for a prostitute: "Em vaig tornar de mil colors i me'n vaig entornar enrabiada, sobretot amb mi mateixa, i amb angúnia perquè sentia que el jove em mirava esquena i em travessava la roba i la pell" [I blushed and I turned away angry, especially at myself, and anguished because I felt that the young man was observing my back and ripping through my dress and my skin] (357). Natalia's body is for her a source of trouble and shame and she can hardly call it her own. Quimet does not help her when he makes a comparison that tries to remove sex from their marriage: "i que ell era com si fos Sant Josep i que jo era com si fos la Mare de Déu" [and that he was as if he were Saint Joseph and that I was as if I were the Mother of God] (359). Probably Quimet feels unsure about himself: his mother wanted him to be a girl, he teases his wife with a real or invented "poor Mary" that he pretends to have left for Natalia, he races his motorcycle, and he is never happier than when he has a rifle. Later, after two children and a married life in which sex does not seem to be pleasurable, Natalia loses her husband, who is killed in battle. Her second marriage is to a man rendered impotent by this same war. Ironically the civil war has served to remove all threats to Natalia's body, allowing her to move on to a contented mature life.[10]

Rodoreda's use of symbols in this novel is a masterful exploitation and questioning of literary tradition. The most obvious is the pigeon, apparently a benign, positive creature, a symbol of peace, faithful love, and the unfailing return home. It had been used before by

Rodoreda in *Vint-i-dos contes*, where Marta, the young girl about to commit suicide in "Abans de morir," did not like pigeons. When her future husband sends her two, she invites him to dinner, and serves roasted pigeons. Later, when she falls in love, she confesses to having grown to like pigeons and he gives her a first-anniversary present of a pigeon made out of diamonds. It is the symbol of a tender trap, of a smothering domesticity. Quimet reduces Natalia to a small pigeon and then to a servant of pigeons when he decides to raise hundreds of them on the roof of their building. Natalia must feed them, and their interminable cooing and strong smell define her life. Rodoreda has effectively shown, in this malevolent and uncontrolled growth of a benevolent creature, the toils and sufferings of unwanted motherhood. Natalia's rebellion against her servitude, the destruction of the pigeons' eggs, is the start of her search for independence. But this quest is not simplified: on the day the news of Quimet's death arrives, Natalia finds the last remaining pigeon dead. She does not throw the body of the pigeon away, just as she has difficulty accepting Quimet's death, because throughout her marriage there had been love, not romantic, not ideal, not liberated, but love nonetheless. All that is left of Quimet is his watch and Natalia's memories of their time together. Although she had resented his continuous watch over her, virtually all the care that Natalia had ever known was stolen from her, first by another woman and then by death. As she grows older the ambiguity of the pigeon symbol, the attractive repugnance, increases: "Si volia pensar en els coloms alguna vegada, m'estimava més pensar-hi tota sola. I pensar-hi com volgués; perquè de vegades pensar-hi em feia posar trista i d'altres vegades no" [If sometimes I wished to think about the pigeons, I liked better to do it all alone. And to think in whatever way I liked, because sometimes to think about them made me sad and other times it didn't] (513). Her thoughts have now become a way to exercise her independence. But in the last, masterful chapter, the pigeon appears again, this time on the shoulder of Quimet's best friend, Mateu, who had been kind to Natalia. Are they the apostle and the Holy Spirit? In a deeply liberating primal scream, Natalia at last expresses all the sorrow she feels for her spent youth, and is able to reject the past and return home to Antoni, her husband/child, to face death with some gratitude for the gift of life. The final image in the novel is given by Natalia, who is anticipating a walk in the park, her space of freedom: there she expects to see birds happily playing in the mud, making whole the heaven and the earth, the female and the male, the past and the present. They are not pigeons, just birds: "o uns quants ocells cridaners que baixaven de les fulles com llampecs, es ficaven al toll, s'hi banyaven estarrufats de ploma i barrejaven el cel amb fang i amb becs i amb ales. Contents . . . ." [or a few chirping birds that descended from the leaves like lightning, got into the puddles of rain, bathed with their feathers all puffed up and brought together the sky and the mud and the beaks and the wings. Happy . . . .] (525–26).

La plaça del Diamant makes good use of Rodoreda's sense of plot and suspense. In chapter 12 Natalia tells her interlocutor that she remembers the pigeons and a funnel together because they both came at the same time to her house. The funnel, a symbol of her increasingly restricted life, had become a weapon in the hard days of hunger after the war when Natalia had contemplated killing her children and committing suicide. She had managed to survive that far by working as the cleaning woman in a large, bewildering, rich house, but after that job ended she was left with no resources to fall back upon except another man that presently came her way. But the suffocating kindness of Antoni was not enough to take her out of the tunnel, or funnel. In the vision she describes in the last chapter, the houses and the pigeons threaten to trap her:

I vaig ficar-me a la plaça del Diamant: una capsa buida feta de cases velles amb el cel per tapadora. I al mig d'aquella tapadora hi vaig veure volar unes ombres petites i totes les cases es van començar a gronxar com si tot ho haguessin ficat a dintre d'aigua i algú fes bellugar l'aigua a poc a poc i les parets de les cases es van estirar amunt i es van començar a decantar les unes contra les altres i el forat de la tapadora s'anava estrenyent i començava a fer un embut.

[And I went into Diamond Square: an empty box made out of old houses and with the sky as a lid. And in the center of that lid I saw fly small specks of darkness and all the houses began to sway as if someone had put everything into water and slowly made waves in the water and the walls of the houses began to stretch up and they grew close together and the hole of the lid shrunk and it became a funnel.] (522)

The primal scream rescues Natalia from the funnel and the temptation of a passive domesticity. She has come through her miseries and is now born again by escaping a new baptism. Her daughter's marriage, however, is obviously off to a shaky start because she confesses to her mother that she will never let her husband know that she loves him, even if she does so, madly. Although the world smiles for Natalia at last, the reader is warned, as in *Aloma*, that each one must find his or her own happiness—not in solitude but among other people, in the open spaces of public squares.

The same motif of the helpless girl who must find her way in life is repeated in her next novel, *El carrer de les Camèlies* (1966), but the narration is closer to that found in popular forms of literature such as the soap opera, than that of the tightly controlled *La plaça del Diamant*. It seems as if Rodoreda is now transposing characters and situations that she had treated seriously in her previous novel into a playful mode. The first sentence sets the reader up for mysteries and revelations: "Em van deixar en el carrer de les Camèlies, al peu d'un reixat de jardí, i el vigilant em va trobar a la matinada" [They left me in the Street of the Camellias, at the foot of a garden fence, and the guard found me there at dawn] (9). A kindly couple adopts the baby, named Cecília Ce, but she grows up lonely and never is sent to school for fear that her uncertain origin may expose her to the repudiation of other children. There is a literal black stain in the place where she was abandoned. One day she escapes from home because she has seen her father's face in the sky. Another time she sneaks away to the Liceo, the opera house of Barcelona, to see *Rigoletto*, an oedipal story of a loving yet destructive father. Cecília notices depressing examples of married life around her: a notary public who has married a woman with the same name as his deceased first wife (59) and a grotesque young couple and their unhappy baby (60–63). Cecília leaves the home of her foster parents to live in a shantytown with the first of a long series of lovers. A few flowers and a forest of colorful umbrellas that protect her shelter from the rain are not enough to defend her from the violence of the men who desire her nor from her own aimless restlessness. After her first lover is put into jail and the second one dies, she tries to work as a seamstress. She discovers, however, that she is not able to survive by selling her labor, so decides to market her own body as a prostitute. Cecília first pairs up with the owner of a restaurant, Cosme, a man who has replaced the photograph of his father with one of a horse. Cosme is thirsty for love and is jealous and tyrannical, so eventually Cecília leaves him, after an abortion and a suicide attempt. She continues "moving up" in her picaresque life, but not without increasing the price she has to pay. Her new lover, a rich young man, forces her to live like a prisoner, spies on her, and plots with two friends to use Cecília for their sadistic games before abandoning her in the middle of the street. There she is rescued by a gentle friend, a handsome and kind rich man, a father figure who restores her to health and freedom, giving her as well a posh villa with a magnificent garden.

Since Cecília needs to finance her good life, she takes control of the exploitation of her body and makes a handsome profit. Now she is ready to return to her neighborhood and talk with the gardener who found her, yet nothing new is revealed in this final conversation. It was the gardener, a self-styled god, who decided to which house she should go and what name she would have. To whom is Cecília talking? Perhaps it is to an expensive psychiatrist in Switzerland. Buried in this flimsy story line are some haunting images that exemplify the helpless condition of women when they become victims of male aggression and mere sexual playthings. Cecília, prisoner of a one-eyed historian and a four-eyed woman servant, forced to live naked and drunk, repeatedly raped and abused, is a disquieting invalidation of the ecstatic but helpless woman found in many forms of pornography.

In May 1967, a new collection of Rodoreda's stories entitled *La meva Cristina i altres contes* (*My Christina and Other Stories*, 1984) confirmed her mastery of the genre. The stories touch on a variety of topics and use an array of narrators: a nurse, a sailor, a young woman, a witch, and a fish. The plots deal mostly with breakdowns in communication, marginal existence and a sense of loss, marked in part by hectic conversation, like the waves of the ocean in "El mar" (The sea) or by the many disembodied voices that seem to address themselves to an impassive interlocutor. But the characters have learned to endure, to tell their stories with gusto, and they are more intrigued and bemused by human folly than repelled or angry. Like the sailor who lived for many years in the belly of a whale in "La meva Cristina" (My Christina), Rodoreda's characters have pride and defiance in being different. New realms open up where human society is boring or repressive: a young man becomes a fish in "El riu i la barca" (The river and the boat), a woman sentenced to die at the stake saves herself by becoming a salamander in "La salamandra," while a woman returns from death as a cat to take revenge on her husband in "Una fulla de gerani blanc" (A leaf of white geranium).

Jardí vora el mar (A garden next to the sea) was published in June 1967, but it had been written from 1959 to 1966. It repeats Rodoreda's theme of the conflict between a happy childhood, associated with the garden, and the desolation of adulthood with the call of death, symbolized here by the sea. The story is told from the point of view of the gardener, who, even if he claims to despise gossip and spying into other people's lives, is curious, wanders through the garden at night, and is always there when someone needs to confess. The central story is trite: Eugeni and Rosamaria met when they were children and grew to love each other in the exuberant garden of Eugeni's kind parents. After they made love and Rosamaria saw life more realistically, she decided to marry a richer man, Francesc, the owner of the house with the garden next to the sea. Eugeni, echoing Lorca's play *Así que pasen cinco años* (Five years from now), promised to return after five years. He does, but Rosamaria is not ready to abandon her husband, even if Eugeni also has become rich by following her model and marrying a rich girl. After Rosamaria fails to appear for a midnight rendezvous at the gardener's house, he commits suicide by drowning in the sea. What saves this story is the limpid and graceful prose, the knowledgeable descriptions of the garden, and the vivid dialogues of the squabbling servants. Pared to its core, this novel develops a frustrated love affair, with romantic flair added by adoring servants. It is obvious that love is here distorted by the power of money that in *El jardí vora el mar*, outside paradise, easily buys men and women or destroys them.

Mirall trencat (Broken mirror) (1974), is an ambitious novel that chronicles the rise and fall of a family. As one might expect, in the beginning there is a flaw. Teresa, the beautiful but poor girl, has had a child out of wedlock, before she accepts a marriage proposal from a rich old man, Nicolau Rovira. Soon a widow, she marries Salvador Valldaura, an independently wealthy, handsome man who was once in love with Barbara, a violinist from Vienna who committed suicide after their affair ended. The same flaw is repeated in the second generation, since their daughter Sofia fondly remembers another man while her husband has had a daughter by a vaudeville artist who remains his true love. There are many naturalistic details such as incest, suicides, detailed sickness, death, and dead rats, thrown in among elegant and discreet love affairs, plush houses, and elusive phantoms. It is difficult to perceive any ironical intent in this long *roman-fleuve* or family saga that is also a *novella rosa*, a romance. Carme Arnau (1979, 256–97) seems to think that it is the culmination of Rodoreda's work and the creation of a myth.[11] Of indisputable importance is the prologue, where Rodoreda recognizes that *Mirall trencat* is written "amb un estil que no era el meu" [with a style that was not mine] (17), and offers the following definition of a novel: "Una novella es fa amb una gran quantitat d'intuïcions, amb una certa quantitat d'imponderables, amb agonies i amb resurreccions de l'ànima, amb exaltacions, amb desenganys, amb reserves de memòria involuntària . . . tota una alquímia" [A novel is made up of a great number of intuitions, with a certain quantity of imponderables, with agonies and resurrections of the spirit, with moments of great joy, with disappointments, with involuntary reservations of memory . . . a whole alchemy] (13). And further: "Escric perquè m'agrada d'escriure. Si no semblés exagerat diria que escric per agradar-me a mi. Si de retop el que escric agrada als altres, millor. Potser és més profund. Potser escric per afirmar-me. Per sentir que sóc" [I write because I enjoy writing. If it would not sound preposterous, I would say that I write to please myself. If as a result what I write pleases others, so much the better. Maybe there is a more profound reason. Perhaps I write to affirm myself. To feel that I exist] (32).

Semblava de seda i altres contes (It felt like silk and other stories) (1978) brings together short stories that span forty years in Rodoreda's career. The first stories show that even when she had not yet found her voice and her texts were invaded by the mannerisms of other writers, Rodoreda was involved in experimentation and in working through the obsessive image of the exploited woman. In "Ada Liz" a young girl sells herself to sailors, but this is not a sad situation for her. On the contrary, it is a way to gain freedom and not depend on any man. "Viure al dia" (Living the moment) pokes fun at the stale and myopic life of the women of Barcelona's bourgeoisie. "Pluja" (Rain) is a surprising study of tension, fear, and inner discourse. While a woman awaits a man that she has invited to her apartment, she realizes that this rendezvous could start a whole chain of events that she could find difficult to break, not because of love, but because of routine. She decides to keep her freedom and evades the meeting. In "El bitllet de mil" (The one-thousand peseta bill) a woman sells her body for that amount, but she is stunned to find out that the bill is a fake. Her sense of despair, desolation, and helplessness compressed to a few lines, the love of flowers that adds a moving touch to the woman's character, and the surprising closing lines (even more than the discovery of the fake) combine to make this a powerful story. "Rom Negrita" (Negrita rum) humorously studies men's enslaving and demeaning sexual impulse. "Paràlisi" (Paralysis) is an interesting story that develops a metafictional counterpoint between the narrator's writer's block and the first signs of paralysis in a woman character, who is aggravated by the realization that she is growing old and losing her hold on men. There is an autobiographical dimension to this story, judging from what Rodoreda told an interviewer in 1966 to explain her own writer's block: "No pas per horror a la literatura, sinó perquè de mica en mica se'm va paralitzar el braç dret. Podia cosir—d'això vivia—, fer totes les feines de casa, el que fos, menys escriure. Quan agafava la ploma, el braç em feia mal, els dits se m'encarcaraven, i la ploma saltava. En va durar quatre anys" [Not because I detested literature, but because little by little my right arm became paralyzed. I could sew—I lived from that—take care of the house, I could do everything, except write. Whenever I took a pen, my arm hurt, my fingers became rigid, and the pen fell. It lasted four years].[12]

Rodoreda's next book, *Viatges i flors* (Trips and flowers) (1980), contains brief descriptions of towns and flowers, showing inventiveness and a lyrical force that blends realistic and acute observation with the emblematic and allegoric tradition. Her novel *Quanta, quanta guerra* (1980) is structured similarly to *Viatges* as a loosely knit series of episodes united by the common presence (as victim or observer) of a boy, Adrià Guinart, an antihero in the picaresque tradition. The novel was begun in 1974 with the tentative title of "The Soldier and the Roses." After Rodoreda rewrote the book three times, neither soldier nor flowers played an important role in the final manuscript, which was a roller-coaster trip through the nightmare of war. Adrià has a mark on his brow that other people interpret as the sign of Cain: he is protected, but has lost his father and is punished for a crime he does not comprehend. He meets a nude, fearless girl in the river, Eve. They are separated and Adrià searches for her until he discovers that Eve had been exploited by an old woman, who enslaved and sold her to soldiers. Eve was carried away by a group of soldiers, gang-raped, and murdered. Adrià discovers he cannot maintain his neutrality any longer. He returns to his father's place where he probably will take up arms. The extreme violence that surfaces in what he sees and hears during his trip is a strong condemnation of the nonsensical myth of war. Even if the alacrity with which everyone receives Adrià and immediately makes full confession of the history of their lives is not believable, the style here is closer to medieval plays and Dances of Death, where all the actors come forth and have their say before being swallowed up by the pestilence of war.

From 1961 until her death in 1983, Rodoreda worked on the manuscript of a novel that recreated a primitive society where surprisingly brutal traditions, strange behavior, and a disquieting primeval nature trace the outline of a nightmarish allegory. The narrator is a boy who witnesses the horrible death of his putative father, who tries to hide inside a specially carved tree but is dragged out and made to swallow pink cement until he expires. Other acts of ritual violence follow until the narrator commits suicide by piercing his heart with a stake. This manuscript was published in 1986 as *La Mort i la Primavera* (Death and spring), accompanied by several of the most important variants of the final draft, which add to the fascination of this starkly primitive yet sophisticated, unique book.

A Catalonian writer, Paulina Crusat, stated in the influential literary journal *Insula*, published in Madrid, that Mercè Rodoreda was a great artist, with such a free and original inspiration that her work placed her among the absolute first rank of writers in Spain or abroad.[13] The many translations of *La plaça del Diamant* and the favorable reception this novel continues to merit will surely establish Mercè Rodoreda's name among the best writers of Spain in this century. It should be clear how much suffering and difficulty she had to endure to attain this distinction, and her triple exile as a Republican, a Catalonian, and a woman should not be forgotten. "El meu exili ha estat dur" [My exile has been hard], she told an interviewer in 1966.[14] Suffering deeply influenced her writing, which may in turn have saved her from the despair of some of her characters. Before Aloma closes down the ancestral house, lost by the folly of one of her brothers, she climbs to the attic where her other brother, a devoted reader, used to live, until he committed suicide. In homage to him Aloma leaves behind a daring book she has bought in a moment of freedom. Then she faces darkness, having decided to live and devote her life to the child who is growing within her. This was also Rodoreda's choice, to leave her work to us as a testimony of both the harshness of existence and the resilience of life.

Notes

1. Rodoreda tells Montserrat Roig in 1972: "Tota la vida he conservat la pena de no haver pogut estudiar" (All my life I have felt the sorrow of not having been able to study), "El aliento poético de Mercè Rodoreda," *Triunfo*, 22 September 1973, 35–39.
2. Mercè Rodoreda, *Cartes a l'Anna Murià, 1939–1956* (Barcelona: LaSal, 1985), 83.
3. "Pròleg" to *Mirall trencat*, in *Obres completes* (Barcelona: Edicions 62, 1984), 3: 16.
4. Nichols 1986, 405–17, develops a unique interpretation of exile in her insightful and intelligent reading of Rodoreda's stories.
5. The comparison is found in Rodoreda 1934b, 36.
6. See Clarasó 1980, 143–52.
7. Rodoreda, *Cartes*, 84–85.
8. Josep Navarro studies these stories in detail in "Ruptura i linealitat temporal als contes de Mercè Rodoreda," in *Actes del Tercer Colloqui Internacional de Llengua i Literatura Catalanes*, ed. R. B. Tate and Alan Yates (Oxford: Dolphin Book Co., 1976), 301–9.
9. Arthur Terry, in *Catalan Literature* (London: Benn, 1972), singles out *La plaça del Diamant* as "perhaps the finest work of fiction to have appeared since the Civil War" (117). Carme Arnau, in "La obra de Mercè Rodoreda," *Cuadernos Hispanoamericanos* 383 (May 1982): 239–57, adds to the critical acclaim the unusually favorable readers' response that made the novel an instant bestseller (244). García Márquez, who struggled through the Catalan original after he read the 1965 Spanish translation by Enrique Sordo, considers *La plaça del Diamant* one of

the most beautiful books written after the Spanish civil war ("Recuerdos de una mujer invisible: Mercè Rodoreda," *Clarín*, 30 June 1983, 6, the cultural section). It is a sad reflection of Castilian centralism that crucial studies such as Gonzalo Sobejano's *Novela española de nuestro tiempo*, 2d ed. (Madrid: Prensa Española, 1975); Ignacio Soldevila Durante's *La novela desde 1936* (Madrid: Alhambra, 1980) (pt. 2 of a series called *Historia de la literatura española actual*); and Santos Sanz Villanueva's *Historia de la novel social española (1942–1975)* (Madrid: Alhambra, 1980) do not consider novels originally written in Catalan. If for "España" and "español" we understand all of Spain, it would then appear that 1962 produced not just one inspiring masterpiece—Luis Martín-Santos's *Tiempo de silencio* (*Time of Silence*)—but two, counting *La plaça del Diamant*.

10. A detailed and perceptive study of the importance of sex and guilt in this novel is found in Busquets 1985, 117–40.

11. Arnau may have been carried away by the narrative framework of her study, since she describes a progression in Rodoreda from a preoccupation with youth to the description of old age and death, from superficial to deep thought, from symbol to myth, and from lesser to greater quality. I am not convinced that this is the case.

12. An interview with Baltasar Porcel, "Mercè Rodoreda o la força lírica," *Serra d'Or* 8 (March 1966): 234.

13. Paulina Crusat, "Un nuevo libro de Mercè Rodoreda," *Insula* 258 (May 1968): 10.

14. Porcel, "Mercè Rodoreda," 232.

Bibliography

1. PRIMARY SOURCES

1932. *Sóc una dona honrada?* Barcelona: Llibreria Catalònia.

1934a. *Del que hom no pot fugir*. Barcelona: Edicions Clarisme.

1934b. *Un dia en la vida d'un home*. Barcelona: Edicions Proa.

1936. *Crim*. Barcelona: Edicions de la Rosa dels Vents.

1938. *Aloma*. Barcelona: Institució de les Lletres Catalanes. Second version: 1969. Barcelona: Edicions 62. Spanish translation (1971) by Montserrat Roig. Madrid: Al Borak Ediciones. A second Spanish translation (1982) by Alfons Sureda i Carrión. Madrid: Alianza Tres.

1958. *Vint-i-dos contes*. Barcelona: Editorial Selecta. Spanish translation (*Veintidós cuentos*, 1988) by Ana María Moix. Madrid: Mondadori.

1962. *La plaça del Diamant*. Barcelona: Club Editor. Spanish translation (*La Plaza del Diamante*, 1965) by Enrique Sordo. Barcelona: Edhasa. English translation (*The Time of the Doves*, 1980) by David H. Rosenthal. New York: Taplinger Publishing Co.

1966a. *El carrer de les Camèlies*. Barcelona: Club Editor. Spanish translation (*La calle de las Camelias*, 1970) by José Batlló. Barcelona: Edhasa.

1966b. *Jardí vora el mar*. Barcelona: Club Editor.

1967. *La meva Cristina i altres contes*. Barcelona: Edicions 62. Spanish translation (*Mi Cristina y otros cuentos*, 1982) by José Batlló. Madrid: Alianza Editorial. English translation (*My Christina and Other Stories*, 1984) and introduction by David Rosenthal. Port Townsend, Wash.: Graywolf Press.

1974. *Mirall trencat*. Barcelona: Club Editor, 1974.

1976. *Obres completes*. Vol. 1, edited by Carme Arnau. Barcelona: Edicions 62. Includes *Aloma*, *Vint-i-dos contes*, and *La plaça del Diamant*.

1978a. *Obres completes*. Vol. 2, edited by Carme Arnau. Barcelona: Edicions 62. Includes *El carrer de les Camèlies*, *La meva Cristina i altres contes*, and *Jardí vora el mar*.

1978b. *Semblava de seda i altres contes*. Barcelona: Edicions 62. Spanish translation (*Parecía de seda y otras narraciones*, 1981) by Clara Janés. Barcelona: Edhasa.

1980a. *Viatges i flors*. Barcelona: Edicions 62.

1980b. *Quanta, quanta guerra*. Barcelona: Club Editor. Spanish translation (*Cuánta, cuánta guerra*, 1982) by Ana María Moix. Barcelona: Edhasa.

1984. *Obres completes*. Vol. 3, edited by Carme Arnau. Barcelona: Edicions 62. Includes *Mirall trencat*, *Semblava de seda i altres contes*, and *Viatges i flors*.

1986. *La Mort i la Primavera*. Barcelona: Institute d'Estudis Catalans. Spanish translation (*La muerte y la primavera*, 1986) by Enrique Sordo. Barcelona: Seix Barral.

2. SECONDARY SOURCES

Arnau, Carme. 1979. *Introducció a la narrativa de Mercè Rodoreda: El mite de la infantesa*. Barcelona: Edicions 62. A comprehensive study offering close readings of the texts.

Busquets, Loreto. 1985. "El mito de la culpa en *La plaça del Diamant*." *Cuadernos Hispanoamericanos*, no. 420 (June): 117–40. An excellent psychoanalytic reading.

Clarasó, Mercè. 1980. "The Angle of Vision in the Novels of Mercè Rodoreda." *Bulletin of Hispanic Studies* 57: 143–52. A good example of applied narratology.

Lucio, Francisco. 1970. "La soledad, tema central en los últimos relatos de Mercè Rodoreda." *Cuadernos Hispanoamericanos*, no. 242 (February): 455–68. Concentrates on *La meva Cristina*.

Nichols, Geraldine Cleary. 1986. "Exile, Gender, and Mercè Rodoreda." *Modern Language Notes* 101: 405–17. A brilliant article with surprising and convincing readings of Rodoreda's short stories.

Porcel, Baltasar. 1966. "Mercè Rodoreda o la forca lírica." *Serra d'Or* 8 (March): 231–35. A moving and revealing interview.

Wyers, Frances. 1983. "A Woman's Voices: Mercè Rodoreda's *La plaça del Diamant*." *Kentucky Romance Quarterly* 30: 301–9. A stylistic and structural reading.

7

Ana María Moix's Silent Calling

Andrew Bush

Ana María Moix first came to the attention of a broad public in Spain through her appearance in the influential 1970 anthology of José María Castellet, *Nueve novísimos poetas españoles* (Nine extremely new Spanish poets), which gave a name and a definition to a significant departure in contemporary Spanish letters.[1] At the age of twenty-one she was among the youngest, and the only woman, to be published in *Nueve novísimos*, and by twenty-six she was already the author of three books of verse, a book of stories, two novels, and a collection of interviews with writers and artists. From 1973 until 1985 Moix did not publish any new book-length work, with the exception of a story for children, a silence little anticipated by those critics who had written of her early promise, and the cause, it would seem, for the scant attention devoted to her work during that long period. Yet it is during this time that Moix served as the cultural coordinator for *Vindicación feminista* (Feminist rights), contributing essays, reviews, and short fiction, and marking her own position in relation to the feminist movement in Spain promoted by that landmark journal.[2] In 1985, however, Moix published *Las virtudes peligrosas* (Dangerous virtues), a new collection of stories that gives evidence of an important shift from her early work; and at the same time, her writing has begun to reenter the focus of critical attention.

Already in the introduction to his anthology, Castellet had remarked the radical break that divided the *novísimos* from their immediate predecessors, the poets of social realism and political protest, a change attested to by all of the contributors to the volume in their statements of poetic principles that introduce the selections from their work. Some years after the publication of Castellet's anthology, Moix herself specified the moment of the rupture: the publication of Pere (then still writing under the Castilian, rather than Catalan, name of Pedro) Gimferrer's *Arde el mar* (The sea is burning) in 1966.[3] The poetry that follows, including her own volumes that preceded the anthology, may be characterized, reductively, by a newly problematized, highly self-conscious understanding of language: language becomes a theme in itself, rather than the bearer of themes. The shift in emphasis that brought the reflexive relation between the poet and language to the fore needs be set in the context of personal and social history. The *novísimos* were all born after the Spanish civil war and largely came of age in a period of rapid economic growth and the first small steps toward restoring social liberties, the results and indicators of the opening of Spain to the world beyond the borders of Franco's dictatorship. Perhaps the most tangible impact that such changes brought to poetry were the renewed contact with foreign literatures, in which French surrealism, Anglo-American modernism, and the Latin American Boom figure with special prominence. Besides these influences one finds the impact and assimilation of the cultural products of mass media, most notably the movies. These new and eclectic sources further account for the parodic tone of the *novísimos*, another marked alteration from the poetry of social realism of the preceding generation. Nevertheless, parody is also opposition politics, and if it takes as its explicit domain cultural rather than social history, the true target may not have changed. For I would contend that the implicit argument of the *novísimos* against the poetry that preceded their own—even if Castellet himself saw no polemic—was a reaction against the intrusiveness of Franco's politics that had dictated terms to poetry; the oppositional voice of poetic protest, that is, was still engaged in debate with the reigning regime. The *novísimos* do not decline to debate with the poets of social realism so much as they refuse to write verse within the parameters of Franco's Spain.

In this moment of renovation, or even revolution, in Spanish poetry, reinforced and in some cases anticipated by associated changes in the fiction of that period, Moix's work has a particular inflection. The general preoccupation with language is filtered through the growing awareness that women's lot has instead been silence, a social fact that Moix portrays in her early fiction within the clearly autobiographical contours of the bourgeoisie of Barcelona of the post-civil war period. In this study I consider Moix's work primarily with regard to its developing meditation on the relations of language and silence, laying stress on the ambivalence that Moix discovers there. She does not offer a vision of the male suppression of the female voice for which a reappropriation of speech could serve as a clear remedial gesture. Rather, the outpouring of speech is precisely what Moix and her autobiographical heroine, Julia, seek to control. Language may itself be the nightmare from which Julia is trying—and failing—to awake; the sweeter dream represents a contrary nostalgia for silence and a wordless world of women. Moix would impose that nostalgia upon her early fiction by formal innovations, which manifest an effort, no less desperate than Julia's psychological struggles, to quiet the insatiable rage and violent torrent of words. I follow this course, beginning with a brief consideration of her poetry and then concentrating on her two novels, *Julia* (1970) and *Walter, ¿por qué te fuiste?* (Walter, why did you leave?) (1973), to the narrative resolution of "Las virtudes peligrosas," a story in which Moix invents the mythical world toward which she was long striving. There she discovers her silent calling. In closing I consider the gains, both actual and potential, and the cost.

Critical attention devoted to Moix's work has been limited—preempted, no doubt, by the gap in the publication of books during the years of her collaboration with *Vindicación feminista*. Such criticism as there has been has concentrated on Moix's prose, rather than her poetry, making an implicit judgment with which I concur: Moix's great achievement to date has been *Walter, ¿por qué te fuiste?*, and, I believe, her short stories. Nevertheless, if *Walter* may be seen to arise out of the striking, but on the whole less successful *Julia*, tempered by the experience of the first book of stories, *Ese chico pelirrojo a quien veo cada día* (That red-headed boy that I see every day) (1971), Moix's early poetry must also be considered as part of the turbulent material out of which the later novel was formed.

Without proceeding to a comprehensive analysis of the poetry, I can nonetheless underline certain features that may serve to delineate both the ethos and the technique of Moix's narrative prose. My first remarks need be directed toward this latter aspect, inasmuch as Moix's formal experimentation, even iconoclasm, will be among the first impressions registered by readers of *Baladas del dulce Jim* (Ballads of sweet Jim) (1969), *Call me Stone* (1969) and *No time for flowers* (1971) (both titles in English in the original). In Manuel Vázquez Montalbán's prologue to *Baladas*, written, as he is careful to point out, in 1968, which is to say a year of revolutionary student turmoil in Europe, the elder *novísimo* stresses that Moix not only eschews meter, as do other defenders of free verse, but goes beyond her peers by breaking with the fundamental typographical convention of poetry, "el sistema columnario" (the columnar system). He goes on to declare: "En una estupenda lección de libertad, he aquí una poesía escrita sin versos" [In a wonderful lesson of liberty, I present a poetry written without verses].[4] In linking aesthetic to political and ethical concerns, Vázquez Montalbán captures the impulse of the historical moment in which Moix began to write, and thus may serve as a corrective to a reading of her poetry in a strictly confessional vein.

The freedom, or more properly the rebelliousness of Moix's "prose poems," as Margaret E. W. Jones has characterized them,[5] is deceiving on several counts. First, while it avoids the metrical corsets of which Vázquez Montalbán had spoken, it employs and at times is even structured by assonant rhyme. This is particularly the case at the outset of the Dulce Jim sequence, where the accented final *o* (*corazón, matón, llegó, traidor, revolcó,* and *yo*) in the first three paragraphs of the first page (*Baladas*, 13) provides a recurrent beat and also functions to integrate "Nueva York," the setting of the poem, into the Castilian scansion.

The technical challenge faced here by Moix, namely the transference of the sound and rhythm of English into her poetry, indicates a larger and enduring issue for her in both poetry and prose. The anecdote and protagonists of *Baladas del dulce Jim*, and even more emphatically the title of *No time for flowers*, target English as the foreign element that both disrupts and renovates Moix's writing. This too must be read as displacement: the more critical issue involves the relation of her Castilian texts to Catalan, the subterranean language that breaks through to the surface now and again—such as in a line from "Una novela" (*Baladas*, 53) or in fragments of dialogue in her interviews (such as her interview with her brother Terenci in *24 × 24*)—but that haunts her every page as a mark of alienation. Juan Antonio Masoliver Rodenas's important insight in this regard with respect to Moix's prose may be seen to touch more deeply the revolutionary character of her formal experimentation than had Vázquez Montalbán, by noting that "Moix ... ha roto con la 'buena escritura' del castellano, una buena escritura que poco tenía que ver con el castellano de Barcelona" [Moix ... has broken with "fine writing" in Castilian, a fine writing that had little to do with the Castilian of Barcelona].[6] The predominance of Castilian in her work and the subversive interference of Catalan reflects, on the one hand, a political reality beyond the linguistic sphere, and on the other, constitutes at the most fundamental level of language a case of doubling or split identity such as will be encountered throughout her narrative work in the form of parallelism and mirroring among characters. Yet the issue, so central

to her writing, is never explicitly thematized. Rather one must read
obliquely to discover, for instance, in her recent rewriting of Joyce's
story "The Dead," the submerged allusion to the conflictive relation
between Irish and English: "'And haven't you your own language
to keep in touch with—Irish?' asked Miss Ivors,"[7] even if her
closest counterpart in Moix's "Los muertos" (The dead), Matilda
Orozco, is given no opportunity to speak for herself.

The form of Moix's poetry is deceiving on a second count as well,
for the continuous prose lines—where they are not interrupted by
punctuating blanks, as in the major five-poem sequence in *No time
for flowers*—mask the jarring discontinuity of their content. Images,
frequently related to dreams, are juxtaposed in a technique that
recalls the surrealists. And in those poems which are primarily
narrative rather than lyric (which is to say the majority of her poetic
production), the changing narrative perspective disrupts the linear
development. These, too, will be characteristic of her novels.

Turning to Moix's central thematic concerns in her poetry, one
discovers the elements that she will explore in both *Julia* and *Walter*,
and characters who are "close cousins" of those in the novels. These
are poems of frustrated love and violent death: fratricide in the
Baladas, as Jim kills his brother Johnny in a rivalry for the love of
Nancy Flor; and the suicide, a death by drowning, of "Aquella
chica" (That girl) in the opening sequence of *No time for flowers*.
The interrelated themes of love and death, of death for love, lead the
young poet to much sentimentality. Most often Moix undermines
this sentimentality with irony, as for instance, when the poem
beginning "El corazón de Charo" (Charo's heart) is overturned in
the closing line: "Qué historia más extraña la de algunas colegialas"
[What strange stories there are about some high school girls]
(*Baladas*, 22); or more subtly in "Los adolescentes mojan de
lágrimas" (Adolescents wet with tears), which concludes: "Es difícil
soñar desde la alcoba blanca sin caer en la monotonía de inventar
sombras tras las cortinas, oír pasos por los tejados y recurrir por fin
a las tres avemarías" [It's difficult to dream in a white room without
slipping into the monotony of imaging shadows behind the curtains,
hearing footfalls on the roof tiles and recurring, finally, to three Ave
Marias] (*Baladas*, 23). On other occasions the irony is lacking and
the result reflects an idealism that is at odds with the overarching
tone of disappointment, pessimism, and pain. Such is the case in the
closing image of the ballad sequence, much celebrated in 1968 by
Vázquez Montalbán: "Eran dos sombras para siempre enamoradas:
Bécquer y Ché Guevara" [They were two shadows in love forever:
[Spanish Romanic poet] Bécquer and Che Guevara] (*Baladas*, 45).

The major sequence of *No Time for Flowers* carries Moix's reader closer to the world of her novels. The sordid ambiance of the bars of Barcelona that one will encounter in *Walter* and a story such as "El inocente" (The innocent) in *Las virtudes peligrosas* lies behind the tale of the suicide of *Aquella chica*. The fleeting figure of "Una Mujer" (A woman) in the poem will be more clearly delineated in the prose, even after the work of the censors.[8] And while the detail of the girl who reportedly "no dormía por las noches, puteaba" [did not sleep at night, she whored around] (1971b, 23), but then proves, if only at her autopsy, to have been a virgin, finds no analogue in the novels—Julia is no tramp and Lea is no virgin—the lesson that nothing is what it may seem is crucial to Moix's work at large. One finds in this sequence the logical culmination of the principal images of Moix's poetry, the sea and shadows, understood here more explicitly than elsewhere as phantoms (1971b, 50)—that is, as images of death; for Moix's poetry, like her prose, has more to do with death than with love.

A final point concerning the poetry is relevant to the study of the novels: the intertwining of texts. To select but one moment of crossing, "Es entonces, Federico, cuando mi corazón tiembla arrinconado como un caballito de mar" [It is then, Federico, when my heart trembles, cornered like a seahorse], Moix writes in *Baladas del dulce Jim* (28), a collection that bears more reminiscences of García Lorca than just a name. The reference is taken up again in *No time for flowers* ("¿recuerdas, Federico?" [Do you remember, Federico?] 13), binding the two books together. Other motifs serve the same end, creating the effect of a single, integrated work. For all her allusive richness, the principal elements of Moix's intertextual strategy are self-referential.

The close interconnection of distinct texts is especially visible in the novels, which both treat the growth and death of isolated members of a single extended family centered in Barcelona in the later Franco years.

Julia is a story of a sleepless night. Julia, a young woman, lies alone and terror-stricken, fleeing her present anxieties through a series of reminiscences that, she finds by daybreak and the novel's end, only serve to rediscover that the source of her anxiety lies in fact in the past. The memories that overwhelm her during the course of the night are punctuated by references to the present moment, so that even if Julia's childhood and adolescence are recounted in chronological order, the retrospective distance is maintained. Only in the closing sequences, when the memories are closest in time to the night of their recollection, does the structure of the novel reveal the overlapping of past and present that is its central motive: "Un resplandor insultante le hirió los ojos" [An insulting splendor wounded her eyes] (214) in the hospital as she awakens from the drug overdose of her attempted suicide, but this will also be the light of dawn, when "La luz empezaba a entrar por el balcón" [The light began to enter through the balcony] (219), bringing her recollections to an end. The traditional metaphor of illumination as an emergence from ignorance is sustained, for Julia will come to realize most clearly on the final pages that she is living under the domination of Julita, herself at age six, a self that she has abandoned and who, in turn, takes revenge. But the implicit trajectory that would carry the older Julia from the fetal position in the dark on the first page to a final rebirth—that is, a narrative actualization of a metaphoric *dar a luz* (literally, to give to light, a Spanish idiom for giving birth)— finds no sequel. Were there any room for hope in this first novel by Moix, a work whose predominant tone is suppressed rage, it is annihilated in *Walter, ¿por qué te fuiste?*, where both Julita and Julia reappear, only to have the protagonist of the first novel die at the age of twenty-three on the final pages of the second.

The rage, the sense of abandonment, the need for revenge, and the barrier to conscious understanding that only a long night of unwilling recollection and two hundred and more pages of narration can penetrate, arise from a single episode in the childhood of Julita. At six she is raped by a young man, a friend of the family, at the summer resort that the family frequents in both novels. Since the mobility of Moix's prose allows her to assume all of the narrative positions that Julia recollects—the whole of the novel is presented as recollection but is by no means limited to monologue—the terrible moment is narrated simply, as if by a child who has no under-standing of the sexual motivation; she comprehends, baldly, the violence of the act. Even so the governing elements of the novel, both with respect to its psychology and imagery, are already present: "No dirás nada, idiota" [You won't say anything, idiot] (61), Julia is told by her assailant as he begins to rape her; and "Recordaba que el sol le caía de plano sobre los ojos, no se atrevía a respirar porque el olor del cuerpo de Víctor la mareaba" [She remembered that the sun fell right in her eyes, she didn't dare breathe because the smell of Víctor's body made her feel sick] (61). The rape, then, traumatizes speech, sight, and breathing, in addition to its consequences for Julia's later sexual development.

It might be enough to recall that the light that welcomes Julia back to life in the hospital many years later appears to her as "insultante" (insulting), as evidence of the enduring effects of each detail of the rape. The more prevalent element of Julia's symptomatology, however, corresponds to the stifled breath at the moment of her violation. Thus a typical description of her unspecified anxiety may be glossed by reference to the crushing weight of the adult male body upon the six-year-old girl: "un peso invisible sobre su cuerpo, una inquietud que le impedía respirar, un dolor en el pecho y en la garganta que necesitaba combatir de algún modo" [An invisible weight on her body, an anxiety that impeded her breathing, a pain in her chest and in her throat that she needed to fight somehow] (64). Julia's breathing is indeed both an obsession and a cause for obsessive acts, and as such it is intimately related to her narrative impulse. In order to distract her attention from her own breathing, Julia will concentrate on a phrase or an image, which becomes obsessive in turn, initiating the sequences of her recollections. The narrative pathway of *Julia*, therefore, follows a tortuous route. It begins with the injunction against divulging the secret of the rape. This obstruction to Julia's access to language is then converted into the symptom, or trope, of stifled breathing. Finally, language returns in the narrative of Julia's recollections, but only by becoming itself an obsession that exceeds Julia's control. The troubled current of Julia's reminiscences is, on the one hand, her defense against the perceived menace of the late night hours and her lonely room, and on the other, her language represents the deferred speech of Julita. In short, if Julia cannot control her recollections and their narration, Julita can and does, drawing any and all reminiscences to herself, the six-year-old victim of a rape who has become the Fate of the narrative.

The specific governing figure of the text is itself an image of obstruction: "Julia, sentada en el portal de una casa, pequeña, delgada, los pies descalzos, las trenzas despeinadas, el pantalón corto y el jersey azul marino con un ancla dibujada en el pecho, la mirada baja, fija en dos piedras que machacaba una contra otra" [Julia, seated in the doorway of a house, small, thin, barefoot, her braids coming undone, in short pants and a navy-blue sweater with a picture of an anchor on the chest, her eyes lowered, staring at two stones that she was striking together] (219–20). Here the girl Julita sits, blocking the doorway, silenced and lonely, and trapped forever in childhood: anchored there, as the attribute or aegis on her undeveloped breast announces. And the image will return: the sweater with its anchor will serve to situate *Walter* within the temporal dimensions of the world depicted in *Julia*. For there one meets the same Julita in the same "jersey azul marino con un ancla dibujada en el pecho" [navy-blue sweater with a picture of an anchor

on the chest] (21), as well as the members of her family, including
a large group of cousins.

As the anchor reveals, taken as a temporal index, the relationship
of *Walter ¿por qué te fuiste?* to *Julia* is more one of overlap than
of succession. The broader time-span of the later novel, which
carries the cousins of Julia's generation, if not Julia herself, to
middle age, is less crucial than the change in point of view that opens
up a critical perspective on the earlier work. The Julita who survives
buried within Julia in the first novel preserves a degree of naiveté in
Walter that is startling, and perhaps finally unconvincing, considering the bitterness that formerly characterized the tyranny of the
younger self for the older. In *Walter* Moix allows that bitterness to
find expression as self-knowledge, and the capacity for reflection
thus signaled creates a metatextual dimension absent in *Julia*. The
opening pages of the second novel may be read as a pointed critique
of the first: "¿Acaso puede una frase arrastrarme a algo? Antes sí
... " [Might a phrase draw me to something? Before it could ...]
(15); before, in *Julia*, sentences had exactly this power—in particular
the description of Julita in the doorway.[9] But in *Walter* the pull of
narrative is frequently arrested by the sharply ironic and skeptical
narrator, Julia's cousin Ismael, who calls into question the validity
of his own experiences and the authority of his memory. Hence the
strictly temporal distinction between Julita and Julia in the earlier
novel cedes priority in *Walter*. Here Ismael as both boy and man
together are set in opposition to the same Ismael in the guise of a
cowboy-clown, "The Great Yeibo" (as he is called in English in the
text) in the Royal Amadeus Circus. The distinction is now the narrow
one between self-consciousness and self-parody. The Julia of the first
novel is a suicidal adolescent who survives her own encounter with
death but remains ineradicably melodramatic. The Great Yeibo is a
failed clown no less than a failed writer (his authorship of a text that
is coextensive with Moix's novel notwithstanding), and his antic
disposition is tragicomic, which makes his the wiser tale.

Anarchism is affirmed in both novels as the single positive value,
but the differing treatment of this theme provides a ready contrast
between the two books. The anarchist proper is Julia's paternal
grandfather, Don Julio, who plays a central role in the earlier work:
he is a renegade living in the mountains of Catalonia, notorious
among the older, conservative members of Julia's family as a killer
of priests and nuns in the days of Barcelona's great social turmoil at
the beginning of the century. In *Walter* the role of the anarchist is
reduced in scope from the political program of Don Julio to the
personal rebellion of Julia's cousin Lea, who, far from assassinating

priests, would rather seduce a seminarist, her cousin Augustín. To investigate this shift is to trace the artistic trajectory of the first period of Moix's writing.

In the first novel Moix recounts how Julia is sent to live with her grandfather when her immediate family is beset by twin crises: the disintegration of her parents' marriage and the deteriorating health of her brother Raphael, who will die of an unidentified illness at the age of twenty, when Julia herself is only seventeen years old. The decision to remove her from her home—originally for a period of months, actually for a period of years—reinforces Julia's deepest cause for pain: her mother's preference for her brothers. She finds, however, the maternal warmth that she has most often been denied at home in the person of her aunt Elena. Elena is willing to share a bed with the frightened girl, thereby recalling Julia's most cherished moments with her mother. And as the reminiscences of Julia return to this period in the life of Julita, her narrative omits, for the first time, an explicit reference to the present moment of insomnia: even as recollection, it is a shared bed with an older woman that represents the only effective remedy for Julia's anxious sleeplessness.[10] While Elena may be situated within the series of female characters whose influence is crucial to Julia's formation, including, first and foremost, her mother but also Señorita Mabel, Lydia, and Eva in *Julia* and Lea in *Walter*, as well as related characters in Moix's early collection of stories, one may begin here more simply by noting that it is in the mountain home of her aunt and grandfather that Julia "catches her breath." "Respira hondo, Julia" [Take a deep breath, Julia], Don Julio advises when they are out for their first walk together, "el aire de las montañas matará los microbios de esa peste que respiráis en Barcelona" [the mountain air will kill the germs from that plague you all breathe in Barcelona] (97), as though the change of social (more than physical) environment were sufficient to purge her. It would seem that Don Julio is right on this point; when Julia returns definitively to Barcelona she finds that "le faltaba aire" [she lacked air] (128).

The predominant figure in determining the quality of this new environment is Don Julio himself, rather than Elena, and more broadly speaking, it is Julia's deep admiration for him, untainted by any irony on Moix's part, that defines the naiveté of the novel. Indeed the solemnity with which Moix allows Don Julio to enunciate his philosophy—"Unicamente somos libres" [The only thing is we are free] (97)—is unparalleled in her work. Masoliver Rodenas had already remarked that Don Julio resembled the grandfather in *Heidi* (1974, 10), and this is so; one might almost consider this episode in

Julia as Moix's first incursion into the fairy-tale genre, without the same conscious intention, it would seem, as in her book for children, nor yet the critical penetration of "Erase una vez" (Once upon a time) in *Las virtudes peligrosas*.[11] One may hardly quarrel with a utopian excursus in an otherwise unrelenting text were it not for the inherent self-contradiction of Moix's depiction of Don Julio. For this reclusive anarchist all forms of authority are anathema, except the authority that he himself exercises over his own household. It is all the more problematic, in light of Moix's work from the period of her collaboration in *Vindicación feminista* to the present, that Don Julio's subservient household is comprised exclusively of women: Julia, his daughter Elena, and the servant Martina. Julita grasps the paradox in part when she belabors her grandfather for intervening in the affairs of Elena: "Eres un tirano, ¿no es ella libre?" [You're a tyrant; isn't she free?] (121). At all other moments, however, Julita is a willing accomplice in Don Julio's authoritarian regime, since he includes her in the ruling elite, or as he expresses his intention: "Haré de mi nieta una persona inteligente aunque sea una mujer" [I'll make my granddaughter into an intelligent person, even if she is a woman] (102).

The most important instruction that Julia receives in this regard are the Latin lessons that constitute part of the curriculum of study under her grandfather's tutelage during these years when she is out of school. Her prodigious mastery of Latin will come to be her identifying trait in her adolescence upon her return to Barcelona. She will be recognized by Mabel, her headmistress, and singled out by her aggressive classmate Lydia for her skills, and even her brother Raphael will introduce her to friends with the words "Es muy lista, a los ocho años sabía latín" [She's very smart, she knew Latin when she was eight] (139). But Latin makes a complex inheritance. As an ancestral language in the double sense of its philological relationship to Spanish and of its source, for Julia, in the grandfather who flourished in the separatist atmosphere of Barcelona in the early part of the century, Latin might be regarded as a displaced figure for Catalan in this Castilian text. Within the context of Don Julio's anarchist utopia, moreover, Latin is a synecdochic figure for language in general—and the mastery of Latin for mastery in general. The infancy that was prolonged by the mother's unwillingness to reciprocate Julia's love and thereafter rendered permanent by the fixating effect of her rape, leaves Julita limited to the alternatives of silence and tears before she comes to Don Julio. Latin, therefore, is in some sense the first language that she truly acquires and represents her emergence into the world of reason.

Learning Latin, in short, identifies Julia with Don Julio, which is both the prerequisite and the goal of the education that he offers her. And if Don Julio promotes Latin for the traditional reasons—"es un buen ejercicio para desarrollar la inteligencia y poder leer a los clásicos" [it's a good exercise for the development of the mind and for reading the classics] (105)—it bears an implicit relationship to writing, of which it is, once again, a trope.

Hence, the inaugural scene that precedes Julia's more formal lessons with her grandfather arises out of a moment when she reacts to a taunting letter from her brothers by banging her fist on the table and exclaiming her anger: "Don Julio sonrió. Julita se había expresado como él, con idénticas palabras y gestos" [Don Julio smiled. Julita had expressed herself like him, with the same words and gestures], to which he replies, "Yo en tu lugar contestaría con una carta" [If I were you I'd answer with a letter] (102), initiating her into a writing career that will extend into *Walter*. Yet for all the value that Latin bears for Julia, it remains a dead language—a language of and for the dead—and, consequently, it neither frees her from the overarching melancholy of this and almost all of Moix's work—a melancholy whose most concentrated exploration is to be found in her story "Dedicatoria" (Dedication) in *Ese chico*, nor does it allow her to overcome her "mudez vocacional" (vocational muteness) (in *No time for flowers*, 11).

A further consequence of this initiation into language may be gleaned by recalling the Lacanian schema for the emergence into the "symbolic" order and its attendant limitation as a paradigm for female subjectivity. The episode in the mountains recreates the oedipal conflict as Lacan construes it: an "imaginary" and so inarticulate unity in Julia's relation to Elena, for which Julia's tears and Elena's sympathetic embrace in their shared bed serve as the narrative emblem; the intervention of the *Nom-du-Père* both in the prohibition against crying and the recognition that Julia is after all the namesake of Julio; and a shift from the mother surrogate to the father surrogate as the price for the acquisition of language. Don Julio thus mediates Julia's relationship to language generally, and through language he continues to mediate even her relationships with women. This is true not only with Lydia and Mabel, but thereafter, on a level of greater intimacy and linguistic complexity, Julia's lesbian relationship with Eva, her literature professor at the university, whom Don Julio had preferred as a wife for his son over Julia's mother, and whom Julia herself first meets through Don Julio in the mountains.[12]

The alternative to Don Julio's domination is a nostalgia for mornings in bed with her mother that would withdraw Julia from the Lacanian symbolic. This radical alienation that leaves Julia with no voice as a woman continues to be felt in Moix's prose; and if one recalls that the explicit prohibition that governs the novels in the form of a grotesque *Nom-du-Père* is the rapist's declaration "No dirás nada, idiota," then both Julia's self-destructive impulse and the violence of Moix's language are readily understood. This psychoanalytic excursis also allows a clearer delineation of Moix's project to discover a symbolic order without language, which is to say an articulate and hence mediated relation for women that obviates the tutelage of men and the alienation of female subjectivity.[13]

A significant step toward the realization of this project is achieved in *Walter* through the figure of Julia's cousin Lea. The wraithlike Lea, willful, imposing, even spiteful, is a more anarchic (if less anarchist) figure than the authoritarian Don Julio. She is also, and for that very reason, by far the more lonely. Her unruliness is expressed most keenly through her sexual activity, and the episode out of which the novel's title grows may serve as an ample illustration of her anarchy in action. The seduction of her cousin the seminarist is gratuitous in most respects: there is no suggestion of love on either side and nothing more than a passing hint that there might even be sexual attraction on Lea's part. And if there is certainly malice aforethought, there is no intent to pervert, since such an intention would imply a recognition of prior innocence. On the contrary, it is the presupposition of innocence, whether in priests or in children, the state of grace or the state of nature, that Lea challenges as a hypocrisy fundamental to the mythology—in Roland Barthes's sense—of the ruling bourgeoisie. Lea does not seek to discover hidden passions for her own sake, but rather to oblige her partners to recognize in themselves what they condemn in others, whether the victim of her seduction be a young man preparing to preach sermons or the child Ismael, jealous of Lea's older lovers. There is a second point to Lea's sexual activity: it proves to those who believe that possession is nine-tenths of the law that she is a law unto herself and cannot be subjugated through sexual relations.

The episode of the seduction of the seminarist is further complicated by a deceit that Lea practices upon her younger cousins. In reference to her clandestine trysts, she speaks to them of a certain Walter, answering questions and telling stories that, as they remind her, are not always self-consistent. Eventually the two youngest, most devoted admirers, Julia and Ismael, follow her on one of her escapades, only to find that the mysterious Walter is cousin

Augustín, looking, in the act, very little like a priest-to-be. A deception aimed at the adults in the family circle would have had a clear practical function since Lea was a minor; and in fact she was as willing to resort to subterfuge as to direct confrontation in order to free herself from familial strictures. The fictions of Walter, however, serve a different end with respect to the younger children. Each in turn imagines a Walter in his or her own fashion; each takes the initial situation, the barest narrative hint—"qué más da quien sea, ¿es interesante, no?" [What does it matter who he is, it's interesting, isn't it?] (107)—and tells his or her own story. For Julia and Ismael in particular, Lea is the muse.

The discovery of the true identity of Walter leads to a scene of writing involving the two young cousins. They have spied upon Lea separately but meet together at home under a favorite tree, where Ismael finds Julia engaged in one of her characteristic pastimes. She is digging small holes in the ground and burying the boxes and other objects that she collects:

Cava el útimo hoyo, de la última tarde, del último verano. ¿No entierra nada en el interior? ¿Por qué lo cubre de grava? Con el resto de las piedras va formando letras hasta componer una palabra Gualter. No se escribe con ge, le dices, sino con doble uve. ...Quieres descomponer la inscripción, de una patada, pero no puedes mover las piernas, sólo dices, ¿o piensas?, Walter soy, seré yo.

[She is digging the last hole, on the last afternoon, of the last summer. Isn't she going to bury something inside? Why does she cover it with gravel? With the rest of the stones she is making the letters that compose the word Gualter. It's not written with a "G," you tell her, but with a "W." ... You want to ruin the inscription with a kick, but you can't move your legs, you only say, or do you think? I am, I will be Walter.] (169)

The cousins, who have otherwise worked in close harmony, distinguish themselves from one another here. Julia domesticates the foreign word into a Castilian orthography, but takes it as a proper name for an empty grave. Walter is, for her, a cipher, a signifier that, like the tale told by an idiot—"no dirás nada, idiota"—signifies nothing. It is at most, as Moix reiterates throughout *Julia*, the name for the experience of loss that has no proper object. Ismael, on the other hand, finds the empty grave inadmissible and chooses instead to take on a foreign identity, even at the price of sacrificing his own, in order to maintain the fiction of plenitude. Analogously he will eventually become The Great Yeibo, but more important, he will always bear the burden of that loss that is perhaps more Julia's than his own. One reads interrelated destinies in this scene: Ismael will become a romantic hero, however ironized, and Julia, however obliquely, will be his author.

The scene will be repeated many years later, following Julia's attempted suicide, which is related again briefly in *Walter*. Julia is hospitalized anew, and without further details in the novel, one can only surmise that she is suffering from psychological and not physiological causes. Be that as it may, Ismael visits Julia's institution twice, and the second time he finds that she has already died, leaving a package with the instructions, "entreguéselo a mi primo Walter" [Deliver it to my cousin Walter] (245). The nuns deliver this package to Ismael, and his acceptance in the name of Walter is vindicated when he finds a note inside addressed "Querido Ismael" [Dear Ismael], which reads, "Seguro que volverás a visitarme. Estas cartas son para Lea. Entrégaselas" [I'm sure that you'll come back to visit me. These letters are for Lea. Deliver them to her] (246). This request, ghostly inasmuch as the dead here communicate with the living, reveals at the close of the novel the key to the narrative action that holds together the panoply of reminiscences and disjointed perspectives. As children she and Ismael had been Lea's couriers, bearing her clandestine notes to her lovers. With her death she has at last desisted from the role of messenger, and, breaking the silence of her self-directed speech, she has addressed another person—Lea.

One hears the echo of Don Julio's counsel to write a letter as a dim prophecy fulfilled. And if the present time of narration, and consequently, the narrative itself, are the mediation between and articulation of the relationship of the two women, Julia and Lea, a man, Ismael, remains the necessary go-between. Ismael is a complex and compelling character, and in this regard he is a major advance over Don Julio in the development of Moix's narrative skill, but for that very reason he presents an even more difficult theoretical impasse for the resolution of the problematic relationship of the female subject to language. By Ismael's intervention, what might have been the story of the love between Julia and Lea becomes instead the mock-romance of his own unfulfilled quest: seven years of carrying about Julia's letters in hopes of delivering them to Lea, a task that culminates rather in the late-night middle-aged confidences of two male cousins, Ismael himself and Ricardo, recollecting a youth of incestuous desire.[14] Like *Julia*, then, *Walter* is primarily the story of the obstruction of female relationships, including the relationship to language, wherein the apparition of

Julita in the doorway is merely displaced to the ghost of Julia, now literally dead, in the second novel.

For his own part, in undertaking to execute Julia's last will, Ismael initiates a return journey both toward Lea, who eludes him, and to writing, which he accomplishes. The prior exile, or out-bound journey, came in response to Lea herself, his contrary muse. Ismael had already achieved some success as a poet, although to the chagrin of his politically-minded cousins and their friends, his verses were too personal. He tried to correct this tendency in prose, but his *intimista* (inner-directed) temperament foiled his efforts. It was in this period, when, having reestablished relations with Lea after some years apart—relations that included one night of sexual intercourse and many, alternating with Julia, of sharing Lea's bed—that Ismael recounted to her a plan for a new story:

> Tendida en la cama, y yo sentado en el suelo, apoyado en el borde te contaba: un escritor le cuenta a su amante la historia que va a escribir: la de un escritor que cuenta a su amante una historia por escribir en la que un escritor abandona a la amante porque ella le dice que es él incapaz de escribirla porque es incapaz de abandonarla aunque le diga que es incapaz de escribir la historia en la que lo abandona.

> [You, lying on the bed, and me, sitting on the floor, leaning up against it, I was telling you a story: the one where a writer was telling his lover the story that he was going to write: that of a writer who tells his lover a story to be written in which a writer leaves his lover because she tells him that he is incapable of writing it because he is incapable of leaving her even though he may tell her that he is incapable of writing the story in which she leaves him. (241)[15]

The project has clear autobiographical resonances for Ismael in his relation with Lea, even if he stretches the truth in imagining her as his lover. Her response is more ironic than anarchic: "qué risa, siempre inventas historias que después eres incapaz de escribir. Tú serías incapaz de dejarme sólo por el hecho de que yo asegure que eres incapaz de hacerlo, por lo tanto eres incapaz de escribirlo" [What a laugh, you always make up stories that you're incapable of writing afterwards. You would be incapable of leaving me simply because I assure you that you are incapable of doing so, consequently, you are incapable of writing it] (241). One cannot have one's muse and write her story, too.

Ismael accepts the challenge and abandons Lea, but the task he receives from Julia gives him new purpose for seeking Lea out again. He wanders in search of her as The Great Yeibo, the cowboy-clown,

and is accompanied by Albina, a woman in the body of a horse. This
latter figure introduces a fantastic element that functions effectively
to guard the text against any reductive reading as a drama of psychological realism that has merely been disguised by the splicing
techniques that disrupt the narrative order.[16] The invention of
Albina allows, moreover, for an extraordinary burlesque passage on
the difficulties encountered in the act of love between a man and a
horse-woman, where the irony cuts more sharply against the social
and sexual role of the woman in Albina than against the fantastic sin
of bestiality. Finally, the white body of Albina, taken in combination
with other elements from Moix's writing, may be read as a particular
intertextual inflection of the quest motif. Recalling the plaintive
request enunciated in her poetry: "Call me Stone, please. Call me
Stone. Walter se pasó la vida suplicando ..." [Call me Stone,
please. Call me Stone. Walter spent his life imploring ...] ("Call me
Stone," 1971b, 54), along with Ismael's declaration that he himself
is, or will be, Walter; the ear, alerted by the shift to English in the
name as well as in the plea, may hear Melville's opening words,
"Call me Ishmael," and see in Albina's white body a ghostly
afterimage of the white whale. The emphatic metatextual dimension
of *Walter*, of which Ismael's project for a story is a reflection, gives
an ironic twist to the echo of *Moby Dick*, however. For beyond the
retrospective narration of Ahab's quest by the American Ishmael,
congruent with Ismael's recollections of the summers in T. and the
subsequent years within the family circle, Moix adds the skepticism
of the middle-aged Ismael who doubts his own retrospective glance
and his capacity to formulate it in narrative. There is a further twist
of Melville's tale: when the white whale, or here the white horse,
turns and becomes pursuer, she finds that Ismael is in pursuit of Lea.
Thus one encounters Moix's typical comedy of errors: Albina loves
Ismael who loves Lea (who loves nobody, as her anarchic sentiment
demands). Thus the metamorphosis, itself a common motif in
Moix's early stories, as Jones has noted (1976, 109), may be seen as
an exacerbated form of the lack of recognition inherent in Moix's
depiction of *amor no correspondido* (unrequited love, but more
literally love without correspondence) such as one finds in the story
"Correo urgente" (Special delivery) in *Ese chico*.

Ismael never does deliver Julia's letters. He fails in his quest for
Lea, as he must, if he is to write about it. But having missed her only
by a day at a family gathering in Barcelona, he learns that Lea
"aseguró que hace años escribiste una hermosa historia, dijo si le
veis decídselo" [swears that years ago you wrote a beautiful story,
she said if any of you see him, tell him so] (252). And if he has not
already, he does so now, as in a dream that cannot come true:

"Anoche soñé que había regresado a T." [Last night I dreamed that I had returned to T.] (9). He and Moix begin the novel so that at the end he/she may arrive "hasta el punto de hacerle sucumbir y escribir anoche soñ ...?" [to the point of making him succumb and to write last night I dre ...?] (259).

A critic must be wary of predicting further developments with regard to a writer as young as Moix, especially since she has proven herself to be given to periods of intense activity followed by intervals of relative silence in the nearly twenty years since she figured among the *novísimos*. Nevertheless, the publication of *Las virtudes peligrosas* marks a brilliant return to fiction, especially the title story, which has already led to an especially rich critical response, Levine's "Behind 'Enemy Lines.'" I close, therefore, with a brief speculation on the trajectory that might be drawn from Moix's earlier fiction to "Las virtudes peligrosas."[17]

I begin by noting that here once again Moix works by oblique allusion to set her text in a critical relation to Cholderlos de Laclos's *Les liaisons dangereuses*, so that both "virtudes" and "peligrosas" become complex tropes upon a canonical expression of the prior tropes of the male erotic imagination. This intertextual pathway also serves to highlight the motif of postal correspondence—Laclos's work is an epistolary novel—that is the implicit crux of Moix's story.[18]

"Las virtudes peligrosas" relates the history of a love affair between two women that literally drives the husband of one of them crazy. The love of the two women is never realized in a sexual liaison; rather their contact is limited to a reciprocal gaze at the opera and elsewhere: a gaze that is fixed forever in two portraits that hang opposite one another in that woman's home. The husband's jealous investigations uncover no means of communication between the two women: they never speak, nor do they write to one another. The uncanny regularity with which they find themselves face to face allows a possible reading that would carry interpretation once again to the realm of the fantastic, more specifically to the area of the parapsychology of telepathy. A further detail supports such a reading for those familiar with Moix's previous work: the husband steals in upon his wife one night and discovers her looking out her window at the other woman, who sits astride a white horse; the husband shoots, missing the woman but killing the horse—if, unlike Albina, they may be separated. The result, however, is to convert a possible reality into the ineradicable fantasy that drives him to his death some time later and far from the scene of his wife's supposed infidelity.

Without trying to resolve this issue in favor of telepathy or of some other means of communication overlooked by the husband, it will suffice here as an indication of the course of Moix's writing to stress that in this story she has returned to familiar problems, but with a different outcome. The theoretical impasse that I have outlined in both *Julia* and *Walter* arises as the result of the alienation of women from language. Julia acquires language under male tutelage through her grandfather's instruction in Latin, but male mastery can always turn language against her, compelling her to silence, as, most brutally, Victor does in the moment that he rapes her. Furthermore, the intervention of the male is an inevitable mediation between women in the novels: Julia is introduced to Eva by Don Julio in the mountains and reintroduced to her in the city by her own father, and her relationship to letters embodied by her love for her literature teacher is shadowed by the projection of their previous sexual desire. In the case of Julia's relation to Lea, Ismael's role as middle-man is patent. The confluence of these twin versions of male mediation is found in the form and focus of the narration of *Walter*. Ismael, rather than Julia, narrates the relation between the two women and in so doing he replaces their story with his own; his words bury rather than bear the letters that he carries and, after all, fails to deliver from Julia to Lea.

"Las virtudes peligrosas" seeks a resolution to this impasse by presenting a mediation other than language for the communication between women: a silent calling. Levine's suspicion concerning the silence of these women is well taken, as is her perspicacious assessment of the son: for it is the son, the male voice, that narrates the story. But the son thus articulates the enduring love of these women for Alice and for the reader—not for the women themselves. At the outset, which is to say at the height of their youthful beauty, their relation may yet be imaginary in both the Lacanian acceptation and as a reference to the fantastic. They are doubles and they meet through the *looking glass*, which Moix has transformed in translation into *prismáticos* (opera glasses), glasses to look through, while at the same time retaining the sense of the allusion manifest in the name of Alice—that is, of a mirror in which a single woman sees herself reflected. The son intervenes at this stage of the story as well, for he is the painter of the twin portraits of the women that face each other on opposite walls of the dining room, thereby moving the imaginary doubles to the level of the symbolic. But just as the wife remains indifferent to the authority of the husband's lawful claim to fidelity, refusing to relinquish the attachment to a woman in favor of a man, so too the women both move beyond the confines of the symbolic achieved previously through the son's mediation. They blind themselves—perhaps a measure of Moix's theoretical limitations in thus accepting castration as the fantasmagoric fate of women in the oedipal conflict—but they thereby remove the portraits as an articulation of their love. Moreover, this rejection of the symbolic does not incur a necessary acceptance of the imaginary as the only expression of their relation: blind though they may be, they keep the mirrors veiled.

The correspondence that transforms the unmediated and fantastic love of their youth into the lover's discourse, the enduring story of love, in their old age is accomplished by the exchange of gifts. Each woman adorns Alice with a trinket from a treasure of memories—a ribbon, a pin; each in turn removes the adornment that she finds by sense of touch on Alice's body and replaces it with one of her own. Thus they dress and undress one another, caressing and embracing, but only through the mediating figure of Alice herself. Employed independently by the blind old ladies to read to each in her solitude, Alice believes herself to be a purveyor of texts, when in fact it is her own body, sealed with ribbons that pass from the one to the other, that becomes the wordless letter that they lovingly exchange.

Notes

1. José María Castellet, ed., *Nueve novísimos poetas españoles* (Barcelona: Barral, 1970).

2. Professor Linda Gould Levine has generously allowed me access to the copies of *Vindicación feminista* in her possession. See also her mention of *Vindicación feminista* in 1987, 108 and 1983, 290 and 308–9, as well as an overview of the history of *Vindicación feminista* written by one of its founders, Lidia Falcón, "Vindicación feminista o el ideal compartido," *Revista de Estudios Hispánicos* 22: 53–65.

3. See Ana María Moix, *24 × 24 (Veinticuatro por veinticuatro) (entrevistas)* [Interviews] (Barcelona: Peninsula, 1972), 207.

4. Manuel Vázquez Montalbán, prologue to Moix 1969, 8.

5. Jones 1976, 106.

6. Masoliver Rodenas 1974, 11.

7. James Joyce, *Dubliners* (New York: Modern Library, 1926), 242.

8. Moix boldly addresses a great many subjects in *Walter* that would have been scandalous in Franco's Spain, particularly with regard to sexual mores. Levine notes that "forty-five cuts were made in the novel by the censors prior to its publication, although many were also of a political nature" (1983, 309). Levine also cites Moix as speaking of "the sensitivity of the critics in not mentioning the homosexual overtones of [*Julia*]" (1983, 304).

9. Masoliver Rodenas also sees *Walter* as "una reelaboración de la primera novela, eliminando las aristas de la inexperiencia para crecer en profundidad y complejidad" (a reelaboration of the first novel, eliminating the rough edges of inexperience to grow in depth and complexity) (1974, 9).

10. The novel is divided into twelve unnumbered chapters. Whereas the first four chapters begin with specific references to the minimal physical activities that

accompany the night-long reminiscence—such as smoking a cigarette, rising from bed to go to the wardrobe, and so on—the fifth chapter, in which Julia remembers her arrival at the home of Don Julio, includes no such framing device. It may be noted in passing that the text in *Walter* breaks neither for chapters nor even for paragraphs. In the terms discussed above, therefore, the text presents itself—impossibly—as a single, sustained breath.

11. The figure of Don Julio may also be compared to Ana María Matute's Jorge de Son Major in *Primera memoria* (First memoir) (Barcelona: Destino, 1960), a novel and a novelist of the greatest importance in Moix's formation. Moix's interview with Matute in *24 × 24* gives ample evidence of the younger writer's admiration; see also the opening paragraph of Moix's 1976 essay "Erase una vez . . . La literatura infantil a partir de los años 40" (Once upon a time . . . Children's literature since the 1940s), *Vindicación feminista* 5: 28. Critics have also cited possible sources of influence in Faulkner and Juan Benet (Jones 1976, 107) and Mario Vargas Llosa and Juan Marsé (Masoliver Rodenas 1974, 11).

12. As Jones has pointed out, Eva is to be included in the set of "individualist and rebel" female characters in Moix's work who are linked by "the tantalizing anagramatic similarity of their names" (1976, 113). Jones includes "Ella" of "Ella comía cardos" (She ate thistles) from *Ese chico* as well as Lea in the set, but one might add Julia herself to the list of anagrams (connecting the final diphthong of her name to an English pronunciation of Lea), and possibly even Ism-ael. The meaning of *lea*, taken as an imperative form of *leer* (to read) is also suggestive.

13. Moix's project for founding a communication between women here described might be aligned with Julia Kristeva's privileging of a preoedipal phase in her conceptualization of the semiotic, and it is subject to much the same theoretical limitations. For a recent feminist response to Kristeva, see Mary Jacobus, "*Dora* and the Pregnant Madonna," in her *Reading Woman: Essays in Feminist Criticism* (New York: Columbia University Press, 1986), 137–93.

14. While Levine considers Julia but a "minor figure" in *Walter* (1983, 308), I find, on the contrary, that her presence in the novel continues to be strong enough to undermine Moix's effort to bring the other cousins to the fore. Ricardo, Ismael's interlocutor in the bar, and María Antonia, the object of Ricardo's incestuous desire, fail most notably in this respect.

15. Note that the translation reduces an ambiguity. By choosing the female "historia" rather than the male "cuento" for "story," Moix sets up an ambiguous female pronoun, such that one might read that the writer is incapable of abandoning his story as much as his lover. In short, story and lover are conflated in the gendered pronoun.

16. Nevertheless, the whole text is introduced under the sign of a dream, and it would be possible to read it in its entirety as being governed by the processes of dream-work.

17. The new poems that Moix published in *Litoral femenino: Literatura escrita por mujeres en la España contemporánea*, edited by Lorenzo Saval and J. García Gallego, a special issue of the journal *Litoral* 169–70 (1986), see especially 319, also bespeak an important development that I merely hint at by noting that Moix has chosen a traditional form, the sonnet, with a distinctly baroque coloration in the second poem, that carries her far afield of the iconoclasm of her first collections of poetry.

18. As a critical reading of *Les liaisons dangereuses*, Moix's story might find a place in recent feminist theoretical debate related to that novel as articulated in

Nancy K. Miller's response to Wayne C. Booth; see Miller, "Rereading as a Woman: The Body in Practice," *Poetics Today* 6 (1985): 291–99; and Booth, "Freedom of Interpretation: Bakhtin and the Challenge of Feminist Criticism," *Critical Inquiry* 9 (1982): 45–76. An even more illuminating theoretical contextualization may be obtained by comparing "Las virtudes peligrosas" to Teresa de Lauretis's *Alice Doesn't: Feminism, Semiotics, Cinema* (Bloomington: Indiana University Press, 1984), in part because Moix introduces the story in relation to the medium of film (see Moix, *Las virtudes peligrosas*, 1985, 9).

Bibliography

1. PRIMARY SOURCES

1969a. *Baladas del dulce Jim*. Prologue by Manuel Vázquez Montalbán. Barcelona: Saturno.

1969b. *Call me Stone*. Barcelona: Esplugues de Llobregat, limited edition.

1970. *Julia*. Barcelona: Barral.

1971a. *Ese chico pelirrojo a quien veo cada día*. Barcelona: Lumen.

1971b. *No time for flowers y otras historias*. Barcelona: Lumen.

1973. *Walter, ¿por qué te fuiste?* Barcelona: Barral.

1976. *La maravillosa colina de las edades primitivas*. Barcelona: Lumen.

1984. *A imagen y semejanza*. Barcelona: Lumen. Contains the author's three previous published volumes of poetry (1969a, 1969b, and 1971b.)

1985. *Las virtudes peligrosas*. Barcelona: Plaza y Janés.

2. SECONDARY SOURCES

Jones, Margaret E. W. 1976. "Ana María Moix: Literary Structures and the Enigmatic Nature of Reality." *Journal of Spanish Studies—Twentieth Century* 4: 105–16. A comprehensive overview of Moix's work published to 1976.

Levine, Linda Gould. 1983. "The Censored Sex: Woman as Author and Character in Franco's Spain." In *Women in Hispanic Literature: Icons and Fallen Idols*, edited by Beth Miller, 289–315. Berkeley and Los Angeles: University of California Press. A fine study of Moix's novels that sets them within the context of contemporary Spanish women's writing in general and relates them more specifically to Martín Gaite's *Retahílas* and Matute's *La trampa*.

———. 1987. "'Behind Enemy Lines': Strategies for Interpreting *Las virtudes peligrosas* of Ana Maria Moix." In *Nuevos y novísimos: Algunas perspectivas críticas sobre la narrativa española desde la década de los 60*, edited by Ricardo Landeira and Luis T. González-del-Valle, 97–111. Boulder, Colo.: Society of Spanish and Spanish-American Studies. An insightful essay on Moix's most recent work; concentrates on the title story.

Masoliver Rodenas, Juan Antonio. 1974. "La base sexta contra Ana María Moix." *Camp de l'arpa* 9: 9–12. A valuable early appraisal of Moix's work, concentrating on the novels.

Schyfter, Sara E. 1977. "The Fragmented Family in the Novels of Contemporary

Spanish Women Writers." *Perspectives on Contemporary Literature* 3: 23–29. Brief discussion of *Julia* in relation to a set of Spanish women's novels devoted to fragmented families: Laforet's *Nada*, Medio's *Nosotros los Rivero*, and Matute's *Primera memoria*.

―――. 1980. "Rites without Passage: The Adolescent World of Ana María Moix's *Julia*." In *The Analysis of Literary Texts: Current Trends in Methodology. Third and Fourth York College Colloquia*, edited by Randolph D. Pope, 41–50. Ypsilanti, Mich.: Bilingual Press/Editorial Bilingüe. A psychoanalytic analysis of *Julia*.

8
Esther Tusquets's Fiction: The Spinning of a Narrative Web
Mirella Servodidio

The Catalan writer Esther Tusquets is a relative newcomer to the literary scene, and her success offers a refreshing departure from more conventionally predictive career trajectories. Born on 30 August 1936 to an upper-middle-class family, Tusquets was first educated at the Colegio Alemán in her native Barcelona and subsequently studied "Filosofía y Letras" at the Universities of Barcelona and Madrid, specializing in history. She is the mother of two children. Until the publication of her first novel at age forty-two, Tusquets's reputation was based on her distinguished record as director of Editorial Lumen, a position she assumed in the early sixties and holds to this day. She has been an active and visible participant in Spanish cultural life and regularly contributes articles to Spanish newspapers.

El mismo mar de todos los veranos (1978) (English translation by Margaret E. W. Jones, *The Same Sea as Every Summer*, 1990), Tusquets's stunningly accomplished first novel, created a stir for its unmistakable autobiographic overtones, explicit eroticism, open treatment of lesbian love, and, especially, for the surprising assurance and masterful craftsmanship of its "novice" creator. A veritable "succès d'estime," it appeared to be a work that could not surpass itself. Tusquets's reputation, however, has been securely anchored by a subsequent string of narratives remarkable for their artistic consistency and congruence. *El amor es un juego solitario* (Love is a solitary game) (1979), recipient of the Premio Ciudad de Barcelona, and *Varada tras el último naufragio* (Washed ashore after the last shipwreck) (1980) complete the trilogy initiated by *El mismo mar*. A collection of stories, *Siete miradas en un mismo paisaje* (Seven glances at the same landscape) (1981), a children's tale *La conejita Marcela* (Marcela the little rabbit) (1981), and the novel

Para no volver (Never to return) (1985) are the most recent fruits of a writer who is clearly still in her creative prime.

Tusquets's work locates itself within the broad parameters of the "new novel," associated with the landmark works of Luis Martín-Santos, Juan Benet, and Juan Goytisolo. It is a genre that since the decade of the seventies has engaged in a fluid process of innovation and change that redefines the relationship of the text to itself, to language, and to referential reality. Bearing the markers of the writerly text, Tusquets's fiction is acutely conscious of itself as a literary act and offers a running commentary on its own condition of textuality. Rich in intertextual references and written in a deliberate, opaque style, it is a narrative that commands the active collaboration and attentiveness of the reader.

Tusquets also continues a vigorous tradition of post-civil war narrative by women initiated by Carmen Laforet, whose benchmark novel *Nada* was awarded the coveted Nadal Prize in 1944. While disavowing a direct engagement with the feminist movement, Tusquets nonetheless associates herself with a second generation of women writers who, unlike such predecessors as Rosa Chacel, Ana María Matute, Elena Quiroga, Carmen Laforet, and Carmen Martín Gaite, expressly sets out to inscribe the alienation of female heroes within patriarchal culture. Indeed, her fiction provides a compelling statement of the paradigmatic fit between individual psychic structure and the social, economic, and sexual arrangements that prevail in post-civil war Spain, and it problematizes the difficulties women face in arousing themselves from the habits of conformity and dependency that are the products of social conditioning. The author's persistent thematic concerns with alienation, decision-making, and death, filtered through a feminine perspective, also bear the unmistakable traces of existential philosophy, that strange bedfellow of Franquism to which she alludes in *Para no volver*.[1]

Offering recurring variants of interlocking themes and characters, Tusquets's opus creates a continuum of diverse yet harmonious parts that form a seamless whole. Novel confronts novel with its own revision or complement, a silent parody and extension of itself. With differences only of emphasis and degree, each becomes a ramification of a single gender-marked tale located within a subsistent order that negates the separation of individuals or the passage of time.

With the exception of the stories of *Siete miradas*, squarely placed in the two decades following the civil war, Tusquets's novels are written from within the framework of the post-Franco period. Nonetheless, the liminal situations in which the female heroes find themselves provoke the review and assessment, for each, of the crucially formative Franco years. The specific referential reality—that of the Catalan upper bourgeoisie—is never foregrounded, yet it remains a consistent target of the author's barbs. Indeed, her combined writings offer a vivid delineation of the ethos of a ruling consumer class (allied with Franco during the civil war) that is insular and complacent. In this "papier mâché" orbit, in which the prevailing sociolect is an empty aesthetic of good form, material wealth is subtended by spiritual impoverishment. It is the site of a saga of failures on both a collective and individual scale: failures of love, of nerve and of imagination, and more important, of the failed leadership of the intelligentsia in shaping a national agenda in the post-Franco era.

By casting the female protagonists as members of an intellectual elite and therefore as readers and assimilators of texts, Tusquets succeeds in highlighting the influence of literary codes on the psychosocial development of women. The question of texts, reading, and interpretation is continuously thematized in her writing, revealing the manner in which fiction and reality intersect, mime each other, and reinforce cultural patterns. Sensitive and painfully aware, Tusquets's marginalized female heroes are as inefficacious as their fellows in striking a blow for change.

El mismo mar de todos los veranos is not only statistically the first novel of Esther Tusquets, it is also the progenitor of all her works to come, for these are no more than the diverse intonations of an artistic universe that is already developed and in place. The shaping sensibility of this first-person confessional narrative is that of a mature, privileged professor of literature who, viewing her life as text, recounts the conflictive tales that define her reality. The novel begins with the displacement of the "fiction" of her happy marriage to Julio, a famous movie director, by another conventional, oft-repeated tale: his blatant infidelity, most recently with a young starlet. Wishing to write herself out of this script, the narrator returns to the vacant first home of her parents that is the synecdochic throwback to a childhood self that is also symbolized by the spring season in which the novel is set. There, in a freely associative "remembrance of things past," she initiates an agonizing quest for an authentic self buried in the myths and fairy tales, both read and invented, of childhood and adolescence. The pre-Oedipal matriarchal substratum of this narrative is unmistakable, for the failure of the mother-daughter mirroring bond is the driving force, both emotionally and scripturally, of the hero's life story. The analogy between mother-daughter bonding and textual bonding is clear. Barred from unity with her mother, the child seeks a compensatory closeness to the tales that are the traditional repertoire of childhood reading. Wishing them to mirror her own existential dilemmas and lacks, she reconfigures them into a single story from which all happy endings have been proscribed.

The failed mother-daughter story is followed, during her university years, by the Jorge story—a tale of dashed illusions and unrequited love that is recounted at the novel's near conclusion. Jorge, the brash outsider, iconoclast, and revolutionary, promises freedom from an asphyxiating social order as well as personal validation. His unexplained suicide, on the eve of their elopement, causes the narrator to question her very existence and reactivates the absence and void created by maternal rejection. Mentally casting herself as the Ariadne to Jorge's Theseus, she is again the victim of a fiction with an unhappy end.

The novel's central story, that of Clara, might well be called "The Bourgeoisie at Play," for it is a tale of the progressive erosion of values of a decadent social class that is engaged in sexual games of power and narcissistic perversion. The cynical, abulic narrator, trapped in the deadly tedium of her nonlife, responds to the seductive description of Clara, a Colombian student, in an erotic plot of lesbian love scripted by Maite, her decadent friend. What finally draws her to Clara, however, is the self-recognition that the young girl stirs, for in her waiflike plainness and frailty, she offers a specular image of the narrator as a young girl. Conversely, as reflected in Clara's eyes, she takes on the centrality and desirability associated with her mother. With Clara as rapt audience, the narrator—like a new Penelope—weaves and reweaves the desolate strands of her past while hovering on the threshold of a new beginning. In their tender lovemaking she arrives at last at a state approximating symbiosis as she becomes mother-lover to herself.

Comprising the novel's central section, this unorthodox love story, which challenges sociocultural norms, inscribes a cyclical, spatialized time that subverts narrative convention. However, the work's concluding episode reinstates linear time and restores a "normal" order, for at the urging of the narrator's mother, Julio returns to claim his errant wife. The narrator proves unable to respond to Clara's challenge to coauthor the last chapter of their common story. Instead, she relocates herself in a patriarchal text that blocks her progression from reader to writer of herself.

Much as the play of light brings into relief the differing facets of a single stone, *El amor es un juego solitario*, Tusquets's prize-winning second novel, reimages the contours of the universe depicted in *El mismo mar*. Like the narrator of the first novel, Elia—the indolent, central character—is a literate woman of a hegemonic, decadent class for whom marriage, motherhood, and privilege do not ward off existential tedium and despair. The conspicuous absence of her husband and children from the space of the novel signals relationships as distant as those of Tusquets's first work.

Located solipsistically in the stifling space of her chamber (mind), Elia yields to the anaesthetizing lethargy that is her defense against the fear of life, time, and death that periodically assails her. Like her predecessor she engages in a looking-back that is rooted in the shaping experience of a childhood reading that encodes deviance and alienation. An innocent book of adventures, contaminated by an obscene interpolation that describes primates mating in springtime, becomes the signifier of a childhood stigmatized by the neglect and scandalous conduct of wealthy parents who flout the conventions of a closed Spain in the 1950s. Elia's life—just as that of the female hero before her—exemplifies the proposition that one is what one reads, for her serial adulteries are irremediably patterned on this originating childhood text. Also set in springtime, the novel finds Elia—like her counterpart—entering into a "game" of love that first involves the sexual initiation of Ricardo, a university student and aspiring poet of a fallen middle-class family, and then expands to include Clara, Ricardo's classmate. Along with Elia, her young lovers embody a psychosexual problem of "difference" marked by the failure of mother-child bonding and which conditions the values and attitudes each brings to love. As in *El mismo mar*, the unorthodoxy of their relationship undermines sociocultural codes, breaking out of all boundaries and exclusions. A final segment of three-way sex and sodomy points unmistakably to the conclusion that the frenetic coupling of the characters has nothing to do with love. Joined sexually, the three nonetheless remain apart, their problematic of difference unaltered and unresolved.

Notwithstanding the direct kinship of *El amor* with its predecessor, the novel offers differing permutations of the game of love. Elia does not strive for radical change or happiness in spring, as does her precursor. Instead, the inalterable otherness that is her ontological reality restricts Elia's dreams and desires, narrowing them ritualistically to these spasmodic episodes of sexual euphoria. This deliberately programed decadence is governed by equally implacable laws of narration that are upheld by a third-person authorial voice. Obeying a rigorously symmetrical design, the unfolding of the story is marked by discernible spatial units that correspond to the differing perspectives of the three players.

Despite the evident correlation between psychosexual codes and the game codes of society, the novel's historic reference is weaker than that of *El mismo mar*. Literature itself is the supreme referent of *El amor*, defining the characters primarily as consumers and producers of literature rather than players, lovers, or citizens. The story of the lives of the three principals becomes the story of the telling of the story. Each is shaped by prior readings that are the intertextual fodder for the production of personal scripts or coauthored scripts in which they are actively creating or being created by one another.

If love is but a game, it is then a game of the imagination, a literary act. It is also very much a "juego solitario" for, while the stories of the three characters are paired frenetically, they ultimately resist integration. Narrative collaboration (like love) proves to be a simulacrum, for each author is, in fact, engaged in a solitary struggle for power of mastery and completion. Their self-referential and disparate texts ultimately shape themselves into a model of literary onanism, the "sucio juego literario" (dirty, literary game, 150) that is identified, at last, in the novel's final sentence and that is its dissimulated referent. Indulging the narcissistic reveries in which copulation is conjured as the stimulant for self-arousal and gratification, each of the principals instigates an endless circuit of fiction, interpretation, and desire that undermines the linearity of mimesis. This literary gamesmanship forecloses the ennobling aspects of love first promised and then denied in *El mismo mar* and instead inscribes the darkly self-defeating side of a human nature that already stands beyond redemption.

Varada tras el último naufragio completes Tusquets's trilogy. Spun from the same thread, the novel reimages the characters and concerns of the previous works and foreshadows the emergent themes of *Para no volver*, published five years later. The novel's consanguinity with *El mismo mar* is especially marked. Locating itself in the same landscape, *Varada* also takes as its central focus the alienation of a middle-aged writer, Elia, who suffers a depression caused by the recent dissolution of her marriage. The placement of the work within a narrow, liminal framework, the rupture of linear time through flashbacks, and the reproduction of an identical referential reality seal the kinship of the two works.

Jorge, the defecting husband who shatters the myth of Elia's ideal marriage, is a direct spinoff of the Jorge recreated in the painful ruminations of the narrator of *El mismo mar*. A romantic stranger like his predecessor, he rescues her from an identical habitat—the "land of dwarfs" that is Catalonia—and childhood pathology—the crippling loss of self-esteem created by failed mother-daughter bonding and paternal indifference. Through the haven Jorge's love provides, Elia is able to blunt the edge of a lifelong obsession with death that echoes that of the Elia of *El amor*. In this paradigmatically Freudian struggle of Eros and Thanatos, love strikes the winning blow, consigning death to the margins of Elia's reality. The dependency this relationship creates fails to prepare Elia for a freedom that she has never sought. With Jorge's departure she develops a reliance on the barbiturates that her psychiatrist, Miguel, supplies and that foster stupor and inertia. The novel charts Elia's gradual recovery, a trajectory that begins with the erasure of her personal history (she destroys all her possessions) but ends with the excavation of that buried, encrypted self upon which any change must be founded.

Like *El amor*, the novel uses a third-person narrative and a shifting point of view to weave in the perspective of the other existentially "ship-wrecked" characters. Elia's experience is repeated in the marital crisis of Eva, her closest friend who is a feminist labor lawyer and a political activist from the time of their shared university years. Eva's liberalism and self-sufficiency are challenged and shattered by the midlife crisis that propels her "free-thinking" husband, Pablo, into a conventionally "machista" relationship with a girl half his age. From a fallen middle-class family, Pablo (the mature version of Ricardo) has sacrificed his gift for writing in the pursuit of the material comfort that will redress the deprivation of his youth. Feeling marginalized by his wife's independence, Pablo dreams of a new beginning, both sexual and artistic, but ultimately suffers from a loss of nerve. The Clara of *Varada*, like the two Claras before her, is the casualty of a pre-Oedipal love fantasy now centered on Eva, who has befriended her for the summer. The shifting viewpoint allows a rotating assessment of every character by each of the others. The result is a fully rounded portrait that captures the ambiguities, contradictions, and complexities of human nature.

As in the other novels, *Varada* engages in self-conscious code-switching designed to dramatize the interactive play of literary codes and social reality. The mythification of love, friendship, and fidelity—shaped by the combined readings of the characters—gives way to a growing awareness of the fissures between reality and imagination. Elia and Clara, in particular, are the heroes (and victims) of their own delusional fictions in which happy endings are invariably prescribed. If Clara is permanently lodged in a fanciful bestiary that recasts her childhood reading, Elia is finally able to break loose from the literary codes that entrap her. She comes to see

Jorge as the fictive construct of her own mythmaking and of her blind faith in the power of his illocutionary speech-acts to eternalize love and to leave death defanged. Her principled resistance to reconciliation with Jorge, at the novel's conclusion, contrasts with the sordid, if pragmatic, compromise struck by Eva and Pablo.

The seven stories of *Siete miradas en un mismo paisaje*, quarried from the recollections of a mature narrator, chart the crucial milestones in the life of a female protagonist, Sara, from the time she is nine until she turns eighteen. The interdependence of the stories creates the equivalence of a fourth novel, the "pre-text" of the Tusquets trilogy, which delineates the inaugural stages of the mature hero's life. The placement of the stories reveals an authorial intent to break with a linear reconstruction of the past, for while they are set in a specific timeframe (1945–57), they jump forward and backward without regard for chronology.

Although they map Sara's "sentimental education," the stories of *Siete miradas* engage in a greater privileging of the cultural text that is the work's determining point of reference. The reader is given a full sweep of the political, ideological, and religious beliefs, the values, habits, and artifacts that are the paraphernalia of culture. The education, tribal customs, and habits of play of the upper bourgeoisie are brought into sharp focus, and dualities of inner-outer, center-margin, superstructure-substructure, female-male are clearly posited, defining the interplay of repressed and master voices as the agon of history.

Aligning herself with the downtrodden, the peripheral, and the misunderstood, Sara opposes the vacuous consumer society to which she belongs. Her social conscience and solidarity with the "losers" in the Franquist text in "Los primos" (The cousins), "La casa oscura" (The dark house), "Orquesta de verano" (Summer orchestra), and "Exiliados" (Exiled) refract the large-scale struggle and contesting of power relationships in civil war Spain. The social facts of history that undergird Sara's youthful protests are expressed figurally through effects of spatialization that delineate the zones separating winners and losers, men and women, servants and masters, adults and children, and which are punctuated by the repeated references to thresholds, doors, and passageways demarcating the border-crossings from power to privation. Sara's forays into the arts (dance in "Giselle" and acting in "He besado tu boca, Yokanaan"—I have kissed your mouth, Yokanaan) are also driven by the desire to break with rigid patterns of class and gender. Her romantic crushes and sexual initiation in "En la ciudad sin mar"

(The city without a sea) and "He besado tu boca, Yokanaan," involving men who are social and ideological "outsiders," describe a similar urge to cut loose the moorings of factuality.

The rebellions and crises that mark Sara's rites of passage are conveyed in overcharged tonalities that take on a heightened life-and-death quality. Ultimately they point only to the excesses of youthful imagination. Sara's idealism, her dramatic impressionability, her faith in love as the ultimate equalizer are but the stuff of adolescent dreams. These aspirations are cruelly subverted by the desultory skepticism of authorial hindsight that registers the inadequacy of human power to shape the world—or even that small part of the world called the self.

Para no volver carries the thematic concerns of Tusquets's opus to a new level by using the psychoanalytic situation in which the protagonist finds herself as the catalyst for pointing conclusively to the link between psychosexuality and the sociocultural realm. In the process the author effectively challenges the proposition that psychoanalysis is ahistoric. She also succeeds in illustrating that the concept of "normality" is itself normative and thereby implicated in sociocultural judgment.

The novel covers a full spectrum of intertextual references ranging from the master texts of Freud and Marx to the popular print media, cinema, and television. While *Para no volver* shares with its immediate predecessor an increased emphasis on referential reality, the case history of Elena, the protagonist, largely reproduces the lives of the mature heroes of the trilogy, as in a game of shifting mirrors.

In the autumn in which she turns fifty, Elena sinks into a midlife depression that is vexed by the departure of Julio, her film-director husband, who has embarked on a promotional tour of the United States with his nubile mistress. Her two sons have also struck out on independent courses, plunging Elena into the unaccustomed solitude of an empty nest. Like her predecessors, Elena uses sex and barbiturates as temporary palliatives for loneliness and a fear of death. However, she moves beyond the pharmacological solutions on which Elia placed reliance in *Varada* when she enters a psychoanalytic situation designed to extricate the causes of her painful self-refutation.

While Elia's experience is embedded in the particularity of the post-Franco years, *Para no volver* raises universal questions relative to the development of the female psyche that find particular resonance in the writings of contemporary feminist theoreticians.

Using a feminist perspective, Tusquets problematizes the dominant concepts of a Freudian mastertext (penis-envy, castration anxiety, and the like) that theorize psycho-sexual development around the experiences of a male child, and that posit women's difference as developmental failure. Tusquets raises important questions about power, discourse, psychoanalysis, and women that turn on the epistemological inequality between the analytic interlocutors.

Because the novel traces the course of Elena's analysis, the reader follows the shape of her beliefs, her evasions and deceptions, her journeys toward and away from the stated truth. We witness her desperate struggle against the protocol of the patient-analyst relationship, her reactions and overreactions to the "wise-one's" maddening silence, which she interprets as indifference to her plea for intimacy. We are especially made to focus on Elena's entrenched resistance to self-knowledge, effected by ironic posturing, banalization, and parody. Elena's odyssey toward truth, after all, exacts a serious penalty—the forfeiture of the cherished myths that sustain her, along with the members of her class and generation.

The first of these myths pertains to the intellectual elite, the academics, professionals, and artists that are part of Elena's circle. No longer the paladins of democracy or the heralds of a new order, they offer a specular image of the pro-Franco establishment they once decried. A second myth, that of an artistic community muzzled by censorship and repression, is overturned by the embarrassing paucity of talent of the post-Franco years. Julio exemplifies the artist who compromises his integrity because he is unable to define himself outside of the socioeconomic system and its rewards. His story shares center stage with those of the novel's other failed artists: Eduardo, a painter and the occasional lover of Elena; Andrea, an actress; and Elena, herself an unpublished writer.

Elena is the product of the "unnatural marriage" of Franquism and French existentialism that unfolds in the 1950s and 1960s. Her bohemian pilgrimages to Paris and Perpignan in which she avidly assimilates the films, erotic magazines, and Marxist texts that are censored back home, fail fundamentally to alter her status as a "burguesita de pro" (a pro-Franco petit bourgeois, 53). With her marriage to Julio she, in fact, renounces her professional identity, becoming adept at "el sucio juego, tan femenino, de adorar a su hombre como si se tratara de un dios" [the dirty feminine game of adoring her man as if he were a god] (101) and she is as guilty of defining herself in a relationship of dependency as the bourgeois wives she has derided. In the course of her analysis, Elena begins to question her "ideal marriage," her deference to the opinion of others and her absorption of the discursive systems of a socio-economic order that excludes her. Having acted as Julio's nurturer, caretaker, helpmate, and muse (the "Woolfian" looking-glass reflecting the patriarch at twice his size), she rages inwardly when he fails to publicly acknowledge the role she has played in his accomplishments. The myth of maternal altruism is also exploded as Elena comes to see that her centrality in the family universe has been largely self-engineered and self-serving.

Elena's resistance to analytic discourse is therefore punctured by stray glimpses of truth and self-recognition that point to her own accountability in a life story of arrested development and failed opportunity. What is the appropriate conclusion in a narrative of female development? Tusquets leaves her readers with mixed signals that eschew tidy endings or facile solutions. With Julio's return, Elena lapses into her habitual role of "angel in the house." Yet her mental resolution to "initiate" analysis suggests a possible pathway to self-actualization.

If *Para no volver* relies explicitly on a psychoanalytic intertext, it is also true that Tusquets's other works draw widely on those principles of psychoanalysis that point to the determinative influence of early childhood and unconscious desire. Freighted with the cargo of a "congoja paradigmática e inicial" [a paradigmatic and initiatory anguish] (*Siete miradas*, 125), Tusquets's protagonists are the keepers of "un personalísimo museo de los horrores, imágenes que hemos ido acumulando ... desde la infancia" [a personal museum of horrors, images that we have been accumulating . . . since infancy] (*Para no volver*, 187) that arrests them psychologically despite their mature years. While they engage in a tireless looking back in search of origins and authentic selfhood, their restless scrutinies, driven by a compulsion toward "lo reiterativo y lo ritual" [the reiterative and ritualistic] (*Siete miradas*, 186), merely certify the conviction, variously expressed, that time is indeed irreversible. The sameness of their reenactments and symptomologies creates a sense of stasis and simultaneity despite the timeline of different serial events depicted by each work. In fact, their combined stories coalesce in extension of a principle of identity that shapes a single tale that might well be described by the title of Freud's key essay "Remembering, Repeating and Working Through."[2]

The crucial distinctions delineated in Freud's essay are effectively represented by the behavioral patterns of Tusquets's characters. The unconscious repetition that occurs when recollection is blocked through repression and resistance, variously demonstrated in Tusquets's trilogy, is explicitly problematized in *Para no volver*.

Here Elena's analyst analogizes this mechanism to the inefficacious reproduction of an erroneous mathematical computation and adds: "De poco han de servirte las repeticiones, puesto que te equivocarás siempre en el mismo punto" [Repetitions will serve you little since you will always err on the same point] (31). Instead Freud holds that only in the as-if realm of transference can the affects of the past be symbolically worked through in the present. Similar to this "fictive" medium of analysis, the same-but-different stories of Tusquets's characters are, in Freud's words, "revised editions" of old texts.[3]

The communicative system of analysis is an axial aspect of this process. However self-absorbed Tusquets's heroines appear, they make an explicit or implicit claim on the attention of an interlocutor or addressee that is crucial in the finding and making of meaning. While the impulse to tell is prompted by a full array of motivations ranging from the erotic to the altruistic, it is almost always driven by the desire to be heard, recognized, and understood—to enunciate a significant version of the story of life, as Elena makes plain: "La gente, muy necesitada de que alguien la escuche, para que anden todos anhelantes por los caminos de la vida a la caza y captura de ... un interlocutor válido" [People, very needy of someone who will listen, so that—in yearning—they travel the paths of life to hunt and capture ... a valid interlocutor] (*Para no volver*, 169).

In *El mismo mar*, the narrator's full recovery of the past awaits the arrival of a sympathetic interlocutor. Clara's silent presence suffices to activate a transferential process that effects a crossover with her childhood: "La historia de Clara y la mía ... un mero pretexto para contar y revivir viejas historias" [Clara's story and mine ... a mere pretext to tell and relive old stories] (104). Here narrative arousal is more narcissistic than erotic. Asking for the admiration and attention denied by her mother, the narrator's story is but "un pretexto ... para ofrecer esta preciosa imagen de mí misma" [a pretext ... to offer this precious image of myself] (179). The narrative transaction that follows allows the events of the past to be symbolically transcribed into the present, and "La casa, Clara, mi infancia son de repente una misma cosa" [The house, Clara, my infancy are suddenly one and the same] (153). Through a process of metaphorical equivalence, the Clara story also unearths the censored text of the narrator's adolescent love for Jorge that has been entombed without a listener. Painfully dredged up in segments, it is eventually reestablished in a circuit of communication. Yet despite the conscious restoration of this past tale, the narrator cannot countervail its insistent and numbing effect on the present and complete the cure, stimulated by transference, that will allow her life story to progress. Clara's single utterance, drawn from Barrie's masterpiece, "Y Wendy creció" [And Wendy grew up] (229), offers a contrast, by semiological implication, with the narrator's psychological stasis. Bereft of transformation, her life remains linked semantically to the sea of the novel's title, *El mismo mar de todos los veranos.*

El amor es un juego solitario engages in continuous rhetorical exchanges shaped by the investments of desire of the three principals. Yet the very centrality of interlocution dramatizes the failures of telling and listening and the attendant failure of cure.

As a speaking subject Elia is her own object of desire. Her erotic narratives addressed to a changing cast of listeners are exhibitionistic in their design: "Necesita siempre oyentes renovados ... Elia necesita verse reflejada" [She needs constantly new interlocutors ... Elia needs to see herself reflected] (93). Yet her stories involve a disavowal of the principles of transference, for they paper over the alienation and fear of death that have tormented her since childhood.

In her first meeting with Ricardo, Elia hovers on the threshold of a genuine re-presentation of the past, as in transference. Viewing him as a potentially valid interlocutor, she initiates a discourse that gives voice to the "niña perdida ... desorientada" [(the) lost ... disoriented child] (35) that resides within her and that elicits a contractual relationship of redemption from her listener. Ricardo's lack of receptivity renders this story inoperable and it is withdrawn and replaced with a self-consciously precious text that is coauthored and that glosses over reality.

More than Ricardo, Clara is the ideal interlocutor who is "Tan atenta, tan sensible, tan respetuosa y receptiva" [So attentive, so sensible, so respectful and receptive] (93). Cast primarily as the compliant receiver of Elia's discourse, Clara is betrayed by her interlocutor, who sacrifices her to the discursive requirements of an erotic tale of three-way sex. When Clara initiates some telling of her own, she is as guilty of narrative dishonesty as Elia, for she does not enunciate her feelings candidly to her lover. The failed tellings and listenings of this novel stand as an analogue of psychosis or neurosis that obstructs the "working through" of a transferential relation. Elia, in particular, is caught in a web of Freudian repetition that mires her in the psychological bog of the past. She remains that desolate child for whom evolution is an impossibility.

Varada tras el último naufragio also addresses the problematic boundaries of telling and listening and the complexities of narrative transmission. The fictions by which Elia dreams, interprets, and constitutes herself as a human subject are largely shaped by the deficits of childhood and by the search for an interlocutor who will serve as a "bridge" to the outside world. The assured and insolent texts she produces in her university years camouflage Elia's pervasive lack of self-esteem. These are followed by a circular love story that deflects the threat posed by a competing text: a linear narrative that lurches forward implacably toward death. Her tale of seduction is designed for Jorge, the ideal interlocutor, who—in receiving it—will confer worthiness upon her as an object of desire. The repetitive insistence and enactment of satisfaction of this story creates a relationship of dependency of the speaker on the listener. It is a story so rigidly drawn as to preclude an evolving reality and leaves no space for alternate addressees (such as her son). When Jorge leaves her, Elena is "incapaz totalmente de escribir" [totally incapable of writing] (48). This narrative silence into which she lapses stands as the signifier of a mechanism of repression that explains her immediate cessation of a lifelong effort to "rescatar los fragmentos de un pasado ... desentrañar la clave, saber cómo fue una en realidad, cómo fueron los otros, por qué se han desarrollado luego así las cosas" [to salvage fragments of the past ... to uncover the key, to know how one was in reality, how others were, why things have developed as they are] (11). Elia's relationship with her psychiatrist exemplifies the polar opposite of Freudian transference for, although Miguel encourages her to submit her emotions to intellectual consideration, he resorts to a lecturing that precludes dialogic exchange or the possibility of his conversion into the fictive object of her past desire. In radical opposition to the talking cure, Elia clings to the belief that "mientras no se formule y reconozca en palabras ... no comenzará el auténtico dolor" [as long as it is not formulated or acknowledged through words ... authentic sorrow will not begin] (44). Unguided, her self-knowledge evolves slowly and incrementally. At the novel's conclusion Elia's progress is directly linked to the restoration of language since she is moved for the first time to draft a letter to her son, an action that betokens a renewal of interlocution, narrative aperture, and desire.

In the stories of *Siete miradas en un mismo paisaje*, the jaundiced narrator engages in a retelling that is predicated on an interchange with her former selves. The idealistic and passionate enunciations of the past are subverted, undermined, or corrected through a process of retrospective assessment that tends to efface the traditional distinctions of narrative transaction, for she is both teller and listener, both the sender and receiver of discourse, both storyteller and story told.

The centrality of interlocution in the finding of meaning is, of course, expressly certified in *Para no volver*. The earlier works explore and rehearse a terrain that is now rendered immediate and from which there is no pulling back. Elena has assimilated a Freudian vocabulary that consciously counterposes the pitfalls of "repetition" with the benefits of "remembering and working through." The greatest challenge she faces is the translation of passive knowledge into the language of action and personal mastery. Though she is schooled in the principles of analytic discourse, Elena is largely unsuccessful, for she warily views the therapeutic situation as a battle of wits and wills. She is intellectually capable of acknowledging the susceptibility of transference to failure if it is allowed to become the principal agency of resistance, but Elena nonetheless endangers the success of her treatment by resisting or faking the free associations that are essential to analysis. The "como si fuera" [as-if] (121) of the transferential process becomes a spurious, self-conscious game designed to safeguard "la última cámara de su intimidad . . . cuya más honda esencia consiste en no saberse" [the last chamber of her intimacy . . . whose most profound essence consists of not knowing herself] (175). *Para no volver* introduces the belief expressed by feminist critics that while analytic transference depends on metaphoric interpretation, it must also achieve a metonymic contiguity with the patient's life to be successful.[4] Thus Elena resists the "symbol-hunting" of Freudian interpretation but is quite open to examining the circulation among the unconscious, history, and gender. Although the novel traces the beginning of a breakthrough, as Elena comes to analyze herself, Tusquets staunchly resists the temptation to delineate a therapeutic success story. Instead she gives us a novel that is faithful to the complexities attendant on the disclosure, through analytic discourse, of unconscious desire and that stresses the important contiguity of the individual psyche and culture.

If Tusquets's self-absorbed characters yield to the need for a listener to engage in narrative exchange, her self-reflexive texts make an equal claim on the attention of the reader, who is called upon to collaborate in the creation of textual meaning. In the encounter with the text, the reader-analyst discovers an unmistakable articulation of psyche and text, for the developmental successes and failures of Tusquets's female heroes impinge upon narrative structure and movement, authorial voice, and style. Content, therefore, is not a freestanding truth but instead converges directly with form.

With repetition as the shaping energy of Tusquets's fiction, the textual present is continuously subtended by the textual past. As in the talking cure, the representation of the unconscious appears in the symbolic realm of language, binding texts rhetorically through similar tropes of psychic desire: images, allusions, comparisons, synecdoches, metaphors, and anaphoras, which are reproduced from work to work, strengthening the web between narrative past and present. On the level of story, Tusquets's works also create an enchainment of signification through a persistent doubling back and zig-zagging movements within and across texts that produce the metaphorical mirroring and metonymic linkage associated with analytic interpretation and transferential reading, respectively. The first of these locates the thematic content of the unconscious that is common to all her works; the second emphasizes the contiguities of text and text, of text and subject in the register of desire. Together they shape an alternate, unitary plot that explores the possibility of female authority and symbolic expression.

Tusquets's fiction establishes a homology between sexuality and textuality that gives shape and substance to an erotics of form. Unlike the forward movement of masculine narrative that leads to a single discharge of erotic energy, her fiction turns back on itself in a prolongation of arousal and appetition. The central section of *El mismo mar*, for example, delineates a pre-Oedipal narrative that unleashes a specifically female libidinal economy expressed in an intonational language that stands outside of patriarchal discourse. However, the lingering voluptuousness of this cyclic tale is subverted by the urgency of a male narrative of entry, violation, and climax that leads to narrative closure. In *El amor*, the correlation between narrative and linguistic structure and the structure of desire is also clear. Elia's first meetings with Ricardo—extended sessions of intimacy and seduction that are conducted exclusively on the level of discourse—highlight the significance of sexual and textual foreplay in a female erotics of form. Anticipation and the deferral of coitus are strategies preparatory to (narrative) climax. However, because (female) desire is multiorgasmic, Elia must reenact this tale of seduction with an ever-rotating cast of readers. In *Para no volver* and *Varada*, the lack of appetition of the inorgasmic female heroes is also illustrated by narrative voice and form. Elia's eroticism in *Varada* is held captive to a self-authored script that no longer has artistic credibility. Her loss and subsequent recovery of (verbal) desire is marked by the transition from a third- to a first-person narrative voice at the novel's conclusion. The abrupt banishment of all signs of punctuation accompanying Elia's final assumption of discourse heralds a freedom of movement through narrative space and a new openness to verbal intercourse. Finally, in *Para no volver*

Elena's free associations are as devoid of authenticity as the orgasms that she simulates. Her eventual resolution to confront herself squarely has both textual and sexual implications, for the initiation of genuine discourse is paralleled by the climax she finally experiences with her lover.

The prominent imaging of lesbian love in Tusquets's fiction is also configured in a continuous interplay of desire and form. Feminist psychoanalytic theoreticians have turned their attention to the tortuous difficulties of female development.[5] Because the mother is the original prototypic erotic image, the homoerotic side has more primitive weight for a girl than for a boy. Girls tend to waver in a bisexual triangle, retaining a continuous mother-daughter identity as well as affective relationships with other women. Female identity, therefore, comes to define itself in relation and connection to others, as Nancy Chodorow has shown.[6] Like the permeability of female ego-boundaries that blur the distinction between self and other, Tusquets's works are melded by continuous migrations, cross-references, and citations that are the signifiers of the privileged metonymic continuity of mother and child. The result is an intratextual fusion of the individual narratives that stands as the structural analogue of gender-marked difficulties of individuation and separation and of a subsistent pre-Oedipal desire. This intratextuality also acts as a compensatory mechanism—on the level of form—for the failure of mother-daughter bonding that is a leitmotiv of Tusquets's work.

The author's persistent thematic concern with death is also linked to narrative form. Repetition, retardation, and ambiguity subvert or pervert the normal passage of time. The very titles of two works, *El mismo mar de todos los veranos* and *Siete miradas en un mismo paisaje*, with their emphasis on sameness, certify the replacement of narrative progression and fluidity with the static patterns and frozen frames of spatial form. The stories of *Siete miradas* create a frozen tableau in which chronology is irrelevant. In *El mismo mar*, the narrated events are not seen in their dramatic or causal character but as part of the total, static pattern of permanent destiny. Here, as in the subsequent works, transitions are perfunctory or ignored, implying the lack of a developmental principle. This stationary quality is heightened by the slow, close-up attention to detail and the enlargement of each minute, inner event.

The syntactic complications, verbal complexity, and density of style that all Tusquets's works share accentuate the effect of retardation by slowing the reader's progress. There appears to be a desire to infinitize the writing process with endless run-on sentences, sometimes taking several pages. Clauses are elongated or held in suspension by digressions, disjunctions, parenthetical insertions and interpolations, and by the persistent use of locutions like "acaso," "tal vez," or "quizá" (all variants of "perhaps") that introduce exhaustive explorations of all the permutations of thought. This type of sentence and Tusquets's refusal to use paragraphs serve an important architectural function of rhythm and sequence that also reduces the reader's speed of reception and arrests the forward lunge of time.

The dread inspired by a discourse of mortality with its "hedor a cosa terminada, a realidades muertas" [(its) stench of a finished thing, of dead realities] (*Para no volver*, 27), is expressed formally through incessant rereadings that do not lay claim to that final plenitude and integration of meaning that only endings can confer. However, as in analysis, these rereadings generate new meanings and new beginnings. Both *Varada* and *Para no volver*, in particular, hold out the prospect of a fresh start (semantically and structurally) and thereby meet a central goal of psychoanalysis: that of engendering greater self-possession, resiliency, and openness to the effects of unconscious desire. Distrustful of the last word in interpretation and history and recoiling from the significant closure that melds understanding with destruction, Tusquets gives us a Scheherazadelike story of stories that instigates a potentially endless circuit of desire and interlocution, thereby holding death at bay.

Just as content is tethered to form, the individual fate and psychology of Tusquets's female characters are part of a larger historical canvas and, therefore, exemplify the connection between the personal and the social that feminist psychoanalysis strives to grasp. As we have seen, the author's persistent themes of alienation, decision-making, and death are explored by markedly similar characters within the sociopolitical frame of post-Franco Spain. Because her masterful narratives are also fictive renderings of the dilemma of the woman writer and reader, Tusquets calls attention to the interpretive strategies that are learned, historically determined, and therefore gender-inflected. The impact of canonical texts on female readers has been amply demonstrated in her fiction. An open question, however, turns on the accessibility to male interpretation of the meaning encoded in texts by and about women. While, as with all contemporary art, Tusquets's fiction awaits the final judgment of history, her place in the pantheon of Spanish letters rests partially with the answer to this question.

Notes

1. See Gemma Roberts, *Temas existenciales en la novela española de postguerra* (Madrid: Editorial Gredos, 1973), for a clear placement of existential currents in post-civil war Spain.

2. Sigmund Freud, "Remembering, Repeating and Working Through" (1914), in *The Standard Edition of the Complete Psychological Works of Sigmund Freud*, ed. and trans. James Strachey, 24 vols. (London: Hogarth Press 1953–74), 12: 154. Peter Brooks's commentary on this essay in "The Idea of a Psychoanalytic Literary Criticism," *Critical Inquiry* 13 (1987): 334–48, has been a useful guidepost for the study of Tusquets's fiction.

3. Freud, "Fragments of an Analysis of a Case of Hysteria," in *Standard Edition*, 7: 116.

4. See Jane Gallop, *Reading Lacan* (Ithaca: Cornell University Press, 1985), for a linking of metonymy and femininity.

5. Juliet Mitchell, Nancy Chodorow, Dorothy Dinnerstein, Jane Flax, Hélène Cixous, Luce Irigaray, and Julia Kristeva have highlighted the mother-daughter relationship as the dominant formative influence on female development.

6. Nancy Chodorow, "Family Structure and Feminine Personality," in *Woman, Culture and Society*, ed. Michelle Z. Rosaldo (Stanford Calif.: Stanford University Press, 1974), 58.

Bibliography

1. PRIMARY SOURCES

1978. *El mismo mar de todos los veranos*. Barcelona: Editorial Lumen. Translated by Margaret E. W. Jones (1990), *The Same Sea as Every Summer*. Lincoln: University of Nebraska Press.

1979. *El amor es un juego solitario*. Barcelona: Editorial Lumen.

1980. *Varada tras el último naufragio*. Barcelona: Editorial Lumen.

1981a. *La conejita Marcela*. Barcelona: Editorial Lumen.

1981b. *Siete miradas en un mismo paisaje*. Barcelona: Editorial Lumen.

1982. "Las sutiles leyes de la simetría" (The subtle laws of symmetry). In *Doce relatos de mujeres*, edited by Ymelda Navajo, 198–212. Madrid: Alianza Editorial.

1985. *Para no volver*. Barcelona, Editorial Lumen.

2. SECONDARY SOURCES

Bellver, Catherine G. 1984. "The Language of Eroticism in the Novels of Esther Tusquets." *Anales de la Literatura Española Contemporánea* 9: 13–27. In addition to studying the figuration of the erotic in Tusquets's fiction, Bellver shows how the author broadens the definition of eroticism in Spanish literature by defining sexuality from a feminine point of view.

Claudín, Victor. 1980. "Esther Tusquets: Conquista de la felicidad." *Camp de l'arpa* 71: 47–53. An illuminating interview with the author that covers a full spectrum of issues relating to her work.

Levine, Linda Gould. 1987. "Reading, Rereading, Misreading and Rewriting the Male Canon: The Narrative Web of Esther Tusquets' Trilogy." In the issue "Reading for Difference: Feminist Perspectives on Women Novelists of Contemporary Spain," edited by Mirella Servodidio. *Anales de la Literatura Española Contemporánea* 12: 203–17. Using a feminist perspective, Levine examines the process by which Tusquets's female characters read themselves in and out of a patriarchal literary canon.

Nichols, Geraldine Cleary. 1984. "The Prison-House (And Beyond): *El mismo mar de todos los veranos.*" *Romanic Review* 75: 366–85. Nichols studies the novel's semiological and cultural codes and analyzes three elements of discourse: the theme of discourse, intertextuality, and literary style.

Ordóñez, Elizabeth J. 1984. "A Quest for Matrilineal Roots and Mythopoesis: Esther Tusquets' *El mismo mar de todos los veranos.*" *Crítica Hispánica*, 6: 37–46. Ordóñez uses this novel as a way to illustrate how feminist archetypal theory provides a demythifying means of reading Hispanic narrative by women.

Servodidio, Mirella. 1986. "Perverse Pairings and Corrupted Codes: *El amor es un juego solitario.*" *Anales de la Literatura Española Contemporánea* 11: 237–54. This essay offers a semiotic analysis and delineates the perversions and subversions that occur within the psychosexual, game, and narrative codes.

———. 1987. "A Case of Pre-Oedipal and Narrative Fixation: Tusquets' *El mismo mar de todos los veranos.*" In the issue "Reading for Difference: Feminist Perspectives on Women Novelists of Contemporary Spain," edited by Mirella Servodidio. *Anales de la Literatura Española Contemporánea* 12: 157–73. The novel is studied through the optic of current feminist psychoanalytic theory that considers the mother-daughter relationship as the dominant influence on female development.

Vásquez, Mary S. 1983. "Image and Linear Progress toward Defeat in Esther Tusquets' 'El mismo mar de todos los veranos.'" In *La Chispa, 83: Selected Proceedings*, edited by Gilbert Paolini, 307–13. New Orleans: Tulane University. Traces the novel's accelerating progression toward defeat that expresses individual, generational, class, national, and generically human experiences of failure.

9

Marina Mayoral's Narrative: Old Families and New Faces from Galicia

Concha Alborg

Marina Mayoral was born in Mondoñedo, Lugo, in the province of Galicia in 1942. She studied in Santiago before going to Madrid, where she received a doctorate in Romance philology at the Universidad Complutense. She also holds a degree in psychology from the Escuela de Madrid. Since 1978 she has taught Spanish literature at the Universidad Complutense and was a visiting professor at the University of Pennsylvania for a year. She was formerly married to the well-known literary critic Andrés Amorós, with whom she had two sons. At present she is married to Jordi Teixidor, an accomplished painter from Valencia.

Mayoral's research activities have been many. She has focused her attention on the Galicians Rosalía de Castro and Emilia Pardo Bazán; in a personal interview, she said that she feels a sense of kinship with these two writers based on their common love for their native land.[1] Her studies on the postromantic poet include *La poesía de Rosalía de Castro* (The poetry of Rosalía de Castro) (1974), which was her doctoral dissertation; *Rosalía de Castro y sus sombras* (Rosalía de Castro and her shadows) (1976); *Rosalía de Castro* (1986); and a critical edition of *En las orillas del Sar* (On the banks of the River Sar) (1978). In addition, she has prepared the critical editions of works by Emilia Pardo Bazán: *Cuentos y novelas de la tierra* (Short stories and novels from the earth) (1984), *Los Pazos de Ulloa* (Ulloa's manor) (1986),[2] and *Insolación* (Sunstroke) (1989). Other major works are *Análisis de textos (Poesía y prosa españolas)* (Textual analyses [Spanish poetry and prose]) (1977) and *Análisis de cinco comedias* (Analyses of five comedies) (1977), which was written in collaboration with Andrés Amorós and Francisco Nieva. Her numerous articles deal with other literary figures as well, such as the poets Miguel Hernández and León Felipe, the Romantic Gustavo Adolfo Bécquer, and Azorín from the Generation of '98.

After her reputation as a literary critic was well established, Mayoral began publishing novels in 1979 and was quickly labeled as one of the most promising of the new women novelists.[3] Before this she had written a few short stories and was included in Francisco García Pavón's anthology, *Antología de cuentistas españoles contemporáneos* (An anthology of contemporary Spanish short stories) (1984). Her first novel, *Cándida otra vez* (Cándida once again) (1979), won second prize in a competition sponsored by Ambito Literario, an innovative publishing house; the novella *Plantar un árbol* (To plant a tree) earned her the 1980 Premio Gabriel Sijé de Novela Corta; and *Al otro lado* (On the other side) was awarded the 1980 Premio Novelas y Cuentos. Her last two novels are longer than her previous ones: *La única libertad* (The only liberty) (1982), and *Contra muerte y amor* (Against love and death) (1985), which was a finalist for the Planeta Prize. Mayoral considers writing fiction her primary goal and in 1987 was working on a new novel that deals with historic and science fiction themes.[4]

It is easy to see at a first reading that Marina Mayoral's novels share common traits; not only do some of the characters reappear in other works and the same story lines continue from novel to novel, but all have the unmistakable presence of Galicia.[5] Even when the novels take place in Madrid, as is the case in *Al otro lado* and *Contra muerte y amor*, the characters are always Galician, having spent their formative years in that setting. Her first two novels, *Cándida otra vez* and *Plantar un árbol*, take place in Mayoral's native land. The author has created, as other well-known novelists have done (Juan Benet's Región or Gabriel García Márquez's Macondo), a fictitious town, Brétema, that embodies all that is meaningfully Galician for her, basically a semifeudal society where social classes are still very much in place. Although admittedly not concerned with social commentary, Mayoral is nevertheless taken with the inequities that exist between servants or the working class and the privileged classes, as exemplified by La Tolda and La Rosaleda in *Contra muerte y amor*.

The strength of Mayoral's novels lies in the richness and originality of her characterizations. A wide range of characters from different social classes, ages, and occupations relate to each other in a weblike pattern. The professional group, represented by doctors, lawyers, and journalists, contrasts with the more unusual boxer, artist, or detective. Strong women protagonists, lending themselves to feminist interpretations, often appear in her novels. Cándida, for whom the short novel is named, is the first of many members of the aristocratic Monterroso de Cela family to appear in her narratives. Laura, in *Plantar un árbol*, is an older woman who returns to her roots. Prominent in *Al otro lado* are the enigmatic, beautiful Silvia and her equally complex sister, Olga. *La única libertad* has several outstanding female characters: Etelvina, the young narrator; the three eccentric grandmothers, Georgina, Benilde, and Ana Luz; and Matilde, the artist's wife. Two other memorable protagonists are the strong lawyer, Esmeralda, and the wealthy woman, Lita Monterroso, of *Contra muerte y amor*. Although Mayoral is not a militant feminist, she does defend a better position for women in society, an attitude that is reflected in her novels.[6]

The themes in Mayoral's novels are the traditional, metaphysical ones of liberty, death, and love that are suggested in her titles. Of the three, death seems to be the most prominent, since violent, untimely, or mysterious endings are the fates of many of her characters. Love and marriage, with introspection into sexuality— explored in several of her works—are less enduring than friendship. Other relationships, such as homosexuality and incest, come into play as well, proving that they are no longer taboo subjects in women's writings. Some critics have interpreted Mayoral's emphasis on emotion as melodramatic, but she claims that this is how she perceives life.[7]

Due to her knowledge of literary criticism, it would be easy for Mayoral to indulge in contemporary narrative techniques, but instead she chooses a more traditional approach to her fiction and dispenses with complex devices. Nevertheless, her novels tend to have involved, intricate action with an element of mystery and intrigue reminiscent of the "novela negra," or detective story. In some instances the reader has to wait for a future novel to uncover the resolution of the plot. Here she follows a new tendency of the Spanish contemporary novel. Detective fiction, a genre associated with capitalistic, democratic societies, had been absent from Spanish writing during the years of "franquismo" (Franco's government), but has flourished in the post-Franco regime.[8]

Also worth noting is Mayoral's technique for the use of perspective, which incorporates different narrative points of view and forces the reader to decide which one is the "real" version. Her use of humor further helps to create the type of novel that has been praised by critics and readers alike.

When I asked Mayoral if she preferred the short story or the novel, she responded that she unequivocally favored the longer narrative. Due to her love of ramifications and complex plots, she finds the conciseness of the short story burdensome.[9] However, she has had some success writing short narrations, having gained substantial recognition by winning the Hucha de Oro prize in 1982 for "Ensayo de comedia" (Play rehearsal). Because they are supremely well-constructed and since they have not been studied before, these narrations deserve to be analyzed here.

Plantar un árbol, a novella in seven chapters,[10] is characterized by the technique of ellipsis. Laura goes back to her native Galicia to find her roots, and while planting a tree she converses with an old woman and with Paco, a close friend from her childhood. However, the reader only reads the protagonist's first-person narration and does not hear the interlocutor's voices. Part of Laura's discourse is also her own thoughts and some words that she addresses to her dead father. This is, then, a situation presented from one person's point of view that creates narrative tension, especially given the protagonist's depressed state of mind, and that forces the reader to discern the truth. Time is a cyclical entity, symbolized in part by Paco's little grandchild, who is named Laura like the older woman. As the narrator says, "El círculo se cierra y vuelvo a donde nací" [The circle closes and I come back to where I was born] (79).

"De su mejor amiga, Celina" (From her best friend, Celina) also uses a woman narrator who, when facing her own death, addresses her deceased friend. Other than having the same elliptic narrative technique, the most interesting part of this short story lies in the nature of the relationship of the women, which surpasses any other she has had, including Celina's marriage to Antonio. The two women were never lovers; both were attracted to men for sexual gratification, but they wish they had been lesbians so as not to need anyone else: "hubiéramos sido muy felices" [we would have been so happy] (13), and therein lies the conflict.[11] Linguistically interesting are the semiaffectionate insults that the narrator uses to address her friend—"Gordita, tragona, tardica, bribona, borrica" (little chubby one, big eater, Johnny-come-lately, rascal, little ass)—which contrast with the loving thoughts she is conveying.

Another unusual relationship, this time between an older man and the film star Greta Garbo, is the subject of "Querida y admirada Greta" (Dear and admired Greta). The entire story is composed of the letter that he writes describing his lifelong obsession for her. The outstanding feature of this story is the sincere, respectful, naive tone of the letter. This apparently simple man has followed Garbo's entire career, movie by movie, from an insignificant Galician town. The silver screen has been an escape from his otherwise dull life.

"Ensayo de comedia" has a cosmopolitan setting. The protagonist-narrator is an actress who imagines how her life could be written as a three-act play. The metafictive element is cleverly introduced since the would-be play becomes the short story with a perfect dramatic structure. Even though the life-as-a-play theme is not new, Mayoral has created a fresh tone with her accustomed touch of humor. The happy ending, totally uncharacteristic, explains the "comedia" (which can mean either play or comedy) of the title.

The most unusual of Mayoral's short stories, due to its incorporation of the supernatural, is "Del amor y de la amistad" (Of love and friendship).[12] A psychologist tells the story of her friend, who is married to a man who does not age. Although she promises not to use the information to further her studies she witnesses the frustration of a wife growing older while her husband does not change. The originality of Mayoral's works and her gift for storytelling can be deduced from these five very different short narratives. Her prose, as is the case throughout her novels, is careful and precise without a hint of artificiality.

Mayoral's novels demonstrate striking consistencies and strong interrelationships, as the following analysis of her novels shows. *Cándida otra vez* tells the story of an aristocratic Galician woman who is involved in a mystery and seeks help to unravel it from an old friend, a lawyer who is also the narrator of this short novel. *Al otro lado* has a far more complex plot since several characters offer conflicting views on Silvia's life and her supernatural powers. The same use of multiple perspectives is evident in *La única libertad* where the young Etelvina goes to the family manor in Galicia to write its history and consequently her own story, which is interwoven with the other characters' experiences. Some of the characters from this novel reappear in *Contra muerte y amor*. Although they are working at a fast pace in Madrid—such as Esmeralda, the successful lawyer, and Manolo, the aspiring boxer—their provincial past is still very evident.

All of Mayoral's characters, like herself, are from Galicia. Whether they have moved to Madrid or still live there, they all share a common past, a way of seeing life that is typically Galician. In her two first novels—*Cándida otra vez* and *Al otro lado*—the aristocratic family is the Monterroso de Cela clan. When Pedro, a lawyer who appears in both of these novels, tries to explain to his foreign secretary what he feels for Cándida Monterroso and his hometown, he finds it difficult:

> ... desde los Reyes Católicos para acá, más o menos. En mi pueblo todo era de los Monterroso de Cela, desde siempre ... No, no era un franquista, bueno sí era franquista, pero sobre todo era un señor feudal

del siglo XV . . . Sí, descendiente directo . . . Un odioso dictador . . . pues
sí, bueno, no. Es decir, yo no lo odiaba, casi nadie, ni a él ni a sus nietos
. . . jugábamos juntos, siempre hemos jugado juntos. . . .

[. . . from the Catholic Kings to here, more or less. In my town everything
has always belonged to the Monterrosos de Cela . . . No, he was not
pro-Franco; well, he was, but most of all, he was a feudal lord from the
fifteenth century . . . Yes, a direct descendent . . . A hateful dictator . . .
yes, well, no. That is to say, I did not hate him, no one did, nor did we
hate his grandchildren . . . we played together, we have always played
together. . . .] (41–42)

This combination of attraction and repulsion, desire and escape, is
what all of Mayoral's characters feel towards their native Galicia.

In the two following novels, *La única libertad* and *Contra muerte
y amor*, Mayoral uses Brétema, which embodies this same Galician
environment. This fishing village has a poor section, La Tolda, with
its unmistakable fish odor, which contrasts with the well-to-do
houses of La Rosaleda. Often the men and women of La Tolda
working as servants in La Rosaleda have a warm relationship with
their employers, even if they are economically enslaved.

The protagonist family in these two novels is the Silva clan. While
the Monterrosos were blond, green-eyed, strikingly beautiful, and
had their share of phobias and illnesses from generation to
generation, the Silvas too had individual characteristics that set them
apart from the other townspeople. One of the tasks of the reader of
Mayoral's fiction is to reconstruct the elaborate genealogy that the
author herself confesses to having traced all the way from don
Ildefonso de Silva, the great-grandfather, through his eight children,
to Etelvina, the great-granddaughter, who tries to write the history
of La Braña, the country manor or "pazo."[13]

Mayoral does not describe the countryside of Galicia in concrete
detail, as a nineteenth-century novelist might do. For example,
Marta, who has a secondary role in *Cándida otra vez*, paints
landscapes that "le gustaban a todo el mundo, eran la expresión de
un pueblo oprimido por un centralismo secular" [were pleasing to
everyone, they were the expression of a country repressed by a
secular centralism] (33). Her portrayal of this region is mainly
sociological, with the exception of La Braña, which she sees as an
exquisite, luxurious paradise full of natural beauty (*La única
libertad*, 27).

One element of the Galician landscape and way of life on which
Mayoral does dwell is the sea. A place of work for the lower class
and recreation for the more privileged one, the sea is where the two

poles of society meet, especially the children, who play there together. There are several scenes in Mayoral's novels that describe what it used to be like to grow up in Galicia. Pedro, in *Cándida otra vez*, remembers their adventures in the "cova do mar" [the sea's cave], a dangerous place where more than one fisherman had lost his life, but nevertheless a fascinating spot for the youngsters. The brave Monterroso children, Cándida in particular, always liked to play there and raced with the tide to avoid getting trapped inside the cave.

Even though the children of both classes play together, most of the characters in Mayoral's fiction marry within their class. The few who break this pattern pay dearly for it. In *Contra muerte y amor*, Esmeralda, married to the aristocratic Daniel, never gets over her feelings of inadequacy, despite the fact that she is a well-known lawyer. And Silvia of *Al otro lado* begins the novel marrying the wealthy outsider, Luis, to the scorn of her family. Despite the changes that have taken place in a democratic society, especially in the capital city, some of the old restrictions still apply.

The differences between the classes are most obvious, however, in the relationships of servants and masters that are described in *La única libertad*. Moreover these distinctions are accentuated by the fact that most of the action takes place in Galicia. The Silva family treats servants with a paternalistic attitude that the servants, in turn, accept happily. For many, especially the women, working in a wealthy household is preferable to the miserable life in the villages where people lack even the basic necessities of life. In the rich manors the servants learn good manners and good taste, although the usefulness of such knowledge is not clear. Etelvina and her great-aunts discuss the situation with this type of remark: "Lo extraño es que no nos odiasen. ... lo normal es que tuvieran apego a 'los señores.' ... El problema, como siempre, era de clases, y de que cada uno se movía en un plano y mientras no intentasen mezclarse todo iba bien" [The strange thing is that they did not hate us. ... normally, they felt close to the 'señores.' ... The problem, as always, was one with the classes, and that everyone moved on their own plane and while they did not try to mix, everything went well] (137).

Once in a while a housemaid would marry, or at least live (as in Matilde's situation), with "el señor," but for the most part they had illegitimate children—easily recognizable by their appearance—who were taken care of by the family. The genealogical lines then get entangled, creating a vast possibility of combinations for the reader to explore. In the case of Manolo Fraiz, three family trees are traced, even though the only known fact is that his mother was La Moura (175). The story of Fraiz deserves further attention, not only because of his genealogical interest, but because he is one of the few main characters from a lower social class and because he becomes a protagonist in *Contra muerte y amor*, Mayoral's next novel. The life of a bastard, no matter who his father may be, is not easy in repressive Brétema, so Fraiz decides to train as a boxer (with the name of Black Fraiz), which for him is the only way he can escape and make a life for himself.[14]

An interesting episode related to the conflict within the classes— one of many subplots in *La única libertad*—is the story of Inmaculada de Silva and Antón do Cañote, a gamekeeper. In this case it is a woman who crosses class barriers and has an affair with a young woodsman. Here again different theories speculate on who killed Antón and why, but it is the servants who most insistently defend the honor of doña Inmaculada.

In *Al otro lado*, which takes place in contemporary Madrid, Nati exposes her elitist class ideology in a diatribe reminiscent of Carmen Sotillo's discourse in *Cinco horas con Mario* (1966) (*Five Hours with Mario*, 1989) by Miguel Delibes. Like Carmen, Nati is characterized by clichés. Although she is in love with a man, she refuses to introduce him to the family because he is a detective without a college degree: "... no para mí, cada uno con los de su clase, ahora eso no se dice, pero yo no soy hipócrita ... a la hora de casarse, cada oveja con su pareja" [... that's not for me, each one with those of his class, now this is not said, but I am not a hypocrite ... when it is time to get married, to each his or her own] (213–14).

In some instances, however, social class differences can be an incentive in a relationship. This is the case for Pedro, in *Cándida otra vez*, who gets much satisfaction from taking a Monterroso to bed in a clever game of master and servant. This fixation is carried to an extreme by Nolecho, in *Contra muerte y amor*. Throughout the entire novel, he chases Lita Monterroso in a sadistic ritual that eventually lands him in the hospital.

Marina Mayoral has succeeded in realistically depicting Galician society, with its old family names and structured social classes, but her real talent lies in presenting the conflict that arises when the status quo is probed. The resolution to this conflict is deliberately not clear because it depends on time and place and, more important, human nature.

Human nature is most vividly captured in Mayoral's creation of female characters. In order not to succumb to the stereotypical criticism that women novelists fail to portray substantial male characters, I point out the weight of Pedro in *Cándida otra vez*, the complexity of Rafael in *Al otro lado*, and the originality of Morais and Black Fraiz in *La única libertad* and *Contra muerte y amor*, respectively. But even so, it is evident that Mayoral excels in the strong portrayals of female characters throughout her narrative. With the possible exception of Cándida, who is somewhat typecast, all of them show unique personalities that could serve as models to the female reader.

Silvia, the less obvious protagonist of *Al otro lado*, stands out as a sensitive woman who has suffered, despite her privileged social status. Her portrayal is partly accomplished through the first-person narration of her sister, Olga, an equally well-developed character. From early childhood Silvia demonstrated special powers in dealing with death. The scene about her grandmother's body in the dining room is described in several instances to illustrate the point when the family, and Silvia herself, become aware of her supernatural qualities. Because Olga accepts Silvia's nature as a matter of fact, so does the reader, and as the novel progresses the psychic element is taken for granted. As the people around Silvia die, foreseen by her, she becomes a personification of the angel of death (also the original title that Mayoral gave to the novel). From the time of her birth Silvia was a beautiful baby, blond and green-eyed, standing out with a "protagonismo especial" (29). Her characterization as an angel is based on the legend that before a person dies, a beautiful being of any sex, in reality an angel, passes by and casts a glance, unnoticed by anyone, not even the person who is going to die (150).

In contrast to the ethereal Silvia is the realistic portrayal of the pragmatic Olga, who narrates four chapters of the novel, including the important opening and closing ones. Olga is a doctor and lives alone, despite the fact that she and Alfonso have been lovers for some fifteen years and he wants to marry her, a situation that contrasts with Silvia's three marriages and the wedding that opens the novel. All of chapter 6 is self-analysis, using the stream-of-consciousness technique, where she questions her attitudes in life. About marriage she asks: "¿Es tan difícil de entender que puedas querer a un hombre, incluso serle fiel toda la vida, sin querer compartir todos los momentos de esa vida?" [Is it so difficult to understand that one can love a man, even being faithful to him all of one's life, without wishing to share all of that life's moments?] (85–86).

It is easy to see Olga as a feminist. Her posture would define her as the type of character that feminist critics like Cheri Register call a good role model for women.[15] She is interested in feminist issues, does not see men as antagonists, likes and cares for other women, and helps to augment a feminist conscience. Interested in improving the situation of womankind, Mayoral feels that most of her female characters are feminists, while very few of the male ones would fall into that category. She assures us, however, that her portrayal of strong women has more to do with the way women—her mother in particular—generally behaved in her family than with any prescribed feminism.[16] To the feminist reader, Mayoral's female characters are of particular interest because they do not follow a stereotypical pattern, each of them having different traits.[17]

Due in part to its length, *La única libertad* has a whole gallery of well-drawn portrayals of women that cannot be exhaustively analyzed here. Notable among them are Etelvina, the inquisitive, suspicious narrator; Matilde, the housemaid turned muse; the daring Inmaculada de Silva; and the repressed Cecilia. However, the most memorable female characters are the three cantankerous great-aunts: Benilde, Ana Luz, and Georgina, whom Mayoral seems to portray with special sensitivity. Their description in chapter 2 is based on the comparison and contrast of their personality traits. Benilde, part of the Silva family by marriage, is nevertheless head of the clan. Although she came from a rich landowning family, she is not as socially refined as the other two women. She met the sisters Ana Luz and Georgina in school and they have been friends since. As a child Benilde was not pretty, but she has improved with age and has a dignified air that is emphasized by her always dressing in black since the death of her husband many years ago.

Georgina has always been the liveliest of the three women. A happy, golden-haired child, she preferred sports over intellectual pursuits. Widowed after a short marriage, she had the unconventional occupation of running of a gym (where Black Fraiz started training) and was hoping to open a detective agency. Ana Luz, despite being the least aggressive, is the most controversial of the three. She not only studied at a university, at a time when women did not, but had a relationship with her senior professor that lasted for several years until she became involved with a handsome French actor. She never married and dressed in beautifully feminine clothes. Throughout the novel, the appearance of the women is refreshing and humorous as they try to interfere in every situation. The three of them, riding in Georgina's old Bugatti, make a memorable picture.

The depth of Mayoral's portrayals seems to be broadening, judging from the characterization of Esmeralda in her last novel, *Contra muerte y amor*. Esmeralda is a socially progressive Madrid lawyer, but despite her successful career she has trouble dealing with her family background and Galician childhood. Although the sign on her door says "María García Novoa," she still feels like the vulnerable Esmeralda (or worse yet, Tunda's daughter), a name that she does not like to use since it brings old memories. In Brétema her family lived in La Tolda and she can still smell the fish odor that permeated that section of town. From the beginning of the novel the discourse of the omniscient narrator is interwoven with the voices of Esmeralda's past. She can still hear her father's words, her mother's advice, and her teacher's comments when she left Brétema to go study in Madrid. As her character develops, thoughts from her past are ever-present. Some of these remembrances have a special significance. The memory of the chewed-up apple cores that the children from La Rosaleda gave to the poor ones from La Tolda still makes her resentful. Part of Esmeralda's characterization is what she calls "poor people's gestures." Some of these are not buying light-colored clothing for fear it will get soiled too quickly; not sitting on one's coat in order to save the cloth from wearing; and putting a magazine on the sofa under one's feet. Well-bred people from La Rosaleda, like her own husband, Daniel Andrade, would never act in this manner.

Other characters, Manolo Fraiz among them, see her from different points of view. To him Esmeralda looks like a tough, unpleasant woman—although she is almost pretty when she smiles—who can beat up a policeman if she wants to. Nolecho, a childhood friend, knew her as the bossiest and bravest of the playmates and the one who boxed him to the ground. Daniel, her ex-husband, thinks of her as an incorruptible woman who loved him but who has always intimidated him. Elvira, a friend who admires her intellect, does not really understand her. Only Enrique could see her vulnerability and love her the way she is. When Esmeralda looks at herself in the mirror, she sees an indifferent, apathetic woman who has stopped caring (95). In fact, she has worked hard to get where she is and is tired of suffering and being hurt. The characterization of Esmeralda contrasts with that of Lita Monterroso, which is more stereotypical, alternating the "poor little rich girl" with the "femme fatale" who has been pampered all her life and is truly ruthless.

Throughout her fiction Mayoral's female and male characters grapple with the fundamental issues of love and death. Although the epigraph by the poet Luis Cernuda to *La única libertad* states that love is the only liberty for which one lives, love in Marina Mayoral's novels is far from this idyllic thought. Germán Gullón has pointed out that the relationships between men and women are all poorly timed (1987, 59–70). Taking *Al otro lado* as an example, one can observe that all the characters are frustrated in their search for love. Silvia only truly loved her cousin Rafael and vice-versa, but dissuaded by their family, they married other people—three others in Silvia's case—which hardly made them happy. Olga loved Alvaro, who left her for the charismatic and deadly Silvia. Nati was forbidden to continue her relationship with Mario because he was a married man. Pedro—Herda's lover since the previous novel— breaks up with her for no apparent reason. Nando, from a younger generation, has even more difficulties relating to the tragic Amelita.

In the other novels, love between men and women does not fare any better. Ironically, in several instances there seems to be happiness in incestuous relationships. This theme is explored early in Mayoral's narrative; in her first novel, Cándida for a short time takes her much younger brother as her lover and, surprisingly for her, professes to love him. *La única libertad* has two cases of incest that are developed more at length. In one of the so-called "dispensable" or optional extra chapters of the book, which in fact parallels the narrator's own story, several characters elaborate on doña Petronila Alonso and her son, Eduardo. Different narrators sometimes offer a conflicting point of view, suggesting that the relationship between mother and son was incestuous. In the course of her inquiries into the history of La Braña, Etelvina finds out that her father is no other than her uncle, her mother's twin brother—a fact that for obvious reasons had been kept from her. This incestuous love is described in detail by Alberto himself in a long exposition that constitutes the climax of the novel. His comment, "Querer a alguien nunca es un crimen, aunque la sociedad lo condene" [To love someone is never a crime, even if society condemns it] (367), proves the futility of love because it so happens that in these few instances where there is love, society has indeed denounced it. A similar situation is depicted through homosexuality, although the love between men is not treated in such caring terms. Rather, their plight is an object of ridicule, as in the case of Benito in *Al otro lado* and less so with Carlos and Arthur in *La única libertad*.

Frequent, violent, premature, and mysterious death is also a major theme for Mayoral. Manuel in *Cándida otra vez* has a similar death to those of Ramón the chauffeur and señorita Adelina of *La única libertad*. The three fall down a cliff in suspicious car accidents in which wealthy people are implicated, though never punished. In this same novel, Antón do Cañote is murdered and it is suggested that Inmaculada de Silva and Eduardo commit suicide.

Besides Rafa's ambiguous death, there are three other suicides in

Al otro lado: the woman in the subway, the man in the gallery and
the unexpected death of Amelita. Her death, coming when she jumps
from the attic of her dormitory, is the most striking feature of this
otherwise inconspicuous character. She is briefly introduced as
Nando's devoted eighteen-year-old girlfriend. Her death comes as a
complete shock to the reader and to Mayoral herself, who disclosed
that Amelita's tragic end came as a surprise to her too. This is a case
where a character seemed to decide his or her own destiny, regardless
of the author's intention.[18]

A similar situation, again according to Mayoral, took place with
Nolecho in *Contra muerte y amor*. This figure characterizes himself
by the three deaths that have scarred his life. The three are grouped
together in the dense narration that makes up chapter 7 of part 1.
First, when he was a small child, his mother killed herself by jumping
into the sea. Then he lost his childhood sweetheart and his lover of
eight years to illnesses, which left him alone and resentful. Other
deaths, like Enrique's dramatic murder in this same novel, which
is related to the detective story or "novela negra," are features
in Mayoral's fiction that Phyllis Zatlin has pointed out (1987).
Although Mayoral's novels do not belong completely to this
genre, an element of intrigue often characterizes her work. Here, as
in other cases, Enrique's death goes unpunished—it is not even
investigated—pointing out the triviality of life against death, as
suggested in the title and the novel's epigraph.

Another death, that of Manolo Fraiz's grandmother, closes the
novel. This poor servant from Galicia had been a character in the
previous novel, *La única libertad*. Her relationship with Manolo, the
footman, had been developed there, but her son's father's identity
was not resolved in a clever game of family trees. Since death is such
an important theme and this one is so explicitly narrated, one can
assume that it has a special significance. Rosa dies in a hospital in
Madrid, far from her friends of La Tolda. When she is dying, don
Carlos Villaurín visits her in what Esmeralda interprets as an act of
recognition that comes too late.

Mayoral's overriding themes are presented in works that are not
characterized by an overuse of narrative techniques. Her novels are
more traditional in form than experimental. Consequently, when she
chooses a particular technique it is due to profound reasons, not to
literary trends. She does, however, utilize a changing point of view
to convey her basic idea that truth is relative. She says: "... la
realidad objetiva, la que vería un dios posible, no existe. Por eso en
mis novelas, el lector tiene que crear su propia realidad, la que surge

de las visiones muchas veces contrarias o contradictorias de los personajes'' [... objective reality, that which a possible god could see, does not exist. That is why in my novels, the reader has to create his own reality, the one that emerges from the often contradictory views of the characters].[19] The three beginning chapters of *Contra muerte y amor* that describe the same exact situation—Manolo's visit to Esmeralda—from three different perspectives, are a good example of this.

In other instances Mayoral applies her knowledge of literature by incorporating classical elements in her works. Thus, each chapter of *La única libertad* is preceded by an explanatory note in Cervantine fashion that piques the reader's curiosity and enhances plot interest. In this same novel Mayoral also effectively handles the metafictional mode.[20] Etelvina, the narrator, is writing the story of La Braña that another relative, Alejandro, had already started. To his notes she adds letters and bits of diaries with the accounts of other narrators who have contributed to the story. Etelvina, an insecure young woman, worries about the veracity and significance of the facts, the length of her writings, and her ability to conclude the project. Encouraged by her family, she begins to add her own story to La Braña's history, but she often "loses the narrative thread" (93) or gets the diverse lines "entangled like cherries" (121).[21]

As if Etelvina did not have enough questions of her own about how to write the story, the situation intensifies when she sends the writings to a former lover. Gilberto, as an internal critic, is ruthless in giving her hints on theory and accusing her of being melodramatic or writing like the conservative, nineteenth-century novelist Benito Pérez Galdós. In contrast, her cousin encourages her to continue in her task, hoping she will be as famous as Rosalía de Castro or Emilia Pardo Bazán. As Etelvina discloses more information about her own life, she is aware that she might become a character out of a novel. She also ponders the job of a writer and the possible subgenre of her work. When in the last page of the novel she wonders if she will ever finish the history of La Braña, the reader has in front of him or her the novel itself.[22]

Humor is yet another trait in Mayoral's writing that enhances the reader's participation. For Mayoral humor is truly a fundamental aspect of her style, despite critics like Santiago Vilas, who state that women authors have less of a sense of humor than men have.[23] Whether it is a witty play on words, a funny episode, or the irony of a situation, the reader is often amused. For example, in *Cándida otra vez*, the German secretary's pronunciation is phonetically transcribed, which creates a satiric effect (8–9). At times biting remarks border on sarcasm, as when a homosexual gets hurt in his mouth and exclaims: "Me has estropeado mi instrumento de trabajo; tendrás que ponerme un estanco ... o casarte conmigo." [You have messed up my working tool: you will have to open a tobacco store for me ... or marry me.] (*La única libertad*, 84). Some anecdotes, such as the one in which the children stick their fingers in the saint's rear end, are intentionally naive (*Cándida otra vez*, 24–25).

One humorous situation is the characterization of Nati's elderly mother in *Al otro lado*. Using an elliptic conversation, Nati talks to her mother whom we do not hear. Through Nati's discourse the reader can construct her mother's comic commentary. She calls her daughter old-fashioned and questions her about her boyfriend. Despite the fact that she is bedridden, she seems to know much of what is going on with the family. She watches television, reads racy magazines, and insists on wearing a pink blouse instead of mourning clothes. These details help to create an amusing contrast between generations in an otherwise sad situation.

A humorous touch that emerges in Mayoral's novels is the cameo appearance of Marina herself as a writer and as an acquaintance of the characters. Coincidentally, Marina sees Nati and her boyfriend rowing in Retiro Park, but "... no es seguro, porque Marina organiza una novela sobre cualquier detalle nimio, nunca se habrá visto un paseo en barca más adornado" [... it is not certain, because Marina makes up a novel over any small detail, there will never be a more elaborate boat ride] (*Al otro lado*, 234). Mayoral's witty contribution of poking fun at herself is in her own words like a wink to the reader.[24] One point is certain, however: her narrative never loses the reader's attention, but instead captures it through the use of humor, suspense, or interesting characters.

Despite her preoccupation with her native Galicia, Marina Mayoral has not been considered a Galician writer in the strict sense of the term because until very recently she did not write in that language (although her novel *Contra muerte y amor* was translated into Galician).[25]

Even if she is not considered a Galician writer, her position in contemporary Spanish literature is that of a young novelist belonging to the generation of writers highlighted by Ymelda Navajo in her 1982 *Doce relatos de mujeres* (Twelve stories by women).[26] With them she has in common the date of her birth (late 1930s or 1940s— that is to say, after the Spanish civil war), her academic training (most of them teach and are journalists or critics), and the fact that she started publishing fiction after Franco's death.

Most important, she shares what Navajo calls "la lucha personal y no mimética con el texto, la aventura individual, la búsqueda del camino y el espacio propios'' [a personal and non-mimetic struggle with the text, an individual adventure, a search for her own way and space] (12). But because her style is personal and original, she cannot really be compared to these other women novelists. Unlike Cristina Fernández Cubas, she does not favor an esoteric narrative, nor is her fiction as lyrical as that of Soledad Puértolas or Carme Riera. Her commitment to feminine causes is not as strong as that of Rosa Montero or Esther Tusquets; neither does she favor the journalistic approach of Montserrat Roig. Marina Mayoral shares more characteristics with Ana María Moix for her interest in the psychology and motivations of human behavior, and with Lourdes Ortiz for her predilection for complex plots with metafictional or detective-novel modalities.

The reader of Mayoral's fiction can observe a definite development in her work; not only have her novels grown in length—from the mere one hundred pages of *Cándida otra vez* to four hundred of *La única libertad*—but they have also grown in complexity. *Contra muerte y amor* is a tour de force of multiple perspectives and, aside from her characteristic themes of love and death, Galicia versus Madrid, and social class differences, it highlights the use of humor and suspense while it explores a new topography incorporating more of the Galician language. Because she has published four novels— short narratives aside—in six years, one can no longer say that she is just a promising writer. Her promise has been fulfilled. On the other hand, because of her age and commitment to writing fiction, that promise will undoubtedly be realized time and again.

Notes

1. Interview with Marina Mayoral in Madrid on 28 December 1987.

2. English translation by Ethel Harriet Hearn (1908), *The Son of the Bond-woman*.

3. Each of her novels received ample attention by well-known critics such as Carmen Martín Gaite, Manuel Cerezales, and Concha Castroviejo, among others, in the daily newspapers (*ABC, Diario 16, Ya*).

4. Interview, 28 December 1987, and personal communication, 7 August 1989. Although having a connection to the Galician world, the novel is set in an altogether new environment for Mayoral's works.

5. Antonio Valencia, in the prologue to *Al otro lado* (1981a, 9), says that in Mayoral's novels there is "Un aire de familia."

6. Interview, 28 December 1987. Although she repudiates the label, she nevertheless describes her feminist feelings as "profound."

7. Ibid. This is especially true for the theme of death, which she calls "omnipresent" and very much on her mind.

8. Phyllis Zatlin points this out in her well-drawn article, "Detective Fiction and the Novels of Mayoral" (1987). The second half of the journal issue in which this article appears is devoted to the "Hispanic thriller." An overview of the current detective genre in Spain, including its relation to politics and capitalism, is offered by Samuel Amell in "Literatura e ideología: El caso de la novela negra en la España actual," *Monographic Review/Revista Monográfica* 3: 192–201.

9. Interview, 28 December 1987. However, she admits that some stories lend themselves better to the shorter genre. For a definition and classification of the Spanish short story, see Erna Brandenberger, *Estudios sobre el cuento español actual* (Madrid: Editora Nacional, 1973).

10. She has just revised this novella, making it a third longer and translating it into Galician.

11. These are the same words spoken by Fernanda and Cristina in a similar relationship in *Contra muerte*, 293. Although Mayoral has said that she does not consider her short stories as a training ground for her novels, there are nevertheless traits in them that are characteristic of her style. In another story ("Querida y admirada Greta") the mythical place-name Brétama appears at the head of a letter; the same epistolary technique resurfaces later in *La única libertad*.

12. After writing this chapter another short story came to my attention, entitled "El final," published in *Miguel y yo y diez cuentos más* (Michael and I and ten more stories) (Madrid: Confederación Española de Cajas de Ahorros, 1979). This very short narrative also deals with the supernatural since the characters see themselves dead after an airplane accident. Mayoral recently published a complete collection of her short stories, including nine new ones (1989).

13. Interview, 28 December 1987. Mayoral points out how careful she is with all of the names, relationships, and ages to make sure that they "all work out."

14. Ibid. Had it been Andalucía, she suggests, he could have been a bullfighter—or a golfer or tennis player, if he belonged to a different class.

15. "American Feminist Literary Criticism: A Bibliographical Introduction," in *Feminist Literary Criticism*, ed. Josephine Donovan (Lexington: University Press of Kentucky, 1975), 1–28.

16. Interview, 28 December 1987.

17. According to Gabriela Mora this lack of stereotyping would also constitute good feminine literature. See "Crítica feminista: Apuntes sobre definiciones y problemas," in *Theory and Practice of Feminist Literary Criticism*, ed. Gabriela Mora and Karen S. Van Hooft (Ypsilanti: Eastern Michigan University, Bilingual Press/Editorial Bilingüe, 1982), 2–13.

18. Interview, 28 December 1987. She relates this same incident in her interview with Angel Vivas. (1985, 37–39).

19. "Algunas notas sobre la novela," unpublished handout. Madrid, 1985, received from the author in November, 1987.

20. See Patricia Waugh, *Metafiction: The Theory and Practice of Self-Conscious Fiction* (London: Methuen, 1984).

21. This would qualify the novel as a self-reflexive text in Kathleen M. Glenn's terminology. See "*El cuarto de atrás*: Literature as 'juego' and the Self-Reflexive Text, "in *From Fiction to Metafiction: Essays in Honor of Carmen Martín Gaite*, ed. Mirella Servodidio and Marcia L. Welles, 149–59 (Lincoln, Neb.: Society of Spanish and Spanish-American Studies, 1983).

22. The metafictional aspects of this novel merit their own article, if we take into account the intertextuality with Cervantes (the dispensable stories, the glosses) and the mention of other authors. For a definition of intertextuality see Gustavo Pérez Firmat, "Apuntes para un modelo de la intertextualidad en la literatura," *Romanic Review* 69 (1978): 1–14.

23. See *El humor y la novela española contemporánea* (Madrid: Guadarrama, 1984), for a classification of humor.

24. Interview, 28 December 1987. She relates it to something like Alfred Hitchcock's appearances in his own films.

25. She is not included, for example, in Juan M. Ribera Llopis, *Literaturas catalana, gallega y vasca* (Madrid: Playor, 1982). Mayoral did not write fiction in Galician until 1988.

26. Madrid: Alianza, 1982. Aside from the ones mentioned in the text, also included are: Clara Janés, Beatriz de Moura, Rosa María Pereda, and Marta Pessarradona. Eight are from Catalonia, but no one is from Galicia.

Bibliography

1. NARRATIVE PRIMARY SOURCES

1979a. *Cándida otra vez*. Barcelona: Ambito Literario.

1979b. "El final." In *Miguel y yo y diez cuentos más*. Madrid: Confederación Española de Cajas de Ahorros.

1981a. *Al otro lado*. Madrid: Magisterio Español.

1981b. *Plantar un árbol*. Orihuela: Ministerio de Cultura.

1982a. *La única libertad*. Madrid: Cátedra.

1982b. "Querida y admirada Greta." *Los cuadernos del Norte*, November–December, 86–91.

1983. "Ensayo de comedia." In *Ensayo de comedia y doce cuentos más*. Madrid: Confederación Española de Cajas de Ahorros.

1984. "De su mejor amiga, Celina." In *Antología de cuentistas españoles contemporáneos*, edited by Francisco García Pavón, vol. 2. Madrid: Gredos.

1985. *Contra muerte y amor*. Madrid: Cátedra.

1987. "Del amor y de la amistad." *Insula* 488–89: 35–36.

1988a. *O reloxio da torre*. Vigo: Galaxia.

1988b. *Unha árbore, un adeus*. Vigo: Galaxia [a longer version of *Plantar un árbol*].

1989. *Morir en brazos y otros cuentos*. Alicante: Aguaclara.

2. SECONDARY SOURCES

Cadenas, C. B. 1983. "Cuando los personajes lo son." *Nueva estafeta*, January, 94. A brief study of *Cándida otra vez* and *Al otro lado*.

Díaz Castañón, Carmen. 1982. "Historia de una familia." *Cuadernos del Norte* 12: 89–90. A worthy study of *La única libertad*.

García Rey, José Manuel. 1983. "Marina Mayoral: La sociedad que se cuestiona en medio de una dudosa realidad." *Cuadernos Hispanoamericanos*, 394: 214–21. A good article comparing themes in *Plantar un árbol* and *Al otro lado*.

Gullón, Germán. 1987. "El novelista como fabulador de la realidad: Mayoral,

Merino, Guelbenzu . . ." In *Nuevos y Novísimos*, edited by Ricardo Landeira and Luis T. González-del-Valle, 59–70. Boulder, Colo.: Society of Spanish and Spanish-American Studies. A deserving article because of its generational point of view.

Sánchez Arnosi, Milagros. 1982. "Entrevista a Marina Mayoral." *Insula* 431: 4–5. Contains some interesting remarks about *La única libertad*.

Valencia, Antonio. 1981. Prologue to *Al otro lado*. Madrid: Magisterio español. An overview of Mayoral's works to 1981.

Vivas, Angel. 1985. "Un paseo con el amor y la muerte." *Leer*, June, 37–39. An insightful interview with Mayoral revealing her ideas about the novel.

Zatlin, Phyllis. 1987. "Detective Fiction and the Novels of Mayoral." *Monographic Review/Revista Monográfica* 3: 279–87. An excellent article relating all of Mayoral's novels to the "novela negra."

10

Lourdes Ortiz: Mapping the Course of Postfrancoist Fiction

Robert C. Spires

Lourdes Ortiz recently said, "My parents were not artists or academicians. In fact my mother was a housewife and my father a newspaper illustrator—although he regularly attended the Café Gijón literary discussion sessions during the 1950s. When at an early age I demonstrated an interest in writing they always supported and encouraged my efforts. I guess once I started writing I never quit."[1] Apparently not. Today Lourdes Ortiz, in addition to being recognized as one of the most important new Spanish novelists, is also a dramatist, translator, literary critic, and communication theorist.[2]

After graduating from the school of philosophy and letters of the Complutense University of Madrid, Ortiz taught communication theory at the university before assuming her present position as professor of art history in the university's Royal School of Dramatic Art. During her tenure there she coauthored the monograph on communication theory in which she expounds the thesis that poetic language is the best and perhaps only defense against the mass media assaults of consumer societies.

A member of the generation immediately following that of the Goytisolos, Benet, Tusquets, and Marsé, Ortiz was born in Madrid shortly after the civil war and was subjected to a vintage Franco-era education. As a result she rejected everything associated with the literary canon: she remembers Sánchez Ferlosio's 1956 neorealist novel *El Jarama* (The Jarama River; English translation, *The One Day of the Week*, 1962) being taught as if it were catechism. She was drawn instead to Spanish-American fiction (Vargas Llosa, Sábato, Cabrera Infante), the French *nouveau roman* (Butor), and the decidedly nonconformist approaches of Juan Goytisolo and Jorge Semprún. From her present perspective, however, she confesses that

198

in spite of her rejection of the neorealist approach of novelists such as Camilo José Cela and Miguel Delibes, that mode probably has influenced her own style to one degree or another.

Active at one time in the Spanish Communist party and then in the feminist movement, she soon became disillusioned and left both organizations. She continues to champion the ideals of antifascism, freedom, and equality, but is reluctant to play the role of high priest or disciple for any dogma. Her current project, entitled "Los motivos de Circe," is a collection of stories all involving women characters discussing women's issues; nevertheless she does not want to be labeled a feminist writer.

In addition to her drama, translations, and critical studies, to date Lourdes Ortiz has published five novels: *Luz de la memoria* (Light of memory) (1976), *Picadura mortal* (Mortal sting) (1979), *En días como éstos* (On days like these) (1981), *Urraca* (Magpie) (1982), and *Arcángeles* (Archangels) (1986). One of the more striking aspects of Ortiz's novelistic career is the degree to which it reflects the various modes in Spanish fiction during the post-Franco era. Within the general label "novela poemática" (poeticized novel) that Gonzalo Sobejano proposes for Spanish fiction from 1975–85, he offers five subcategories: memory fiction, detective or erotic literature, testimonial, historical, and metafiction (1985, 1, 26). Without forcing the issue too much, one can match Ortiz's novels with each of these five subcategories.

Yet such a categorization is not without the inherent dangers of pigeon-holing, of reductionism for the sake of symmetry. That danger can be mitigated with a modification of Sobejano's basic paradigm. By selecting two of his categories as poles, as binary opposites as far as novelistic modes are concerned, the other three can be plotted in relative terms to one or the other polar positions. These poles may be defined as the literary mode emphasizing discourse and the mode highlighting story. Although a certain amount of reductionism is still involved in the polar representatives, the works falling in between escape that danger since they reflect a relative position between one of the poles and the hypothetical center point of perfect balance. The two poles, then, are represented by novels published the year of the dictator's death (1975) and constitute respectively the two major trends in post-Franco Spanish fiction.

Although the authors of the two key novels share the distinction of being native Barcelonians, their novels have little in common other than the date of publication. Juan Goytisolo's *Juan sin tierra* (*Juan the Landless*, 1977) and Eduardo Mendoza's *La verdad sobre el caso Savolta* (The truth about the Savolta case) are true binary opposites, the first a radical "writerly" and the second a classical "readerly" text. Between them they help define the boundaries of Spanish fiction since the end of the dictatorship.

Juan sin tierra is a novel about itself, about the process of its own coming-into-being.[3] Although there are references to family history, historical events concerning most notably Lawrence of Arabia and Père Foucault, and to popular art figures, all the references noted become signs pointing at the act of creating the novel. Indeed, the primary "story" of *Juan sin tierra* concerns the writing of the novel at hand. Such a transformation of the conventional concept of story is what justifies placing Goytisolo's revolutionary work at one of the poles on the map of recent Spanish fiction.

La verdad sobre el caso Savolta deserves credit for initiating the other major novelistic trend in postfrancoist Spain, and therefore serves as pennant for the opposite boundary. Whereas Goytisolo's novel exemplifies what Sobejano labels "escriptiva" fiction (language itself is foregrounded and the process of narrating eclipses what is narrated), Mendoza's novel privileges story over storytelling. It involves the mystery surrounding the assassination of a wealthy industrialist, Savolta, during the politically and socially explosive years of 1917–19 in Barcelona. The recreation of the past is effected by means of the protagonist's memories, the narrator's discourses, and the presentation of documents and letters. But it is mystery, not history, that best characterizes this novel. Indeed, Mendoza's novel gave artistic respectability to the mystery genre, long disdained by the literati as merely commercial pop art, and thereby served as precursor to what continues to be a major trend in Spanish fiction.[4]

In addition to the distinctions noted, *Juan sin tierra* rhetorically proclaims the connections between art and society, while *La verdad sobre el caso Savolta* scenically suggests it. That analogy does not imply a value judgment à la Henry James and Percy Lubbock, but rather is designed to define further the polar positions represented by these two key novels. To a large degree Spanish fiction from 1975 to the present can be seen as an effort to reconcile the conflict between process and product, between discourse and story.

The polarity between discourse (metafiction) and story (mystery fiction) accounts for the most acclaimed novels and short stories published during the period noted. Leaning toward the metafictional pole are works such as Luis Goytisolo's *Antagonía* (1973–81), Gonzalo Torrente Ballester's *Fragmentos de Apocalipsis* (Fragments of the Apocalypse) (1977), José María Vaz de Soto's *Fabián* (1977), José María Merino's *Novela de Andrés Choz* (Andrés Choz's novel)

(1976), Javier Tomeo's *El castillo de la carta cifrada* (The castle of the coded letter) (1979), Esther Tusquets's *El amor es un juego solitario* (Love is a solitary game) (1979), Carmen Martín Gaite's *El cuarto de atrás* (1978) (*The Back Room*, 1983), and José María Guelbenzu's *El río de la luna* (Moon River) (1981). In descending order the works mentioned tend to be more story-oriented than Juan Goytisolo's standardbearer, and Guelbenzu's is definitely closer to the center than to the metafictional extreme.

On the opposite pole are all of Manuel Vázquez Montalbán's best-selling series featuring the detective Carvalho, Beatriz Pottecher's *Ciertos tonos del negro* (Certain tones of black) (1985), José Millás's *Visión del ahogado* (Vision of a drowned man) (1977), Alvaro Pombo's *El héroe de las mansardas de Mansard* (The hero of the mansards of Mansard) (1983), Juan Benet's *El aire de un crimen* (The atmosphere of a crime) (1980), Antonio Muñoz Molina's *El invierno en Lisboa* (Winter in Lisbon) (1987), and the stories in Ignacio de Pisón's *Alguien te observa en secreto* (Someone is secretly watching you) (1985) and *Antofagasta* (1987).[5] With the exception of Vázquez Montalbán's novels, each work in the latter group is less conventionally enigma-driven, and therefore tends increasingly more toward the center than Mendoza's precursor. Indeed this drifting from the poles toward the center seems to define the prevailing trajectory of the most recent Spanish fiction, a vivid example of which is Luis Goytisolo's fine 1987 novel, *La paradoja del ave migratoria* (The paradox of the migratory bird). In short, as the latter novel demonstrates so effectively, Spanish novelists seem to be defining a solution to the conflict between discourse and story; they tend to be discovering the formula for creating texts that foreground the act of narrating without sacrificing the art of telling a story.[6] Lourdes Ortiz's novelistic trajectory, on the other hand, does not flow chronologically from one pole toward the center, but rather reflects a conscious effort to touch each point on the spectrum. Ignoring chronology, therefore, I begin with analyses of the two polar novels and then turn to the remaining three to determine just how each fills a spot in the center of the spectrum.

Ortiz's most recent novel is also her most radically "writerly" or metafictional. In effect *Arcángeles* attempts to redefine the very concept of story. There is, however, a more or less conventional anecdote appearing in the second part. It concerns Manolo, an aspiring botanist, who is being forced to abandon his studies to search for a job in a stagnant economy. He rejects the offer for some easy money on a drug deal, as well as the efforts of his sister's boyfriend to recruit him for homosexual prostitution. His sister and girlfriend, on the other hand, are clearly in the process of prostituting themselves as the only viable means of advancing in the Spanish socioeconomic system. This section ends with Manolo proposing that he would be willing to become a gigolo for the frustrated wife for whom his girlfriend works.

Notwithstanding the Manolo anecdote, the real "story," and by far the most prominent one, concerns the process of writing the novel. It all begins with the angel Gabriel addressing the "author," followed by the announcement: "Y el ángel del señor se instala en el libro" [And the angel of the lord settles himself into the book] (9). From then on the author and Gabriel engage in a discussion of what the novel should be about and how to gather material for it. The female author, true to the stereotype, proposes to write about idyllic love, but Gabriel is skeptical, saying he is not right for the part. When they agree that what they have to this point is the initiation phase, Gabriel moans, "Supongo que, inevitablemente me harás descender a los infiernos" [I suppose that inevitably you will make me descend into hell] (21). Hell in this case is Madrid, through which Gabriel travels and describes with Stygian imagery. Included in this current version of the mythic adventure is an interview of the author by an American journalist concerning the novel (when this caricatured feminist critic appears on the scene, Gabriel conveniently disappears). When the reporter departs Gabriel reappears to continue his peripatetic adventure. He describes with bitter irony what he sees and what happens to him. A totally materialistic world emerges where success for men as well as women requires some form of prostitution. There are also parodies of historians, literary critics, dramatists, and poets. After the first part follows the Manolo anecdote of part 2 summarized above, and then in part 3 again the focus returns to the process as opposed to the product. Manolo reappears first with a job as a waiter and then as a street vendor on Paseo de Recoletos. Yet he and Gabriel change identities at various times or merge into a single character until their fusion leads to almost total confusion. Near the end Gabriel turns to the author and reminds her that although she was supposed to write a love novel, "se te llena el libro de muchachitos explotados" [your book has become filled with little exploited children] (196). Then, as the process draws to a conclusion, Gabriel speculates that, true to form, it will all end dramatically in tears (after all, the author is a woman). If she had left things to him, on the other hand, he would have written her a happy ending.

Arcángeles, then, is about its own process of creation. In fact the strategy is designed to make the second part appear as the product of the first one; the discussions between Gabriel and the author and the search for material result in Manolo's story. Then in the third section the distinction between process and product becomes blurred as the story that was told begins to influence the act of telling. The author is manipulated by rather than being the manipulator of what she narrates.[7] In any case the emphasis is on process, on the act of narrating as opposed to its product. *Arcángeles*, therefore, defines one of the boundaries enclosing Lourdes Ortiz's novelistic production to date.

Whereas *Arcángeles* foregrounds the process of narrating and therefore belongs on the metafictional pole, *Picadura mortal* features what is narrated and as a result constitutes the polar opposite to *Arcángeles*; a "who-done-it," *Picadura mortal* represents a story novel in the most conventional sense of the term.[8] Bárbara Arenas, the first-person narrator, works for a boss named Juan Carlos (any analogy with the Spanish king would seem to be encouraged). She is in bed with an insistently virile friend when Juan Carlos calls to ask her to take a case. Since she has tired of her amorous companion she immediately accepts the assignment: "di un cálido beso de desagravio a mi voluntarioso acompañante y le puse de patitas en la calle en cuanto estuvo vestido y peinadito" [I gave my persistent partner a warm reassuring kiss and booted him out as soon as he was dressed and had his curls arranged] (11). She then catches a flight to the Canary Islands, where she is to investigate the disappearance of a wealthy industrialist named Ernesto. She is met at the airport by Adolfo, Ernesto's eldest son.

Adolfo takes Bárbara to the mansion, where she meets the other members of the family. Margarita, the twenty-three-year-old recent bride of Ernesto, seems to have an unusually close relationship with Adolfo. Roberto, the second eldest son, is having an affair with Adolfo's wife, Rosario. Roberto's wife Adela spends most of the time in her room yet she exerts an intimidating influence over the others. Roberto and Adela have two daughters, Nora, married to Guillermo, a mobster type shunned by the other members of the family, and María, a fifteen-year-old "swinger." Although Carlos, the youngest son, is absent initially since his father disowned him when he became involved in some illicit activity, he emerges dramatically near the end of the story. Finally there is González, the father's trusted foreman, who in effect has run the family tobacco industry since it was founded.

The police believe that Ernesto was kidnapped by politicians (he was intending to run for office in the next elections), while the members of the family are convinced he was murdered. Until a body is found there can be no inheritance and meanwhile the family business is exclusively in the hands of González. Roberto points the finger at Adolfo and Margarita, claiming that they killed Ernesto and have targeted him and Rosario next. Since he is having an affair with Rosario, however, the same plot could apply to him.

In her investigation Bárbara discovers that various of the principals are involved in smuggling operations, drug dealings and use, political intrigue, blackmail, and murder (Adela, González and two secondary characters are disposed of before the case is completed). There is a series of twists in the plot and a surprise ending.

Picadura mortal is, then, a formula novel with the exception of featuring a female detective.[9] Although her gender is different, her character is very similar to male models. The opening scene in which she rids herself of a bedmate whose services are no longer appreciated could be taken out of a Vázquez Montalbán or any other macho detective novel. In fact, essentially a female plays what is conventionally a male role—complete with judo punches, narrow escapes, and casual sexual encounters. On the other side of the coin, Bárbara's task is made more difficult precisely because she is a woman. She notes that Roberto's gaze communicates a disdainful attitude toward women (15), she realizes that González is the type that viscerally hates women (44), the police inspector is uncooperative in part because he also does not trust women (100), and finally, when Adolfo becomes upset with the direction of the investigation he declares that he should never have hired a woman to do the job (112). That she does the job, however, and uncovers the complicated web of intrigue serves as a statement in itself. One can argue that an imitation of male role models is not exactly the kind of statement women need to hear, but if one looks beyond the fictitious protagonist to the posited author, the statement changes. It is not really a question of imitating male models, but of reviving the art of storytelling in Spanish fiction; the message, in short, does not concern the protagonist within but the posited author outside the novel. Together, then, *Arcángeles* and *Picadura mortal* provide a useful frame from which to view Ortiz's novelistic production.

Closest to the metafictional mode of *Arcángeles* is the 1982 novel *Urraca*, whose operative verb is "to write." The action takes place in a prison cell in the twelfth century where the imprisoned Queen Urraca is writing a chronicle of her reign with the goal that "los juglares recojan la verdad y la transmitan de aldea en aldea y de reino en reino" [the minstrels can gather the truth and transmit it from village to village and from kingdom to kingdom] (12). What she writes about is not heroes and heroines but hedonists and harlots; not victories on the battlefield but in the bedroom. She chronicles examples of sordidness and sodomy, intrigue and incest, all a history of how she wrested the power to rule from her father and then her husband, only to lose it to her son. But the focus constantly shifts from the product to the process as what is written becomes overshadowed by the question of writing itself. In the final analysis *Urraca* has more to say about written communication than about eleventh- and twelfth-century Spanish history.[10]

Almost immediately the first-person narrator realizes that an attempt to chronicle her story is far from simple. There are two obstacles to overcome, the first involving the conflict between satisfying the historical narrative expectations of a chronicle and the second dealing with her need to express the very personal aspects that determined her life. Although in effect everything she narrates constitutes highly personal rather than historical narrative, she repeatedly feels compelled to remind herself that certain themes are not appropriate for a chronicle. She feels she must apologize for the lack of chronological order (51), and admits that "una crónica no debe detenerse en sentimientos y en personajes secundarios" [a chronicle should not pause to deal with sentiments and secondary characters] (48). Finally she is forced to make a confession: "Me doy cuenta de que las crónicas, Roberto, son siempre incompletas, mentirosas" [I realize, Roberto, that chronicles are always incomplete and untrue] (67). She is realizing that so-called historical narrative is a fraud; the word can never be the idea, object, or person it represents. "Mientras escribo tengo la impresión de que el tiempo desgasta y el relato convierte a los protagonistas en muñecos de feria; les roba la palabra, el gesto, y mi juicio les despoja, les desnuda" [While I am writing I have the impression that time is being wasted and the story is converting the characters into puppets; it is robbing them of their speech and gestures, and my opinions pluck them clean, leave them naked] (68). She realizes, in short, that she is being betrayed by the very mode she had hoped to control and to manipulate.

But mode is not the only thing that betrays her. The second obstacle to her goal is Roberto, the monk assigned to look after her in the cell and the direct recipient of her narrative. When she begins to tell how her husband, Raimundo, in the presence of the Bishop, began to fondle her after drinking too much wine, she interrupts herself: "No te preocupes, monje, que tu reina no va a seguir por ahí ... No enrojezcas ..." [Don't worry, Monk, your queen is not going to continue along this line ... Don't blush ...] (26). Later she blames the disorder in her story on Roberto's innocence (79), and claims that for his benefit she is increasing expectations and dramatic tension by emphasizing key moments (85). In short, Urraca is forced to concede that the object to whom her narrative is directed, her narratee, exerts almost as much influence over her text as she does; he is a challenge to her sovereignty over the narrative.

Yet Urraca as narrator is no more inclined than she was as queen to be ruled by her subjects. And in imitation of her strategy as a sovereign, she begins to conquer her rival by means of seduction: "Aben Ammar debía parecerse a ti, monje; tenía seguramente tus mismas manos largas, esas que yo presiento destinadas a recorrer la piel; tenía ese talle delgado y firme que tú castigas con cilicios y que él seguramente bañaba con óleos" [Aben Ammar must have looked a lot like you, Monk; almost certainly he had your same long hands which I can just tell are destined to caress skin; he had that firm and slim body that you punish with hair shirts and that he no doubt bathed with fragrant oils] (37). Then when she begins to describe the scene where Zaida, the Moorish princess, seduced her father she draws a provocative analogy: "Cojines de seda, monje, donde tú podrías recostarte, mientras yo, tumbada a tu lado, iría recorriendo tu cuerpo con mi lengua" [Silk cushions, Monk, where you could lie down while I, stretched out at your side, would be exploring your whole body with my tongue] (38). Compared to the stylized verbal foreplay, the seduction itself is totally prosaic: "Bien; por fin ha sucedido. No ha sido demasiado gratificante, pero me he traído la calma. La carne blanca y sin vello de mi monje me he traído la huella de otros cuerpos" [Well it finally happened. It wasn't especially gratifying, but it calmed me. The white and silky flesh of my monk brought with it the traces of other bodies] (121). Rather than literature serving as an erotic stimulus, here is the opposite; the monk's passion allows Urraca narratively to recreate Raimundo's passion: "aquel alarido que ahora vuelvo a oír tras los jadeos precipitados, asustados del hermano Roberto, aquella garganta joven de animal en celo" [that moan that I now hear again over the rapid, frightened panting of Brother Roberto, that young voice of an animal in heat] (121). Although the inexperienced cleric leaves Urraca physically unsatisfied, he allows her to revel in the pleasure of the text. Indeed, since she is now limited to reliving her sex life as a text life, Roberto is more important to her as a reader than a lover.

Urraca, however, does not learn from past mistakes. As queen her seductive strategies brought her only temporary authority, and so as narrator she suffers a similar fate. In fact, even before the seduction she was dependent on her recipient: "Hoy no ha acudido a mi celda el hermano Roberto y le echo de menos y, de repente, esta crónica me parece vacía" [Today Brother Roberto did not come to my cell and I miss him and, suddenly, this chronicle seems empty to me] (66). When Roberto's absences become more frequent, Urraca becomes desperate: "Te necesito a ti para que me escuches; no puedo pasarme ya sin tu sorpresa y tu ignorancia" [I need you to listen to me; I can't go on now without your surprise and ignorance] (110). Roberto the narratee is now not only equal to but indeed superior to Urraca the narrator. Her very reason for being now depends on him.

The subservience implicit in Urraca's dependence on Roberto soon becomes clear even to her as she pleads, "no puedes abandonarme. Tú eres mi testigo, el que ha alentado mi escritura" [you can't abandon me. You are my witness, the one that has inspired my writing] (200). But she knows he is more than mere witness and finally she is forced to ask him to assert his inexorable authority: "De este modo quisiera yo, Roberto, que tú completaras mi crónica, introduciendo la metáfora, jugando con las palabras" [In this way I would like you, Roberto, to complete my chronicle, introducing metaphors and plays on words] (203). Urraca's machinations to assure her authority finally serve to deprive her of it. Ultimately she must surrender her text to her reader.

Although it may seem to be stating the obvious, *Urraca* is fiction, not history; it celebrates invention by means of metaphors and plays on words, and parodies the very concept of a chronicle as a documentation of reality. Yet this novel is less radically metafictional than *Arcángeles*; it has been read, after all, as an historical novel and such a reading can be defended. Yet as the preceding analysis demonstrates, the crucial verb is "to write," and in the final analysis Urraca's act of telling her story overshadows what she tells. The novel, therefore, falls to the metafictional side of center.

Leaning toward the story pole represented by *Picadura mortal* is *En días como éstos*. The latter novel concerns the experiences of Toni, who is a member of a militant guerilla organization. The work is divided into three parts. The first relates an incident in the mountains, where one member of the guerilla band is gravely wounded, another is lost and abandoned, and two policemen are killed as Toni and his friend Carlos carry the wounded man to a village. Part 2 focuses on Toni in his own village after he has left the movement. Finally the police arrive and arrest him, and he is led away, assuming that he was identified by the companion abandoned in the mountains. The third part begins with Toni in prison, where

another member of the organization masterminds an escape. Toni
discovers that his freedom, however, is in effect an imprisonment as
he is assigned to another guerilla band. When he announces his
intent once again to leave the movement, he is asked as a final
assignment to arrange to meet and talk with Carlos. They meet in a
warehouse and die under a rain of bullets as their hands touch.

Although *En días como éstos* concerns one of the more sensitive
political issues in contemporary Spain—militant opposition to the
central government—the renegade organization is never identified
and ideologies are totally eschewed. The key strategy for defusing the
political question is the use of an extradiegetic narrating voice—the
narrator is not a character in the novel—and an intradiegetic point
of focalization—the reader is offered the protagonist Toni's
perspective on what transpires.[11] Since Toni is what can best be
described as a simple soul, it is apparent that the narrator
understands far more than the character. Yet whatever the narrator
knows and understands is only implicitly revealed; all explicit
explanations are limited to Toni's level of comprehension. As a
result the focus switches from the topical question of terrorism in
Spain to a more universal one concerning political change by means
of military action.

The combination of exterior voice and interior vision is apparent
from the very beginning as Toni, having awakened to discover that
two of his three companions have left the campsite, begins to ponder
his situation. He recalls the inability of his mother to understand
when he tried to tell her why he was joining the rebels: "Tampoco
Toni habría sabido qué decirla; él no sabía del todo por qué estaba
allí pero intuía ya, con el paso del tiempo—mientras sus ojos y sus
oídos se plegaban al bosque—que era mejor no preguntárselo.
Carlos y otros como él sí parecían saberlo" [Toni wouldn't have
known how to tell her, either; he didn't fully understand why he was
there but he now sensed, with the passing of time—while his eyes and
ears were trained on the woods—that it was better not to ask oneself.
Carlos and others like him did seem to understand it] (11). Since the
narrator merely reports Toni's thoughts, the source of knowledge is
shifted to "Carlos and others like him," with the result that the
reader finds him or herself in Toni's position. Just as Toni does, the
reader must look to Carlos for clarification and guidance.

Carlos's authority within the text is underscored when Toni, as the
two labor to carry their wounded comrade to a village, finally voices
his confusion and announces that he intends to return home. To this
his friend replies, "ellos no te dejarán marchar. Sabes muchas
cosas" [They won't let you leave. You know a lot of things] (34).

Again the narrator's voice enters to reveal Toni's reaction: "Toni movió la cabeza apesadumbrado. Los de arriba. Había olvidado también a los sin rostro, a los sin nombre" [Toni moved his head dejectedly. Those at the top. He had forgotten also those faceless and nameless people] (34). A marked contrast is formed between those anonymous and even invisible leaders and Carlos, who not only is beside him but who insists on personally carrying their wounded companion. And of course it falls to Carlos to explain that those champions of the cause for which Toni blindly is risking his life now hold him captive. Little wonder that the reader's sympathy and loyalty, just like those of Toni, are with Carlos.

After the wounded man is successfully deposited in the village, the two friends part company, Carlos heading for the French border and Toni, despite the warning, returning to his home. There he cannot resist the need to narrate his adventures to his younger brother, Pedro, even though he knows that in doing so he runs the risk of glamorizing his experiences and thereby encouraging Pedro to follow his footsteps. Whereas he can recreate the events, Toni is frustrated in his narrating role because he cannot recreate Carlos: "Había intentado explicarle a Pedro cómo era y se daba cuenta de que sus rasgos se desdibujaban, de que apenas conservaba anécdotas, palabras que pudieran devolverle a Carlos y hacerle real ante el hermano. Era un buen tipo, dijo al terminar" [He had intended to describe to Pedro what he was like, and he realized that his characteristics were becoming blurred, that he hardly had any stories or words that could bring back Carlos and make him real for his brother. He was a good guy, he said as he finished] (53). Then in one of the few examples in the novel where the narrator provides access to someone else's thoughts, we are told that Pedro realized that "la imagen de Carlos era la parte más grata que intentaba transcribirle Toni" [Carlos's image was the most gratifying part that Toni tried to convey to him] (54). As opposed to the phantasmal leaders of the movement, Carlos is too real to be captured by mere words, and so the narrator feels obliged to tell us that Pedro can sense what his brother is trying to convey. Such a textual strategy allows the reader to experience the affection and loyalty Toni feels toward his friend. That loyalty, in turn, forms the basis for the ultimate irony of the story.

Toni's previous fears are realized when Pedro runs off to join the movement. Later the police come for Toni and instead of trying to run from them he turns himself over. The reader quickly shares his suspicions that the man they abandoned in the mountains revealed his identity to the police since that man, Agustín, has been characterized as arbitrary and often in conflict with Carlos. Even so Toni does not blame Agustín for what he did.

In prison there is an unexpected twist when a fellow comrade informs Toni that Agustín was killed. This man, Andrés, then claims that Carlos is responsible for giving Toni's name to the police. First Toni responds by excusing Carlos, just as he did Agustín, then he convinces himself that his brother Pedro was taken prisoner and tortured until he revealed what Toni had told him. Next he begins to suspect Andrés of lying when he said Agustín was killed. Finally he can no longer deal with the problem "y tras finalizar todas las posibilidades y descartar aquéllas que le dolían, se quedaba con la más fácil, la que servía para devolverle la calma" [and after considering all the possibilities and discarding those that made him feel bad he picked the easiest one, the one that brought him serenity] (85). Again the reader is placed in Toni's position. There is no way to know who the traitor was and so the reader, as he, must opt for the least painful choice, which of course has to be Agustín. And again if it was Agustín he was not guilty of a crime for in Toni's mind, "no había hecho sino poner en marcha un mecanismo que de antiguo le estaba destinado" [he had only started in motion a machine that since antiquity was headed straight at Toni] (80). By virtue of the narrator's neutrality the whole question of guilt or innocence, villain or hero has been eliminated from *En días como éstos*; the focus falls instead on the victims of the timeless process called revolutionary change. Toni and Carlos, therefore, are not victims of one another or of their own comrades, but of a tragic process defying rational explanation. At least that seems to be one of the messages of *En días como éstos* conveyed by the narrator's silence.

Whereas *Urraca* falls clearly on the process side of center, and *En días como éstos* on the product side, *Luz de la memoria* finds itself almost squarely in the center—since it is Ortiz's first novel this center position again puts her at odds with the trend of her colleagues. A reflection of the novel's central position is the search within it for unity, on both the story and the discourse level. The anecdote concerns Enrique García Alonso, born in 1942 into a conservative family. The second of three sons, he was supposed to be a girl, according to his parents' hopes and expectations. A misfit in his own family since he preferred reading to the masculine games championed by his father and brothers, he was allowed to enroll in the university provided he major in something "practical." His choice, physics, proved unsatisfactory and he dropped out of school and joined a Communist cell. During that time he married Pilar, but after the birth of their daughter she abandoned him for a mutual friend and political colleague, Carlos. Eventually Enrique is arrested and imprisoned for two years, a punishment that does not seem to be related to his apparent assassination of an old man, the motives and details of which are never provided. Sometime after his release he meets Pilar on the street, kills her dog, and is committed to a mental institution. While there he temporarily loses his ability to talk and when he regains it and is declared sane, he begins to work at the Ministry of Information, a position arranged for him by his father but one he soon leaves. Finally Pilar joins him for a weekend at the home of friends in Ibiza. After a night of drinking and lovemaking they go to a deserted tower, which he climbs and from which he then plunges to his death.

This summary makes clear that *Luz de la memoria* is about Enrique and the story of his life. Yet especially in the second half of the novel the reader's attention is divided between what is told and how it is told. Even in the first part there is an awareness of the narrating source since the *histoire* must be reconstructed from a series of flashbacks to nonsequential moments in the past, and since there are several changes in the viewing perspective. For example, the first part has ten chapters and the narrative present concerns Enrique's sessions in the hospital with a psychiatrist. Because at this point Enrique is mute, the narration represents his thoughts and memories triggered by the doctor's comments. What results are a series of flashbacks and at times the scene changes with no clear transition from the hospital to his previous confinement in prison. Similar shifts involve his early childhood and his clandestine political activities, with frequent references to the old man he apparently assassinated. To complicate matters further, there are interspersed scenes that seem to be taken from movies, and chapters 2, 4, and 8 contain, respectively, his mother's, father's, and wife's testimonies to the psychiatrist. Such a fragmentation of the *histoire* seems clearly designed to enable the reader to experience Enrique's conflicts and personal sense of a fragmented existence.

The aesthetic experience of fragmentation is most dramatically created at the beginning of chapter 5: "Yo soy éste, yo era aquél, soy éste que lee, era ese que lee, que desmenuza las palabras, que está sentado frente a los cuatro, que les mira, les miro. . ." [I am this one, I was that one, I am this one who is reading, I was that one who was reading, who dismantles the words, who is seated facing the four at whom he looks, at whom I am looking. . .] (55). The scene involves Enrique meeting with four other members of the clandestine organization, all of whom use an alias. By virtue of the switches in verbs and demonstratives all personal and temporal identity is obscured; an unreal, even make-believe atmosphere is conveyed. The characters seem to be playing revolutionaries and trying to convince themselves that their charade bestows upon them divine insight to lead the masses ("nos hace, nos hacía como dioses" [it makes us, it made us god-like]) (55). From the perspective of his narrative present Enrique makes the reader experience the absurdity of that whole enterprise. Thus, although the reader is aware of these syntactical manipulations, they serve, rather than undermine, the conventional suspension of disbelief.

In the first part (spanning approximately the first half of the novel) the narrative present pertains to the hospital, while the remaining seven chapters primarily deal with what happens after Enrique's release. Accompanying this switch in time and place is a change of emphasis from the story being told to the act of telling it.

The first chapter of the second part is again narrated by Enrique, but the next chapter, designated with the letter A, begins with the following question: "¿Cómo narrar el ácido de Enrique? Es algo intransferible, nos diría él, algo que transcrito pierde valor" [How should Enrique's "acid trip" be narrated? It's something that is not transferable, he would tell us, something that once it is transcribed loses its value] (165). The next chapter, B, also contains a series of similar questions: "¿Cómo expresarlo? ¿Cómo narrar cuando ni siquiera él podría hacerlo...? ¿Cómo describir ese momento difícil . . .?" (How can it be expressed? How can it be narrated when not even he could do it...? How can that difficult moment be described...?] (171). Such questions shift attention from the story to the discourse; indeed, at this point the "story" concerns the method of narrating.

In the following chapter (designated with a number rather than a letter) Enrique himself reassumes the role of narrator and for a while his story is once again foregrounded. He tells of his visit to Ibiza and of Pilar's arrival to spend the weekend, which signals a type of reconciliation between them. Yet it is mutual boredom rather than rekindled love or passion that seems to draw them together. On their fateful night together Enrique confesses a dramatic secret desire: "He pensado que podría escribir mis memorias. A veces juego a que escribo sobre una persona, sobre una vida cualquiera que luego resulta ser la mía. He pensado que contarlo podría resultar divertido, pero me falta siempre el final ... Me gustaría que me ayudases a encontrar un buen final para mi posible novela" [I have been thinking that I could write my memoirs. At times I pretend that I am writing about a person, about any life at all which then turns out to be mine. I have been thinking that it would be fun to tell it, but I am always at a loss for a way to end it ... I would like you to help me find a good ending for my possible novel] (180–81). At this point the line between discourse and story is almost totally blurred. It seems as though the character has fused with the author, that creation and creator have become one and the same.

The fusion of story and discourse leads directly to the problem of an ending. As Enrique gazes at the sea he finally realizes how to solve the dual problem of his life and of that of the narrative: "Mira por dónde, ése podría ser un buen método: entrar despacito, mirando la imagen que se refleja en el agua, fundiéndose con ella poco a poco hasta el momento mismo en que cesa la esquizofrenia, el desdoblamiento, y uno es uno al fin" [Look there, that could be a good way: enter slowly, looking at the image that is reflected in the water, fusing with it little by little until the very moment in which the schizophrenia, the bifurcation, ceases, and one is finally one] (202). Suicide seems to be the only solution to the fragmentation that has characterized both the narrative and Enrique's life. When Enrique then throws himself from the tower one wonders if such a suicide responds to a psychological need in the character or an artistic one in the novel (a leitmotiv is the image of an anonymous woman who met a similar fate and whose death Enrique witnessed as a child). Is he playing the role of protagonist or author at this point? Those are inescapable questions since the novel ends with the very description offered earlier of the body of the anonymous woman. In *Luz de la memoria* it is difficult indeed to draw the line between story and discourse. One is all but forced to conclude that the novel is simultaneously about the characters and about its own creation; Ortiz's first novel straddles the line between the metafictional and story poles.

Lourdes Ortiz's novelistic production dramatically reflects the discourse/story conflict of post-Franco fiction. On the discourse pole is her latest effort, *Arcángeles*, and on the story pole her experiment with the detective genre, *Picadura mortal*.[12] Although *Urraca* creates an historical setting, it really addresses the need to write, which places it on the discourse side of center but short of the polar position occupied by *Arcángeles*. *Días como éstos*, on the other hand, falls to the story side of center. Toni's biography is definitely the focal point, but in the final analysis the extreme care to maintain narrative objectivity almost becomes a focal point itself. In other words, the craft of fiction is much more evident here than in *Picadura mortal*. Finally, the dual search for psychological and artistic unity, as protagonist and author fuse, justifies plotting *Luz de la memoria* at or near the center; in this novel what is told and the process of telling it strike a felicitous balance.

Although the labels "history," "testimony," and "memory" applied respectively to *Urraca, Días como éstos,* and *Luz de la memoria*[13] are not inaccurate, perhaps they are inadequate. Each novel evinces a conflict between discourse and story that is central to the experiences and messages they convey. *Arcángeles* and *Picadura mortal,* on the other hand, clearly privilege one over the other and in so doing invite a more definitive classification.

One can truly say that Lourdes Ortiz's novels are "all over the map." As a result they serve better than any other current novelist's work as a revealing microcosm of post-Franco fiction.

Notes

1. As stated by the novelist in a conversation with me on 21 July 1987. Much of the information on Ortiz that follows was provided by her in this conversation.

2. To date only one of her three plays has been published: *Las murallas de Jericó: Farsa en tres actos y un prólogo* (The walls of Jericho: A farce in three acts with a prologue) (Madrid: Ediciones Peralta, 1980). Her translated works include a translation from French of Jean Jolivet's *La filosofía medieval en Occidente* (Madrid: Siglo XXI, 1974); from German of Jacques Le Goff's *La Baja Edad Media* (Madrid: Siglo XXI, 1970); and from Italian of Aleksandr Romanovich's *Lenguaje y comportamiento* (Madrid: Fundamentos, 1980). As a literary critic she has written *Conocer Rimbaud y su obra* (Understanding Rimbaud and his work) (Barcelona: Dopesa, 1979); "Prólogo y cronología" to *La piel de zapa* by Honoré de Balzac (Madrid: Edaf, 1981); and with Fernando Moreno, *Sociedad 80* (Madrid: Santillana, 1980). In the field of communication theory, with Pablo del Río, she published *Comunicación crítica* (Madrid: Pablo del Río, 1977).

3. I refer the reader to my analysis of this aspect in *Beyond the Metafictional Mode: Directions in the Modern Spanish Novel* (Lexington: University Press of Kentucky, 1984). In addition to offering a modal definition of metafiction and analyses of *Juan sin tierra,* plus several post-Franco examples of the genre, I also cite other studies of Goytisolo's work.

4. As evidence in support of this statement, Constantino Bértolo, in a brief article entitled "Vinos ligeros," *El País,* 16 July 1987, p. 3 of the section "Libros," says the following in reference to Antonio Muñoz Molina's *El invierno en Lisboa*: "sin duda es la novela más significativa de la narrativa española reciente, pero es al tiempo un buen ejemplo de cómo nuestros jóvenes escritores acaban siempre por recurrir a una trama policíaca. . . ." [without question it is the most significant work in recent Spanish narrative, but at the same time it is a good example of how our young novelists always end up relying on a detective plot. . . .] Although one can argue that Vázquez Montalbán deserves credit for the detective or "novela negra" movement, he really did not receive recognition from the literary establishment— and some are still reluctant to recognize him as a real artist—until his 1979 *Asesinato en el Comité Central.* As a reflection of his status with the literary establishment see

his comments, "No escribo novelas negras," in *El Urogallo* 9–10 (January–February 1987): 26–27.

5. A very lucid definition of the modal components of this genre is provided by María-Elena Bravo, "Literatura de la distensión: El elemento policíaco," *Insula* 472 (March 1986): 1, 12–13. In her article Bravo discusses Mendoza's *El laberinto de las aceitunas*, Vázquez Montalbán's *Asesinato en el Comité Central*, and Benet's *El aire de un crimen* as she analyzes the degree to which these novels adhere to the conventions of the genre (in effect Benet subverts more than adheres to them). Also of value on the subject are William V. Spanos, "The Detective and the Boundary: Some Notes on the Postmodern Literary Imagination," *Boundary 2* 1 (Fall 1972): 147–68; and Salvador Vázquez de Parga, "Novela policíaca," *El Urogallo* 9–10 (January–February 1987): 19–25. For a list of novels of this type that have failed in general to make it into the canon see Tébar (1985, 4).

6. The conflict I have been defining serves as one of the principal discursive themes of Martín Gaite's *El cuarto de atrás* as the first-person narrator and her mysterious visitor engage in an extended discussion of how to integrate what Emile Benveniste, *Problems in General Linguistics*, trans. Mary Elizabeth Meck (Coral Gables: Univ. of Miami Press, 1971) labels "historical narrative"—in which the personality of the speaker or writer is almost totally effaced—with the existential need to write "personal narrative" (see Benveniste's chapter "The Correlations of Tense in the French Verb" pp. 205–15). Martín Gaite's masterpiece serves as striking evidence that at least in this case the thesis being proposed is not totally a critic's invention.

7. All this can be seen, of course, as a variation of Unamuno's game of characters creating authors. A much more immediate precursor and one with striking structural similarities is the very novel proposed as the standardbearer for the metafictional pole, Goytisolo's *Juan sin tierra*.

8. Ortiz wrote the novel as a response to certain critics who claimed that the new generation of Spanish novelists was incapable of writing interesting plots. Although she is not particularly pleased with the result, she feels that writing *Picadura mortal* was a necessary and valuable experience for her development as a novelist (conversation of 21 July 1987). The novel appeared in the series "Club de crimen: La novela policíaca española" of Sedmay Ediciones. The series and the publishing house are no longer in existence.

9. Tébar (1985) claims that Bárbara Arenas, the protagonist of *Picadura mortal*, is the only female detective in the new Spanish examples of the genre.

10. Ortiz is not the first to write a fictional account of this famous queen. One precursor to her novel is Francisco Navarro Villoslada's 1849 version entitled, *Doña Urraca de Castilla*. I am indebted to Teresa Chapa for calling my attention to Navarro Villoslada's novel.

11. Gérard Genette, *Narrative Discourse: An Essay in Method*, trans. Jane E. Lewin (Ithaca: Cornell Univ. Press, 1980), defines such a technique as fixed internal focalization in which the narrator tells only what the character knows (see the chapter "Mood").

12. The author herself confirms the classification I am proposing for these two novels in her interview with Gregorio Morales Villena, "Entrevista con Lourdes Ortiz," (1986). At the same time she also labels *Urraca*, cited by Sobejano as one of the prototypical historical novels, as metafictional. By virtue of the graph concept I am proposing with two poles or boundaries, one can accommodate this apparent contradiction by plotting *Urraca* on the discourse side of center but not on the pole.

In short it qualifies as both a metafictional and an historical novel, and therefore should not be limited to either category.

13. Suñén (1985) calls *Luz de la memoria* an autobiographical novel. I should clarify that Suñén apparently means fictitious autobiography since the protagonist is male and the life events recalled are very different from the author's.

Bibliography

1. PRIMARY SOURCES

1976. *Luz de la memoria*. Madrid: Akal.

1979. *Picadura mortal*. Madrid: Sedmay.

1981. *En días como éstos*. Madrid: Akal.

1982. *Urraca*. Madrid: Puntual.

1986. *Arcángeles*. Barcelona: Plaza and Janés.

2. SECONDARY SOURCES

Morales Villena, Gregorio. 1986. "Entrevista con Lourdes Ortiz." *Insula* 479: 1, 10. In an interview this critic first questions Ortiz about the "metamorphosis" of her fiction and then asks about common themes and techniques.

Sobejano, Gonzalo. 1985. "La novela poemática y sus alrededores." *Insula* 464–65: 1, 26. Includes *Urraca* among the "historical novels" of the post-Franco era.

Suñén, Luis. 1985. "Escritura y realidad." *Insula* 464–65: 5–6. Mentions *Luz de la memoria* in calling Ortiz one of the promising new novelists.

Tébar, Juan. 1985. "Novela criminal española de la transición." *Insula* 464–65: 4. Makes passing reference to *Picadura mortal* in citing its uniqueness in having a female detective-protagonist.

11

Montserrat Roig and the Creation of a Gynocentric Reality

Catherine G. Bellver

Montserrat Roig is a prominent member of the sizable group of female narrators who emerged in Spain in the early 1970s. Less bound to the civil war and more geared to political change than their predecessors, this generation of writers stands as a professionally active and socially committed collection of women. Roig, a professional journalist, has won national recognition for her work in both the print and electronic media. In addition to her nonfiction works, she has published a collection of short stories, *Aprendizaje sentimental* (Sentimental apprenticeship) (1971), and four novels: *Ramona, adiós* (Good-bye Ramona) (1972); *Tiempo de cerezas* (The time of cherries) (1977); *La hora violeta* (The violet hour) (1980); and *La ópera cotidiana* (The everyday opera) (1982) (see Bibliography for original Catalan titles). Her journalistic training, involvement in feminist issues, and the historical moment in which she writes are all reflected in her fiction. Along with her female contemporaries, Roig deals with female sexuality and related topics with a formerly unknown frankness; and as a product of an era of sociopolitical change, she openly explores some of the traditional concepts of gender.

Born in Barcelona in 1946, Roig taught literature at universities in Spain and Great Britain, but her prime occupation has been that of journalist and television interviewer. Since her early collaboration in the Catalan magazine *Serra d'Or*, she has written for many Catalan and Spanish newspapers and magazines including *El Món*, *El País*, and *El Periódico*. Her articles treat literary topics, current events, and feminist issues. Her television interview programs have included the successful "Personatges" (People) show of 1978–79, a series of political interviews in 1980, "Los padres de nuestros padres" (Our parents' parents) in 1984–85, and a more recent program called

"Búscate la vida" (Look out for yourself) devoted to the problems of young people.

While Roig's work in television has brought her popularity, her journalistic books have begun to establish her reputation as a humanistic investigator. In 1977 she published *Els catalans als camps nazis* (Catalans in Nazi concentration camps), the first thorough and documented study of Catalans in Nazi concentration camps, and in 1985 *La agulla daurada* (The golden needle), the product of her visit to Russia, in which she recounts the story of her stay as well as the tales of death and deprivation related to her by the survivors of the siege of Leningrad during World War II. *¿Tiempo de mujer?* (Woman's time?) (1980), a collage of articles, interviews, and feminist reflections, reveals the same desire to tell the unwritten story of women that motivates her novels. In these essays Roig reviews the concept of women portrayed by male society over the centuries and considers the dilemma of today's woman who wants to discard the negative roles assigned her without losing her own unique identity.

Roig's journalistic activities have both enhanced and hampered her work as a fiction writer. In a 1977 interview she complained that her excessive involvement in journalism and her unavoidable commitment to nonliterary issues were preventing her from concentrating on creative writing.[1] Yet she has also explained that the rigors of newspaper writing have helped her acquire mental discipline and learn the mechanics of her craft.[2] Ultimately the literary and nonliterary facets of her life intertwine in her writing. While the literary side may account for the emphasis Roig places in her nonliterary work on the personages of history, her journalistic training has undeniably left its mark on her fiction.

Journalistic influences abound in her prose style, narrative structure, authorial perspective, and in frequent references to topical social issues. The variety of voices that speak throughout the novels suggests the stance of a disinterested reporter. Like the presenter of a television human interest story, she focuses upon a few events and faces in an effort to explore the individual drama beneath the surface of historical fact. The result is a flickering montage, a fragmented view of reality whose ultimate meaning is left for the reader to discern. Within her montage effect, Roig often structures the individual episodic elements of her human chronicle along the loose lines of an interview or of a collection of notes. Her unadorned and unencumbered prose moves swiftly and effectively. Sentences are short, vocabulary simple and timely, syntax uncomplicated, and the general tone conversational. Emphasis on the referential or informative function of language stems from an avowed belief that form must follow content: "No soy de las que enfrentan puerilmente

contenido a forma. . . . Creo, no obstante, que las ideas tienen que
ser anteriores a la forma" [I am not one of those who naively pits
content against form, but I do however believe that ideas must
precede form].[3]

Beneath its surface of objective social testimony in Roig's fiction
lies a commitment to the two groups with whom she intimately
indentifies: women and Catalonians. Like many of her female
contemporaries, Roig has seized the new freedoms of the post-
Franco era as an opportunity to redefine woman and to level
indictments against a phallocentric society. By doing so she
contributes to the formation of a new type of social novel. Any social
novel is based on the desire to unmask social evils and the belief that
fiction can influence the world. However, unlike the social novelists
of the 1950s, Roig treats problems arising from deep-rooted mental
attitudes and firmly established conventions and not from
changeable circumstantial difficulties. Furthermore, in her novels
collective social concerns do not preclude identification with
psychological or personal issues. The weight of class struggle was not
generally experienced by the novelist in former social novels, but in
the new social criticism by women, authors become the articulate
spokespersons of their group and writing becomes an act of
aggression. If it is true, as Sandra Gilbert and Susan Gubar have
said,[4] that the pen represents autonomy and writing an aggression,
then one can say that by writing, this new breed of Spanish women
writers makes a vigorous assault on male constructs and begins to
sketch out autonomous female portraits.

Roig writes as a Catalan as well as a woman. The advent of
democracy in Spain has brought about the official recognition of
regional autonomy and the affirmation of linguistic independence.
The Catalan language, long forbidden as a public vehicle of
expression during the Franco regime, has been adopted by many
Catalan writers as an assertion of their regional power. By writing
all her novels in Catalan, Roig confirms the legitimacy of Catalan
literature and actively contributes to its growth. The fact that she
writes in Catalan does not mean she celebrates all aspects of
Catalonia, for, as I will show, she consistently deflates the image of
the middle-class Catalan businessman. What her use of Catalan
indicates is the close relationship between the vindication of her
language and her sex. As Geraldine C. Nichols points out, today's
Catalan women writers were brought up with the notion that both
as females and as Catalans they were inferior.[5] Thus the use of a
previously repressed language has both personal, psychological
implications and a collective, political purpose.

Through the Catalan language Roig recounts women's stories

from their own point of view in order to rewrite the traditional gender-bound definitions and thereby create a female-centered reality. Her novels record the struggles of women for freedom, self-identity, and love. Because their goals are never realized or only temporarily achieved, their common quest is continual and an elegiac cloud hovers over their lives. The frequency with which she presents passive, alienated, and unfulfilled women may serve indirectly to reaffirm stereotypes and discount change, but as a realist, Roig feels compelled to register the pervasiveness of repression because it constitutes women's reality: "No hemos alcanzado la auténtica libertad para crear la autonomía frente al mundo" [We have not achieved the authentic freedom necessary for the creation of our autonomy in the world].[6] The thread of unfulfillment that runs through her novels manifests itself in the form of both existential tedium and sexual frustration. The tedium stems from postmarital suffocation, and the sexual frustration results from situations adverse to the fulfillment of the psychic necessities of women. In Roig's novels erotic exchange most often proves to be an example of the troublesome antithesis between the situations and psychic orientations of women and men. Roig stresses the divergence of male-female perspectives not merely to chronicle the hierarchical ordering of reality but basically to override the devaluation of women. To reverse the valuation given to each sex she demythifies the patriarchal hero by revealing his deficiencies, and she vindicates woman by showing her to be unselfish, capable of real love, idealistic, and strong. The positive female qualities Roig highlights do not prevent frustration or even derangement and death from becoming the ultimate fate of her women. The dilemma for women, as she sees it, is not so much the avoidance of psychic devastation as the search for authenticity. For Roig, feminine consciousness begins by ceasing to "existir para *lo uno*, siendo *lo otro*" [to exist for the *one*, being the *other*],[7] by acknowledging the feminine order as distinctive and valid unto itself.

Part of this process of redefinition of women must be a reevaluation of history, a rereading that consists of an almost archaeological search for the vestiges of female history buried under millennia of masculine dominion, male military history, and the partiality of tradition. With the zeal of an investigative reporter, Roig uncovers in her novels the hidden story of a broad network of women whose lives span almost a century and whose history has remained neglected and therefore unknown. Her stories of lost love and its corollaries of unfulfilled expectations, betrayal, and death establish a common existential bond among women. The retrospective orientation of her novels, by placing women on a shared temporal continuum, gives them a written history previously denied them. Roig alters the peripheral role of women within the story of male achievements by making women the central focus of her narrative and the determinants of genealogy. This type of restructuring of history constitutes an important part of feminism because, in the words of one feminist scholar, feminism is "less the after-image of an obsolete theory of history as the record of great personalities than it is a tribute to intention, individual action and will."[8]

Roig uses fiction to subvert the reduction of woman to passive other in traditional male-authored historical accounts. Not only does she decentralize the masculine position in her novels, she also increases the sense of female history by incorporating into her works a variety of female texts—diaries, notes, monologues, and third-person accounts. Because female texts, like female history itself, have been ignored, submerged, and excluded from the canon, they are different from sanctioned literature, fragmentary, and inaccessible. These nonofficial, nonliterary texts become archaeological finds that bring to light a neglected culture. All the female texts Roig includes, whether they be confidential scribblings or ephemeral conversations, give a voice to those who have been obliged to keep silent and give form to the unformulated. In addition, as a writer herself, Roig produces a text with which to record, interpret, and reshape the social and cultural signs surrounding her. Through the act of writing, then, she follows her own advice to no longer "existir para *lo uno*, siendo *lo otro*" and becomes the creative subject of her own fictional world.

From the start Roig makes evident her efforts to design a gynocentric reality by shifting the focus of history from public to private activities, from history's masculine participants to its female players, and by creating a sense of female identity through repetition, parallelism, and similarity. The very titles of her first three novels single out words connoting temporal reality as change, succession, or repetition— "adiós" in *Ramona, adiós*, "tiempo" in *Tiempo de cerezas*, and "hora" in *La hora violeta*. Novel by novel she evolves a matrilineal society with a real existence validated by historical events and substantiated by the genealogical chart provided at the beginning of her third novel.

In *Ramona, adiós* Roig interweaves the stories of three generations of women named Ramona (and nicknamed Mundeta)—a grandmother married in 1894, a mother maturing during the Spanish civil war, and a granddaughter belonging to the 1960s. Roig's insistence in this novel on assigning a precise date to many of its episodes may reflect the journalist's commitment to documentation and detail, but it also lends concreteness to the female experience. By placing them on the temporal grid of chronology, Roig removes women from the shadowy zone of anonymity, conceptualized abstraction, and generalized configuration and places them within the verifiable confines of history. Women emerge from the shadows in this novel not because they assume the roles traditionally illuminated by the limelight but because Roig shifts her narrative spotlight. As one critic has suggested, more than a saga, she writes a countersaga, for while in the traditional saga women are reduced to subordinate companions, in *Ramona, adiós* it is the men who are "la pantalla o el frontón sobre el que las tres Mundetas se proyectan, rebotan o entrelazan" [the screen on which the three Mundetas project, bounce, and interconnect themselves].[9]

The events of official history—the declaration of the Second Republic (1931), the civil war (1936–39), and the student disturbances of 1966—serve in *Ramona, adiós* as a structural frame and as a point of psychological reference for its female characters. Roig clearly establishes the importance of the relation between women and history by beginning and closing the novel with an italicized first-person narrative by the mother recounting the events of 17 March 1938, the day Barcelona was bombed. Pregnant and alone, this Ramona wandered among the rubble, talking with strangers and visiting hospitals in hope of finding her husband. From her point of view this tragic event provided her a rare moment of excitement and an opportunity to feel assertive and self-sufficient. In later years, only when she spoke of this experience would she become unusually animated and would her face briefly acquire radiance. Moments of political crisis, such as war, can prove positive for women like this Ramona because they destabilize the rigidity of the patriarchal social structure. They represent a period of liberalization because, as Robert Jay Lifton has shown, historical changes give women new kinds of accomplishments for the development of new forms of knowledge.[10]

In her search to refocus history Roig discovers that for the most part women are the silent spectators or the emotional victims of political events. In *Ramona, adiós*, the grandmother does not even mention the Spanish-American War in her diary. Confined to domestic settings, women of her generation were barely aware of politics and certainly not permitted to engage in external affairs. The mother, for her part, is aware of the declaration of the Republic, but she assesses it only in terms of its effect on her personal daily routine.

She later becomes an indirect victim of political events when her lover commits suicide for political reasons. For the youngest Ramona, the male, external world shapes her intellect and precludes free choice. She espouses leftist causes during the 1960s, not because of any autonomous ideological conclusions, but because of her emotional ties to her political-activist boyfriend. Each one of these Ramonas becomes increasingly more involved in the political sphere, but none becomes the architect of her sociopolitical world; they are all obliged to react and not enact.

The fact that the hidden female stories of this novel appear within the physical marks of parentheses, formed by the opening and closing sections with their precise historical references, illustrates the disconnection between female and male histories and implies the need to piece together woman's story with nonhistorical texts. History by definition is a systematic written record of public concerns and by implication a confirmation of existence. Since women have been excluded from the public arena as well as discouraged from writing, the reality of their history becomes problematic. Sufficient studies have been written for us to know now that a female infrastructure has long existed, albeit different and separate from masculine tradition.[11] Not only is women's story different from men's, but also are their means and degree of access to it. As Roig shows in *Ramona, adiós*, in the face of a lack of historical documentation, women's history must be sought in private texts and in ephemeral, oral discourse. Authorial omniscience, of course, allows her also to resort to third-person narration and first-person interior monologue. Between the narrative frame of the opening and closing sections of her novel Roig interweaves, in alternating fashion, bits and pieces of the lives of her three Ramonas. The grandmother's diary entries dated between 6 December 1894 and 2 January 1919 are interspersed with sections focusing on one or the other Ramonas. The frequent shifts in chronology, narrative mode, and point of view create a disordered and fragmentary text that, as Elizabeth S. Rogers says, "complements a basic enterprise which she undertakes in the novel—the reconstruction of the fragmentary and hidden past in order to achieve a new consciousness and a sense of wholeness."[12] In addition, the disconnection among these texts corroborates the incompleteness of contemporary knowledge of female history, an incompleteness reinforced within the novel by the ignorance on the part of the mother and the daughter of the existence of the grandmother's diary and, therefore, of essential information. By upholding the ignorance concerning women, fictional reality duplicates the isolation, the misconceptions, and the repression they share. The grandmother's suppressed autobiography, her diary, becomes her only vehicle for self-expression and ultimately the reader's key to the recovery and interpretation of this silent, unknown world. The grandmother's text, Roig's novel, and one's reading form a triple-layered opportunity for discovery and reevaluation.

Once Roig has confirmed the existence of a female history, she can examine the specific episodes that give it complexity and continuity. In her novels she presents a gallery of different women united by ties of family or friendship and by similar circumstances or experiences. They form a paradigmatic community of women, who despite the advance of time, share a comparable frustration in love and unfulfillment in life. Roig follows the line of thinking of past folk wisdom and the recent statistical study of Carol Gilligan, which hold that psychic wholeness depends for women on affective attachment and for men on worldly achievement.[13] Roig explains in her book of essays that while some women today have begun to adopt a partial, masculine attitude toward love, these women "Se salvan más pero viven menos" [They save themselves more but live less fully].[14] Love for Roig is an all-consuming passion, known primarily to women, that devastates yet gives meaning to life. In her novels female desire remains unfulfilled because men's contrasting psychological perspective does not accommodate women's psychic needs and because the social norms of family, marriage, and class promote psychological atrophy.

While establishing this uniformity among women, Roig also traces women's progression toward conscious liberation from that very uniformity. The first Ramona in *Ramona, adiós* can only resort to fantasy to subvert the rules of conformity imposed upon women. As a child she defied the restrictions placed on a young girl's intellectual development by reading books on the sly. Once married she lives by all appearances the romantic high life of the period, but in her private world, as revealed through her diary, her yearning for passion and excitement is suffocated by her husband's dullness, orderliness, and placidness. Bored by reality, she dreams of the ideal, pure love suggested by the marble cupids in her entry hall. When the opportunity for corporal love presents itself, wifely duty, guilt, and the admonitions of a priest serve as agents of self-administered repression. Her daughter shares her name and much of the same daily routine, but she initiates a process of rebellion with a love affair that temporarily gives her a feeling of psychic fulfillment and of secret retaliation against an environment hostile to her sexual well-being. Before marriage she has a brief affair with Ignasi, a young liberal who commits suicide out of guilt for a political failure. The case of this Ramona illustrates two important constants in Roig's fiction: the different priority given to love by women and by men and the realization of love outside marriage, either as an adulterous act or as an episode prior to marriage. Roig's portrayal of marriage as an unhappy ordeal of subordination reflects the demythification process many of Spain's youngest writers have applied to numerous traditional institutions. It also conforms to the negative portrayal of marriage Annis Pratt has found characteristic of novels by women.[15] The example of the third and youngest Ramona goes beyond the archetypical patterns of novels of marriage to show that the repression of female desire is symptomatic of the dialectic of gender. Beguiled by Jordi's skill as a campus leader and sensing a father figure in him, this Ramona subordinates herself to him sexually and adopts his political ideology. Jordi, for his part, infantilizes her with his deceptive terms of endearment and consistently belittles her. Unlike her grandmother and mother, however, she frees herself from patriarchal domination; she leaves both him and her family. With this dual gesture of abandonment, she breaks the silence in the face of dissatisfaction maintained by her female predecessors and symbolically pronounces the farewell of the book's title.

The growing consciousness of women of their right to self-determination and the persistent challenge of authority by young people make it possible for some of Roig's younger women to free themselves from the patterns followed by their predecessors. But these liberated women, as Manuel Cerezales says, are left by their very liberation without a supporting system of common values.[16] This sense of moral void becomes more evident in *Tiempo de cerezas*, Roig's second novel. The book opens with Natalia Miralpeix's return to Spain following a twelve-year stay in England, where she had fled after her abortion. Now a photographer of forty, she feels the need to reexamine her past, renew her family ties, and reconstruct her life. Once again Roig crafts a novel of recovery of the past, of female history, and of self.

Although years have passed, Natalia discovers that many constants endure in Spain. Just as for the women in *Ramona, adiós*, for Spain in *Tiempo de cerezas* the advance of history brings increased freedom, but it does not eliminate all dilemmas nor solve all moral issues. Symptomatic of the questionable extent of change in Spain is Natalia's aunt's house: the garden and the lemon tree have disappeared, but the house itself is as musty and decrepit as ever. As Natalia reacquaints herself with her family, she finds they have remained basically unchanged: her Aunt Patricia is spiritless, her sister-in-law Silvia is frustrated, her brother Luis is self-centered, and her father is estranged. A review of the political climate of Spain corroborates this same immutability. As a friend tells Natalia, "encontrarás libros marxistas en los quioscos . . . pero, ¿qué más da, si todo sigue igual?" [you will find Marxist books in the newsstands . . . but what difference does it make, if everything is the same?] (99).

Roig stresses the comparison between the past and present by the way she structures her book. The past is kept at a perceptible distance by its segregation into parts 2, 3, and 4 of the novel. Yet ultimately the author reinforces her basic premise that while separate, the past and the present are interrelated. The action of the novel begins in the present, but the narrator continually reverts to the past. The third-person omniscient narrator lends objectivity to the text, but it also serves to bind together its disjointed facets. And finally the incorporation of dialogue into the discursive flow of the narration creates a tensive unity between the actual and the recalled.

The constant temporal shifts are duplicated by numerous changes in narrative perspective. For example, part 1 of the novel begins by focusing upon Natalia; then it shifts to Patricia and her maid, switches abruptly to the artist Harmonia, and finally jumps from Silvia to Luis and back to Silvia. Roig juxtaposes in her novel, much as she would in her television interviews, a series of disconnected, individualized accounts ostensibly free of the imprint of the assembler. As an objective social document, her novel records the sense of political crisis, the changing morality, and the emerging new woman of the post-Franco era. She indicates that the legalization of the Communist party seems to have diffused the commitment of party members and disclosed the contradictions of the motives of many militants. By including members of different age groups, Roig can also easily contrast divergent sexual mores. Roig's open, matter-of-fact references to intercourse, homosexuality, masturbation, and abortion reflect the testimonial orientation of the reporter-journalist as well as Spain's release from much of the puritanism and rigid censorship that characterized the Franco era. For a writer who is also a woman, this frank treatment of sex and related taboos also represents a confrontation with a long tradition denying women knowledge of, access to, and enjoyment of their own sexuality. If it is true, as Michel Foucault has said, that men have reacted to sexual repression by talking about sex, then the attention given to sexuality in novels like Roig's is a sign of that same rebellion.[17]

The social changes begun in Spain in the 1960s and expanded in the 1970s altered to a certain degree the relation between women and official history. Unlike Ramona Ventura, whose participation in historical events in *Ramona, adiós* was limited to a spectator's role, Natalia, in *Tiempo de cerezas*, participated in the demonstrations at the University of Barcelona on behalf of the striking Asturian workers, witnessed police brutality, and suffered detention. Nevertheless Natalia still views history as a framing structure for the individual incidents in her personal life and not as a separate substantive concern. For her, the detention of the political dissident Grimau marked her departure from Spain and the murder of the anarchist Puig Antich her return. She sees her participation in the Parisian student and worker demonstrations of May 1968 as a stage for her sexual liberation rather than as a social contribution. Although Natalia remains politically a secondary player, her awareness of political events makes the inclusion of certain issues a legitimate extension of her experiences.

The journalist's desire to chronicle her times helps the fiction writer reach her goal of creating a gallery of portraits of women united by personal ties and comparable experiences. Other than the protagonist, two women stand out: Natalia's Aunt Patricia, a former friend of Ramona the mother in *Ramona, adiós*, and Natalia's sister-in-law Silvia, the oldest child of the same Ramona. Through Patricia and Silvia, Roig continues her disclosure of the silent struggle of women with the passivity society imposes upon them and the pain that burden places upon them. Patricia and Silvia endure the frustrating constraints of the patriarchal cage built around them by seeking inadequate and temporary avenues of relief or by assuming postures that negate life itself. They both fulfill their wifely duties of abnegation, faithfulness, and submission. And both are trapped in marriages equated with domestic enclosure and insufficient or deficient love. Programmed to submit to male desire, Patricia stoically endures her husband's laziness, infidelity, and whims. Her reflection years later on the abuse she suffered only leads to tortuous depression, drink, and physical debilitation.

The dramatization of imprisonment and escape that feminist critics Gilbert and Gubar find to represent a uniquely female tradition is evident throughout *Tiempo de cerezas*.[18] Any thoughts Silvia might have had about becoming a dancer were dashed by her husband upon their marriage. As she confesses to Natalia, her husband was a father figure, without the latter's minimal encouragement of self-development. True to the archetypical patterns outlined by Pratt, Roig depicts matrimony "as one of the primary tools for dulling a hero's initiative and refraining her maturation."[19] No matter where Silvia and her friends find themselves, their conversations revolve around the restrictions placed upon them by their husbands, the imperfections of their bodies, or their lost past. Shunned and scorned by their husbands, Silvia and her friends remain confined within women's quarters—the beauty shop, the gym, the well-decorated home. Psychic release from oppression comes to them only temporarily in an alcohol-induced game with erotic and sadistic overtones. The traditional gender-bound partition of the world—outer space for men and inner place for women—is effectively shown by Roig through the use of counterpoint. When Silvia and Luis's friends occupy virtually the same locale, sexual separation along with the comparable banality of their conversations only underscores the formalized distance between the sexes.

While Roig consistently contrasts differences between men and women, she also points out the gap in communication separating women. In Silvia's eyes Natalia stands as an enviable free woman, unhindered by a husband and domesticity, economically independent, and sexually liberated. In Roig's next novel, Natalia will discover that she and women like Silvia have more in common than they realize. Throughout her works Roig presents a few women who cast off woman's role of submissive, sexless, silent wife. In the 1930s there was Judit's friend Kati, a daring and energetic woman whose dress, sexual behavior, and political activities scandalized her middle-class compatriots. In Natalia's generation there is Harmonia, a strong, charismatic painter. These alternative models of female conduct are isolated examples that do not reform basic gender-bound structures; and, as Nichols points out, these Lilith figures are invariably condemned to infecundity and eventually to absolute silence for their transgression of taboos.[20]

Beyond being a social document and novel of marriage, *Tiempo de cerezas* is an account of one woman's search for her self through a confrontation with her family. In this novel her mother is still the invalid toward whom she feels indifference, and her father is a hostile figure toward whom she has mixed feelings. From the omniscient narrator the reader begins to learn some details about her mother: her role in relieving her husband's sexual anxieties, her aberrant behavior after her friend Kati's death, and her gradual withdrawal into silence and insanity. We discover that Natalia's father, beneath his social image of triumphant rich man, was actually a negligent architect and an insecure, cowardly man. Natalia's brother completes Roig's tarnished portrait of male heroes; Luis is a successful and innovative architect, but an insensitive, self-centered, and domineering person. At the end of this novel, Natalia has not yet related the subjugation of women and the psychological inadequacies of men to her own intimate experiences.

The issue becomes a matter of open debate in the discussions between Natalia and her friend Norma in Roig's next novel, *La hora violeta*. Five years after her return home, Natalia asks Norma to write a book based on some notes of her Aunt Patricia's, a few of Kati's letters, and her mother, Judit's, incomplete diary of 1942 to 1948. The discovery of her mother's diary gives Natalia the opportunity to reappraise her mother and to reflect upon her own life as she continues her search for her own identity and the meaning of womanhood.

Again in this novel Roig often shifts perspectives and time frames to cede center stage to a number of different women. The novel contains five parts. The first consists of a letter from Natalia to Norma describing her desire to understand the baffling love between her parents and the undying love between Judit and Kati. Part 2 presents the triangle involving Natalia, her lover, Jordi, and his wife, Agnes; and part 4 considers a triangle involving Norma. The central part, incorporating the material entrusted to Norma, belongs to the period 1936 to 1964. Almost an epilogue, the last part coincides with the end of Natalia's reading of the *Odyssey*, which throughout the novel provokes reflection upon archetypical female roles. Roig accentuates the fractured structure of her novel by interpolating within her fictional account fragments from her factual study on Nazi concentration camps. This mixture of fact and fiction lends verisimilitude to her invented stories, and by making Norma the collector of these facts, Roig leads some to see Norma as her mask.[21]

The novel's structure may be fragmented but its message is uniform: all women share a common reality and the differences between the sexes are significant. Roig's brand of feminism, as Elizabeth J. Ordóñez rightly observes, is more psychological than political;[22] she is more interested in rendering the female experience and establishing a bond among women than in exacting social change. For Roig, the first step toward liberation from the partiality of tradition and the weight of male domination must be for women to return to their origins and look at women in their actual everyday reality without the distortion of idealism.[23] Espousing the gynocentric focus of the most recent feminist trends,[24] Roig stresses the heterogeneity of the sexes over androgeny; she celebrates a uniquely feminine consciousness; and she looks at women as creating subject rather than as Other.

Roig's gynocentrism decentralizes the phallocentric order and

reduces the marginality of women. This intentional deviation from
the male-centered system makes one reviewer deduce that her male
characters are the elusive masculine other half.[25] However, unlike
the female Other, Roig's men do not serve as avenues of fulfillment,
but contrarily as obstacles to desire. The men in her novels demythify
the archetypical perfect hero, and in turn, their psychological
deficiencies underscore the alientation of women and the
unreconciled differences between the sexes. Reading for this
difference as a means to finding a genuine female identity cannot
preclude a consideration of male psychology, constructs, and roles,
for as Stimpson has said, "The unravelling of male hegemony, the
knitting up of a female heterodoxy at once independent and
interdependent, is inseparable from . . . the study of sexual difference
itself, of what is 'male' and what is 'female,' of the causes and
inscriptions of difference."[26] In her process of self-exploration,
Natalia ponders this very issue. She and Norma discover that they
share with all women an overriding need for the preservation of
relationships, while men base their lives on isolation and individual
achievement. This discrepancy in world view is what leaves Roig's
female characters with a sense of void or incompleteness. "Para un
hombre," Natalia says, "la soledad puede ser el primer escalón hacia
el poder y el arte. Para una mujer es el vacío, la locura o el suicidio"
[For a man loneliness can be the first step toward power and art. For
a woman, it is emptiness, insanity or suicide] (18). Whether married
or unmarried, whether from a past or present generation, Roig's
female characters are united in their failure to find the lasting
love needed for their psychic wholeness. Love proves to be for
them unstable, ephemeral, limited—in short, contrary to female
requirements.

As in her previous two novels, Roig presents contrasting yet
complementary sets of women. In a first generation are Kati and
Judit, two very different women who both resort to self-destruction
to escape disappointments in love. Denounced by patriarchal society
for her audacious independence and disregard for conventional
female behavior, Kati nonetheless succumbs to the power of love,
committing suicide when her lover is killed in war. Kati's example
reconfirms Roig's underlying premise that intense and lasting
personal attachment is the key to woman's sense of wholeness and
at the same time to her destruction. Kati's suicide can be seen as an
attempt to escape the void of life, but of course her search for
liberation expresses itself through an act of nullification. Judit also
rebels against life. She obliterates the memory of past joys by
withdrawing into an impoverished, empty existence resembling

death. Her insanity constitutes a disavowal of self-affirmation, for as Showalter has shown, madness is essentially a desperate communication of powerlessness.[27] Judit's entire life was a series of losses and disappointments. Only with Kati during the civil war and her husband's detention did she enjoy a feeling of self-identity, of active participation in the world around her, and of supportive connection with another person. Powerless to affirm her own identity after Kati's death and then after the death of her retarded son, she deteriorates both physically and mentally until her own death.

In today's generation, Norma and Natalia form a pair with differing outlooks yet similar outcomes; together they complement Agnes, Jordi's wife. Unlike their earlier counterparts, these contemporary women are not destroyed physically by losses in love, but they share the same discontent with regard to men. Agnes's case is analogous to that of Ramona Claret of *Ramona, adiós*; besides being married to the man Ramona Claret loved, she reiterates Ramona's example of rejection. When her husband leaves her, Agnes decides to await his return patiently, but a taste of loneliness and autonomy helps her discard her role as Penelope.

Natalia and Norma form a complementary pair whose intellectualized feminism and conscious noncompliance with traditional patterns of female behavior contrast with Agnes's unpremeditated renunciation of victimization. However, they discover that their greater autonomy does not guarantee emotional satisfaction. Natalia openly rejects the role of woman as passive victim and submissive wife, having avoided marriage and unconsciously patterned herself in many ways on the male personality. Norma welcomes her total female identity of professional writer, wife, and mother. They both believe they have escaped the Penelope syndrome and achieved sexual liberation, but they both fall in love with men who return to their wives, leaving them to assume the conventional role of the woman who waits. However, rather than losing their sense of self as their female predecessors did, they acquire a deeper awareness of their feminine identity. They learn that feminism does not reconcile their need for independence with their need for lasting love and that although women are no longer trapped, like Judit, by the permanence of marriage, the temporariness of today's relationships creates new dilemmas. Milagros Sánchez Arnosi maintains that this novel raises a shout of protest against the passivity and resignation of so many women who renounce their identity.[28] However, by defining women's identity as emotionality and their destiny as patience, Roig reiterates a number of familiar stereotypes. Her purpose is to transform the elements of those images into positive signs, but the predominance of frustration in her novels compromises her homage to women.

Roig vindicates women more effectively through the inscription in her novel of female-generated texts. Without a written chronological record of experiences significant to their group, women have been deprived of history. In this light, the female documents incorporated in Roig's novels constitute the missing pages of human history, the valuable vestiges of a forgotten culture. Their fragmentary and incomplete nature only reconfirms the disregard, disdain, and darkness that have surrounded women's history. In her previous novels, a lack of written accounts on women was responsible for the ignorance and misconceptions shared by women about each other. In *La hora violeta* a rudimentary sampling of female texts—letters, notes, and diaries—helps bridge those gaps of communication.

A self-propagating phenomenon, knowledge leads to additional questions that bring additional enlightenment. By reading Judit's diary, Natalia and Norma not only comprehend it and its relationship to her social context, they also interpret it in terms of their own psychosocial experiences. Both learn they are not as liberated or unconventional as they thought. Natalia recognizes that she has embraced the passive stance she had condemned in her mother. Norma realizes that beneath her modern attitudes lies a bond to women of all times. Their reading of Judit's text becomes an act of rereading, of discovering the world anew. They engage in what Adrienne Rich has called a "re-vision—the act of looking back, of seeing with fresh eyes, of entering an old text from a new critical direction." What begins for Natalia as a drive to self-knowledge becomes a part of one woman's efforts to dismantle the "lies, secrets, and silence" that Rich identifies as the elements of "self-destructiveness of male-dominated society."[29] Natalia's new knowledge subverts the ignorance long considered becoming to women. By asking Norma to write a book from the notes she has found, Natalia initiates a process by which a large audience will undo the lies long told about women, the secrets they kept, and the silence to which they have been restricted.

Over the centuries women have been compelled to silence protest and self-expression. Because the unheard is unknown and the unknown can easily be construed as nonexistent, women's silence has contributed to their being defined as lack, absence, and void. Definitions of women, having been penned primarily by men and conditioned by male needs, desires, and fears, have made women products of male imagination, objects created for the use of men, and, as Susan Gubar observes, the sheet of blank paper written upon by male authors.[30] What Roig attempts to achieve in her fiction is to give a voice to an otherwise mute existence and to allow the words spoken to be self-generated, intimate, and free.

The rereading evident in *La hora violeta* becomes a comprehensive act of discovery, consciousness, and reevaluation of woman as writer, reader, and actor. The triple layer of creating, self-defining authors comprised of Judit, Kati, Patricia, of Natalia and Norma, and of Roig herself transforms woman from substance into the thinking, speaking, doing, and writing agent of which Julia Kristeva speaks. The text of a novel can be conceived as both practice (actor) and product (author), process and effect. While the actor is the momentary conveyor of a message, the author is the owner, the determinating originator of that message.[31] Thus through her characters and as an author herself, Roig represents woman as a subject who writes herself onto the blank page left after erasing the misconceptions, secrets, and silences.

Roig's fourth novel, *La ópera cotidiana*, reiterates the salient features of the rest of her narrative: a disclosure of gender-based dichotomies implying the vindication of women and the demythification of men, and a presentation of a series of loosely organized enunciations revealing repeated struggles for personal satisfaction and self-identity. Missing from this novel are the fragmentary, written female texts that offset recorded history in her previous novels. New is an element of fantasy, of distorted reality. Except for *Tiempo de cerezas*, this is Roig's only novel with a fully developed male character. *La ópera cotidiana*, as its title and the names of its divisions suggest, is an opera of everyday situations and ordinary people. The principal players in this operatic drama pronounce arias and cavatinas and initiate duets in an attempt to recount their life and divulge their feelings. For the most part, they are confused dreamers who act out their delusions trying, through love, to escape their boring and unsatisfying daily existence. Like most operas, Roig's work is tinged with disaster, melodrama, and verbal outpourings. Roig uses the operatic format not only to underscore her unifying theme of life as a series of divergent and incurable illusions but also to blend together a number of different human voices. Although including at times a third-person narrative voice, Roig's very short chapters are usually built around the dramatic monologues of one of her three central speakers: Horaci Duc, Mari Cruz, and Señora Altafulla.

Altafulla, an eccentric old lady, rambles on, telling her stories of fantasized romance to Mari Cruz, who feigns attention. Mari Cruz, a homeless young girl working as a maid for the Patricia seen in Roig's previous novels, recounts her past and present to an unidentified plural "you." Horaci Duc, a widower and Patricia's boarder, engages her in conversation during their breakfasts together, but these conversations are basically monologues because Patricia plays the part of the patient listener, the consoling friend, and the absolving priest to whom Duc confides his anxious feelings of failure, guilt, and fear. Each one of these three main stories revolves around failed love and ends in disaster. By jumping from one story line to another, the author obliges readers to interweave in their own minds the various threads running through the novel and to make their own concluding psychological interpretations. Once again Roig's journalistic training is detectable in this authorial detachment and in the brevity of her chapters. Ultimately, however, the novel's broken structure reinforces its themes of confusion, anxiety, and alienation. All the principal characters of the novel are interrelated as companions of one sort or another, but no one is united to anyone.

Horaci Duc is a man who alienates himself from his beloved by his own inability to love freely and deeply. He culminates Roig's exploration of male psychology, but unlike her previous male figures, he is not outwardly a successful, forceful, and admired person, but is instead either scorned or pitied by those around him. If, as Natalia maintains in *La hora violeta*, the basic female archetype is Penelope, then as outlined in the present novel, the basic male archetype is Pygmalion. Duc sees his wife as unpolished matter awaiting his creative hands: "Era una joya sin pulir, y me sentía como el escultor que puede modelar una obra de arte con el barro primitivo" [She was an unpolished jewel, and I felt like the sculptor who molds a work of art out of ordinary clay] (34). Like Shaw's Professor Higgins, he gives a proper voice to a socially inferior woman (in this case a Catalan pronunciation to a nearly illiterate Andalusian) with a conviction combining gender superiority with cultural elitism. Susan Gubar tells us that Pygmalion creates female life as he would like it to be—"pliable, responsive, purely physical. More important, he has invaded the humiliation, shared by many men, of acknowledging that it is *he* who is really created out of and from the female body."[32] The Catalan woman Duc molds becomes a product of his own imagination, his work of art, and a trophy meant to impress his rival. Duc's repetition of this same syndrome with Mari Cruz after his wife María's death reconfirms the deep-rooted persistence of his view of woman as inert matter subject to his urge for possession.

This same urge for domination explains the gnawing, destructive jealousy Duc himself describes as a vulture that devours us from within. The obsessive nature of his jealousy is graphically conveyed by his brutal killing of his cat. His overwhelming jealousy expresses itself toward his wife as a desire for exclusive possession. He confesses to Patricia, "La quería encerrada, quería que viviese sólo para mí" [I wanted her shut up, I wanted her to live only for me] (67). His inability to see María as anything but "pliable, responsive and purely physical" leads him to presume that her assumption of independence concealed sexual infidelity. María's autonomy challenges his illusory concept of woman's dependency and exposes his cowardliness.

His lack of courage produces a debilitating sense of guilt in him. Of particular importance in his psychological torment is the occasion when his overpowering fear drove him to burn the political leaflets he was to distribute. This episode, along with the memory of a father who fought for the losing side in the civil war and the contempt of a boss who called him a "red," fills him with self-loathing. When María herself begins to deliver the subversive leaflets, he loses her respect and his dominion over her. The contrast between María and Duc could not be greater; she is strong, fearless, full of vitality, and above all free, while he is weak, cowardly, passive, and decidedly obsessed. As he puts it, María was an eagle, but he was only a poor owl. One critic sees in their story the reversal of the myth of women as the cause of the Fall: woman here is an innocent, pure, and natural being, and man is a jealous and lustful person who destroys their paradisiacal bliss.[33] Significantly, his damage breaks his spirit but not hers.

Along with the contrast between María and Horaci, the parallelism between María and Mari Cruz furthers the author's efforts to evolve a definition of woman and to establish sexual opposition. Beyond the resemblance in their names, both women's lives are influenced by the smallness of Duc's spirit. María takes an assertive stance; she rebels against his cowardice even though her psychological independence means the sacrifice of her sexual life. Mari Cruz becomes the victim of Duc's fear of making a personal commitment after his wife's death. Mari Cruz falls in love with him because she sees him as a liberating father figure, but turns to drugs after his rejection of her love. Beyond their existential parallelisms, María and Mari Cruz present certain social implications. Both are poor Andalusians transformed into working class Catalonians. The discrepancy between these outsiders' loyal attachment to Catalonia and the disloyalty of the chauvinistic Duc undoubtedly carries a call for self-reflection upon ethnic responsibility on the part of the author's compatriots.

Pursuing the free and natural expression of their sexuality, María and Mari Cruz reiterate, within the scope of Roig's novels, the example of women like Kati. They confirm, on a broader scale, the trend among today's Spanish women writers to reevaluate the myth of Lilith. Even though they both lose the object of their love, their failure is not blamed, as in the past, on their disregard for conventional female behavior. The restrictions traditionally placed on female sexuality and the inaccurate, incomplete, and partisan discussions of the subject have made an inclusion of female sexuality imperative for women authors wanting to free women from patriarchal biases.

In *La ópera cotidiana* female sexuality emerges as a source of inner energy, as a means of self-fulfillment, spiritual nourishment, and regeneration, while male sexuality manifests itself as an agent of power, as a means of self-assertion, acquisition, and destruction. For both María and Mari Cruz sexuality is a natural, effervescent force, a strong yet soothing pleasure not unlike the *jouissance* discussed by French feminists. María, as Duc recalls with belated self-recrimination, was joyous harmony; "todo en sola una mujer, el placer y la ternura ... ¿Qué más quería?" [everything in one woman, pleasure and tenderness ... What else did I want?] (66). For Mari Cruz sex was a means of liberation from her repressive upbringing and an avenue of rebirth. Discovering her body she experiences a new sense of self-knowledge and self-identity. This sense of renewal contrasts markedly with Duc's life-annihilating attitude toward sex. Riddled with guilt and crippled by fear, his relationship with Mari Cruz became a conscious effort to forget his past and escape reality. In *La ópera cotidiana* Roig explores the "Dark Continent" of feminine sex and discovers, as Hélène Cixous does, that it is neither dark nor unexplorable. Following Cixous's mandate to women to discover the "infinite and mobile complicity" of their eroticization, Roig creates in Mari Cruz a fictional character who boldly proclaims "cuerpo es la mujer" [woman is body].[34]

This self-affirming attitude does not, however, guarantee Mari Cruz self-fulfillment. In keeping with the prevailing structures established in her previous novels, Roig's characters in this novel end up alienated from reality one way or another. The novel closes with Mari Cruz roaming the streets in a drugged stupor, muttering incoherently. Señora Altafulla is declared insane and sent to an asylum. Duc, for his part, also verges on insanity. Only two people emerge with sound minds: María, whose inherent vitality leads to her violent death, and Patricia, whose fundamental endurance seems to prevent her from dying. As a chronicler of her times, Roig cannot contradict the basic alienation she finds endemic to her environment.

I must concur with the reviewer who affirms that Roig "successfully risks combining social circumstances with psychological dimensions."[35] Journalistic training undoubtedly accounts for her testimonial perspective, for her tendency to chronicle the political climate, the new morality, and the emergence of feminism in Spain today. And Roig's own feminism clearly explains her exploration of the psychology of women. Her reading for difference fulfills a fundamental desire, common among many feminists of recent years, to delineate the uniqueness of female identity and thereby override the devaluation of women. Both story and history—the experiences of individual women and their shared reality over time—are important to Roig's efforts to refocus the past and re-form the present. Recognizing the incompleteness, partiality, and ignorance that have colored the accounts on women written by men, Roig allows women themselves to speak out in her novels. Their voices assume subdued, intimate forms—conversations, letters, and diaries—because social restrictions have excluded them from the masterly occupation of writer. The disjointed structure of these diverse statements may reflect Roig's journalistic training or the *écriture féminine* defined by French feminists as fluid, nonlinear, decentralized, and many-voiced. Whatever the source, its effect is to reinforce the gaps still left in our re-vision of women. The novels of Montserrat Roig reveal that women's history is still a blank page, not the passive artifact Gubar examines, but an ancient story not yet committed to paper, a vital spirit not yet settled into the body of written history, and a life about to make itself manifest.

Notes

1. Francesc Castells, "Montserrat Roig: Escriptora Compromesa," *Serra d'Or*, February 1977, 26.

2. Kathleen McNerney, "Journalism, Feminism and Creativity: Catalan Women Writers," *Proceedings of the Eleventh Annual Conference of Hispanic Literature*, ed. J. Cruz Mendizábal (Indiana, Pa.: Indiana University Press, 1986), 213.

3. Montserrat Roig, "A modo de confesión," in her collection of interviews *Los hechiceros de la palabra* (Wizards of the word) (Barcelona: Ediciones Martínez Roca, 1975), 16.

4. Sandra Gilbert and Susan Gubar, *The Madwoman in the Attic* (New Haven: Yale University Press, 1979), 87, maintain that women authors have always tended to reflect the literal reality of their own confinement in the constraints they depict.

In accordance with this observation, the solidarity of which I speak can be seen as part of an ongoing female tradition.

5. Geraldine C. Nichols, "Mitja poma, mitja taronja: Génesis y destino literarios de la catalana contemporánea," *Anthropos* 60–61 (1986): 120.

6. Montserrat Roig, *¿Tiempo de mujer?* (Barcelona: Plaza y Janés, 1980), 156.

7. Ibid., 154.

8. Catharine R. Stimpson, "Feminism and Feminist Criticism," *The Massachusetts Review* 2 (1983): 281.

9. C. B. Cadenas, "Historia de tres mujeres," *Nueva Estafeta*, no. 18 (May 1980): 76–77.

10. Robert Jay Lifton, *History of Human Survival* (New York: Random House, 1970), 279.

11. For an excellent summary of this point see Elaine Showalter, "Feminist Criticism in the Wilderness," in *Writing and Sexual Difference*, ed. Elizabeth Abel (Chicago: University of Chicago Press, 1982).

12. 1986, 104. In her study Rogers analyzes in particular the role and importance of language in this novel.

13. Carol Gilligan, *In a Different Voice* (Cambridge, Mass.: Harvard University Press, 1982).

14. Roig, *¿Tiempo de mujer?*, 286.

15. See Annis Pratt, *Archetypal Patterns in Women's Fiction* (Bloomington: Indiana University Press, 1981), chap. 3.

16. Manuel Cerezales, review of *Ramona, adiós* in *ABC* (Madrid), air mail edition, 27 May 1980, 22.

17. Michel Foucault, *The History of Sexuality*. Vol. 1: *An Introduction* (New York: Vintage Books, 1980), 84.

18. Gilbert and Gubar, *Madwoman*, 85.

19. Pratt, *Archetypal Patterns*, 41.

20. Nichols, "Mitja poma," 121.

21. Janet Pérez, review of *L'hora violeta* in *World Literature Today* 55 (1981): 659.

22. Elizabeth J. Ordóñez, "Reading Contemporary Spanish Narrative by Women," *Anales de la Literatura Española Contemporánea* 7 (1982): 241.

23. *¿Tiempo de mujer?*, 154–55.

24. The shift in recent years from androcentric to gynocentric feminism is discussed by Showalter, "Feminist Criticism in the Wilderness," 9–35.

25. David Ross Gerling, review of *La hora violeta* in *Anales de la Literatura Española Contemporánea* 8 (1983): 245.

26. "Feminism and Feminist Criticism," 275.

27. Elaine Showalter, *The Female Malady* (New York: Pantheon Books, 1985), 5.

28. Milagros Sánchez Arnosi, review of *La hora violeta* in *Insula* 36 (April 1981): 8.

29. Adrienne Rich, *On Lies, Secrets, and Silences* (New York: Norton, 1979), 35.

30. Susan Gubar, " 'The Blank Page' and the Issues of Female Creativity," in *Writing and Sexual Difference*, ed. Abel, 75.

31. See Juia Kristeva, *Desire in Language*: *A Semiotic Approach to Literature and Art*, trans. Thomas Gora, Alice Jardine, and Leon S. Roudiez (New York: Columbia University Press, 1980), 36–91.

32. Gubar, " 'The Blank Page,' " 73.

33. Nichols, "Mitja poma," 124.

34. Hélène Cixous, "The Laugh of the Medusa," trans. Keith Cohen and Paula Cohen, in *The Signs Reader: Women, Gender and Scholarship*, ed. Elizabeth Abel and Emily K. Abel (Chicago: University of Chicago Press, 1983), 279–97.

35. C. B. Cadenas, "Historia de tres mujeres," *Nueva Estafeta*, no. 18 (May 1980): 17.

Bibliography

1. PRIMARY SOURCES

1971. *Molta roba i poco sabó ... i tan neta que la volen*. Barcelona: Editorial Selecta. Spanish translation (1981) *Aprendizaje sentimental*. Barcelona: Argos Vergara.

1972. *Ramona, adéu*. Barcelona: Edicions 62. Spanish translation (1980) *Ramona, adiós*. Barcelona: Argos Vergara.

1977. *El temps de les cireres*. Barcelona: Edicions 62. Spanish translation (1980) *Tiempo de cerezas*. Barcelona: Argos Vergara.

1980. *L'hora violeta*. Barcelona: Edicions 62. Spanish translation (1980) *La hora violeta*. Barcelona: Argos Vergara.

1982. *L'òpera quotidiana*. Barcelona: Planeta. Spanish translation (1983) *La ópera cotidiana*. Barcelona: Planeta. Excerpts translated into English by J. M. Sobrer (1988) and published as "The Everyday Opera (Selections)" in *On Our Own Behalf: Women's Tales from Catalonia*, ed. Kathleen McNerny, 200–234. Lincoln: University of Nebraska Press.

2. SECONDARY SOURCES

Bellver, Catherine G. 1987. "Montserrat Roig and the Penelope Syndrome." *Anales de la Literatura Española Contemporánea* 12: 111–21. Compares Roig's major female characters with their mythological archetype Penelope, to investigate the author's depiction of women in their romantic relationships with men.

Rogers, Elizabeth S. 1986. "Montserrat Roig's *Ramona, adiós*: A Novel of Suppression and Disclosure." *Revista de Estudios Hispánicos* 20: 103–21. Examines the techniques Roig uses in *Ramona, adiós* to recover and reveal the stories of three generations of women.

12

Rosa Montero: From Journalist to Novelist

Joan L. Brown

Rosa Montero belongs to the generation of female writers who came to prominence in the late 1970s. Of the dozen or so women authors who once were designated as "rising stars," Montero is among the select group that includes Ana María Moix, Esther Tusquets, Lourdes Ortiz, and Montserrat Roig, who by now have recognized places in the Spanish literary firmament.[1] Her position is based on four novels that have attracted critical attention at the same time that they have amassed a huge popular audience in Spain.

Like many of her generational colleagues, Rosa Montero is a journalist, although unlike some others she did not set out to become one. Born in 1951, she belonged to a middle-class family in Madrid, one that she described in an early interview as "media modesta" (modestly middle class.)[2] She studied psychology at the Universidad Complutense, the most respected university in Madrid. In response to a question about psychology majors, Montero has affirmed that she too enrolled to find the answer to personal problems, in her case adolescent panic attacks. However, she gradually became disillusioned with the uses to which the study of psychology was put, and abandoned her university career in her fourth year (*Ozono*, 6). She then turned to journalism, graduating from the Escuela Oficial de Periodismo in Madrid and beginning her career in 1969.

Since she entered the field, Montero has worked as a journalist in various media: on four newspapers, over half a dozen magazines, and for Televisión Española. From 1977 she has worked exclusively for *El País*, Spain's most respected newspaper. She has held various positions on the paper, including that of special correspondent (traveling to the United States, Latin America, Greece, Iraq, Sweden, France, and elsewhere) and editor-in-chief of the paper's Sunday magazine (in 1981 and 1982, the first woman to hold this position). She is currently a staff writer.

Rosa Montero has received a number of journalism awards and honors for her achievements as an interviewer. These include the 1978 Mundo Prize and the 1980 Premio Nacional de Periodismo. Her first book, published in 1976 (the year after Franco died), was a collection of interviews entitled *España para tí para siempre* (Spain, for you always). She published a second anthology of interviews in 1982 entitled *Cinco años de País* (Five years of The Nation). These interviews, and especially those of the second volume that chronicle Spain's first years after Franco's death, deal primarily with political and social issues. As a reporter who specializes in politically oriented questioning, Montero's technique is allied with New Journalism, the movement that originated in the United States in the 1960s and that emphasizes journalistic involvement. A textbook definition of this orientation is that the "involved" journalist (as opposed to the "aloof" one) "desires to bring himself, his intelligence, his sensitivities, his judgments to bear on the news of the day; he is not satisfied to be a bystander, an observer, a recorder or a neutralist."[3] This commitment did not become possible in Spain until six years after Montero's career began, since the sensitivities and judgments of reporters were censored during Franco's rule, from 1939–75. Beyond overt censorship, the press was used as a "political and ideological instrument" to transmit values that would uphold the fascist regime.[4] Montero's insertion of her own unabashedly liberal point of view in her interviews, through her challenging questions, descriptions of the subjects, and depictions of her interactions with them, was at the time a new and courageous use of what traditionally was regarded as a "soft" news genre.

In addition to her success as a journalist and to her achievements as a writer of fiction, Montero has engaged in what she terms "other literary activities," such as working briefly in independent theater, writing a forward for a 1982 Círculo de Lectores (an important publishing club) edition of Tolstoy's *Anna Karenina*, translating a novel and a play from English to Spanish, and writing a thirteen-episode series of programs for Spanish television that aired in 1985. She was a visiting professor in the United States at Wellesley College in 1985 and has given lectures and readings at a number of universities and cultural institutions in Spain, France, Switzerland, Germany, and the United States.

For all her visibility in Spain and abroad, Rosa Montero maintains a private personal life. The only facts to be gleaned from interviews are that she is single and lives in Madrid. The scarcity of details about her private life is ironic, since her legions of fans feel that they know her intimately because of her accurate depictions of their world. In a recent article on literary talent scouts who have "bagged" best-selling authors, Montero's publisher describes the phenomenon as unique: she is beloved by her readers because she deals with (their) real life.[5] With one futuristic exception, all of her fiction is set in Madrid in the 1970s and 1980s; her novels depict the urban social strata of post-Franco Spain with a careful and knowing eye. She is especially astute at capturing the details of both work and social life for a woman in her thirties.

Because readers know Montero's age, she is assumed to be a model for her young women protagonists. Similarly, her reputation as a journalist has led critics as well as readers to accept another assumption: that Rosa Montero writes fiction as a newspaper reporter. The opinion expressed by critic Javier Villán is widely held: "Por bien o para mal, y nada está escrito quo obligue a este último, su condición de periodista se va a proyectar siempre sobre su vocación de novelista" [For good or for ill, and nowhere is it written that it has to be the latter, her identity as a journalist will always be projected onto her vocation as a novelist].[6] The form that this "projection" takes is a "commitment to responsible journalism" whereby "her desire to create a work of art is ... less important to her than the need to express her ideas, sentiments and concerns about a number of issues ranging from sex to politics."[7]

While the popular suppositions about Rosa Montero—that her novels depict her own life and that they are based on factual reporting—are largely true, it would be naive to accept them as wholly correct. Refutation of the assumption that her works are slavishly autobiographical can only come from the author, and it does. Montero distinguishes between the "autobiographical" and the "biographical," and explains with reference to her first novel that her "biographical" fiction is an imaginary and intermingled account of events that have happened within her social group.[8] The author also counters the notion that she writes journalism in the guise of novels. She is acutely aware of the requirements of the two genres and considers them to be diametrically opposed to one another. Although she credits journalism with teaching her a certain dexterity with words, she feels that the clarity and precision of journalism are detrimental to good novel-writing, and that they must be overcome in the more abstract and ambiguous realm of fiction.[9]

In fact, in her novels Rosa Montero grows progressively stronger in her rejection and subversion of the conventions of journalism. Her development from journalist to novelist is incremental, as I will attempt to show in the following chronological discussion of her four major novelistic works. From her first heavily journalistic narrative to her most recent antijournalistic novel, Montero's fiction demonstrates a gradual renunciation of journalistic clarity. Ironically, in addition to the nonjournalistic narrative techniques that assume increasing importance in her novels, Montero also overtly parodies newspaper reporting and newspaper management with mordant humor and the outrage of an idealist.

Assumptions about Rosa Montero's private life and her limited (journalistic) narrative range were formulated in response to her first novel, *Crónica del desamor* (1979) (Chronicle of disaffection; English translation by Cristina de la Torre and Diana Glad, *Absent Love: A Chronicle*, forthcoming). This novel has the most direct ties to Montero's first vocation: she began it while under contract to prepare a nonfiction book of interviews with women, a project with which she became bored and for which she substituted the finished novel, gambling that her publisher would accept it instead (*Ozono*, 7). The work focuses on a young journalist, a single mother named Ana Antón, and on the lives of her wide circle of friends in contemporary Madrid. *Crónica del desamor* is based on a slim metaliterary conceit—the novel is the chronicle that Ana thinks of writing at the beginning of the book and knows she will write at its close. Within this framework the narrative is a collection of descriptions, brief scenes, and recorded speech through which the main characters share their lives as well as their views. The plot is propelled by Ana's year-long wait for a well-deserved permanent job slot that does not materialize, and for the resolution of an attraction to the owner of the newspaper where she works.

The ground-breaking story of the *Crónica del desamor* is the situation of women in modern Spain, a "chronicle of disaffection" that in 1979 constituted a revolutionary exposé. Women's plots are the subject of Ana's projected book; someday she plans to write about "manos babosas, platos para lavar, reducciones de plantilla, orgasmos fingidos, llamadas de teléfono que nunca llegan, paternalismos laborales, diafragmas, caricaturas y ansiedades. Sería el libro de las Anas, de todas y ella misma, tan distinta y tan una" [greasy hands, dishes to be washed, staff cutbacks, feigned orgasms, telephone calls that never come, diaphragms, caricatures, and anxieties. It would be the book of Anas, of all of them and of herself, so different and so singular] (8).

Details of female existence that were always kept out of literature, such as menstruation, sexual harassment, and visits to a (male) gynecologist are described in detail, in frank language, and often with black humor: if men gave birth, Ana muses early in the novel, abortions would have been legal since the beginning of time (21).

Women's roles in society and the evolution of the women's movement are primary topics in *Crónica del desamor*. Feminist philosophizing is introduced in characters' extended discourse. An example of this is the series of observations spoken by Candela, one of Ana's friends, late in the work: she reflects that women's liberation initially represented a devaluation of women as they tried to emulate men; only recently have women come to value their bodies and their gender (230–31). The author's own feminist stance has been the subject of debate. Although she defines herself as a feminist, she differs from many feminist writers by placing a high value on heterosexual love and commitment; in this she has been aptly compared to her venerated colleague Carmen Martín Gaite.[10]

Relationships between women and men are another central subject of *Crónica del desamor*, and they are portrayed as unsatisfying for both. Among Ana's friends are a "broken doll" who has been shattered by the end of her marriage, an independent woman who ends a live-in relationship because she feels stifled, and a woman who craves a succession of younger lovers. The protagonist's own romantic history is sad: she ended her relationship with the father of her son before he was born, and at age four he is tormented by the lack of a father. The man who had left her ten years earlier returns with declarations of love, but she is unmoved. Her polished boss, Soto Amón, whom she privately calls Ramsés (as one of his slaves), disappoints her with his predictable self-absorption, although her realization that he possesses no hidden reserves of sensitivity serves to liberate her from his thrall. Homosexual relationships fare no better in the novel; to Ana, her gay friend Cecilio's "torturada espera homosexual no es más que el último símbolo ... del hundimiento de la fe en la pareja" [tortured homosexual waiting is only the ultimate symbol ... of the collapse of faith in the couple as a unit] (133).

The thematic emphasis of Montero's first novel is so strong that its artistic achievement has been questioned. Eunice D. Myers has called it "an uneven work; in some places polemics obscure its artistry" (1988, 99). Montero's own book-jacket commentary on the work, perhaps a reflection of her lack of confidence at the time, has fueled this criticism. She announces there that she does not consider her book to be a novel, but rather a "crónica sin pretensiones, una mirada rápida al mundo que nos rodea, una aproximación a los problemas y afanes cotidianos de todos nosotros" [a chronicle without pretensions, a quick look at the world around us, an approach to the daily problems and desires that we all have]. Despite the often lengthy feminist discourse of the women who dominate its

pages, the work does fulfill the traditional expectations of a good
novel: it depicts one main character, Ana, who undergoes a series of
experiences that change her. At the beginning of the novel, the
heroine can only dream of writing her story, but by the end she has
acquired sufficient resources to begin it.

Technically, *Crónica del desamor* is closely associated with the
genre of the nonfiction interview that Montero cultivated so
successfully as a reporter. Phyllis Zatlin has called the novel "a
collage of interviews."[11] This assessment is accurate, although it is
as much a reflection of Montero's novelistic introductions to her
interviews as of her reportorial stance as an omniscient narrator.
Instead of featuring politically important national figures, the
interviewees in Montero's first novel are an amalgam of ordinary
people, most of them female, whose lives traditionally have gone
unnoticed. These characters, and the feminist views they hold as a
matter of survival, are reflections of the "involved" author who
claims them as part of herself.[12]

Notwithstanding its stylistic and ideological debt to New
Journalism, Montero's first novel features trenchant criticism of the
modern Spanish newspaper. Ana Antón is an able journalist who
works harder than anyone else, yet she is denied a permanent job at
the newspaper that prefers to exploit her. Although he is most readily
seen as a caricature of male supremacy, the owner of Ana's
newspaper also symbolizes the thoughtless magnates who control
the media. Soto Amón, Ana's boss, is handsome, ambitious, and
controlling, a member of the dominant class who is already training
a precocious young man to succeed him. His complete insensivitity
is at once frightening and seductive. The character of Soto Amón is
one that will reappear in Montero's work nearly a decade later, a
subject of enduring fascination: the powerful boss who is simultaneously hated and adored.

Rosa Montero's documentary of the lives of contemporary
Spanish women met with enormous success when it appeared, and at
last count it has gone through thirteen editions. The triumphant
reception of *Crónica del desamor* startled Montero, who was not yet
thirty when she found that suddenly she was a public figure. Soon
after the publication of her first novel, she remarked in an interview
that she felt that a character named Rosa Montero was being
imposed on her, "que se ha inventado la gente y que no soy yo" [that
people have invented and that is not me] (*Ozono*, 5). She also became
aware of the tyranny of public expectations and resolved to maintain
her independence with regard to giving her reading audience what
they expected from her. Montero's eagerness to explore new ground

and to take risks as a writer of fiction is apparent in each of her subsequent works.

La función Delta (1981) (English translation by Kari Easton, *The Delta Function*, forthcoming) is much more complex than its predecessor. Whereas her first novel poses as a chronicle of the real world, her second explores the elusive nature of reality. *La función Delta* is narrated in two strands. One is a first-person account of the daily life of a sixty-three-year-old woman named Lucía Ramos in the year 2010, as she approaches death in a hospital. The second narrative consists of Lucía's recently begun memoirs, in which she is describing a crucial week in her life in the 1970s, when she was thirty years old. An account of the protagonist's life gradually emerges from her parallel narrations, which do not converge until the work's close. However, Lucía's story is not straightforward. Her perceptions of both her past and her present are subject to changing interpretations as she gradually falls in love with a lifelong friend, Ricardo, who also becomes her literary critic. The question of "reality" with regard to both the past and the present is further complicated in the novel by the fact that Ricardo, who frequently challenges Lucía's recollections and interpretations, is himself a superb storyteller who delights in "recalling" imaginary events. The metafictional aspects of the novel focus overtly on the nature of narrative and on the continuum of truth on which "reality" and "invention" are opposite poles.

Within this metaliterary orientation, Montero allows the reader to retrieve the milestones of the protagonist's life easily; the central events in Lucía's life are not disputed, although their significance is subject to different interpretations. Lucía was a filmmaker who dropped out of the field after her successful first movie, a film entitled *Crónica del desamor* (Chronicle of disaffection), which was identical to the real author's first novel, except for a dramatic finale in which the main character drowns. Lucía's "real job" consisted of working at an advertising agency, where her special niche involved creating ads for women's products that would not offend feminists. She describes herself as having a talent for falling in love with inappropriate men (122), including a married man who refuses to make a commitment to her. Lucía's one successful relationship was with a nurturing, sensitive mathematics professor named Miguel, with whom she lived until his untimely death, and for whom she chose to sacrifice her film career.

Social themes predominate in this novel, as in *Crónica del desamor*. Relations between the sexes are a primary topic. In *La función Delta*, unlike its predecessor, relationships are depicted as having the potential for mutual fulfillment. The nature of women's roles in contemporary Spanish society also is addressed at length. Lucía's central conflict in life has been her ambivalent definition of what it means to be a woman. Ricardo points out to Lucía that her dualistic definition of love as "amor cómplice" [passive love] versus "amor pasión" [passion] is a reflection of her "problema de identidad como mujer" [problem of female identity]: "entre la mujer independiente que querías y creías ser, y la mujer 'esposa de' que llevas dentro de ti y para lo que fuiste educada" [between the independent woman that you wanted to be and believed you were, and the "somebody's wife" that you carry within you and for which you were educated] (213). Ricardo's perceptive recognition of Lucía's inability to reconcile her assertive, "masculine" side with her submissive, "wifely" side is a telling reflection of the new type of male character who inhabits *La función Delta*. Unlike the male characters who populated Montero's first novel, two of this work's male leads, Ricardo and Miguel, are egalitarian and sensitive in their treatment of women. Not coincidentally, these are the two men with whom the narrator falls in love.

Social criticism voiced by Ricardo on a personal level is echoed on a broad scale through the classic device of description set in the future. In Lucía's hospital room, Ricardo offers an incisive disquisition on the greatest achievement of the technological revolution: having created a perfect system for repression. Spain in the year 2010 is an Orwellian nightmare, a rigidly monitored environment in which an Order Squad commits murder but Official Security Rules prescribe that people must act as if nothing has happened (176). Old people are scarce and devalued, and young people, as represented by Lucía's nurse, are uninvolved in political issues.

The metafictional technique through which social analysis is presented in *La función Delta* has become increasingly common among current Spanish women writers such as Esther Tusquets, who find its "subversive potential" useful "to defamiliarize cultural conventions."[13] In her second novel, Montero again reports on life for a middle-class Spanish woman in her thirties in contemporary Spain, leading reviewers to prolong their earlier association of her fiction with journalism: "In *La función Delta*," wrote Phyllis Zatlin in 1985, "Montero continues to demonstrate her journalist's capacity for vivid description and characterization."[14] However, the novel represents a substantial departure from objective reporting. The work's imaginative framework calls into question the very nature of reality, emphasizing the multiplicity of interpretations that contribute to its definition.

In *La función Delta* Montero moves beyond the documentary realism of *Crónica del desamor*, leaving behind clarity in favor of ambiguity. She has said that in her second novel "lo que me interesaba no era contar ... era el cómo" [what interested me was not telling the story, but how it was told].[15] The work's title reflects the author's acceptance of randomness and mystery: it refers to a mathematical function "que describe fenómenos discontinuos de gran duración" [that describes discontinuous phenomena of long duration] (118).

The complexities of *La función Delta* aroused the interest of literary critics in Spain and the United States, and the novel was received enthusiastically by the Spanish reading public. Montero's second novel also brought increased critical notice to *Crónica del desamor*. Her first two novels are often considered together, as evidence of her preoccupation with her own world, in contrast with her most recent novels, which have taken her farther afield. Between these two "phases," Montero tried the short-story form. Her one contribution to this genre, entitled "Paulo Pumilio" and published in 1982, presents a shift in subject matter from the world of the urban middle-class to that of the outer fringes of society. It is a jocose, first-person rendition of the life story of an outcast, told from the prison in which he awaits sentencing as a murderer. Humorous and fast-paced, the story is reminiscent of contemporary writer Camilo José Cela's now-classic 1942 novel, *La familia de Pascual Duarte* (Pascual Duarte's family). Like Cela's novel, "Paulo Pumilio" is picaresque: it details the dishonorable adventures of someone on the bottom rung of the social ladder, often to hilarious effect.

Montero's short story presages the "escape from her own skin" that the author maintains she did not achieve until her third novel, *Te trataré como a una reina* (I'll treat you like a queen) (1983). Like her previous book, this novel combines various narrative strands and invites the reader to assemble them. Unlike her other novels, *Te trataré como a una reina* is a richly atmospheric mystery novel, set in parts of present-day Madrid that presumably are far removed from the author's respectable middle-class orbit. It is a novel of suspense that is also poignant, ironic, witty, and comic.

Te trataré como a una reina begins with a magazine account of how an upstanding man, Don Antonio Ortiz, was pushed from a high window by a woman of questionable repute, Isabel López ("La Bella"), a bolero singer in a seedy nightclub. The magazine is a sensationalist journal named *El criminal*; transcriptions of interviews that ostensibly shed light on the crime are inserted in the novel in

three places. Parallel to this investigation, the characters in the novel
reveal themselves through their actions and interactions. Bella, the
nightclub singer, is a pathetic but brave middle-aged woman who has
been allowed to sing at the Club Desiré, the rundown nightclub
where most of the novel takes place. Menéndez is the owner of the club,
who has tried to clean it up by firing its former prostitute-waitresses;
he spends his days reading pornographic novels hidden behind a
copy of *The Three Musketeers*. Poco is an habitué of the club who
also works there as a guard, helping the owner in his efforts to keep
the police from investigating the drug business that is probably being
conducted there by patrons (who inject drugs in the lavatory). Poco
dreams of leaving the cardboard palm trees of the Desiré and
returning to the Cuba he left long ago, symbolized for him by the
magnificent Tropicana nightclub of Havana in the 1950s. One other
woman comprises the cast of the Desiré, an eighteen-year-old vamp
who calls herself Vanessa (her real name is Juana). She supports
herself as a maid while she dreams of being a star.

Outside the Club Desiré, other principal characters are introduced
in cinematographic fashion as they act out their often ridiculous
lives. Don Antonio works in the field of perfume development as a
"professional nose," and he is immensely proud of his superhuman
sense of smell. He amuses himself by having brief affairs with
women whose husbands are out of town, relying on a travel agent
as his source, and keeping detailed records of his conquests. His
factotum, Don Benigno, a man older than he who has been stripped
of most of his dignity, has for years secretly been in love with
Antonio's sister, Antonia. She knows nothing of this. She has settled
into the role of a spinster, managing her brother's household as if she
were a servant. Secretly, she pleasures herself with a favorite stuffed
animal, then reprimands the toy and confesses to a deaf priest. A
simple teenage boy in her building, Damián, watches her in this
activity until she invites him in one day and they begin an affair that
gratifies them both.

Relations among the characters in *Te trataré como a una reina*
have been compared to the boleros that are featured prominently in
the text. Couples change partners frequently. Poco is intimate
with Bella and flirts with Vanessa, whom he would like to take with
him to Cuba; Vanessa has an affair with Antonio; Bella (who is a
lifelong friend of Antonia's) has sex with an anonymous young
man who asks for a gift in return. Although older male characters'
relations with a woman young enough to be their daughter is not
questioned, Antonia's relationship with Damián is intolerable to
those around them. As Concha Alborg points out, the social

repercussions for promiscuity are determined by the participant's gender (1988, 72). This inequality underlies the rage that leads Bella to push Antonio out of a window; like the other questions in the novel, the mystery surrounding Bella's action is resolved as the plot unravels in the final pages of the novel.

Boleros are more than a metaphor for characters' liaisons in *Te trataré como a una reina*. These romantic, idealized love songs are an ironic foil to the degraded lives of the protagonists, who cling to the lyrics as a representation of their dreams. The boleros become intertextual references to the characters' most cherished myths. Their exotic nature is heightened by the way in which they are sung, using South American pronunciation (with sibilant c's and z's) instead of Castilian Spanish, a fact that is indicated in the text by substituting the letter *s* for all c's and z's in transcriptions of the songs. The novel's title, a verse from a bolero, underscores the ironic use of this musical genre in the novel. Male characters use the promise "I'll treat you like a queen" to manipulate women. Antonio brags to a friend who admires his conquests: "Hay que tratarlas como si fueran reinas. Son muy románticas, las mujeres" [You've got to treat them as if they were queens. They're very romantic, women are] (100). Women, however, are wise to this ploy: when Poco, entreating Vanessa to come away with him, says "Te trataré como a una reina" [I'll treat you like a queen], she replies, "Oh, sí, la reina de las pulgas, la emperatriz de las escobas" [Oh, sure, the queen of the fleas, the empress of brooms] (207).

The theme of the difficulty of true communication between men and women is present in this novel as in the author's earlier ones, although it illustrates with greater poignancy Montero's conviction that men and women "se separan por abismos terribles de desconocimientos, no nos conocemos para nada" [are separated by terrible abysses of misunderstanding, we don't understand each other at all] (*Córdoba*). In its treatment of women characters and in its portrayal of life for certain members of the lower middle class, the novel also illustrates the author's belief that "el grupo realmente marginado es aquel que ni siquiera es consciente de su marginación" [the group that is truly marginalized is the one that isn't even aware of its marginal status] (*Córdoba*). So successful are her characterization of the netherworld of her protagonists and her parody of magazine reporting that the novel has invited familiar references to her journalistic expertise.[16]

The primary use of journalistic skill in Rosa Montero's third novel is to satirize the profession brilliantly. Reporter Paco Mancebo's magazine pieces are glaring examples of journalistic bias: he consistently demonstrates what journalism manuals caution against, namely the "*distortion* of news ... through stereotyping."[17] Glenn has observed that in the novel male writing leads to a "misreading" of women (1987, 191). The reporter's bias leads him to conclusions that are opposite from the truth: it is really Bella, and not Antonio, who is a victim, despite the fact that she is neither petite nor virginal. In addition to being a parody of investigative reporting, *Te trataré como a una reina* also plays with the conventions of the *novela negra* (detective novel), especially in its gender reversal of victim and perpetrator.

Except for its satiric function, Rosa Montero's "first genre" is unequivocally left behind. In *Te trataré como a una reina*, Montero for the first time assembles a cast of characters who are totally unlike herself and sets them in motion in their own world. Before this novel, she has revealed, she attempted to express herself "por medio de personajes a los que yo movía. Pero en esta novela quise meterme en la piel de unos personajes que, al serme lejanos, tiraran de mí" [by means of characters whom I led. But in this novel I tried to get under the skin of characters who, because they were so distant from me, would pull me along].[18] Reviewers have generally agreed that she fulfilled the difficult goals she set for herself with her third novel. Tellingly, her success has been expressed in terms of her dual careers. In the words of Javier Villán, "Rosa Montero [es] una periodista de raza y una novelista a la que, a partir de 'Te trataré como a una reina,' hay que ampliarle el crédito y la credibilidad de narradora" [Rosa Montero is a born journalist and a novelist who, since the publication of "*Te trataré como a una reina*," deserves greater credit and credibility as a narrator] (*Córdoba*). General readers in Spain, who never found Montero's "credibility" to be wanting, again honored the author by vaulting her novel to the best-seller list.

Rosa Montero's next novel also became an immediate best-seller, despite the fact that she continues her refusal to pander to fans by giving them what they liked before. *Amado amo* (Beloved master) (1988) is technically far removed from any of her earlier work. It is a closely observed narration of a critical period in the life of a commercial artist who is a longtime employee of an advertising agency. Stylistically, the novel is distinguished by a lack of punctuation that would mark the main character's thoughts or others' reported speech. Although it is narrated in an omniscient voice, events and dialogue flow together as they are experienced and perceived by the man whose stream of consciousness is reported; dramatic revelations are repeatedly buried in the protagonist's often trivial train of thought. Chapters are differentiated by the various

settings in which César Miranda, the protagonist, moves. He himself
remains virtually static over time.

César is not a likable figure. He is a dissolute, self-indulgent
middle-aged man who is terrified that others at his agency have
caught on to his uselessness. In the past he had not always felt like
such a "dwarf and a worm" (79), having once been a successful pop
artist. Now paranoia and depression plague him constantly. Because
the firm allows artists a great deal of latitude in the hours they keep,
César often stays at home instead of going to work. He spends his
days alone in his apartment, looking at magazines and oversleeping.
His anxiety, exacerbated by his low self-esteem, threatens to paralyze
him. He manages to sustain a relationship with a colleague, Paula,
although her constant complaining about work annoys him and he
longs for his former lover, Clara. He also beds a college student.
César's "adventures" are usually humiliating. On occasion, they
reveal his creator's talent for black humor, as when César forces
himself to attend a party at the home of his young rival, Nacho, only
to spend the evening trying to pry the host's masturbating dog loose
from his leg.

The business culture in which César attempts to survive is all-
powerful. The Golden Line, the English name of César's advertising
agency, is a rigidly hierarchical society in which nuanced cues are
crucially important in indicating workers' changing status. Parking
spaces, office size, secretarial assignments: all indicate official
approval or disapproval. The agency is controlled by foreigners.
Americans own the firm, having bought out the Spanish parent
company during César's tenure; César's boss is an Englishman
named Morton who does everything correctly, including speak
Spanish flawlessly. César feels disadvantaged because of his modest
birth, sensing that he can never compete on equal footing with those
more privileged than he. All around him he witnesses the caprice that
determines who is on the way up and who is on the way out. A
colleague's horrible suicide leaves him shaken and with a lesson in
the terror of losing one's job; when called upon to betray a friend
in order to keep his, César does not hesitate.

Amado amo is as intensely thematic as Montero's first novel,
Crónica del desamor. It offers a scathing critique of the de-
humanizing business culture of the large firm, ironically known in
Spanish as the Casa (which also means home), in which the quality
of peoples' lives is determined. The heartless newspaper business
enterprise that appeared in Montero's first novel is now examined at
length as an advertising agency, and the figure of Soto Amón is
reprised in more detail in Morton. Reflections on the power of bosses

are frequent. "Los jefes eran los dioses de un mundo ateo" [Bosses were the gods of an atheist world], César muses early in the novel (39). The figure of the boss who exercises power through seduction is also overtly criticized. "El Poder poseía esa energía secreta, esa asombrosa alquimia: la capacidad de aparejar amor y sufrimiento ... Amado amo" [The Power possessed that secret energy, that amazing alchemy: the ability to join love and suffering ... Beloved master] (142–43). César becomes so depressed that he defines living as fearing someone, within a hierarchical succession of humiliations (144). He defines The Golden Line as "un molde de servidumbre" [a mold of servitude] (158).

Through the character Paula, it becomes clear that the situation for women in this corporate culture is even worse than it is for men; perhaps most damaging is the fact that her feminist demands are dismissed as whining and repetitive by the man she considers her ally, and who ultimately betrays her. Montero's treatment of the one feminist character in *Amado amo* appears to confirm her own ambivalence about the feminist movement (although not about feminist beliefs), a position that Roberto Manteiga has documented in her previous three novels (1988). Relationships between men and women are depicted negatively in *Amado amo*. César, whose thinly veiled machismo and paranoid self-absorption preclude a relationship with a successful woman, reflects that the prospects for compatibility between the sexes are slim. "Por ejemplo," he asks rhetorically, "qué futuro podía tener la relación sentimental entre un pulpo y un pájaro ..." [For example, what kind of future could there be for an emotional relationship between an octopus and a bird ...] (108).

As a novel of social criticism, *Amado amo* is reminiscent of the neorealistic "social novel" of the 1950s in Spain, by authors such as Armando López Salinas, José Manuel Caballero Bonald, Ignacio Aldecoa, Carmen Martín Gaite, and Dolores Medio, which focused on the alienation of everyday people and frequently chronicled the plight of anonymous workers.[19] It further recalls Miguel Delibes's 1969 novel *Parábola del náufrago* (English translation by Frances López-Morillas, *The Hedge*, 1983), in which a hapless worker is tyrannized by the Casa that has subsumed the socializing and also the spiritual functions of the home, with disastrous personal results. *Amado amo* also bears an existential stamp. At one point, without directly mentioning the myth of Sisyphus, César describes a military assignment that had him move small rocks from one pile to another, then move them back again; by inference, his existence at The Golden Line is the same. Despite perceptible links to earlier traditions, *Amado amo* is a quintessential novel of the 1980s, chronicling the cynical careerism that may have reached its apex in this decade.

Amado amo applies scathing social criticism to the field of journalism. It offers a brief but important treatment of the conflict between business and ethics that characterizes the newspaper business and that has been called a prime symbol of the modern opposition between materialism and idealism.[20] The heinous betrayal with which the novel culminates is brought about by the action of a newspaper editor, who calls the chief of The Golden Line to warn him that a traitor has leaked internal agency governance documents that attest to the firm's sexism. The editor calls as a matter of courtesy, since he will already do his friend the favor of killing the story. The symbolism of the conclusion of *Amado amo* is cynical and bitter. Inequality for women is perpetuated through the self-interest of men in power, and the institution that could expose injustice instead reverts to conducting business the way it was done under Franco. Although journalism has great symbolic value, journalistic technique is absent from the oblique narrative of Rosa Montero's fourth novel. *Amado amo* achieves the ambiguity that Montero has called the goal of her "apprenticeship" as a writer of fiction.

In speaking about the relationship of literature and journalism, the author has observed that "Cuando del periodismo pasas a la novela entras en un camino nuevo y, en buena medida, tiene que aprender a reeducarte" [When you go from journalism to the novel you embark on a new path and, to a certain extent, you have to reeducate yourself] (*Córdoba*). As we have seen, Rosa Montero's "reeducation" has meant a gradual rejection of the conventions of journalism in favor of novelistic ambiguity and invention. Her first novel, *Crónica del desamor*, was very closely allied with her journalistic technique; the characters present themselves in imaginary interviews that reflect the lives of professional women in Madrid in the late seventies. In her second novel, *La función Delta*, the author continued to report on the world around her, but she did so partly from the vantage point of the twenty-first century and within an imaginative metaliterary structure that questioned the very nature of reality.

Montero's short story, "Paulo Pumilio," presaged the leap in subject matter from her own world to a world she did not inhabit, which would be explored at length in her third novel, *Te trataré como a una reina*. The novel detailed the lives of a group of misfits on the fringes of the lower middle class, in the context of a mystery story. Journalism was parodied through the insertions of biased news accounts as counterpoint to reality, just as romantic boleros were used to highlight the disparity between characters and their dreams. In her most recent novel, *Amado amo*, an unlikable protagonist is studied in glaring detail as he struggles for survival in the powerful corporate culture of an advertising agency. The narrative is technically oblique and thematically clear in its social criticism. Journalism, in the form of the editor of a newspaper, is present only as a symbol of ethical bankruptcy.

Throughout Rosa Montero's evolution from journalist to novelist, she has maintained her preoccupation with social issues. Foremost among these are the roles of women, relations between the sexes, and the abuses committed by those with power. Beyond these observable phenomena, Montero is concerned with the conflict between ideals and reality and with the social construction of "truth." She approaches these issues by using a variety of novelistic techniques, ranging from straightforward omniscient narration to a sophisticated memoir-in-progress that is transformed as the writer falls in love with her critic. Montero's characters are diverse. They include men and women who share her own experience, but extend to characters whose lives scarcely intersect with their creator's, even though they all live in Montero's native city of Madrid. Her characters' lives are at the center of her fiction: they are at times ridiculous, often poignant, always riveting.

The fiction of Rosa Montero has grown in complexity and sophistication since her first novel was published in 1979. She has emerged from a background of political journalism to become one of the most interesting and provocative novelists of the post-Franco era.

Notes

1. A dozen of the female novelists who began publishing around this time were featured in the first anthology of short fiction by women in Spain, which appeared in 1982. In addition to the writers mentioned, others in that collection are Cristina Fernández Cubas, Clara Janés, Beatriz de Moura, Rosa María Pereda, Marta Pessarrodona, Soledad Puértolas, and Carme Riera. See Ymelda Navajo, ed., *Doce relatos de mujeres* (Madrid: Alianza, 1982.)

2. Interview by Alvaro Feito, Valeriano García Rivera, and Juan González Alvaro, "Al pobre pez le falló la lucecita, ¿no?," in *Ozono*, vol. 4, pp. 4–7. The copy of this document in my possession, given to me by the author, does not contain a date; however, it is apparent from the content of the interview that it was

conducted just after the publication of her 1979 first novel. Subsequent references to this interview will be cited in the text as *Ozono*.

3. John Calhoun Merrill, *The Imperative of Freedom: A Philosophy of Journalistic Autonomy* (New York: Hastings House, Studies in Public Communication, 1974), 147.

4. Javier Terrón Montero, *La prensa de España durante el régimen de Franco: Un intento de análisis político.* (Madrid: Centro de Investigaciones Sociológicas, 1981), 11.

5. Jesús Lucía, of Debate (a publishing house), in an interview in *Tiempo* 316, 30 May–3 June 1988, 159.

6. Javier Villán, interview in *Córdoba*, 12 November 1983, n.p. Subsequent references to this interview are identified as "*Córdoba*."

7. Manteiga 1988, 114. The statement refers to Montero's first three novels.

8. Lynne K. Talbot, "Entrevista con Rosa Montero," *Letras Femeninas* 14 (1988): 94.

9. Interview by Angel Fernández Santos, "Rosa Montero: Narrar es una inutilidad necesaria," *El País*, 21 November 1983; also in *Córdoba*.

10. Manteiga 1988, 119. On the subject of her own feminism, Montero has said that to her feminism is a fundamental attitude with which she faces life, as basic to her as her age or the era in which she lives. She defines feminism as a continual search, and not an ideology (Villán interview in *Córdoba*).

11. Phyllis Zatlin, in a review of *Crónica del desamor* and *La función Delta*, *Hispanófila* 84 (May 1985): 121–23.

12. Angel Fernández Santos, *El País* interview.

13. Phyllis Zatlin, "Women Novelists in Democratic Spain: Freedom to Express the Female Perspective," *Anales de la Literatura Española Contemporánea* 12 (1987): 29–43; quotation is on 37. See also Alborg 1988.

14. Phyllis Zatlin, *Hispánofila* review, 123.

15. Lynne K. Talbot, *Letras Femeninas* interview, 95.

16. For example, in an essay on the intercalated "magazine segments" in the novel, Kathleen M. Glenn writes that "Montero's experience as an interviewer stands her in good stead. She has an eye for the telling detail, an ear for statements that do not ring true, and a gift for puncturing inflated egos" (1987, 193).

17. Gary Atkins and William Rivers, *Reporting With Understanding* (Ames: Iowa State University Press, 1987), 213.

18. "Rosa entre espinas: En su tercera novela, Rosa Montero aborda un mundo ajeno." Interview in *Cambio 16*, 19 December 1983, 167.

19. The social novel of this period has been defined variously by literary historians. Pablo Gil Casado restricts the classification to novels that meet five criteria: they deal with injustices in society, they focus on social groups rather than individuals, they describe reality through testimony, they present only the version of reality that supports their world view, and they create a protagonist-class or multiple hero. Gonzalo Sobejano broadens the definition of the genre to include social criticism that also focuses on the individual protagonist. This more ample definition of the social novel is the one that best applies to Montero's *Amado amo*. See Pablo Gil Casado, *La novela social española (1942–1968)* (Barcelona: Seix Barral, 1968), xvi, and Gonzalo Sobejano, *Novela española de nuestro tiempo* (Madrid: Prensa Española, 1975), 517–45.

20. José Acosto Montoro, *Periodismo y literatura* (Madrid: Guadarrama, 1973), 57.

Bibliography

1. PRIMARY SOURCES

1979. *Crónica del desamor.* Madrid: Editorial Debate. Page references are from the 8th ed., 1981. Translated by Cristina de la Torre and Diana Glad as *Absent Love: A Chronicle.* Lincoln: University of Nebraska Press, in press, 1990.

1981. *La función Delta.* Madrid: Editorial Debate. Page references are from the 5th ed., 1982. Translated by Kari Easton as *The Delta Function.* Lincoln: University of Nebraska Press, in press, 1990.

1982. "Paulo Pumilio." In *Doce relatos de mujeres,* edited by Ymelda Navajo, 69–73. Madrid: Alianza.

1983. *Te trataré como a una reina.* Barcelona: Seix Barral. Page references are from the 8th ed., 1984.

1988. *Amado amo.* Madrid: Editorial Debate. Page references are from the 2d ed., 1988.

2. SECONDARY SOURCES

Alborg, Concha. 1988. "Metaficción y feminismo en Rosa Montero." *Revista de Estudios Hispánicos* 22: 1, January, 67–76. Analyzes the subversive use of metafiction in transmitting feminist criticism in Montero's first three novels.

Gascón Vera, Elena. 1987. "Rosa Montero ante la escritura femenina." *Anales de la Literatura Española Contemporánea* 12: 59–77. Relates the characterizations of women in Montero's first three novels to the writings of French feminist theorists.

Glenn, Kathleen M. 1987. "Victimized by Misreading: Rosa Montero's *Te trataré como a una reina.*" *Anales de la Literatura Española Contemporánea* 12: 191–201. Interprets the three "nonfiction" magazine interviews in the novel as representations of masculine failure to comprehend female texts or feminine reality.

Manteiga, Roberto C. 1988. "The Dilemma of the Modern Woman: A Study of the Female Characters in Rosa Montero's Novels." In *Feminine Concerns in Contemporary Spanish Fiction by Women*, edited by Roberto C. Manteiga, Carolyn Galerstein, and Kathleen McNerny, 113–23. Potomac, Md.: Scripta Humanistica. Identifies and explores the duality of the characters that populate Montero's first three novels, who have strong feminist goals but still search for fulfillment through romantic love.

Myers, Eunice D. 1988. "The Feminist Message: Propaganda and/or Art? A Study of Two Novels by Rosa Montero." In *Feminine Concerns in Contemporary Spanish Fiction by Women*, edited by Roberto C. Manteiga, Carolyn Galerstein, and Kathleen McNerny, 99–112. Potomac, Md.: Scripta Humanistica. Examines Montero's first two novels in terms of their multifaceted feminist themes.

13

Writing Ambiguity and Desire: The Works of Adelaida García Morales

Elizabeth J. Ordóñez

As the ghosts of the Franco dictatorship slip evermore into the hazy contours of memory, so go the phantoms of sociorealism, that novelistic experiment of the postwar period that sought to reflect faithfully and reject roundly society's oppressive restraints. But if the techniques for recreating the culture in text have changed, the desire to do so has not. Today's generation of young writers still wage battle against ghosts, but the language of that struggle is different. It borrows from the ghosts themselves; it speaks to them and of them in their own language, and it invents opponents who have the uncanny capacity to slip and slide among layers of culture and the imagination. Call them postmodern, semiotic, multiplicitous, self-conscious—these writers and their fictions are no longer filed easily away in clearly defined categories nor contained by glib or simple formulae. Instead they gesture subversively in their challenge to whatever may have once been comfortably certain. Among these troops is Adelaida García Morales.

García Morales spent the formative years of her life in locations she later evokes in her writings: Badajoz, her birthplace, and Seville, where she spent her childhood. Her intellectual and artistic preparation is varied, for she holds a degree in philosophy from the University of Madrid and has also studied script writing at the Escuela Oficial de Cinematografía. Her professional experience is no less diverse: she has been a teacher of Spanish language and literature and of philosophy in the Instituto de Enseñanza Media (secondary school), translator for the OPEC nations in Algiers, and model and actress in the Esperpento (farce) theater of Seville and in various short subjects. She lived for five years in a small village of La Alpujarra in the province of Granada. Apparently influenced by her childhood experiences, García Morales's first published book, *El Sur seguido de Bene* (South followed by Bene) (1985), was a critical and commercial success. *El Sur* was also successful as a film directed by Víctor Erice. *El silencio de las sirenas* (The silence of the sirens) (1985), García Morales's second published work, bears the mark of her years in La Alpujarra. It was honored by the Herralde Prize for the novel during the same year of its publication.

Drawing thus from her experience and her imagination, García Morales has created fictional worlds in *El Sur seguido de Bene* and *El silencio de las sirenas* that are both of and beyond what is most familiar to their readers. *El Sur* and *Bene*'s domestic confines are situated on a lonely stretch of road, cut off from village or town. The village of *El silencio* is similarly secluded, perched among the surrounding peaks of Las Alpujarras. Silence reigns over these isolated spaces, and into the gaps left by the absence of speech, the whispers of ghosts and the spirits of the past insinuate themselves. The listeners of these voices of silence are three young women whose characters closely resemble one another, especially in their almost absolute physical and ontological solitude. Theirs is an introverted, internalized world—even a confining and restricted one—and whatever they say about the world beyond them becomes colored and shaped by their solitary imaginations. In the narrative space of *El Sur*, *Bene*, and *El silencio* there hovers always a lurking presence of unspecified evil and intimations of prohibited desire. Allusions to incestuous desire link Adriana (*Sur*), Angela, and Bene (*Bene*), and strange psychic powers and evil spells surround the obsessive passion of Elsa (*El silencio*). Into this rarefied atmosphere, ghosts of fathers, lovers, and father/lovers seem to emerge uncannily; they float in rhetorical ambiguity, evading attempts to grasp at them and pin them down as the either/or of reality or fantasy. And the young narrators or protagonists (Adriana, Angela, Bene, and Elsa) are at times seen as monsters, to be pitied yet to have no lasting place in a world only reluctantly tolerant of the elusive, the unmanageable, the unclassifiable, and most disconcertingly the inexplicable.

If anything is clear, what one encounters in the narrative worlds of Adelaida García Morales are the familiar characteristics of the unfamiliar worlds of fantastic literature. Many of the recurrent features of the fantastic that Tzvetan Todorov has classified and analyzed are present in the narratives that I analyze here. All three texts in some way occupy that "duration of uncertainty," the temporal-spatial realm in which the need to choose between the natural and the supernatural is often held in abeyance.[1] The reader is thus obliged to hesitate between opposing explanations of occurrences, the rhetorical ambiguity of the fantastic text rendering such options untenable. On this ambiguous middle ground, then, the fantastic examines "desire in its excessive forms," and its "preoccupations concerning death [and] life after death are linked to the theme of love."[2] As we shall soon discover, these themes identified by Todorov are also those that link *El Sur, Bene,* and *El silencio de las sirenas.*

The works of García Morales might be sufficiently served if one were to analyze them solely in terms of these structural and thematic constants of the fantastic. However, without reference to the fantastic genre's cultural implications, an analysis and assessment could only partially address how this mode of expression serves also as a vehicle whereby today's contemporary woman writer perplexes and challenges her readers. The fantastic has long been repressed and marginalized, and for good reason:[3] it characteristically operates outside dominant value systems, subverting laws and beliefs that seek to insure cultural order and established ideological hegemony.[4] So if the fantastic is a literature of desire—which Todorov establishes and Jackson reaffirms—it is so primarily because it dares to articulate the unsaid or give voice to that which is customarily prohibited by culture.[5] The fantastic therefore violates "normal" or commonsense perspectives, as it insists on its discourse of transgressive desire. To achieve this disconcerting mode of articulation, practices such as sadism, incest, necrophilia, murder, and eroticism recur as themes structuring interrelationships and ultimately the text itself. And recurrent motifs like ghosts, shadows, vampires, werewolves, partial selves, reflections, enclosures, monsters, beasts, and cannibals all serve to erase rigid markers of dream and reality, gender and genre (Jackson). The presence of cultural prohibitions thus assails the reader into perceiving reality as shifting—perhaps even shifty—and by no means predictable and stable.

As indicated by Jackson (104), one of the ways in which women writers have employed the fantastic is "to subvert patriarchal society—the symbolic order of modern culture." Our female narrators must, of course, also grapple with this symbolic order, for that cultural given presents itself over and over again as the unavoidable hurdle for all writing. Yet as woman seeks to convert the content of her imagination into the symbolic order of culture, her desire collides repeatedly with the contradictory tensions of the text. Her gender-inflected voicing may elicit costly negotiations. One way out of entirely sacrificing her imaginary realm for the strictures of the symbolic is to opt for a rhetoric of ambiguity. Though such a posture is by no means gender-specific, it is one effective way woman can elude the often rigid demands of the symbolic order. With this in mind, along with Andrés Amorós's conclusion that "lo fantástico supone, desde luego, el deseo de profundizar en la realidad para captar sus estratos más íntimos" [the fantastic assumes, after all, the desire to delve into reality to capture its most intimate levels][6] I would like to explore, by means of the narratives of García Morales, how the cultural dis-ease often felt by woman inscribes itself into the ambiguous or subversive fantastic text. I approach García Morales's texts as a continuum, guided by my reading of the central concerns of each: *El Sur* traces the seductive power of the paternal enigma and the father's law, discourses that initially hold the daughter's desire in their sway; *Bene* also reveals insistent ambiguity as, this time, the enigma of the mysterious housemaid is left elliptically incomplete; and finally, *El silencio de las sirenas* offers a meditation on the sources, processes, and pitfalls of love story writing, as woman attempts to negotiate the treacherous terrain between the symbolic order and her imagination.

> ... it is his desire which prescribes the force, the shape, the modes, etc. of the law he lays down or passes on, a law that reduces to the state of "fantasy" the little girl's seduced and rejected desire—a desire still faltering, barely articulate, silent perhaps, or expressed in signs, a desire that must be seduced to the discourse and law of the father.
> —Luce Irigaray, *Speculum of the Other Woman*

Every daughter is "daddy's girl." Sooner or later every female becomes enfolded into the embrace of her father's discourse. She absorbs its terms perhaps unconsciously, and so her utterances may seem entirely her own. Yet at some time her search for self-articulation must at least attempt to come to terms with this invasion, or perhaps less sensationally, this permeation. *El Sur* is the story of just such a reckoning.

Narrated by the daughter, Adriana, and addressed to the deceased father, *El Sur* recounts the narrator's formative years under the authority of her father, his suicide, and her later investigation into the nature of his secret past life—his former lover, Gloria Valle, and her son, Adriana's half-brother. Through the course of the daughter's maturation and investigation the father loses his apparently magical powers and takes on more human proportions. He acquires poignancy as one who has made mistakes and paid dearly for them. But if he begins as an enigma for his daughter ("para mí eras un enigma") [you were an enigma to me] (6), he is never fully clarified. As García Morales herself has observed, the figure of the father remains "de una manera ambigua, conflictiva" [in a certain way ambiguous, conflictive] (Sánchez Arnosi, 1986). In his ambiguity he reflects the daughter's own ambivalent attitude toward him. For though she comes to understand her father better, understanding is somehow not sufficient ("comprender no era suficiente") (51). Like the masked image in an old photo, the father can never be fully revealed; something deeper remains hidden and continues to insinuate itself uncannily into the deeper levels of the daughter's consciousness. Desire for the father and his betrayal leave their mark upon the daughter and her text.

During her early childhood the daughter was at odds with others in her perception of the father. She believed him to be a magician ("pensaba entonces que tú eras un mago") [I thought then that you were a magician] (5), but between him and other women in the household there was great enmity. The mother complained of isolation and imprisonment while the daughter was oblivious to the suffering of other females under the aegis of paternal rule. For her, the father signified nothing less than a tender and luminous presence. She believed she shared his magical powers, that she was different and special. While she felt ambivalence toward her mother, her father was the object of unqualified adoration. Mesmerized by the magical pendulum that functioned as the external signifier of the father's power, Adriana accepted her own virtual imprisonment (her father prohibited her from attending school) as a sign of her difference and even superiority.

Adriana's narration of her childhood feelings toward her father are revealing to the reader, even if they remain for her the blind spot of her captivity and her text. We see how she placed the father-daughter bond beyond the familiar and normal, or into what has been identified as the space of the fantastic: their special union was "familiar y mágica a un tiempo" [at once familiar and magical] (16). She was seduced by their eerie sharing of prohibition: "me sentía hermanada contigo en aquello que teníamos en común: el mal" [I felt joined to you in that which we shared in common: evil] (16). And she felt the frightening thrill of her transgressive posture reconfirmed by those outside the magical circle: her mother's gaze was like a mirror that reflected "aquel monstruo que ya veía yo aparecer en mi interior" [that monster that I already saw appear inside me] (15). At that time the daughter perceived her father in the traditionally maternal role of comforter offering unconditional love, while others—females—appeared censorious. She could not see that she was being set up for a fall, that the father was hiding behind his enigma and could not tolerate, indefinitely, such challenges to his law.

Things inevitably change, then, as Adriana's narrative follows the master plot for female development. The father-daughter bond has to be broken, at least from the father's side; prohibition has to be invoked. The father's imposition of silence on the household becomes all-enveloping, not even exempting or privileging the daughter. A family secret that definitively separates the spouses (something to do with that woman from the past) also severs the secret bond between father and daughter. Still, while rhetorical ambiguity veils the ghosts of desire past ("silencios tensos, palabras con segundas intenciones") [tense silences, words with double meanings] (25), it fails to erase the daughter's desire for her father: "me sabía tu cómplice y eso me acercaba de nuevo a ti" [I was convinced I was your accomplice and that drew me closer to you] (26). To borrow from the words of Jane Gallop: "the daughter's desire for her father is desperate".[7] She is reluctant to give up his discourse, whatever form it may take. More than ever she wants to fill herself with the father's texts and find words to bridge the gap that divides them: "libros, cuadernos, carpetas. Deseaba tanto leerlas" [books, notebooks, folders. I wanted so much to read them] (26). His texts—his discourse—seduce her in his absence, for physically he has already abandoned her: "sentí que me habías abandonado" [I felt you had abandoned me] (27). But sometimes he returns, if only to impose severe prohibitions: "imponiéndome brutalmente unas normas rígidas" [brutally imposing rigid rules] (31). As a result, she hates him and desires him at once: "surgió en mí un amago de odio hacia ti. Entonces tuve un deseo: casarme contigo" [signs of hatred loomed up in me. At that time I had one desire: to marry you] (31, 34). Hatred and incestuous longings well up simultaneously, for ambivalence becomes the only possible response to paternal evasion. Finally the possibility of dialogue or closeness is ruptured definitively. The father commits suicide.

Unable to bear the loss, the daughter again invokes the fantastic and erases the distinction between this world and the next: "en un acto supremo de voluntad decidí no creer en la muerte. Tú existirías siempre" [in an act of supreme willpower I decided to not believe in death. You would exist always] (38). Though she newly desires closeness with her widowed and unloved mother, some obscure force divides them: "deseé acercarme a ella, pero me sentí paralizada" [I wished to approach her, but I felt paralyzed] (39). The unnamed ghost of the father separates mother and daughter (at least for the moment) and impels the daughter to reject all signs of division between life and death. She is driven to seek the father among traces he left behind in the city of his past, Seville.

Seville provides other texts from other perspectives (the other woman, the "medium," the half-brother) that weaken and eventually rupture the absolute hold of the father's discourse on the daughter. By chance Adriana discovers the letters of Gloria Valle, writings that hold answers to the secret of the father's other life. From Gloria's differing point of view, they tell a story of abandonment, of the father's cynical insensitivity to Gloria's plight, of Gloria's strength and bravery. And they imply to the daughter the abandonment of both families, a kind of infinitely reversible "Catch 22" in which the son, the daughter, and the two women were all the objects of the father's brooding manipulations. Adriana discovers a situation, then, that the silent, enigmatic father never fully disclosed and one that the daughter ironically never suspected: "Yo sabía tan poco de tí" [I knew so little about you] (42). Like a medium, the old housemaid, Emilia, conjures up another aspect of the past. Telling of the father's childhood and youth, she evokes for the daughter the "living ghost" (45) of the father. And Miguel, the father's abandoned son, writes a diary on the margins of the father's discourse: "la imagen de un padre era algo extraño e innecesario para él" [the image of a father was something strange and unnecessary for him] (47). The father is thus never fully unveiled by these "Sevillan texts," but their pieces of ambiguity assemble a puzzle that begins to reshape the dead father's image. The daughter discovers the cynic, the coward, the man forever hidden by a carnival mask. This is enough to restore the threshold dividing the living from the dead. The revelations of those from the past sufficiently alter the paternal enigma to drive a wedge between father and the daughter's desire: "Y en este escenario fantasmal de nuestra vida en común, ha sobrevivido tu silencio y también, para mi desgracia, aquella separación última entre tú y yo que, con tu muerte, se ha hecho insalvable y eterna" [And in the phantasmal scene of our shared life, your silence has survived, and to my dismay, [so has] that ultimate separation between you and me, which with your death, has become insurmountable and eternal] (52). Thus read the final words of the daughter's narrative and the end of her epistle to a father who finally is allowed to die.

The ending of *El Sur* is painful; its sense of total loss is profound. Yet this pain, unlike its previous avatars, promises birth and rebirth. But how can such a dismal conclusion seem hopeful? Consider this: besides its links with the fantastic, *El Sur* has much that recalls the Gothic novel. Familiar Gothic themes in *El Sur* include the enclosure of female figures in a gloomy space controlled by masculine authority; the existence of a mysterious family secret; and the daughter's ambivalent fear and desire of a paternal figure who confines her, along with a maternal figure who shifts between nurturance and indifference.[8] Like the traditional Gothic novel, *El Sur* moves toward the release of its captive females, the explication of the family secret, and the freeing of the daughter from danger and unholy desire. And as the following analysis of Rafael Llopis coincidentally reconfirms, the novel also ends characteristically: "el mundo del padre, deseado en la infancia y rechazado definitivamente en la juventud, se convierte en un mundo arcaico y corrompido pero amenazador ... la mujer se erija en figura racional, como portadora de luz contra las sombras de un pasado exclusivamente varonil" [the world of the father, desired in childhood and definitively rejected in youth, transforms into an archaic, corrupt, and menacing world ... woman rises as a rational figure, as the bearer of light against the shadows of an exclusively masculine past].[9] When Adriana raises the "círculo luminoso de mi linterna" [the luminous circle of my lantern] (52) to light the abandoned objects of her dead father, she performs the same ritual of separation and renewal. And this rebirth implicitly frees her to establish future bonds and articulate other discourses outside the restrictive boundaries of the father's law.

After the father's death, when Adriana's mother is released to visit Santander and the daughter decides to make her pilgrimage to Seville, there is some promise of rapprochement between mother and daughter. The gap left by the absence of the father may, in future, be filled with a newly forged bond between mother and daughter. And in Seville the incestuous longing for the father is displaced by Miguel's attraction to Adriana. Though she escapes from her half-brother's physical presence, she leaves a note that she loves him, confusedly beginning to shift the locus of her desire away from the father. Though another forbidden object, this fraternal one—as noted above—is outside the ambit of the father's law. He is the product of an exclusively maternal world ("aquel mundo que Gloria Valle había tejido para vuestro hijo" [that world that Gloria Valle had woven for your son] (51). If Adriana tries to insure the permanence of her brother's desire, she is, in a sense, creating the inverse of the prohibition that tormented her. By setting up another transgression, this time the image of a union defying the paternal prohibition, she creates a signifier perhaps more friendly to the expression of female or feminine desire.[10] Or as Jane Gallop has concluded: when woman's complicity with father-love is curtailed, then she may "rediscover some feminine desire, some desire for a masculine body that does not respect the Father's law."[11] The desire to insure her continued presence—spiritually, if not physically—within the aura of the brother's maternal "atmósfera de encantamiento" [magical atmosphere] (52) is thus born of a separation from the father's house of the dead. In the luminous circle of her lantern's light Adriana bids farewell to the abandoned objects (the signs of death) of her father and places herself metonymically into the realm of the maternal fantastic. The paternal affair is over.

> Transgression belongs neither to day nor to night ... No
> before, no during, no afterwards. It is as if it were another
> region, a place different from all places.
> —Maurice Blanchot, *Le pas au-delà*

Opening *Bene* is a dream sequence in which the first-person narrator addresses her brother, Santiago. She dreams of him walking at her side through a eucalyptus grove, having returned to stay with her. They see Bene holding a missal with the burned imprint of a human hand on its cover. The brother disappears, leaving the narrator alone with Bene. Now Bene's eyes blaze intensely and the narrator attempts to flee. Instead, as a result of her exertion, the dreamer awakens without having solved the mystery of Bene's sudden departure. Outlined thus is the enigmatic axis of the novella. In keeping with the volume's title, *El Sur seguido de Bene*, an enigma continues to structure the narrative, though now its locus shifts from the paternal figure to that of a woman named Bene. The narrator's desire continues to fix itself implicitly upon a fraternal object, Santiago. This highly charged first passage thus "dreams" its reader into a strange and uncanny realm of prohibitions and concealed desires. Bene somehow threatens disruption of the established order; here, at least, her association with the burned holy book casts her as a fearful accomplice in some unholy desecration of consecrated textuality. Yet, as will the entire text, the oneiric passage refuses to solve its enigma. A microstructure of what follows, the opening dream inscribes a rhetoric and structure unceasingly protective of its ambiguous undecidability.[12]

Much like Adriana of *El Sur*, *Bene*'s Angela is an isolated young adolescent. During the time of the narrated events, age and education began to separate the girl and her older brother, whose intimacy she desperately desired. Angela was rarely able to experience life except as it passed by on the lonely road beyond her iron gate enclosure. Bulls frequently passed, flaunting their powerful masculine gait. Caravans of silent gypsies passed, wordlessly signifying ethnic and class differences, unspoken dimensions beyond the girl's economically privileged yet highly restricted world. The spatial disposition of the girl's sphere vis-à-vis the outside world thus establishes at the outset of the novella a world of gender and class divisions, a world that exerts great power over the narrator's imagination and an uneasiness that can only intimate the unspoken regions of culture.

The culture underlying the girl's observations is thus understated, implied, and part of the perplexing nature of her perspective. She can only describe what she sees, and that from the point of view of one for whom reality has been consistently censored and repressed. As a result, the narrator's observations of Bene reflect that same hesitancy or incertitude: Bene's expression has something "indefinible, inaprehensible" (58) to it, and the deathlike mask that suddenly clouds Bene's visage lies beyond the narrator's powers of description; it is "inexplicable" (61). Similarly, Bene's widely dissimilar reactions to the conditions of her servitude (from authoritative self-possession to complete helplessness before her employer) may say as much about the narrator and her text as about the character. Unnameable fears and unspoken impotence link the child narrator and her family's new servant: both are marginal, both "déclassé" because of gender, age, and in Bene's case, social status. Either or both lie outside the boundaries of cultural certainties; the narrator, as a female child without authority, is denied the position of unequivocal purveyor of truth.

Others in the household suspect Bene of some heinous past, and their rhetoric, in contrast to Angela's, is more like that of the governess in *The Turn of the Screw*. Aunt Elisa and Doña Rosaura, each in her way, would impose what Shoshana Felman has called "the vulgar, literal and unambiguous" on their textualizations of the enigmatic Bene.[13] Tellingly, when Angela reflects upon Aunt Elisa's suspicions of Bene, her words seek to reflect the degree to which Elisa reduces the ambiguity of her subject: "tía Elisa dudaba de la bondad de Bene o, más bien, estaba convencida de su maldad" [Aunt Elisa doubted the goodness of Bene or, rather, she was convinced of her evil] (63). While Angela produces a text that privileges ambiguity and "won't tell,"[14] Elisa reduces rhetoric and represses the chances of uncertainty. Her moral vision is largely restricted to concerns about her widowed brother's amorous exploits, but professorial doña Rosaura warns Elisa about less visible sources of Bene's putative evil. Doña Rosaura's reality lies on the other side of Todorov's schema; she is convinced that Bene's dead lover/father was a demon and that he still holds Bene in his power. She cannot accept the "duration of uncertainty" of the fantastic, but seeks to convince

Elisa of the certainty of supernatural presence. As Angela explains, the language of doña Rosaura "parecía destinado sólo a nombrar lo obvio"[seemed destined only to name the obvious] (68), and though Angela finds doña Rosaura's bold assertions compelling, her own observations of Bene cause her to hesitate before the others' rhetorical certainty: "no podía concebir que anidara en ella algo tan terrible como insinuaban las palabras y las voces temerosas de aquellas mujeres" [I couldn't conceive that she harbored something so terrible as the words and fearful voices of those women insinuated] (68).

Bene and the children have a custom of picnicking in some nearby eucalyptus groves. These excursions give rise to more contradictory feelings, for while Bene brings along delicious desserts and serves them attractively, some incomprehensible tension (at least for Angela) grips the threesome. Santiago, as he becomes more estranged from his sister, seems to share in some uncanny conspiracy with Bene. And when Bene suddenly dons her deathlike expression, Angela is further repelled and frightened. Something here lies beyond the girl's capacity to understand and articulate. That inexplicable and unnameable something that drains Bene's countenance and leaves upon her a look of deathlike suspension in "un extraño sueño de encantamiento" [a strange dream of enchantment] (87) recalls the mysterious, inexplicable force that overcomes the schoolgirls in Peter Weir's 1975 film *Picnic at Hanging Rock*. Does a spirit similar to the one that haunts and bewitches the girls of that film exercise a similar force here on Bene and Angela? Does that unnamed and elusive disrupter of Victorian order similarly insinuate itself into the Extremaduran patriarchal bourgeoisie in the guise of Bene and her phantom lover? Bene's haunting by the doomed ghost of her gypsy lover also recalls the irresistible pull of the ghostly lover in da Falla's *El amor brujo* (Bewitched love). Do both ghosts say something about man's possessive hold on woman, even after death? The questions suggested by these textual echoes all point in the same direction: to cultural and sexual forces that evade the mastery of direct and unequivocal replies.

More and more Bene comes to occupy the region of these and other unanswered questions. When she is missing from her bedroom, she may or may not be with the children's father. Her absence is never balanced by an alternate presence, and intimations of adult sexuality remain for the narrator "algo misterioso y casi diabólico" [something mysterious and almost diabolical] (73). Expectedly, then, Angela's conjecture about the compelling enigma of her father's pleasures is followed by the apparition outside her window. As in *The Turn of the Screw*, unnamed sexual desire apparently transforms into phantasmal signs visible only to those for whom sexuality is still repressed in ignorance or irresolution (Angela, the governess).

The sign of sexuality, the least verbal in *Bene*, is nevertheless the most pervasive as it is the most elusive. After the father leaves the household on one of his customary "pleasure" trips, he leaves a vacuum into which Santiago is drawn. Angela has already observed Bene's signs of seduction on the picnics ("los detalles de seducción que ella dirigía a mi hermano") [the details of seduction that she directed at my brother] (83). But as the separation between brother and sister becomes definitive in the father's absence, it seems to Angela that her brother has fallen completely under Bene's spell. She sees him as a body without a soul, one whose love was like "una posesión sobrehumana" [a superhuman possession] (99). In a kind of oedipal displacement for both children, Bene comes to occupy the place of rival, the mature woman whose powers appear as superhuman or even supernatural to the young girl. Angela is no match for adult sexuality, and the brother slips entirely out of her range: "tu olvido de mí era irremediable" [your obliviousness to me was irremediable] (98). The thwarting of Angela's incestuous desires is somehow transferred and translated into Santiago's uncanny necrophilia, an amorous desire on his part that seems to come from "la misma muerte" [death itself] (99). One transgression is thus subsumed into another while sexuality continues to function as a negation of rhetorical and—implicitly—cultural restraints.

Something unspeakable lies always beyond the boundaries of the household gates. Try as she might, when Angela attempts to pry information from her poor friend and Bene's sister, Juana, she is thwarted. The barriers of class and privilege separating them perforce separate their very use of language, so Angela can never solve the enigma of the "other side." Juana only reinforces the enigma of Bene, reaffirms her sister's difference ("no es como los demás") [she is not like others] (81); and Juana's later insinuations about Bene's work (she supported the family) and love life (it was said Bene had many sweethearts) only play against the reader's most conventional expectations and prejudices. Sexual innuendos and rumors, things that people say, might simply be based on cultural divisions and bias: "la gente es muy mala y odia a los gitanos" [people are evil and hate the gypsies] (94). Bene's putative evil may be entirely "positional," coinciding, as Jameson has observed, "with categories of Otherness."[15] So as Juana refuses to surrender all the secrets of her class to Angela—virtually her only possessions—she insists upon her right to conceal ("se negaba a revelarme algo ... era como si se le hubiera impuesto la sagrada obligación de ocultarme algo") [she refused to reveal something to me ... it was as if someone had imposed on her a sacred obligation to conceal something from me] (92). That obligation to conceal is Juana's right to self-protection. The narrator's inability to ascertain secrets and share her own uncertainties reaffirms once again the text's refusal to bow before the interrogations of cultural dominance and reduce its rhetoric to simple or comfortable answers.

In spite of prohibitions by those who would seek to master meaning by keeping the inexplicably demonic at bay—doña Rosaura with her "no te asomes a la cancela, ni hables con desconocidos ... no escuches ni mires a nadie" [don't appear at the gate, don't talk to strangers ... don't listen to nor gaze at anyone] (99)—the signs of the Other or the gypsy apparition multiply. Even closed doors become ineffective barriers against the forbidden; having lost their capacity to cordon off the culturally undesirable, they have become permeable. As meaning thus splits and divides and the sole source of it resides in the narrator's and reader's reception of the phenomena, the only precise, unquestionable thing is the narrator's panic: "sus señales eran inaprehensibles. Sólo mi pánico era preciso, incuestionable" [his signs were inapprehensible. Only my panic was precise, unquestionable] (101). Even the narrator herself is decentered, deprived of ontological certainty: "ya no sabía quién era él ni tampoco quién era yo" [by now I didn't know who he was nor even who I was] (101–2).

The horrified household finally expels Bene, and Santiago joins her. Two weeks later he is returned forcibly, however. He seems safe and Angela is delighted to have him to herself again. But the veil of his secret return is quickly removed by Aunt Elisa, who demands a full accounting of his activities: "que me vas a contar todo lo que ha pasado con esa fulana" [you're going to tell me everything that went on with that hussy] (107). Again occupying a position similar to that of the governess in *The Turn of the Screw*, Aunt Elisa attempts to grasp at meaning; her suspicions demand interpretation, a posture that can result only in suffocating, stifling, and killing the ambivalence before her.[16] Her insistence on resolving the enigma of Santiago's flight has as its sole consequence a reactive stance by Santiago: his total self-enclosure into a realm of silence and, finally, death. Like the text itself, Santiago refuses to surrender to easy explanations. Santiago's need for "silencio total" (110) mirrors what Felman has called the "reserve of silence"[17] or that which literature is incapable of speaking (or refuses to disclose). The narrator, too, surrenders to a kind of death, a perfect blackness, in her ostensible desire to join the brother, and in so doing she recapitulates his challenge to a unified, unequivocal reality. By embracing death, or a kind of ghostly semblance of death, the fraternal pair underscore the text's insistence on its culturally transgressive role.

As the ghost, that indeterminate specter of meaning, hovers in the reader's mind, we realize that what we have just "witnessed" (read) is the unnameable, elusive slippery stuff that is the "bogeyman" of all writing, most especially that of women. The "ghost" is that which defies articulation, try as the narrator might to join the ranks of the sensible majority. But the marginal element—the female, the child—is never guaranteed such a comfortable cultural position. As Jackson observes, her job is often to "make visible that which is culturally invisible and which is written out as negation and as death."[18] (In *Bene* those areas of invisibility are disclosed by the ghostly apparitions, the brother's death, and Angela's figurative death.) Most important, as Jackson continues, "the cultural, or countercultural, implications of this assertion of non-signification are far-reaching, for it represents a dissolution of a culture's signifying practice, the very means by which it establishes meaning."[19] To voice such a horror as a woman is to transgress to "another region," is to flee the circle of determinate meaning that culture underwrites by force of its (patriarchal or paternal) law.

> They no longer had any desire to allure; all that they wanted was to hold as long as they could the radiance that fell from Ulysses' great eyes.
> —Franz Kafka "The Silence of the Sirens"

As García Morales's writing evolves it resonates with echoes of itself. The mountainous world of *El silencio de las sirenas* is another solitary and isolated place, in the words of the novel's narrator: strange, intemporal, silent. Here, in the harshness of village life, hardy widows live stoically beyond desire, and the presence of ghosts is just as natural as the breath of the living. Into this space, far from urban culture and within the shadowy presence of exotic Africa, comes María to serve as teacher. But more important than María's ostensible professional function in the village is her role as ad hoc hypnotist of Elsa, another outsider, who is experiencing a deeply passionate love for a man she hardly knows. With María's regular assistance, Elsa tells and increasingly embellishes her account of love, eventually transforming it into a nineteenth-century romantic fiction.

El silencio de las sirenas thus tells an old story from a new angle: this love story is as much a meditation on its generation as on the nature of love itself. Though Peter Brooks emphasizes that "texts are always implicitly or even explicitly addressed to someone," *El silencio*'s explicit use of the Lacanian "dimension of dialogue" makes of it a self-reflective text in ways its predecessors were not.[20] While Adriana's epistle to her deceased father and Angela's recounting of a dream and reflections to her late brother Santiago express at least one side of the dialogic transaction, *El silencio* depends for its very existence on multiple dialogues. María draws out the threads of Elsa's tale, playing at analyst and enthralled by her role as interlocutor. She also transmits, comments upon, and rewrites Elsa's notebooks. Multiple as is María's "intervention"[21] in Elsa's obsessive narrative, it facilitates the text's "transference" and contributes to its interpretation. This collaborative enterprise of two women is consequently rich in implications about the sources, processes, and pitfalls of love story writing (and living) for women.

Prompted by Lacan, Shoshana Felman asks if all stories, all narratives imply a transferential structure—that is, a love-relation that both organizes and disguises, deciphers and enciphers them.[22] While Felman's question or hypothesis is more a rhetorical introit to *The Turn of the Screw* than a firmly answerable proposition, it serves well here as a suggestive entrance to *El silencio*. Elsa is blatant in her affirmation of the "love-relation" structuring her narrative. Even more, in her notebook she interrogates the process whereby imagined love becomes a more potent organizer of her narrative than anything she has actually experienced: "Me pregunto cómo pueden los sueños tejer una historia que me va enredando más que la vida misma" [I ask myself how dreams can weave a story that ensnares me more than life itself] (51). She also ponders the sources of her imagery: "Y me pregunto también de dónde provienen estas imágenes ..." [And I also ask myself where these images are coming from ...] (51). One answer to her queries precedes the questions themselves: "he visto y ahora ensueño" [I saw and now I envision] (51). By the end of her notebook entry she realizes that an initial visual experience has taken on its greatest power within her imagination.[23] But at the same time she is impelled to enunciate the content of that imagination—her desire—and must resort to enciphering its imagery through the mediating function of the symbolic order. Elsa's powerlessness to name this ("esto") that is more than love ("no sé qué nombre dar") [I don't know how to name it] (52), articulates the difficulty of applying the symbolic order to the imaginary. Worse still, as Juliet Flower MacCannell states, crossing over into the symbolic often entails a sacrificial positioning for woman. But has she another option? Perhaps, in her desire to bridge the alienating gap between the two orders, she may attempt to position herself astride them; for woman may imagine herself, as Kristeva has advocated, "at the threshold between the imaginary and the symbolic."[24] Elsa and María's collaboration temporarily achieves this synthesis, but ultimately it fails.

To achieve and maintain this position is demanding since the symbolic order traditionally expects to speak for woman. If she tries to speak for herself she may find herself subject to dangerous crosscurrents. Elsa is buffeted in just this way. At one moment, a brief communication between Elsa and Agustín results in her elated recollections of the fullness of language: "no recuerdo en toda mi vida que la palabra hubiera sido algo tan pleno para mí [I don't remember any other time in my life when the word was so full for me] (60–61). She seems to participate fully in the symbolic order. But later, when Elsa's speech is met with Agustín's indifference and even silence, her discomfiture in this role causes her to rail against her feelings of oddity: "¡No soy un monstruo! ¡No soy un monstruo!" [I'm not a monster! I'm not a monster!] (62). Elsa's eccentricities frighten Agustín, and he takes refuge in the posture of Ulysses: he fills his ears with metaphorical wax, deafening himself to her words. For Elsa's expression of desire seems the traditional siren's call to him: seductive and treacherous. The novel's allusion to Kafka suggests, however, that another perspective is in order here. The sirens of Kafka are silent; initially they wield a power outside the symbolic order of language. But as Ulysses eludes them, they lose their desire to allure. They instead fall dependent on the hero's radiance (the symbolic order) in the same paradoxical gesture which is that of the woman who seeks to write. If Kafka's sirens could speak, their words might lament how woman, desiring to speak (or write), is necessarily cast within the symbolic order and then regarded by it as a monster. Elsa, as another casualty of the symbolic order's deafness to woman's eccentricities, finds her desire ignored, frustrated, and even misread.[25]

As in García Morales's other narratives, the monstrosity of *El silencio*'s encipherment is underwritten by a layering of fantastic elements in the text. The village setting, the presence of magic and ghostly echoes in Matilde's (an older village woman's) rituals and stories, and not of least importance the collaboration between María and Elsa produce levels of strangeness that make the monstrousness of Elsa's desire more potent and poignant. Its transgression against rational restraint could never be contained by the restrictions of a less ambiguous realism. Even when Elsa's notebook shifts from the village to Venice, that setting is also phantasmal and ghostly. There, too, the lover emerges as a product of fantastic space, as an emanation of an imaginary realm. As Elsa writes in Venice, she feels herself a monstrous siren again, deciphering her feeling as a sign of prohibition announcing the impossibility of physical or concrete union with her lover. Within the framework of this reading, her monstrosity is no less a sign of the difficulty of woman's writing herself out of the imaginary and into the demanding contract that the symbolic imposes.

María acts as a kind of midwife for the symbolic order, ushering Elsa's imagination into the realm of language. But this ritual or ceremony will have its price for Elsa. Foreshadowings of the sacrifice appear in more and more ornate renderings of the ongoing story. Once Elsa dreams of "Eduardo" (Agustín) receiving a manuscript written by various authors that he will have to rewrite in a different way. Though the dream is set amid the romantic intrigue of late-nineteenth-century Germany, Elsa feels "anulada" (annulled) (109) by the mysterious transactions of the dream. Could it be that her collaborative text eventually will be rewritten? Later in her notebook Elsa records that her love cannot be realized in any other way than to be written for Agustín. Somehow, as the concrete lover becomes more shadowy, his power over what and how she writes increases. When inquisitorial soldiers pursue her in another dream, she suspends her narration in terrified mystification. Silence is her escape from these threatening agents of the symbolic. Inexorably, Elsa's estrangement causes her to retreat more and more from word or action: "ella no era capaz de decir, ni de pensar nada" [she was not capable of saying, nor of thinking anything] (132).

María finally urges Elsa to face the prosaic notion that the narrative of her love participates in that old literary tradition in which women die or go crazy. Elsa refuses to see her own passion—or the literary models she chooses as analogues—in such simplistic terms, but her insistent obsession may rule out other discursive options. Attempting to wrench Elsa out of her obsession, María reminds her that the tragic love plot "es casi una ley" [is almost a law] (146). Under that portion of the symbolic order (or "father's law") that governs narrative convention in our culture this has long been the customary contract. There may be no escape once a woman has submitted to it. Eventually, under its provisions, Elsa may have to die or go crazy.

And so she does. Elsa becomes but a phantasm occupied by the image of her lover. Having completely internalized him, she herself is nothing. Accordingly, Lacan has voiced such a predicament: as the subject installs his (in this case, her) demand in the Other, "the phantom of the Omnipotence" is introduced.[26] So when the concrete "lover" makes his appearance to articulate his stern prohibition of Elsa continuing her communications to him, her sense of selfhood is definitively obliterated. Severing the thin thread of words connecting her to life, Agustín's demand erases Elsa's remaining will to live, for she lived to write to and about him. As Elsa's dreams foretold, Agustín effectively ends her text for her and implicitly chooses its inevitable conclusion: insanity *and* death. But the plot of *El silencio* is signed with a cautionary paradox: to face the demands of the symbolic may be eventually to cede all, but to desire outside the symbolic order may be to regress to absolute silence and, in this case, literal death. Here the works of Adelaida García Morales seem to hang in abeyance, caught in the impasse of this disquieting paradox. The only way out of this impasse would seem to be to demand the unifying richness of the threshold position between the two orders. Though it may prove treacherous and slippery terrain, its successful negotiation may also be the only means to stake a claim on writing and indeed on life.

As I conclude this overview of Adelaida García Morales's interrelated narrative corpus, one should also remember what might be more than an insignificant detail: *El silencio de las sirenas* was conceived and its writing was begun in 1979, before the beginning of *El Sur* and *Bene* (1981). This chronology of the works' inception rather than of their publication might explain why *El silencio* seems a perplexing regression. It would also allow *Bene* the last and more accomplished word in García Morales's challenge to our culture's ordering of the imagination. In any case, this beginning corpus of a young writer's work is fascinating indeed. García Morales, by engaging in the writing or rewriting of fantastic texts and the discursive renderings of love, is able to explore the varied manifestations of desire: from the enthralled daughter isolated in Andalucía to the unsolved enigma of the other woman to the obsessively passionate single woman of Las Alpujarras, the author circles round and round the multiple faces of [female] desire. In these flights of imagination, she reveals unspoken regions of the culture as well as the challenges and pitfalls that lie in wait, inevitably, when one is daring or mad enough to attempt their articulation.

Notes

1. Tzvetan Todorov, *The Fantastic: A Structural Approach to a Literary Genre*, trans. R. Howard (Cleveland, Ohio: Case Western Reserve University Press, 1973), 25.

2. Ibid., 13.

3. Fredric Jameson, *The Political Unconscious: Narrative as a Socially Symbolic Act* (Ithaca, N.Y.: Cornell University Press, 1981), 106.

4. Rosemary Jackson, *Fantasy: The Literature of Subversion* (New York: Methuen, 1981).

5. Ibid., 54.

6. Andrés Amorós, *Introducción a la novela contemporánea* (Salamanca: Ediciones Anaya, 1966), 159.

7. Jane Gallop, *The Daughter's Seduction: Feminism and Psychoanalysis* (Ithaca, N.Y.: Cornell University Press, 1982), 70.

8. See Norman N. Holland and Leona F. Sherman, "Gothic Possibilities," in *Gender and Reading: Essays on Readers, Texts, and Contexts*, ed. E. A. Flynn and P. P. Schweickart (Baltimore: Johns Hopkins University Press, 1986), 215–33.

9. Rafael Llopis, *Esbozo de una historia natural de los cuentos de miedo* (Madrid: Ediciones Jucar, 1974), 160–61.

10. See my article "Paradise Regained, Paradise Lost: Desire and Prohibition in *La madre naturaleza*," *Hispanic Journal* 8 (1986): 7–18, for a more extensive study on the sister-brother bond as a mode of defying the father's law.

11. Gallop, *The Daughter's Seduction*, 79.

12. Given certain similarities of theme and tone between *Bene* and Henry James's *The Turn of the Screw*, I have been inspired in many of my observations by Shoshana Felman's brilliant study of this James novel, "Turning the Screw of Interpretation." Felman's argument rests on the premise that the James novel never resolves its ambiguity, and from Edmund Wilson's three ways in which the text sustains its "questioning" or ambiguous stance (through its rhetoric, thematic content, and narrative structure), she constructs her elaborate examination into this threefold refusal of the Jamesian text to tell all. See Shoshana Felman, "Turning the Screw of Interpretation," in *Literature and Psychoanalysis: The Question of Reading—Otherwise*, edited by Shoshana Felman (Baltimore: Johns Hopkins University Press, 1982), 94–207.

13. Ibid., 107.

14. Ibid.

15. Jameson, *The Political Unconscious*, 115.

16. Felman, "Turning the Screw."

17. Ibid., 193.

18. Jackson, *Fantasy*, 69.

19. Ibid.

20. Peter Brooks, "The Idea of a Psychoanalytic Literary Criticism," *Critical Inquiry* 13 (1987): 343.

21. Ibid., 345.

22. Felman, "Turning the Screw," 133.

23. Frederic Jameson has charted this process in Lacanian terms: "In any case, whatever the nature of the Lacanian Symbolic, it is clear that the Imaginary—a kind of pre-verbal register whose logic is essentially visual—precedes it as a stage in the development of the psyche" ("Imaginary and Symbolic in Lacan: Marxism, Psychoanalytic Criticism, and the Problem of the Subject," in *Literature and Psychoanalysis: The Question of Reading—Otherwise*, 353). Though Jameson clearly is thinking of the "mirror stage" of psychic development when he refers to the visual, I think it is safe to assume that if the subject sees the image of one it subsequently desires, a gap similar to that formed between the individual and its own self, a gap that never can be bridged, may form. This is the desire that becomes

the "motor of narrative" (Ronald Schleifer, "The Space and Dialogue of Desire: Lacan, Greimas, and Narrative Temporality," in *Lacan and Narration: The Psychoanalytic Difference in Narrative Theory*, ed. R. C. Davis [Baltimore: Johns Hopkins University Press, 1983], 844), and the force impelling Elsa's love story.

24. Juliet Flower MacCannell, *Figuring Lacan: Criticism and the Cultural Unconscious* (Lincoln: University of Nebraska Press, 1986), 135.

25. Barbara Johnson has studied this fearful circumstance of the woman writer whose "autobiographical reflex" often engenders images of monstrousness as a result of the "difficulty in conforming to a female ideal which is largely a fantasy of the masculine, not the feminine, imagination" ("My Monster/My Self," *Diacritics* 12 [1982]: 10).

26. Jacques Lacan, *Ecrits: A Selection*, trans. A. Sheridan (London: Tavistock, 1977), 311.

Bibliography

1. PRIMARY SOURCES

1985a. *El Sur seguido de Bene*. Barcelona: Anagrama.
1985b. *El silencio de las sirenas*. Barcelona: Anagrama.

2. SECONDARY SOURCES

S., L. 1986. "En pos de la quimera: Una nueva novela de Adelaida García Morales." *El País* 4 (145): 6–7. Generally positive review of *El silencio de las sirenas* that points to ineffable qualities of the novel.

Sánchez Arnosi, M. 1986. "Adelaida García Morales: La soledad gozosa." *Insula* 472: 4. Revealing interview with the author that includes insights into the salient aspects of *El Sur* and *Bene*.

Works Available in English Translation

Laforet, Carmen. 1958. *Nothing* (*Nada*). Translated by Inez Muñoz. London: Weidenfeld and Nicholson.

———. 1963. *Andrea* (*Nada*). Translated by Charles F. Payne. New York: Vantage Press.

Martín Gaite, Carmen. 1983. *The Back Room* (*El cuarto de atrás*). Translated by Helen R. Lane. New York: Columbia University Press.

———. 1990. *Behind the Curtains* (*Entre visillos*). Translated by Frances López-Morillas. New York: Columbia University Press.

Matute, Ana María. 1963a. *Awakening* (*Primera memoria*). Translated by James Holman Mason. London: Hutchinson and Co.

———. 1963b. *School of the Sun* (*Primera memoria*). Translated by Elaine Kerrigan. New York: Pantheon Books. Reissued in 1990; New York: Columbia University Press.

———. 1965. *The Lost Children* (*Los hijos muertos*). Translated by Joan MacLean. New York: Macmillan Co.

———. 1989. *The Heliotrope Wall and Other Stories* (*Algunos muchachos*). Translated by Michael Scott Doyle. New York: Columbia University Press.

Montero, Rosa. In press, 1990. *Absent Love: A Chronicle* (*Crónica del desamor*). Translated by Cristina de la Torre and Diana Glad. Lincoln: University of Nebraska Press.

———. In press, 1990. *The Delta Function* (*La función Delta*). Translated by Kari Easton. Lincoln: University of Nebraska Press.

Rodoreda, Mercè. 1967. *The Pigeon Girl* (*La Plaça del Diamant*). Translated by Eda O'Shield. London: Deutsch.

———. 1980. *The Time of the Doves* (*La Plaça del Diamant*). Translated by David Rosenthal. New York: Taplinger.

———. 1984. *My Christina and Other Stories* (*La meva Cristina i altres contes*). Translated by David Rosenthal. Port Townsend, Wash.: Graywolf Press.

Roig, Montserrat. 1989. "The Everyday Opera (Selections)" (*L'òpera quotidiana*). Translated by J. M. Sobrer, in *On Our Own Behalf: Women's Tales from Catalonia*, ed. Kathleen McNerny. Lincoln: University of Nebraska Press.

Tusquets, Esther. 1990. *The Same Sea as Every Summer* (*El mismo mar de todos los veranos*). Translated by Margaret E. W. Jones. Lincoln: University of Nebraska Press.

Contributors

CONCHA ALBORG is associate professor of Spanish at Saint Joseph's University in Philadelphia. She was born in Valencia, Spain, and lived in Madrid until moving to the United States in 1961. She earned an M.A. from Emory University and a Ph.D. from Temple University in 1981. She has published *Temas y técnicas en la narrativa de Jesús Fernández Santos* (1984) and a number of articles on Spanish contemporary novelists, with emphasis on the most recent women writers.

CATHERINE G. BELLVER is professor of Spanish at the University of Nevada, Las Vegas. She received a B.A. from Northwestern University and M.A. and Ph.D. degrees from the University of California, Berkeley. She has published *El mundo poética de Juan José Domenchina* (1979) and *Rafael Alberti en sus horas de destierro* (1984), as well as many journal articles and book chapters on modern Spanish literature.

JOAN L. BROWN is associate professor of Spanish at the University of Delaware. She received a B.A. from Vassar College and M.A. and Ph.D. degrees from the University of Pennsylvania. She is the author of journal articles and book chapters on contemporary Spanish literature by women, and of *Secrets From the Back Room: The Fiction of Carmen Martín Gaite* (1987).

ANDREW BUSH is assistant professor of Hispanic Studies at Vassar College. He received a B.A. from Brown University and a Ph.D. from Yale University. He has published essays on topics in Latin American, Peninsular and comparative literatures. He is the editor of the scholarly journal *Revista de Estudios Hispánicos*.

MARGARET E. W. JONES is professor of Spanish at the University of Kentucky. She received a B.A. from the State University of New York (Albany) and M.A. and Ph.D. degrees from the University of Wisconsin. She has published books on Ana María Matute, Dolores Medio, and the contemporary Spanish novel. Her articles include essays on Ana María Matute, Ana María Moix, Carmen Laforet, and on general feminist issues applied to Spanish literature.

ELIZABETH J. ORDÓÑEZ is associate professor of Spanish at the University of Texas, Arlington. She received a Ph.D. from the University of California, Irvine. She is the author of over twenty-five articles and book chapters on Spanish and Chicano literature and has two books in progress on Spanish narrative by women in the nineteenth and twentieth centuries.

JANET PÉREZ is Paul Whitfield Horn Professor of Spanish and associate dean of the Graduate School at Texas Tech University. She holds M.A. and Ph.D. degrees from Duke University. She has past or present service on thirty editorial boards. She has edited or coedited approximately one hundred volumes in the Spanish section of the Twayne World Authors Series and is the author of books on Ortega y Gasset, Ana María Matute, Miguel Delibes, and Gonzalo Torrente Ballester. Her books also include the edited volume *Novelistas femeninas de la postguerra española* (1983) and *Women Writers of Contemporary Spain* (1988). She has published more than one hundred articles and book chapters, many on the subject of modern Spanish women writers.

GUSTAVO PÉREZ FIRMAT is professor in the department of Romance Studies at Duke University. He is the author of *Idle Fictions: The Hispanic Vanguard Novel* (1982), *Literature and Liminality* (1986), *Triple Crown: Chicano, Puerto Rican and Cuban-American Poetry* (with Roberto Durán and Judith Ortiz Cofer) (1987), *The Cuban Condition: Translation and Identity in Modern Cuban Literature* (1989), *Equivocaciones* (1989), and the edited volume *Do the Americas Have a Common Literature?* (1990).

RANDOLPH D. POPE is professor of Spanish and Comparative Literature at Washington University in St. Louis, and chair of Comparative Literature. He is the author of *La autobiografía española hasta Torres Villarroel* (1974) and *Novela de emergencia: España, 1939–1954* (1984). His many articles deal with the narrative of Spain and Latin America. He was the director of the Spanish Summer School at Middlebury College for five years and has directed programs from American universities in Granada, Madrid, and Salamanca.

MIRELLA SERVODIDIO is professor and chair of the Spanish Department of Barnard College, Columbia University. She is the author of *Azorín, escritor de cuentos* (1979) and *The Quest for Harmony: The Dialectics of Communication in the Poetry of Eugenio Florit* (1979), and of articles on Carmen Laforet, Carmen Martín Gaite, Esther Tusquets, Pío Baroja, Ramón del Valle Inclán, and others. She has edited *Gabriela Mistral, Texto Crítico* (1981) and edited and contributed to *From Fiction to Metafiction: Essays in Honor of Carmen Martín Gaite* (1982) and the issue of *Anales de La Literatura Española Contemporánea* "Reading for Difference: Feminist Perspectives on Women Novelists of Contemporary Spain" (1987). She is on the editorial boards of *Anales de la Literatura Española Contemporánea* and *Revista Hispánica Moderna*.

ROBERT C. SPIRES is professor and chair of the Department of Spanish and Portuguese at the University of Kansas. He is the author of *La novela española de posguerra: Creación artística y experiencia personal* (1978); *Beyond the Metafictional Mode: Directions in the Modern Spanish Novel* (1984); *Transparent Simulacra: Spanish Fiction, 1920–1926* (1988); and articles in several journals. He has held research fellowships from the National Endowment for the Humanities and the U.S.–Spain Joint Committee for Cultural Exchange.

PHYLLIS ZATLIN is professor of Spanish at Rutgers, The State University. She holds a B.A. from Rollins College and M.A. and Ph.D. degrees from the University of Florida. A specialist in contemporary Spanish women writers and the contemporary Spanish theater, she has published extensively in these areas and has prepared editions of works by several playwrights for publication in Spain. She has authored books on Elena Quiroga, Victor Ruiz Iriarte, and Jaime Salom, and with Martha Halsey is coeditor of *The Contemporary Spanish Theatre: A Collection of Critical Essays* (1988).

Index

Abandonment, 46, 54, 142, 211, 264
Abel, Los (1948), 95, 97, 98–99, 103, 104, 111
Abortion, 128, 243
"Ada Liz," 131
Adultery, 119, 163. *See* Love affairs
Aging, 131
Agraphia, 28, 30, 33
Agulla daurada, La (1985), 218
Agustí, Ignacio, 116
Aire de un crimen, El (1980), 201
Alas, Leopoldo (Clarín), 61, 78
Alborg, Concha, 249
Aldecoa, Ignacio, 73, 253
Algo pasa en la calle (1954), 45, 46, 47, 48–50, 52, 53, 55
Alguien te observa en secreto (1985), 201
Algunos muchachos (1968; *The Heliotrope Wall and Other Stories,* 1989), 111
Alice in Wonderland, 97
Alienation: in Martín Gaite, 83, 88; in Matute, 94, 95, 98, 99, 102, 107, 111; in Medio, 62, 64, 65, 69; in Moix, 139; in Quiroga, 43, 44, 46, 50, 51, 53, 54, 55, 56; in Roig, 236, 237; in Tusquets, 160, 164, 176
Aloma (1938), 117, 120–22
Alós, Concha, 20
Al otro lado (1980), 180, 183, 185, 187, 190, 191, 193
Amado Amo (1988), 251–54, 255
Amor es un juego solitario, El (1979), 159, 162–64, 165, 171, 174, 201
Amorós, Andrés, 179, 261
Análisis de cinco comedias (1977), 179
Análisis de textos (1977), 179
Anarchy, 144–45, 146, 148
Andersen, Hans Christian, 97
Andrés (1967), 60
Androgeny, 101, 229

Anna Karenina, 241
Antagonía (1973–81), 200
Antofagasta (1987), 201
Antología de cuentistas españoles contempóraneos (1984), 180
Aprendizaje sentimental (1971), 217
Aquella chica, 141
Arcángeles (1986), 199, 201, 202–3, 204, 207, 213, 214
Archetypes, 229, 230, 234
Arde el mar (1966), 136
Arnau, Carme, 130
Arrepentido, El (1961), 111
Así que pasen cinco años, 130
Asturias (1973), 60, 69
Ataduras, Las (1960), 78, 87
Atrapadas en la ratonera: Memorias de una novelista (1980), 66, 69
Autobiography, fictionalized: in Laforet, 30, 39; in Martín Gaite, 77, 85, 88; in Matute, 96, 103, 111; in Medio, 61, 62, 66, 67; in Moix, 137; in Montero, 242; in Rodoreda, 131; in Tusquets, 159
Azorín, 180

Baladas del dulce Jim (1969), 138, 139, 140, 141
Balneario, El (1954), 75–76, 87, 88
Battle of the sexes, 15
Bearn, 116
Benavente, Jacinto, 101
Bene (1985), 266–71
Benet, Juan, 116, 160, 180, 198, 201
Béquer, Gustavo Adolfo, 16, 140, 180
Bibiana (1963), 60, 61, 67–68
Bible, 98, 107, 108, 110, 266
Bicicletas son para el verano, Las (1982), 48
Bildungsroman, 32, 33, 62, 67
Bisexuality, 175
"Bitllet de mil, El," 131

283

Blanquerna, 120
Böhl de Faber, Cecilia (Fernán Caballero), 14, 15, 19
Boleros, 249, 250, 255
Borges, Jorge Luis, 93
Bourgeoisie: Catalan, 161, 162, 166; Galician, 181
Buero Vallejo, Antonio, 51
"Búscate la vida," 218
Búsqueda de interlocutor y otras búsquedas, La (1973), 74
Butor, Michael, 48

Caballero, Fernán. *See* Böhl de Faber, Cecilia
Caballero Bonald, José Manuel, 84, 85, 253
Cabrera Infante, Guillermo, 198
Caciquismo, 100, 102, 107, 109
Cain, 132
Cain-Abel motif, in Matute, 95, 97, 98, 99, 100, 104, 107, 109, 112
Call me Stone (1969), 138, 152
Cambio 16, 42, 45
Cándida otra vez (1979), 180, 183, 184, 185, 186, 187, 190, 192, 193, 194
Canon, Spanish literary: Laforet's place in, 27; women in, 13, 14, 16, 17, 18
Careta, La (1955), 45, 46, 47, 50–53, 54
Carpentier, Alejo, 116
Carrer de les Camèlies, El (1966), 120, 128–29
"Casa oscura, La," 166
Castellet, José María, 136, 137
Castillo de la carta cifrada, El (1979), 201
Castro, Rosalía de, 14, 15, 19, 179, 192
Catalan language, 219; repression of, 23, 95, 116, 120, 219; subversive interference of, 139
Catalan nationalism, 94, 95, 103, 116, 219
Catalans als camps nazis, Els (1977), 218
Catholicism: Franco era, 48, 49
Catholic school, 43, 44
Cela, Camilo José, 26, 30, 110, 199, 248

Censorship: and Martín Gaite, 73, 77, 83, 85; and Matute, 97, 98, 101, 102, 103, 104, 111; and Moix, 141; and Montero, 241; and Quiroga, 45; and Roig, 226
Cerezales, Manuel, 26
Cernuda, Luis, 189
Cervantes, Miguel de, 15
Chacel, Rosa, 160
Characters, multiple, 65, 66
"Chico de al lado, El," 97
Childbirth, 119, 120
Childhood, 129, 141
Children, 68, 69, 94, 98; estranged, 94, 111; illegitimate, 48, 130, 185, 186; motherless, 43, 44, 46, 53, 56 n.3. *See* Orphanhood
Chodorow, Nancy, 175
Ciertos tonos del negro (1985), 201
Cinco años de País (1982), 241
Cinco horas con Mario (1966; *Five Hours with Mario*, 1989), 186
Cinema: influence of, 48, 66, 77, 85, 87, 137, 249; Italian neorealist, 73, 78
Civil code, 48
Civil war, Spanish: aftermath, 45, 48, 51, 52, 88, 103, 104, 106 (*see* Postwar Spain); and Catalonia, 95; causes of, 46, 99, 104, 112; demythification of, 52; two sides in, 100, 104, 107; victims of, 28, 52, 60, 103, 104, 105
Clarín. *See* Alas, Leopoldo
Clarisme, 117
Club dels Novellistes, 117
Colmena, La (1951; *The Hive*, 1953), 47
Comedia, 183
Commedia dell'arte, 101
Communication, theme of: in Martín Gaite, 72, 75, 81, 83, 86; in Matute, 95; in Medio, 62, 65, 69; in Montero, 250; in Ortiz, 205; in Quiroga, 54, 56; in Rodoreda, 129; in Roig, 228; in Tusquets, 170, 171
Communist Party, Spanish, 199
Conde, Carmen, 16, 42, 45
Conejita Marcela, La (1981), 159
Contra muerte y amor (1985), 180, 181, 183, 184, 185, 186, 187, 188–89, 191, 192, 193, 194

"Correo Urgente," 152
Crim (1936), 120
Crónica del desamor (1979; *Absent Love, A Chronicle*, forthcoming), 243–45, 246, 248, 252, 254
Crusat, Paulina, 132
Cruz, Sor Juana Inés de la, 16
Cuarto de atrás, El (1978; *The Back Room*, 1983), 83–86, 87, 88, 201
Cuento de nunca acabar, El (1983), 74
Cuentos y novelas de la tierra (1984), 179
Cumbres, 97

"Dead, The," 140
Death, theme of: in García Morales, 260, 271; in Matute, 110, 111; in Mayoral, 181, 189, 190; in Moix, 140; in Quiroga, 51; in Rodoreda, 132; in Tusquets, 165, 176
"Del amor y de la amistad," 183
Delibes, Miguel, 98, 186, 199, 253
Del que hom no pot fugir (1934), 119
Democracy, Spanish, 82, 83
Demythification of men, 233
Desde la ventana (1987), 74
Destino, 97
"De su mejor amiga, Celina," 182
Detective novel (*novela negra*), 82, 120, 181, 204, 248, 251
Día en la vida d'un home, Un (1934), 119
Dialogue, use of, 83, 87, 272
Diario de una maestra (1961), 61, 66–67
Divorce, 45, 48, 49, 50, 55
Doce relatos de mujeres (1982), 24 n.3, 193, 255 n.1
Domingo, 60
Double standard, 83, 88

Education: abandonment of, 78, 97, 117; convent, 46, 94; self-education, 43; traditional, 68; tutors, 96; women's, 16, 73
El Saffar, Ruth, 30
En días como estos (1981), 199, 207–10, 213, 214
Enferma, La, 45, 46
En las orillas del Sar (1978), 179
"Ensayo de comedia," 182

Entre visillos (1958; *Behind the Curtains*, 1990), 76–78, 86, 87
Environmental determinism, in Quiroga, 62, 63, 64, 68, 69
Eroticism, 159, 174
Escapism, 86, 87
Escribo tu nombre, 44, 46, 47
Ese chico pelirrojo a quien veo cada día (1971), 138
España para ti para siempre (1976), 241
Esperpentos, 102
Espina, Concha, 16
Estrangement, 94, 95, 111, 268
"Exilados," 166
Exile, 46, 116, 117, 118, 133, 151
Existentialism: in Laforet, 20; in Matute, 95, 98; in Montero, 253; in Quiroga, 51, 54; in Tusquets, 168

Fabián (1977), 200
Fabuloso imperio de Juan sin tierra, El (1981), 60, 68
Fairy tales, 97, 146
Familia de Pascual Duarte, La (1942), 26, 30, 248
Family dynamics, 62, 67, 78
Fantastic literature: by García Morales, 259, 260, 262, 263, 266, 267, 273, 274; by Martín Gaite, 75, 76, 84, 86, 87; by Moix, 152, 153, 154
Farsa de verano (1973), 60, 66
Fascism, 83
Father-daughter bond, 261–63
Father's law, 261
Faulkner, William, 48; influence on Quiroga, 44, 45, 56
Feijoo, Fray Benito Jerónimo, 15
Felipe, León, 179
Felman, Shoshana, 267
Female characters: by García Morales, 259; by Martín Gaite, 77–78; by Matute, 98, 101, 102; by Mayoral, 180, 181, 186, 187, 188; by Medio, 69–70; by Moix, 146; by Montero, 245; by Ortiz, 204; by Rodoreda, 119, 128, 129; by Roig, 219, 222, 230, 232, 235; by women writers, 21, 22, 56 n.2
Female experience, literary rendering of: in Martín Gaite, 85, 88; in

Montero, 243, 253; in Quiroga, 45, 46; in Roig, 220, 221, 222, 227, 229, 232, 237; in Tusquets, 160
Female literary tradition, 13, 14, 16
Feminism, 181, 221, 231, 237, 244, 245
Feminist criticism, 21, 22
Feminist movement, Spanish, 160, 199, 253
Fernández Cubas, Cristina, 20, 194
Fernández Santos, Jesús, 73
Fernán-Gómez, Fernando, 48
Fiesta al noroeste (1959), 95, 99, 100–101, 102, 103, 104, 111
Flashback technique: in Martín Gaite, 78; in Matute, 106; in Ortiz, 211; in Quiroga, 48, 50, 51, 53, 54; in Tusquets, 164
Fragmentos de Apocalipsis (1977), 200
Fragmentos de interior (1976), 82–83, 87, 88
Fraile, Medardo, 73
Franco era: growth of women writers during, 13–14, 19, 24 n.3; laws of, 106; prominent women writers of, 20, 93 (*see* Postwar Spain)
Francoist ideology (Franquism), 50, 168
Freudian theory: and feminist criticism, 22; and Martín Gaite, 85; and Quiroga, 51; and Tusquets, 165, 168, 169, 171, 173
"Fulla de gerani blanc, Una," 129
Funcionario público (1956), 60, 64–65
Función Delta, La (1981; *The Delta Function*, forthcoming), 246–48, 254
Fundación Ana María Matute, 96

Galdós, Benito Pérez, 192
Galerstein, Carolyn, 16
Galicia: in Mayoral, 180, 183, 184, 186, 193, 194; in Quiroga, 43, 44, 46
Galician language, 194
Gallop, Jane, 263, 265
Garbo, Greta, 182
García Morales, Adelaida, 20, 21, 23, 258–77
García Pavon, Francisco, 180
Gaviota, La (1856; *The Sea Gull*, 1965), 15

Gender studies, 21, 22; in Roig, 217, 229, 230, 233
Generation of Mid-Century, 73, 87
Gilbert, Sandra, 219, 227
Gilligan, Carol, 224
Gimferrer, Pere, 136
Gómez de Avellaneda, Gertrudis, 14, 15
Goytisolo, Juan, 160, 198, 199, 200
Goytisolo, Luis, 200, 201
Goytisolos, Juan and Luis, 198
Grimm Brothers, 97
Gubar, Susan, 219, 227, 234, 237
Guelbenzu, José María, 201
Guevara, Ché, 140
Guilt, 51, 52, 53
Gullón, Germán, 189
Gynocentric reality, 221
Gynocentrism, 229

Heidi, 145
Hernández, Miguel, 179
Héroe de las mansardas de Mansard, El (1983), 201
Hijos muertos, Los (1958; *The Lost Children*, 1965), 95, 96, 99, 101, 102–4, 105, 106, 111
Historias de Artámila (1961), 94, 111
History, female: in Roig, 220, 225, 237
Homosexuality: in Laforet, 35; in Martín Gaite, 82; in Matute, 100; in Mayoral, 181; in Montero, 244; in Ortiz, 201; in Quiroga, 50; in Roig, 226
Hora violeta, La (1980), 217, 221, 229, 232–33
Humor, 183, 192, 193, 252
Hypocrisy, criticism of: in Martín Gaite, 79; in Matute, 101, 104; in Medio, 62; in Moix, 148; in Quiroga, 46, 52

Imprisonment, 60, 61, 208, 211
Incest, 150, 181, 190, 259, 263, 265, 269
"Inocente, El," 141
Insanity, 231
Insolación (1889; ed. by Mayoral, 1989), 179

Insolación, La (1963), 26, 27, 35
Institució de les Lletres Catalanes, 117
Insula, 132
Intereses creados, Los (1909), 101
Interlocutor, 75, 127, 129, 170, 171,
 173
Intertextuality: in Moix, 141, 153; in
 Tusquets, 160, 164
Invierno en Lisboa, El (1987), 201
Isabel II of Spain, Queen, 60, 69
Isla y los demonios, La (1952), 26, 27,
 32–34, 35, 36, 37, 39

James, Henry, 78, 200
Jaque mate, 26
Jarama, El (1956; *The One Day of the
 Week*, 1962), 47, 198
Jardí vora el mar (1967), 129–30
Jones, Margaret E. W., 139
Journalism: and Montero, 240, 241,
 242, 247, 250, 255; and Roig, 217,
 218, 227, 234, 237
Joyce, James, 140
Juan sin tierra (1977; *Juan the
 Landless*, 1977), 199, 200
Julia (1970), 138, 140, 141–44, 145,
 146, 147, 149, 150, 154

Kafka, Franz, 273
Kharjas, 17
Kronik, John, 75
Künstlerroman, 32, 36

Lacan, Jacques, 22
Lacanian theory, 22, 154, 272, 274
Laclos, Cholderlos de, 153
Laforet, Carmen, 19, 20, 22, 26–41,
 42, 160
Lagerlof, Selma, 60, 69
Language: theme of, in García
 Morales, 273; theme of, in Laforet,
 28–29, 30; theme of, in Martín
 Gaite, 81, 87; theme of, in Moix,
 137, 143, 146, 147, 148, 154; theme
 of, in Tusquets, 172; use of, in
 Laforet, 38; use of, in Martín
 Gaite, 77; use of, in Moix, 139; use
 of, in Tusquets, 175–76
Lesbianism, 108, 153, 159, 162, 175,
 182
Liaisons dangereuses, Les, 153

"Liberated woman," 55, 63, 67, 70,
 88, 224
*Libro de juegos para los niños de los
 otros* (1961), 111
Literary tradition, 125, 274
Literature by women, scholarship on,
 18–19
Llamada, La (1954), 26, 27, 34–35, 37
Llopis, Rafael, 265
Llul, Ramon, 120
López Salinas, Armando, 253
Lorca, Federico García, 93
Los que vamos a pie, 67
Love, theme of: in Mayoral, 181, 189;
 in Moix, 140; in Rodoreda, 122,
 123, 124; in Roig, 230;
Love affair: biographical, in
 Rodoreda's life, 117, 123; fictional,
 in Laforet; 37; fictional, in
 Rodoreda, 120, 121, 122, 130
Lubbock, Percy, 200
Luciérnagas, Las/En esta tierra (1955),
 95, 96, 99, 101, 103–4, 110
Luz de memoria (1976), 199, 210–13,
 214

Macananz, Melchor de, 74
*Macananz como otro paciente de la
 Inquisición* (1975), 74
Machismo, 13, 18, 253
Manteiga, Roberto, 253
"Mar, El," 129
Marks, Martha A., 55
Marriage: in Laforet, 37; in Matute,
 104, 105, 108; in Mayoral, 181, 185;
 in Medio, 64, 68; in Rodoreda, 119,
 121, 122, 123, 124, 125, 128, 130; in
 Roig, 224, 225, 227
Marsé, Juan, 198
Martín Gaite, Carmen, 19, 20, 22, 42,
 72–92, 160, 201, 253
Martín-Santos, Luis, 45, 160
Masoliver Rodenas, Juan Antonio,
 139, 145
Masturbation, 226, 249
Matute, Ana María, 19, 20, 22, 42,
 51, 93–115, 160
Mayoral, Marina, 20, 23, 44, 179–97
Medio, Dolores, 20, 22, 42, 59–71,
 253
Memoirs, 34, 83, 84

Memory, theme of: in Laforet, 33, 34; in Martín Gaite, 86; in Matute, 98; in Moix, 141, 142, 143; in Montero, 246; in Tusquets, 161, 163
Mendoza, Eduardo, 199, 200
Menstruation, 122, 243
Mercaderes, Los, 105–6, 107
Merino, José María, 200
Metafiction: in the contemporary Spanish novel, 200, 201; in Martín Gaite, 87; in Mayoral, 183, 192, 194; in Montero, 246, 247; in Ortiz, 203, 204, 207
"Meva Cristina, La," 129
Meva Cristina i altres contes, La (1967; *My Christina and Other Stories*, 1984), 129
Middle class, Spanish, 59, 63, 64, 240
Millás, José, 201
Mirador, 117
Mirall trencat (1974), 118, 130–31
Mismo mar de todos los veranos, El (1978; *The Same Sea as Every Summer*, 1990), 159, 161–62, 163, 164, 170, 171, 172, 174, 175
Mobility, social, 185, 186
Moby Dick, 152
Modern Language Association, 19, 72
Modificación, La (1957), 48
Moers, Ellen, 13
Moix, Ana María, 20, 23, 136–58, 194, 240
Mon, El, 217
Monologue: interactive, 80, 81, 108; interior, 47; short story, 122
Montero, Rosa, 20, 23, 194, 240–57
Moradas del castillo interior (1588; *Interior Castle*, 1961), 14
Mort i la Primavera, La (1986), 132
Mother, influence of, 14, 63, 125
Mother-daughter bond: in García Morales, 265; in Tusquets, 161, 162, 165, 170, 175
Motherhood, 98, 126
"Motivos de Circe, Los," 199
"Muerta, La," 37
"Muertos, Los," 140
Mujer llega la pueblo, Una (1956; *The Eyes of the Proud, 1960*), 46
Mujer nueva, La (1955), 26, 37
Muñoz Molina, Antonio, 201
Murià, Anna, 118

Nada (1944; *Nothing*, 1958), 26, 27, 28–31, 32, 33, 34, 35, 37, 39, 160
Narcissism, 162
Narrator: first person, in Laforet, 28, 30; first person, in Martín Gaite, 77, 79, 80; first person, in Mayoral, 182, 187; first person, in Ortiz, 205; first person, in Quiroga, 44, 47, 53, 54; first person, in Roig, 222; first person, in Tusquets, 161, 174; omniscient, in Laforet, 34; omniscient, in Martín Gaite, 77; omniscient, in Montero, 245; omniscient, in Quiroga, 48; omniscient, in Roig, 226; second person, in Quiroga, 47, 54; third person, in Laforet, 32, 38; third person, in Martín Gaite, 77; third person, in Medio, 67; third person, in Quiroga, 47, 50; third person, in Tusquets, 163, 165, 174
Navajo, Ymelda, 24 n.3, 193, 255 n.1
Neorealism, 87, 198, 199, 253
Neruda, Pablo, 93
Nichols, Geraldine C., 219
Nieva, Francisco, 179
"Niña," 60
Niña, La, 38, 39
Niños tontos, Los (1956), 110
Nobel Prize, 93, 101
"No hacer nada," 99
Nom-du-Père, 147, 148
Nonconformist individual, 49, 55, 75, 78, 79
Noria, La, 47
Nosotros los Rivero (1953), 60, 61, 62–63
No time for flowers (1971), 138, 139, 140, 141, 147
Nouveau roman (French new novel), 48, 198
"Novela, Una," 139
Novela de Andrés Choz (1976), 200
Novelas ejemplares y amorosas (1637 and 1647; *A Shameful Revenge and Other Stories*, 1963), 15
Novella (novelette or *novela corta*): and García Morales, 266, 267; and Martín Gaite, 75, 76, 78, 87; and Matute, 100, 101; and Mayoral, 180, 182; and Quiroga, 42; and Zayas, 15

Novella rosa, 130
Novísimos, Los, 136, 137, 138, 153
Nueve novísimos poetas españoles (1970), 136

Obiols Armand, Joan, 117
"Objective" realism: in Martín Gaite, 76, 87; in Medio, 69, 70; in Quiroga, 47, 56
O'Connor, Patricia W., 49, 50
Oedipal conflict, 155, 269
Opera cotidiana, L' (1982), 217, 233–36
Ordoñez, Elizabeth J., 98, 229
Orphanhood, theme of: in Laforet 32, 35; in Matute, 98, 105, 111; in Quiroga, 43, 44, 46, 53, 56; in Rodoreda, 128
"Orquesta de verano," 166
Ortega y Gasset, José, 66
Ortiz, Lourdes, 20, 23, 194, 198–216, 240
Otra circustancia, La (1972), 60, 68

"Padres de nuestros padres, Los," 217
País, El, 217, 240
Parábola del náufrago (1969; *The Hedge, 1983*), 253
Paradoja del ave migratoria, La (1987), 201
Paralelo 35 (1967), 27
"Paràlisi," 131
Para no volver (1985), 160, 164, 167–70, 173, 174, 176
Pardo Bazán, Emilia, 14, 16, 19, 44, 110, 179, 192
Parody, 144, 160, 202, 243, 250
Patriarchy, theme of: in García Morales, 271; in Quiroga, 50; in Roig, 220, 227; in Tusquets, 160
"Paulo Pumilio," 248, 254
Pazos de Ulloa, Los (1886; *The Son of the Bondwoman*, 1908), 16, 99, 179
Penelope syndrome, 162, 231
Pequeño teatro (1954), 96, 97, 101–2, 110
Pérez, Janet, 16, 18
Periódico, El, 217
"Personatges," 217
Perspectives, multiple: in Mayoral,

181, 183, 194; in Medio, 64, 65; in Moix, 150; in Quiroga, 45; in Roig, 229
Perspectivism, Ortega's philosophy of, 66, 67
Peter Pan, 97
Peter Pan complex, 98, 171
Pez Sigue flotando, El (1959), 60, 61, 65–66
Phallocentric order, 229
Picadura mortal (1979), 199, 203–4, 207, 213, 214
Picnic at Hanging Rock (1975), 268
Pisan, Christine de, 15
Pisón, Ignacio de, 201
Plaça del Diamant, La (1962; *The Time of the Doves*, 1980), 116, 119, 120, 124–27
Plácida, la joven (1956), 46
Plantar un árbol (1980), 180, 181, 182
"Pluja," 131
Poesía de Rosalía de Castro, La (1974), 179
Politics, theme of: in Martín Gaite, 82, 83, 84; in Moix, 137; in Ortiz, 208; in Quiroga, 46, 47, 53; in Roig, 222, 223; in Zayas, 15
Polizón del Ulises, El (1965), 110
Pombo, Alvaro, 201
Post Franco era, 181, 242
Post Franco novel, 200, 213; and Matute, 95; and Moix, 137; and Ortiz, 199, 210, 213, 214
Postwar generation, 105, 106
Postwar novel (social novel), 61, 65, 73, 160, 219, 258
Postwar Spain, depiction of: in Martín Gaite, 74, 77, 78, 80, 84, 85; in Medio, 64, 65, 69
Potteccher, Beatriz, 20, 201
Pre-oedipal phase, 161, 165, 174, 175
Presente profundo (1973), 46, 47, 51, 54–55
Primera memoria (1960; *School of the Sun*, 1963), 96, 106–8
"Primos, Los," 166
Prizes, Spanish literary: Ambito Literario, 180; Biblioteca Breve, 80; Ciudad de Barcelona, 159; Victor Catalá, 119, 122; Crexells, 120; Critics', 42, 93, 104; Concha Espina, 60; Rómulo Gallegos, 47;

Gijón, 75, 100; Hucha de Oro, 182;
Mundo, 241; Nadal, 26, 42, 44, 47,
60, 76, 98, 106, 160; Nacional de
Periodismo, 241; National, 83, 93;
Novelas y Cuentos, 180; Planeta,
101, 180; Sant Jordí, 119; Sésamo,
60; Gabriel Sijé, 180; Tertulia Café
del Turia, 100
Proceso de Macanaz, El: Historia de
un empapelamiento (1969), 74
Prostitution: in Medio, 68; in Ortiz,
201, 202; in Rodoreda, 125, 128,
129, 131, 132
Psychoanalysis, 167, 168, 169
Publicitat, La, 117
Puértolas, Soledad, 20, 194

Quanta, quanta guerra (1980), 118,
132
"Querida y admirada Greta," 182
Quevedo, Francisco, 15
Quiroga, Elena, 19, 20, 22, 42–58, 160

Rambla, La, 117
Ramona, Adiós (1972), 217, 221–25,
231
Rape: in Matute, 100; in Moix, 142,
143; in Rodoreda, 125, 129, 132
Real Academia de Historia, 43
Real Academia Española, 42, 43
Rebellion, theme of: in Medio, 62, 63;
in Moix, 144; in Ortiz, 208; in
Rodoreda, 126; in Roig, 224, 226;
in Tusquets, 167
Register, Cheri, 187
Religion (Catholic): in Laforet, 37; in
Matute, 100; in Medio, 63; in
Quiroga, 49, 50, 52; in Santa
Teresa, 14
Repression of women by men, 121
Retahílas (1974), 80–82, 87, 88
Riera, Carme, 20, 194
Río, El (1963), 111
Río de la luna, El (1981), 201
Ritmo lento (1962), 79–80, 87, 88
"Riu i la barca, El," 129
Rodoreda, Mercè, 20, 23, 116–35
Roig, Montserrat, 20, 23, 194, 217–39,
240
Role model, female, 49, 63, 242, 255
Role(s) of women, theme of: in
Laforet, 27; in Montero, 244, 247;

in Ortiz, 204; in Rodoreda, 119,
125; in Roig, 218, 220, 221, 222,
228, 231
Role reversals, 118, 204
Romance, novels of, 85, 121, 124,
264, 265, 271
Roman-fleuve, 130
Romero, Luis, 47
"Rom Negrita," 131
Rosalía de Castro (1986), 179
Rosalía de Castro y sus sombras
(1976), 179
"Rosamunda," 37–38

Sábato, Ernesto, 198
"Salamandra, La," 129
Salisachs, Mercedes, 20, 46
Sánchez Arnosi, Milagros, 231
Sánchez Ferlosio, Rafael, 47, 73, 198
Sangre, La (1952), 44, 45
Sastre, Alfonso, 73
Seduction, 148, 206–7, 269
Self-reflexive text, 84, 141, 173, 272
Semblava de seda i altres contes
(1978), 131
Semprún, Jorge, 198
Serra d'Or, 116, 217
Servodidio, Mirella, 72
Sex, theme of: in Matute, 101; in
Mayoral, 182; in Moix, 151–52; in
Quiroga, 49; in Rodoreda, 119, 120,
121, 125; in Roig, 225, 226, 236; in
Tusquets, 162, 163, 175
Sexuality: in García Morales, 268,
269; in Matute, 102; in Mayoral,
181; in Moix, 148; in Rodoreda,
131; in Roig, 225, 226
Shame, 125
Siete miradas en un mismo paisaje
(1981), 159, 166–67, 169, 172, 175
Silence, theme of: in García Morales,
270; in Matute, 107; in Moix, 137,
143, 146, 153, 154; in Roig, 232
Silencio de las sirenas, El (1985), 259,
260, 261, 271–75
Sobejano, Gonzalo, 18, 199
Social classes, theme of: in García
Morales, 266, 267, 269, 270; in
Martín Gaite, 83; in Matute, 111; in
Mayoral, 180, 185, 186; in Quiroga,
46, 53, 54, 56
Social criticism: in Martín Gaite, 80,

87; in Matute, 104, 106; in Montero, 247, 253, 254; in Quiroga, 49, 52, 56; in Roig, 219
Sóc una dama honrada? (1932), 119, 120
Soldados lloran de noche, Los (1964), 96, 107, 108
Soledad sonora, La, 43
Solo un pie descalzo (1983), 107
Soriano, Elena, 20
Spinster, 63, 88
Stereotypes, 70; of women, 186, 220, 231, 250, 251
Stream of consciousness, 45, 50, 80, 187, 251
Structure, novelistic: avant garde, 76; complex, 84; conversational, 81, 84, 87; fragmented, 65, 211, 229; traditional, 35, 44
Style, novelistic: lyrical, 44, 45, 56, 93, 98; "nineteenth century," 44, 61, 99, 271
Suicide: in García Morales, 261, 263; in Martín Gaite, 83; in Matute, 102, 105, 108; in Medio, 67; in Ortiz, 211, 213; in Quiroga, 54, 55; in Rodoreda, 120, 122–23, 127, 128, 130, 132, 133; in Roig, 230
Sur, El (1985): film, 259; novella, 261–66
Sur, El, seguido de Bene (1985), 259, 260, 261, 275
Surrealism, 76, 137, 140
Surveys of women writers, 14, 18
Svevo, Italo, 80
Symbolic order, 148, 260, 261, 272, 273, 274

Teixidor, Jordi, 179
Televisión Española, 240
Teresa de Jesús, Santa, 14, 19
Te trataré como a una reina (1983), 248–51, 254
Tiempo, El (1957), 111
Tiempo de cerezas (1977), 217, 221, 225–31
¿Tiempo de mujer? (1980), 218
Tiempo de silencio (1962; *Time of Silence*, 1964), 45
Todorov, Tzvetan, 76, 259, 260, 267
Tolstoy, Leo, 241
Tomeo, Javier, 201

Torrente Ballester, Gonzalo, 44, 200
Torre vigía, La (1971), 95, 107, 109–10
Tovar, Antonio, 83
Trabal, Monserrat, 118
Tragaluz, El (1967; *The Basement Window*, 1981), 51
Trampa, La (1969), 107, 109
Trayecto uno, 47
Tremendismo, 29
Tres pasos fuera del tiempo, 26
Tres y un sueño (1960), 96, 111
Tristura, 42, 44, 46, 47, 53–54
Turn of the Screw, The, 267, 270, 272
Tusquets, Esther, 20, 23, 159–78, 194, 198, 201, 240

Ultima corrida, La (1958), 46
Unamuno, Miguel de, 93
Unica libertad, La (1982), 180, 181, 184, 185, 186, 187, 188, 189, 190, 191, 193, 194
Unión General de Trabajadores (UGT), 117
"Upstairs, Downstairs," 83
Urraca (1982), 199, 204–7, 210, 213, 214
Usos amorosos de la postguerra española (1987), 74
Usos amorosos del siglo XVIII en España (1972), 74

Valente, José Angel, 88
Varada tras el último naufragio (1980), 159, 164–66, 167, 171–72, 174, 176
Vargas Llosa, Mario, 198
Vaz de Soto, José María, 200
Vázquez Montalbán, Manuel, 138, 139, 140, 201, 204
Verdad sobre el caso Savolta, La (1975), 199, 200
Vernacular languages, Spanish, 95
Viatges i flors (1980), 132
Viento del Norte (1951), 42, 43, 44, 45, 47
Villalonga, Lorenç, 116
Villán, Javier, 242
Villegas, Juan, 50, 51, 53
Vindicación feminista, 136, 138, 146
Vindication of women, 233
Vint-i-dos contes (1958), 119, 122–24, 126

Virtudes peligrosas, Las (1985), 136, 141, 146, 153
"Virtudes peligrosas, Las," 138
Visión del ahogado (1977), 201
"Viure al día," 131

Walter, ¿por qué te fuiste? (1973), 138, 140, 141, 142, 143, 144–45, 147–50, 152, 154
Weir, Peter, 268
Welles, Marcia, 72, 79
Widowhood, 130, 267, 271
Women's demonstrations, 67, 227
Women's issues, themes of: in Mayoral, 188; in Medio, 67, 69; in Montero, 243; in Ortiz, 199; in Roig, 217, 218; in twentieth century novelists, 21
Women Writers of Spain, 16
Woolf, Virginia, 14
"Writerly self," 30
Writerly text, 160, 201

Zambrano, María, 16, 19
Zayas y Sotmayor, María de, 14, 15, 19
Zola, Emile, 16

More Spanish women writers have come to prominence in the last fifty years than in all of the preceding eight centuries. In *Women Writers of Contemporary Spain,* edited by Joan L. Brown, eminent scholars in the field of twentieth-century Spanish literature introduce thirteen of the major women writers of modern Spain. This volume of essays is addressed not only to Hispanists but to all readers interested in women and literature.

The book opens with an overview of Spanish women authors and their place in the national literary canon from the tenth century forward. The periods covered by the essays include the Franco regime (1936–75) and the post-Franco era to date. Modern Spain forms the backdrop for the works of the thirteen writers who are presented in the order in which they appeared on the Spanish literary scene. Each chapter features original, provocative literary analysis; it also provides an overview of the author's works, fundamental biographical data, and both primary and annotated secondary bibliographies.

First come the richly baroque depictions of psychological development and postwar alienation created by Carmen Laforet, which are explored by Gustavo Pérez Firmat. The fiction of Elena Quiroga, with its innovative technical experimentation and oblique presentation of censored themes, is analyzed by Phyllis Zatlin. Dolores Medio's unflinchingly realistic documentation of middle-class postwar Spanish society is discussed by Margaret E. W. Jones. Carmen Martín